THE NORTH – VE

Vegetarian Guides are the most com[plete in the] world, carried and relied on by tens of [thousands] and recommended by all the leading [...]

Veggie Guides offer vegans, vegetar[ians and their] partners a huge choice of places where everyone will enjoy a delicious, memorable and great value night out or weekend away.

Featuring...

99 vegetarian restaurants, cafes, even pubs
190 more restaurants, cafes and pubs that veggies and vegans love
23 vegetarian B&Bs
45 more places to stay with great veggie grub
290 delis, wholefood and other stores where local veggies shop
Vegetarian caterers
Local vegetarian groups to meet new friends

See what's in your area:

	Guest Houses		Restaurants Cafes & Pubs			
	Veggie	**Omni**	**Veggie**	**Omni**	**Shops**	**Page**
Cheshire		2	1	20	15	4
Cumbria	10	9	14	13	20	10
Derbyshire	2	5	7	19	14	49
County Durham	1	1	1	5	12	62
Lancashire	1	1	10	13	45	68
Lincolnshire		3	1	11	16	83
Manchester			8	29	13	89
Merseyside		2	3	16	16	103
Northumberland	1	5	3	9	8	117
Nottinghamshire			9	12	17	125
Tyne & Wear			3	10	16	136
North Yorkshire	6	7	6	4	17	146
York		3	2	6	9	158
East Yorkshire		1	6	3	12	167
South Yorkshire			8	9	17	174
West Yorkshire	2	6	17	14	40	186
Isle of Man		1		2	6	217
TOTAL	**23**	**46**	**99**	**195**	**290**	

Contents iv, Vegetarian Index vi, Top Places viii-xi
Booze 2, A-Z Index 221, Locations Index 226

For latest openings visit
www.vegetarianguides.co.uk/updates

The perfect present for vegetarians, vegans, meat reducers and those who love them (but never knew where to take them)

Vegetarian North of England, 1st edition

by Alex Bourke & Ronny Worsey
ISBN 978-1-902259-11-6

Photos by Sophie Fenwick-Paul, Zuki Fenwick-Paul,
Patricia Tricker, the entries themselves

*Published October 2010 by Vegetarian Guides Ltd,
reprinted with corrections December 2010, February, April 2011
PO Box 2284, London W1A 5UH, England
www.vegetarianguides.co.uk   info@vegetarianguides.co.uk
Tel 020-3239 8433 (24 hours)   Fax 0870-288 5085 skype veggie_guides*

Design and maps by Mickaël Charbonnel, Alexandra Boylan,
Andrea Mattioli, Rudy Penando & Jenny Carp
Vegetarian Guides logo design: Marion Gillet

Cover photos (clockwise from top left):
Lakeland Pedlar front, Cumbria
Newcastle upon Tyne by Zuki Fenwick-Paul
Organic Heaven, Chesterfield
Yewfield B&B, Cumbria by Sophie Fenwick-Paul
Lakeland Pedlar inside, Cumbria
Lake District by Sophie Fenwick-Paul

Printed and bound in Great Britain by QNS, Newcastle upon Tyne
www.qnsprint.co.uk

For free information on the region's attractions:
**www.visitengland.com
www.visitnortheastengland.com
www.visitenglandsnorthwest.com
www.visitnorthwest.com
www.primenorthwest.co.uk
www.enjoyenglandseastmidlands.com
www.carfreewalks.org**
Tourist information sites for counties are listed in those chapters.

© Vegetarian Guides 2011. No part of this book may be reproduced or transmitted in *any* way or by any means, *including the internet*, without the prior permission of the publisher in writing, other than brief quotations for review purposes. **What that means in practice:** We spent a year compiling this book. If you sub the text down, move the sentences around and change a few words before posting it on the internet to rake in advertising revenue, then our intellectual property lawyer will sue you for every piratical thieving penny you take plus damages and legal costs, and we will ensure the whole veggie world knows what you did. We will also pay 10% of the damages as a bounty to anyone who reports pirates. If you want to review and recommend our books with a link to us, we will happily pay you commission, see www.vegetarianguides.co.uk/affiliate

Join the team: If you have updates, or a group, shop or cafe and want copies to resell or give as gifts, we will do you a very attractive discount. Contact updates@ or sales@vegetarianguides.co.uk or call us on (+44) (0)20-3239 8433 (24 hours, we call back).

Disclaimer: Restaurants are continually changing their owners and opening hours and sometimes close for holidays. Every effort has been made to ensure the accuracy of information in this book, however it is impossible to account for every detail and mistakes can occur. Before making a special journey, we recommend you call ahead to check details.

Vegetarian Britain 4th edition
part 2:

NORTH
of England

Cheshire, Cumbria, Derbyshire, Co. Durham, Lancs, Lincs, Manchester
Merseyside, Northumberland, Notts, Tyne & Wear, Yorkshire, Isle of Man

600 places to eat, sleep and shop veggie

by Alex Bourke & Ronny Worsey
with special thanks to Philippa Lennox and Patricia Tricker

Contributors:

Cheshire: Chris Olivant, Samantha Calvert

Cumbria: Sophie Fenwick-Paul

Derbyshire: Manjit Biant

Durham & Cleveland: Peter Burdess, Joa Ninan Chloë

Lancashire: Alwynne Cartmell

Lincolnshire: Linda Wardale

Manchester: Rochelle Gunter, Chris Olivant,
Donna Siverns, Anna Stanley

Merseyside: Niki O'Leary

Northumberland: Mark Morley

Nottinghamshire: Alex Claridge, Patrick Smith

Tyne & Wear: Mark Morley

Yorkshire: Natalie Leodis, Morgan Golf-French, Sophie Krank

Isle of Man: Bryony Whipp

Vegetarian Guides

Vegetarian North: Contents

Highlights	i
Contributors	ii
Contents	iv
Veggie Index	vi
Top 10 Trips	viii
Crème de la Crème	x
Quirky Places	xi
Pies and Prejudice	1
Beer	2

Cheshire

Alderley Edge	5
Altrincham	5
Bramhall	5
Cheadle	6
CHESTER	6
Crewe	7
Hale	7
Knutsford	7
Lichfield	8
Macclesfield	8
Nantwich	8
Sale	8
Tarporley	9
Warrington	9
Wilmslow	9
Chain stores	9

Cumbria

Map	11
Introduction	12
Accommodation	14
Ambleside	33
Appleby-in-Westmoreland	36
Barrow-in-Furness	36
Brampton	37
Caldbeck	37
Cockermouth	37
Grasmere	39
Kendal	40
Keswick	41
Milnthorpe	43
Penrith area	43
Ulverston	**44**
Whitehaven	46
Wigton	47
Windermere	47
Workington	47
Chain stores	47

Derbyshire

Introduction	49
Accommodation	50
Etwall	51
Ashbourne	52
Bakewell area	52
Buxton	53
Chesterfield	54
DERBY	55
Edale	58
Glossop	58
Hathersage	59
Matlock	59
Scarthin	60
Caterers	60
Chain stores	61
Local groups	61

County Durham

Accommodation	63
Chester-le-Street	63
Darlington	63
DURHAM	64
Guisborough	65
Middlesbrough	65
Stockton-on-Tees	66
Chain stores	67
Local groups	67

Lancashire

Introduction	68
Accommodation	69
Ashton-under-Lyne	70
Bispham Green	71
Blackburn	71
Blackpool	72
Bolton	72
Burnley	73
Bury	73
Chorley	74
Colne	74
Euxton	75
LANCASTER	75
Preston area	77
Rossendale	79
Tarleton	79
Todmorden	79
Wigan	80
Chain stores	82

Lincolnshire

Accommodation	84
Boston	84
Bourne	84
Cleethorpes	85
Grimsby	85
Holbeach	85
LINCOLN	85
Louth	87
Tealby	87
Chain stores	88
Local groups	88

Manchester

Introduction	89
Vegetarian	91
Pubs	95
Omnivorous	97
Shops	99
Caterer, Chain stores	
Local groups	102
Manchester Map	103

Merseyside

Introduction	104
Liverpool Map	105
Accommodation	106
LIVERPOOL	106
Southport	112
Wirral	113
Chain stores	116
Delivery services	116
Local groups	116

Northumberland

Introduction	117
Accommodation	118
Amble	120
Berwick upon Tweed	120
Falstone	121
Hexham	122
Hedley on the Hill	122
Morpeth	123
Thropton	123
West Woodburn	123
Chain stores	124
Local groups	124

Nottinghamshire

Introduction	125
NOTTINGHAM	126
Chain stores	134
Caterer	134
Local groups	135

Tyne & Wear

Gosforth	137
Heaton	137
NEWCASTLE	140
Whitley Bay	144
Chain stores	145
Local groups	145
Caterer	145

North Yorkshire

Introduction	146
Accommodation	147
Grassington	150
Harrogate	151
Helmsley	151
Knaresborough	152
Northallerton	152
Pocklington	153
Ripon	153
Saltburn by the Sea	153
Scarborough	154
Skipton	156
Whitby	156
Chain stores	157
YORK (Map	158

East Yorkshire

Introduction	167
Accommodation	168
Beverley	168
Bridlington	168
Goole	170
HULL	170
Local group	173
Chain stores	173

South Yorkshire

Introduction	174
Bawtrey	175
Doncaster	176
SHEFFIELD	176
Chain stores	185
Local groups	185

West Yorkshire

Introduction	187
Hebden Bridge	188
Accommodation	194
Boston Spa	194
BRADFORD	195
Brighouse	197
Cleckheaton	198
Denby Dale	198
Dewsbury	198
Halifax	199
Haworth	200
Holmfirth	201
HUDDERSFIELD	201
Ilkley	203
Keighley	204
LEEDS	204
Otley	211
Shipley	213
Slaithwaite	213
Sowerby Bridge	213
Wakefield	213
Wetherby	215
Chain stores	216
Local groups	216

Isle of Man

Introduction	217
Accommodation	218
Castletown	218
Douglas	218
Port Erin	219
Ramsey	219
St Johns	220

Caterers Index	220
A–Z Index	221
Locations Index	226

v

99 VEGETARIAN RESTAURANTS, CAFES & PUBS

CHESHIRE
The Greenhouse, Altrincham 5

CUMBRIA
Fellinis, Ambleside 33
Zeffirelli's, Ambleside 33
Rattle Gill Cafe. Ambleside 34
Review, Barrow-in-Furness 36
Quince & Medlar, Cockermouth 38
The Green Valley, Grasmere 39
Meeting House Cafe, Kendal 40
Waterside Wholefood, Kendal 41
The Lakeland Pedlar, Keswick 42
The Heights Hotel, Keswick 26
The Watermill, Little Salkeld 44
Gillam's Tearoom, Ulverston 44
World Peace Cafe, Ulverston 45
Conservatory Cafe, Ulverston 46

DERBYSHIRE
World Peace Café, Etwall 51
Caudwell's, Rowsley 52
Buddhist Café, Buxton (2011) 53
Elliotts's, Chesterfield 54
Yaffle vegan cafe, Derby 55
The Globe vegan pub, Glossop 58
Green Way Cafe, Matlock 59
The Cafe in Scarthin Books 60

COUNTY DURHAM
The Waiting Room,
  Stockton on Tees 66

LANCASHIRE
Topaz, Ashton-under-Lyne 70
Lily's, Ashton-under-Lyne 70
V-Fresh, Blackburn 71
Kitchen on Gt Moor St, Bolton 72
Surya Snack Bar, Bolton 73
Red Triangle, Burnley 73
Jim Skaffy, Colne 74
The Whale Tail, Lancaster 74
RK Sweets, Preston 77
Bear Cafe-Bar, Todmorden 79

LINCOLNSHIRE
Pimento Tearooms, Lincoln 85

MANCHESTER
Earth Café 91
Eighth Day Café 92
The Greenhouse 93
Greens 93
Fuel Café Bar 94
Unicorn Hot Dog Stall 95
Bistro 1847 pub 95
The Thirsty Scholar pub 95

MERSEYSIDE
Egg Café, Liverpool 106
Food From Nowhere, Liverpool 107
Green Fish Café, Liverpool 107

NORTHUMBERLAND
The Garden Station, Hexham 122
The Learning Shed, Hexham 122
Hexham Tans, Hexham 122

NOTTINGHAM
Alley Café 127
Crocus Cafe 126
The Flying Goose 126
Roya's at Flying Goose 126
Mm... Deli 128
Cafe Nomad 128
Squeek 128
Sumac Centre cafe & bar 128
World Peace Cafe 129

TYNE & WEAR
Jack Sprats 137
The Sky Apple 139
Bob Trollop's Pub 141

NORTH YORKSHIRE
The Retreat Cafe, Grassington 150
Vinehouse Cafe, Helmsley 151
World Peace Cafe, Pocklington 153
Nutmeg Cafe, Scarborough 154
Cafe Venus, Scarborough 154
Wild Oats, Skipton 156

YORK
El Piano 161
Goji 163

EAST YORKSHIRE

Bean There, Bridlington	168
Seasalt & Passion, Bridlington	169
Bempton Cafe, Bridlingotn	169
Zoo Cafe, Hull	170
Hitchcock's, Hull	171
Green Ginger, Hull	172

SOUTH YORKSHIRE

Eating Whole, Doncaster	176
Airy Fairy, Sheffield	176
Blue Moon Cafe, Sheffield	177
Homemade Cafe, Sheffield	177
Cafe Number 9, Sheffield	178
Heeley City Farm, Sheffield	179
New Roots, Sheffield	179
World Peace Cafe, Sheffield	180

WEST YORKSHIRE

Greens, Hebden Bridge	190
Nelson's Wine Bar, Hebden Br	191
Prashad, Bradford	195
South Square, Bradford	195
Treehouse, Bradford	196
Ginger Veg Cafe, Halifax	199
World Peace Café, Halifax	199
World Peace Cafe, Huddersfield	201
The Veggie, Ilkley	203
Hansa's, Leeds	204
Roots & Fruits, Leeds	205
The Common Place, Leeds	205
That Old Chestnut, Leeds	206
Cheerful Chilli, Otley	211
Dandelion & Burdock, Sowerby Bridge	213
Mango cafe, Wetherby	214
Mango restaurant, Wetherby	215

The Heights Hotel, Cumbria p26

VEGETARIAN ACCOMMODATION

CUMBRIA

Yewfield, Ambleside	14
Hall Croft, Appleby-in-W	17
Lakeland Living, Cockermouth	19
Lancrigg, Grasmere	20
Beech Tree GH, Coniston	22
Fox Hall Vegan B&B, Kendal	24
Heights Hotel, Keswick	26
Ardrig B&B, Kendal	32
Sefton House, Ulverston	32
Conishead Priory	45

DERBYSHIRE

The Barn at Ashe Hall, Etwall	51
Sheldon's Luxury Retreat	51

COUNTY DURHAM

Vegge B&B, Durham	63

LANCASHIRE

Crazi Carrots, Bolton	69

NORTHUMBERLAND

The Long View, near Berwick	118

YORKSHIRE

Lidmoor Farm, Bransdale	147
The Women's Holiday Centre Horton-in-Ribblesdale	147
The Wolds Retreat, Pocklington	147
The Orange Tree, Rosedale	148
Falcon Guest House, Whitby	148
Shepherd's Purse, Whitby	148
Myrtle Grove, Hebden Bridge	189
Thorncliffe B&B for Women Hebden Bridge	190

SELF-CATERING

www.cottageguide.co.uk

Yewfield, Cumbria	14
Keswick Holiday Homes	32
Upfront, Cumbria	43
Nag's Head, Derbyshire	58
Chester-le-Street area	63
Sanders Yard, Whitby	150
Acorn GH, Hull	168
Lumb Cottage, Hebden Bridge	189

Top 10 Veggie Trips

Welcome to the first vegetarian guide to the North of England. If you're overwhelmed by the huge choice of places to visit, stay over and eat out in these 16 counties, here are our suggestions to get you started.

Country Weekends

1. CUMBRIA and the Lakes, page 10
One of Britain's top walking destinations, the **Lake District National Park** has stunning scenery, stone houses, boat trips on Lake Windermere, ten vegetarian or vegan bed & breakfasts from budget to luxury, and a dozen vegetarian cafes and restaurants. Hotspots include **Ambleside, Grasmere, Kendal, Keswick** and **Ulverston**.

2. DERBYSHIRE and the Peak District, page 49
Most of the Peak District National Park is in Derbyshire. This rugged landscape of the **Pennine** hills, bogs and wooded valleys is one of the most visited areas in Britain for day trips, as it is within 3 hours drive of around half the population. There are some lovely veggie cafes and even a pub with only vegan food.

3. NORTHUMBERLAND, page 117
In total contrast to Cumbria, Northumberland is relatively unspoilt by tourism yet has Hadrian's Wall, stunning coastline and lots of ancient castles and ruins to visit.

VegiVentures Holidays

Great Vegetarian/Vegan Food

Annual holidays in:

PERU **TURKEY** **ENGLISH LAKE DISTRICT**

Plus Creativity Weekends and
CHRISTMAS CELEBRATION

FOR **FREE** DETAILS ☎ **01760 755888**

VegiVentures, Castle Cottage, Castle Acre, Norfolk PE32 2AJ
www.vegiventures.com

4. NORTH YORKSHIRE, page 146
There are several each of vegetarian B&Bs and cafes, either in the country or by the seaside. The big attraction is **York**, see below, while **Scarborough** and **Whitby** both offer a great weekend by the sea.

5. WEST YORKSHIRE, page 186
The county is packed with a huge diversity of big city and country town vegetarian delights. Big cities **Bradford** and **Leeds** have lots of terrific places to eat, but we would start with counterculture capital **Hebden Bridge**, just outside Halifax. Rural locations have four of Britain's best vegetarian restaurants: **Cheerful Chilli, Dandelion & Burdock, The Veggie** and **Mango**.

City Nights Out

6. LIVERPOOL, page 104
The north's capital of culture offers the Beatles, museums, art and lots of veggie-friendly places to eat.

7. MANCHESTER, page 89
Along with York, this is one of the five most visited cities in Britain. (The others are London, Birmingham and Edinburgh.) Popular for music and drinking, there are several pubs specialising in vegetarian food and two gourmet vegetarian restaurants.

8. NEWCASTLE UPON TYNE, page 136
Tyneside has two of Britain's best veggie cafes and, right by the Tyne Bridge, a vegetarian pub. The Alternative Stores vegan shop carries a massive range of hard-to-find delights.

9. NOTTINGHAM, page 125
This university city has more veggie cafes than any other medium-sized city and is quite popular with vegans.

10. YORK, page 158
York is history heaven with Romans, Vikings, lots of museums, and two superb vegetarian eateries.

Also good for eating out are **Sheffield** (page 176), and **Hull** (page 170) which is worth visiting just for Hitchcocks.

Romantic dinners, birthday and anniversary celebrations don't have to be limited to your county. Why not whisk your loved one, or just yourself, off to a veggie hotspot? Each has its own character and there are enough here to keep you coming back every month for years. Turn the page for the very best restaurants and vegan specialists.

Crème de la Soya Crème

GOURMET RESTAURANTS

CUMBRIA
Fellinis, Ambleside	33
Zeffirellis, Ambleside	33
Quince & Medlar, Cockermouth	38
Green Valley, Grasmere	39

COUNTY DURHAM / CLEVELAND
The Waiting Room, Stockon-on-Tees	66

MANCHESTER
The greenhouse, Rusholme	93
Greens, West Didsbury	93

NOTTINGHAM
Roya's at The Flying Goose	126
Squeek	128

TYNE & WEAR
The Sky Apple, Heaton	139

YORK
El Piano vegan restaurant	161

EAST YORKSHIRE
Hitchcock's, Hull	171

WEST YORKSHIRE
Greens, Hebden Bridge	190
Prashad, Bradford	195
The Veggie, Ilkley	203
Hansa's, Leeds	204
The Cheerful Chilli, Otley	211
Dandelion & Burdock, Sowerby Bridge	213
Mango Restaurant, Wetherby	214

TOP B&B

Readers consistently rate **Lancrigg** in Cumbria as their favourite, with four poster beds, whirlpool baths and 4-course dinner in their mainly organic vegetarian restaurant Green Valley. Page 20.

100% VEGAN FOOD

CHESHIRE
Vegonia Wholefoods, Nanṭwich	8

CUMBRIA
Fox Hall B&B, Kendal	24

DERBYSHIRE
Yaffle cafe & tea shop, Derby	55
Sound Bites shop & deli, Derby	57
The Globe pub, Glossop	58

MANCHESTER
Earth Café	91
Unicorn grocery	95,102

MERSEYSIDE
Studio2 breakfast & buffet	106
Food From Nowhere cafe	107
Honest to Goodness shop	115

NORTHUMBERLAND
The Long View B&B	118

NOTTINGHAM
SUMAC Centre cafe & bar	129
Screaming Carrot bakery	134

TYNE & WEAR
Alternative Stores shop	143

YORK
El Piano vegan restaurant	161

WEST YORKSHIRE
The Common Place, Leeds	205
That Old Chestnut, Leeds	206
Dandelion & Burdock Sowerby Bridge	213

Quirky and Special Places

Scarthin Books, Derbyshire
Peering round stuffed bookshelves to find hidden staircases pays off in the bookshop, as if you keep going up, you'll eventually hit the top floor cafe, an all-vegetarian gem. The walls are decorated with children's artwork, a set of stocks and a ball and chain, amongst other random oddities. Staff are chirpy and the handwritten signs playfully grumpy. Page 60.

The Globe, Glossop, Derbyshire
A real ale pub characterised by faded Victorian splendour and vases of flowers. The seldom-changing menu is entirely vegan and main meals cost as little as £2.50. The place atracts a very mixed crowd, especially on the weekend evenings when there is a DJ or World music act upstairs. Page 58

The Bear, Todmorden, Lancashire
An old-fashioned cafe in a beautiful building reached by a wooden winding staircase. There's a big stack of secondhand books to read (and buy for around £1 donation to charity, if you form an attachment). Whiling away an afternoon here feels like stepping back in time. Todmorden is also home to both a straw bale building co-op and a microbrewery you can visit to buy bottled beers and enjoy the stylised nude art on the walls. Page 79.

Odder, Manchester
This lives up to its name, with fake buffalo heads on the wall and confusingly-placed mirrors. Not the cheapest joint in town, but a really chilled out and comfortable place to enjoy a pint with a full vegan breakfast or a pizza. Sister venue to nearby Odd and Oddest, which have a very similar menu. Page 96.

The Sumac Centre, Nottingham
The 'People's Kitchen' on Saturday nights quickly fills up with hungry people seeking a three-course vegan meal for three pounds. If you're prepared to venture off the beaten track in search of a bargain and don't mind scuffed upholstery and no tablecloths, this is the place to come. There's also a vegan real ale bar and often live music and other events. Page 129.

Hitchcocks, Hull, East Yorkshire
All you can eat buffet restaurant run by a couple who've travelled all over the world collecting recipes. The first to book choose which country the menu of the night will be from. Page 171.

The Globe vegan pub, p58

VEGETARIAN SHOES

I don't eat the inside and I won't wear the outside. Pick up non-leather shoes at:

Alternative Stores, Newcastle, p143
The Olive Branch, Bradford p197
The Third Estate, Leeds, p208
www.beyondskin.co.uk
www.bboheme.com
www.ethicalwares.com
www.freerangers.co.uk
www.neoncollective.com
www.veganline.com
www.vegetarian-shoes.co.uk

Do you love all-day breakfasts?

Are you any of the following? A vegan, a trainee vegan, someone who lives with a vegan, a kitchen scientist, a student, a cartoon lover, a lazy cook or a vegetarian wanting to ride the 'cool wave'?

Do you like the sound of the following? Egg-free eggy bread, gourmet wheat-free sosages, yoghurt that wants to be cheesecake, geek crumpets, power smoothie and chocolate fudge cake?

If so, you need the brand new 20 page cookbook:

The *(all-day)* Breakfast Scoffer

Available now from Vegetarian Guides for £1.50, see page ii or 228

Wholesale orders visit www.activedistribution.org
Bulk orders (50+) at a big discount, contact the publisher: **scoffer@chef.net**
or write to: Scoffer Towers, c/o 245 Gladstone St, Nottingham NG7 6HX

Pies and Prejudice

Ronny *is a Merseyside lass now living in Derbyshire who has worked in a number of vegetarian cafes and restaurants all round the region.*

It isn't actually grim up north. We don't spend our days toiling in mills, scrubbing our front steps and adjusting wrinkled stockings and hair rollers. We're too busy dining and supping in a wide range of cafes, restaurants, pubs and takeaways that serve good veggie food from all round the world, often at half the price you'd pay down south.

We've got all of England's most beautiful mountains, many of the lakes and forests, and some stunning beaches. We also have a down to earth outlook on life, friendly approach to visitors and a much more dry, witty take on life than them Southerners (though maybe I'm just biased).

This guide includes the sprawling urban centres of Leeds, Manchester, Sheffield, Newcastle and Liverpool, showing you where to find good grub amongst the crowds and traffic. It also takes in more s erene places such as Northumberland, The Peak District and the Yorkshire Dales.

The Lake District, which encompasses the Cumbrian fells, is the second most visited part of Britain outside London with good reason: the scenery is stunning. Bear in mind when visiting that public transport is limited and accommodation tends to be booked up well in advance during summer months.

Finally, a word on the weather. Yes, northern England does in general get more wind, snow and rain than the south, particularly if you stay to the west of the Pennine mountain range. However, this is more than made up for by the landscape, top scran and warm welcome you'll encounter. Just remember to pack boots and a waterproof coat and you'll be reet.

Ronny has written various books including the legendary Scoffer series, magazine features and information packs about veggie cooking and living. She can sometimes be found locked up in a vegan cake laboratory. A keen hillwalker, she is currently on a quest to find the perfect vegan pie.

Beer and Pubs

by Sagar Kirit Shah of Real Ale for All *& Ronny Worsey*

Beer and cider production, like wine, often involves animal products in the fining process to help remove impurities and improve the appearance of the final product. Fining aids include fish isinglass (a collagen from the swim bladder), gelatine, egg whites or casein. Unfortunately this renders many beers unsuitable for vegetarians, vegans, and many others such as those suffering from seafood allergies.

EU and UK legislation does not require breweries to list ingredients in any drinks with an alcoholic content of more than 1.2% volume – so usually you don't know by the label if it is vegetarian or vegan. This is unlikely to change in the future, as many breweries and wine-makers are fighting hard to keep the law as it is – so customers will not see all the chemicals they use.

Fortunately many beers and ciders are suitable for vegetarians and vegans and use either a non-animal fining agent such as bentonite (a type of clay) or pea extract, or are not fined at all. Unlike wines, popular beers and ciders are generally branded clearly and it is nearly always possible to find some in a pub or supermarket.

Bottle conditioned real ales are almost always vegan because they are not filtered. Yeast needs to be in the bottle in order for it to continue fermenting.

As a general rule of thumb, **cask conditioned ales** (and even many bottled ales) are not suitable for vegetarians or vegans. This is because fining is required to clear the material held in suspension in the liquid. Real Ale for All (RAFA) has been working with the Vegan Society to encourage breweries to go vegan but progress may take a long time.

These websites list many popular beers and ciders and indicate whether they are suitable for vegetarians and/or vegans. The first one displays emails and letters received from breweries so you can verify the information.

www.veggiewines.co.uk
www.vegansociety.com/AFSSearch.aspx
www.enchant.me.uk/Vegetarian_beers.html

When visiting a pub, especially if it is part of a major chain, you can generally find at least one or two popular beers or ciders that are suitable for vegetarians or vegans. Some pubs exclusively serve beers and ciders produced by their own breweries – so it may be worthwhile getting in contact with the brewery to find out in advance.

YOUR CUT OUT AND CARRY VEGETARIAN BEER GUIDE

BEER YES
Becks, Brakspear
Budweiser
Carlsberg, Cobra
Grolsch
Heineken
Hoegaarden
Holsten Pils
Lowenbrau
Miller
Shepherd Neame
Stella Artois

BEER NO
Boddingtons
Carling, Fosters
Greene King
Guinness
John Smiths
Kronenbourg
Newcastle Brown
Red Stripe
San Miguel
Staropramen
Tetleys

CIDER YES
Magners pear cider
Scrumpy Jack
Strongbow
Westons
Woodpecker

CIDER NO
Blackthorn
Diamond White
Kopparberg
Magners apple cider
Strongbow Sirrus

Source: www.veggiewines.co.uk & The Vegan Society

Most cheap pubs sell vegan beers such as Carlsberg, and many sell vegan ciders too, though very few offer any vegan food beyond chips.

The **Wetherspoons** chain of over 700 pubs sells several vegan beers and ciders and does a chickpea and spinach curry, vegan if you have extra popadoms instead of naan. See for example page 86. www.jdwetherspoon.co.uk

The **Sam Smiths** pub chain sells a variety of beers from their own breweries at affordable prices, and 90% are certified with the Vegan Society, though they do not offer vegan food. www.samsmiths.info

Vegan Pubs
The Globe, Glossop 58
(food but not all beers vegan)
Sumac Centre, Nottingham 128
(everything 100% vegan)

Vegetarian Pubs
Zeffirelli's jazz bar, Ambleside 33
Bistro 1847, Manchester 95
Thirsty Scholar, Manchester 95
Bob Trollop's, Newcastle 141
Nelson's Wine Bar,
 Hebden Bridge 191

Other Pubs
with veggie/vegan food
The Red Cow, Nantwich 8
The Headless Woman, Tarporley 9
Lucy4 Wine Bar, Ambleside 35
The Farmers Arms, Ulverston 46
Sycamore Inn, Matlock 52
Dog & Partridge, Derbys 52
Nag's Head, Edale 58
The Strawberry Duck, Bolton 69
Farmers Arms, Lancs 71
Plough Inn, Euxton, Lancs 75
Gregson Centre, Lancaster 76
Pyewipe Inn, Lincoln 84
JD Wetherspoon (3), Lincoln 86
The Olde Barn, Lincs 87
The Kings Head, Lincs 88
Fuel Cafe-Bar, Manchester 94
Kro (5), Manchester 96
Marble Brewery, Manchester 96
Odd, Odder, Oddest, Manc 96
Marina Arms, Northumberland 120
Feathers Inn, Northumberland 122
Three Wheat Heads, Thropton 125
Bay Horse Inn, Northumberland 123
Victoria Hotel, Nottingham 132
McQueens, Knaresborough 153
Stone House Inn, N Yorks 156
The Fat Cat, Sheffield 181
Mooch Cafe, Hebden Bridge 192
The Kings Arms, Haworth 200

For a guide to vegetarian wine:
www.vegetarianguides.co.uk/wine

To find out if your favourite drink is
suitable for vegetarians or vegans consult:

www.veggiewines.co.uk
www.vegansociety.com/AFSSearch.aspx
ww.enchant.me.uk/Vegetarian_beers.html

For a guide to vegetarian wine:
www.vegetarianguides.co.uk/wine

The informationan on this card is provided in good faith based on information supplied by veggiewines.co.uk and the Vegan Society August 2010, who have contacted the manufacturers. Vegetarian Guides cannot be held liable for any inaccuracy. You are advised to make your own enquiries to confirm the latest situation.
www.vegetarianguides.co.uk

Alderley Edge	**5**
Altrincham	**5**
Bramhall	**5**
Cheadle	**6**
Chester	**6**
Crewe	**7**
Hale	**7**
Knutsford	**7**
Macclesfield	**8**
Nantwich	**8**
Sale	**8**
Tarporley	**9**
Warrington	**9**
Wilmslow	**9**
Chain stores	**9**

Cheshire

Alderley Edge
Gusto

Omnivorous Italian restaurant

75 London Road, Alderley Edge SK9 7DY
Tel: 01625-583 993
Open: Mon-Thu 11.00-23.00
www.gustorestaurants.uk.com
www.athomewithgusto.com (deliveries)

In the glamorous, wealthy Cheshire village, frequented by footballers and WAGs if you want to see how the beautiful people live. No more expensive than an average pizzeria with a lively buzz about it and relaxingly chilled on a Sunday afternoon. Sunny outside terrace.

Starters and salads £2.75-4.50 include red pepper and tomato soup, raisin bread bruschetta, garlic pizza bread, roasted almonds. Mains £5.95-8.59 include wild mushroom risotto, pasta dishes, pizzas, all dishes made to order and can be adapted.

Fabulous bar. Wine from £14.50. Lots of champagnes from £24 to Cristal £275. Cocktails and champagne cocktails £6-9. Beers from four continents.

Children's menu. Free wifi. Private hire. Previously called Est Est Est. Also in Knutsford, Heswall (Wirral), Liverpool and beyond.

Altrincham
The Greenhouse

Vegetarian restaurant and health food shop

41/43 Oxford Rd, Altrincham WA14 2ED
(10 minutes walk from the Metro station)
Tel: 0161-929 4141 restaurant
Tel: 0161-928 4399 shop
Open: Mon-Sat 08.30-17.30
Now offer a take away service

Soups £3.25 such as spicy African soup, £5.50. Ten different salads. Savouries are mainly vegetarian rather than vegan, but some of the daily bakes are vegan such as winter vegetable and bean £6.15 with bread and side salad. Lots of desserts, including dairy-free Bakewell tart. Gluten-free available. Also takeaway, catering size orders, and outside catering.

The **shop** has lots of allergy-free food, including wholemeal bread. Fridge and freezer with hummus, tofu, sprouts, dairy-free ice-cream. Vegan chocolate by Plamil, and Booja Booja at Christmas. Over 100 kinds of tea. Lots of gluten-free food. Wholemeal bread.

Some bodycare and Natracare. Supplements by Solgar, Quest, Bioforce/Vogel, Pharmanord. Weleda and Nelson homeopathy. Ecover. Big leaflet display. Visa, MC. Two gyms upstairs.

Dilli

Omnivorous Indian restaurant

60 Stamford New Rd, Altrincham, WA14 1EE
Tel: 0161-927 9219
Open: Mon-Sun 12.00-15.00, 17.30-23.00
(22.30 on Sund) www.dilli.co.uk

They have a separate veggie menu, and even a vegan set meal. Starters £4.25-5.50 or have a platter for two £9.50. Mains £5.50-7.50, rice 2.25-2.45, veg biriyani £5.25. 10% discount to Vegetarian Society members.

Bramhall
Ego, Bramhall

Omnivorous Mediterranean restaurant

38- 40 Bramhall Lane South, Bramhall
SK7 1AH. Tel: 0161-439 0693
Open: Mon-Sun 12.00.22.30
www.egorestaurants.com

Modern chain of restaurants in the north-west which cook everything to order, so they are happy to adapt for special diets. Typical vegetarian dishes include roast aubergine with peppers;

pasta with pumpkin, oregano and pine nuts; and mushroom risotto. All around £8. House wine £3.75-5.95 glass, £13.95-16.45 bottle. Beer and cider from £3.25. Cocktails £4.95. Children welcome.

Cheadle

Pizza Express, Cheadle

Omni pizza restaurant & take-away

83 High Street, Cheadle, Cheshire SK8 1AA
Tel: 0161-491 1442
Open: Mon-Sat 11.30-23.00, Sun -22.30
www.pizzaexpress.com for menus and ingredient lists with vegan suitability

This is the description referred to for other branches of this national chain throughout this guide.

Pizza Express is open long hours and is a handy standby in areas like Cheshire without veggie restaurants. Pizzas have vegan bases and can be made without cheese for vegans. In some branches you can bring your own vegan cheese. Vegan starters £2.15 include roasted tomatoes with herbs and olive oil; nuts and seeds roasted with chilli, salt and rosemary; marinated olives. Pizzas £6.25-9.95. Loads of desserts but alas not a single one is vegan.

Wine from £3.75 glass, £12.95 bottle. Italian beers £3.40 (330ml bottle). Low alcohol lager £2.65. Spirits £2.60. Soft drinks £2-2.25. Tea and coffee £1.70-2.50.

Children welcome and they have their own menu which is almost all veggie but not vegan.

Vegetarian but not vegan items marked on menu, so consult the very detailed ingredient list or their website if you have a problem with nuts, garlic, tomatoes etc. Vegans beware that some items that are normally vegan in other restaurants aren't here such as bruschetta. However the chain as a whole are more aware of vegan needs than most restaurants and we hope with further encouragement they could become the first national pizza chain to start stocking vegan cheese and offer vegan ice-cream and reap a tidy increase in customers.

Chester

Hotel Roma

Omnivorous hotel & Italian restaurant

51 Lower Bridge Street, Chester CH1 1RS
Tel: 01244-325091 / 320841
Restaurant open: Mon-Fri 12.-14.30, 17.30-23.30, Sat-Sun 12.00-23.30
www.hotel-roma.co.uk

A central base for exploring Chester. Ensuite rooms, single from £42.50-52, double/twin £55-72, 4-poster £85, family room with double and single £95 with children or £35 per person adult. Breakfast, let them know your requirements when booking, vegan and gluten-free no problem. Parking. Baby listening.

Lunchtime pasta for two with garlic bread or salad £7.90, evening a la carte has Italian dishes which can be made to order and also vegetarian paella, risotto or stroganoff for around £8. MC, Visa.

The Granary, Chester

Health food shop

108 Northgate St, Chester CH1 2HT (off city walls, near Odeon cinema and cathedral)
Tel: 01244-318553
Open: Mon-Sat 9.00-17.00, Sun closed
www.thegranaryhealth.co.uk

Really good for vegan stuff - they have all the fake cheeses, frozen mince, sausages, sausage rolls (all the Fry's range), egg replacers, soya milk and margarine, yoghurts, all the Redwoods sliced fake meats and occasionally there are sos rolls, pasties etc.

Crewe
Lam's Chinese Takeaway
Omnivorous Chinese take-away

17 Nantwich Rd, Crewe, CW2 6AF
Tel: 01270-216 400
Open: Mon-Sun 17.00-23.00,
Tuesdays deliveries only

Crewe was possibly the worst town in Britain for veggies until we heard about this place near the rail station with tofu and lots of veggie options. Seaweed soup £1.60, 5 tofu and 10 veggie dishes £3.50, veg curry or 4 kinds of mixed veg with fried rice £4.50.

Crewe Hall
Hotel and omnivorous restaurants

Crewe Hall, Crewe Green, off Weston Road, Crewe, Cheshire CW1 6UZ
Tel: 01270-253333
Open: Mon-Fri 19.30-21.30; Sat 08.00-22.00; Sun 08.00-11.00, 17.00-21.30
www.qhotels.co.uk/hotels/
crewe-hall-crewe-cheshire/dining.shtml

Very upmarket hotel with restaurants. A regular vegan customer reports "We've always called in advance and received a separate vegan meal with 3 or 4 options on each course (including pudding and not just fresh fruit salad)." High chairs. Licensed. Wheelchair access.

A vegan living in Crewe tells us it is truly grim for vegetarians. Apart from the Holland and Barrett, your best chance in town is to go for beans on toast at **Morrisons Café**, Dunwoody Way, Crewe CW1 3AW. Tel: 01270-253624. Open: Mon-Wed 08.00-19.00, Thu-Sat 08.00-19.00, Sun 9.30-16.00.

Hale
Man Zen, Hale
Omnivorous Chinese restaurant

84 King Street, Knutsford WA16 6ED
Tel: 01565-651537
Open: Mon-Sat 17.30-23.30, Sun 14-23.00
www.manzenhale.co.uk

Lots of vegetarian options including "vegetarian chicken". Vegetarian banquet £21. Sun-Thu until 19.00 two courses for £9.90. Licensed. MC, Visa, Amex. Another branch in Knutsford.

Pizza Express, Hale
Omnivorous Italian restaurant

142 Ashley Road, Hale, Cheshire WA15 9SA
Tel: 0161-928 6644
Open: Mon-Sat 11.30-23.00, Sun 12-22.00
www.pizzaexpress.com

See Cheadle for menu.

Knutsford
Gusto
Omnivorous Italian restaurant

81 King Street, Knutsford WA16 6DX
Tel: 01565-755 487
Open: Mon-
www.gustorestaurants.uk.com

See Alderley Edge above.

Man Zen, Knutsford
Omnivorous Chinese restaurant

84 King Street, Knutsford WA16 6ED
Tel: 01565-651537
Open: Mon-Sat 17.30-23.30, Sun 12-22.00
www.manzenknutsford.co.uk

See Hale branch above.

Pizza Express, Knutsford
Omnivorous Italian restaurant

117a King Street, Knutsford WA16 6EH
Tel: 01565-651 898
Open: Mon-Thu 12.00-22.00, Fri 12.00-22.30, Sat 11.30-22.30, Sun 12.00-22.00

See Cheadle.

Macclesfield
Pizza Express, Macclesfield
Omnivorous pizza restaurant

4 Market Place, Macclesfield SK10 1EX
Tel: 01625-425 175
Open: 11.30-23.00

Vegan pizza bases and can leave off the cheese for vegans.

Nantwich
The Red Cow
Omnivorous pub

Beam St, Nantwich CW5 5NA
Tel: 01270-628 581

Lively and popular pub in a beautiful old building. Offers at least 7 vegetarian main meal options for £6.95, some of which are, or can be, vegan. Typical dishes include pasta with roast pepper sauce, chickpea curry; and veg kievs.

Vegonia Wholefoods
Vegan wholefood shop

8 Oat Market, Nantwich CW5 5AL
Tel: 01270-618 647
Open: Mon-Sat 9.00-17.30, Sun closed
www.vegonia.co.uk

Thousands of vegan foods, many organic, Fairtrade, gluten-free, herbs and spices, Oriental foods. Fridge and freezer with most of the vegan cheeses and meat substitutes such as Redwood, Bute Island, Frys, Taifun, ice-cream by Booja Booja, Swedish Glace, Tofutti.
Lots of vegan chocolate by Plamil, Seed & Bean, Organica, Booja Booja, Montezuma, Xylitol, raw Conscious Chocolate.
Bodycare by Faith In Nature, Yaoh, Weleda, Suma, Natracare. Weleda, Green People and Nature Babycare.
Supplements by Lifeplan, Nature's Aid, Viridian, Quest, Kordells, Vogel, Lifestream. Helios homeopathy, essential oils.
Cleaning by BioD, Suma Ecoleaf, Faith In Nature, Earth Friendly, and some refills. The Vegan magazine. Candles, incense, bamboo socks. Mail order. MC, Visa.

Sale
Hanni's
Mediterranean restaurant

4 Brooklands Road (by Brooklands Metrolink), Sale M33
Tel: 0161-973 6606
Open: 17.30-22.00 Mon-Sat

Friendly restaurant on the Manchester to Altrincham tram line, with a well-stocked bar. At least 8 veggie starters, which you can order as a mezze. Options include hummus; falafel; tabouleh; mixed salad; and dolmades. A typical mezze of about 6 starters between two people will cost about £12 each. Vegans should just ask for no yoghurt dips on the side.

Sokrates
Omnivorous Greek restaurant

25a Northenden Road, Sale M33 2DH
Tel: 0161-282 0050
Open: Sun 15.00-22.00 (last orders 21.00),
Mon-Thu 17.30-23.00 (last orders 22.00)
Fri-Sat 17.30-24.00 (last orders 22.30)
www.sokratestaverna.co.uk

Sister restaurant to one in Bolton, see Lancashire chapter.

Tarporley

The Headless Woman

Gastro pub with massive menu

Tarporley Road (just off A51), Duddon,
Tarporley CW6 0EW
Tel: 01829-781 252
Open: Mon-Sun, food served 12.00-14.00
and from 18.00.

A cosy pub noted for its food, which offers vegetarian and vegan options, including foccacia with roast peppers, tomato and olives; mushroom risotto; and Thai vegetable crumble. Sandwiches around £3, mains £10-11.

Warrington

Ego, Warrington

Omnivorous Mediterranean restaurant

25 Walton Road, Stockton Heath,
Warrington WA4 6NJ
Tel: 01925-60 26 06
Open: Mon-Sun 12.00-22.30
www.egorestaurants.co.uk

Outside dining in summer. See Bramhall.

Wilmslow

Pizza Express, Wilmslow

Omnivorous Italian restaurant

26 Alderley Road, Wilmslow SK9 1PL
Tel: 01625-540 055
Open: Mon-Thu 11.30-23.00,
Fri-Sat 11.30-23.30, Sun 12.00-22.30
www.pizzaexpress.com

See Cheadle.

Tourist information:
www.visitcheshire.com
www.chesterwiki.com

Chain stores

Holland & Barrett

Health food shop

70 George Street, **Altrincham** WA14 1RF
Tel: 0161-929 6716
Open : Mon-Sat 9.00-17.30, Sun 10-16.00

7 Paddock Row, Grosvenor Precinct
Chester CH1 1ED
Tel: 01244-348 153
Open: Mon-Sat 9.00-17.30,
Sun 10.30-16.30

Unit 25 Foregate Street, **Chester** CH1 1HD
Tel: 01244-401 126
Open: Mon-Sat 9.00-17.30,
Sun 11.00-17.00

25 Victoria Street, **Crewe** CW2 2JE
Tel: 01270-253 022
Open Mon-Sat 9.00-17.30 (Fri 17.00),
Sun 11.00-16.00

Mill Street Mall, **Macclesfield** SK11 8AJ
Tel: 01625-424 256
Open Mon-Sat 9.00-17.30, Sun 9.00-16.00

39 High Street, **Nantwich** CW5 5DB
Tel: 01270-610 041
Open: Mon-Sat 9.00-17.30

72 High Street, **Northwich** CW9 5AG
Tel: 01606-42073
Open: Mon-Sun 9.00-17.30

Unit 77, Town Square, Holton Lea
Runcorn WA7 2EU. Tel: 01928-791188
Open: Mon-Sat 9.00-17.30, Sun closed

Unit 4, The Mall, School Road, **Sale** M33 1XZ
Tel: 0161-905 1894
Open: Mon-Sat 9.00-17.30, Sun closed

97/99 Princess Street, **Stockport** SK1 1UR
Tel: 0161-480 2314
Open: Mon-Sat 9.00-17.30, Sun 10-16.00

85 The Mall, Golden Square Shopping Centre
Warrington WA1 1QE. Tel: 01925-418 424
Open: Mon-Sat 9.00-18.00 (Thu 19.00),
Sun 11.00-17.00

31c Grove Street, **Wilmslow** SK9 1LD
Tel: 01625-531 626
Open: Mon-Sat 9.00-17.30, Sun 10-16.00

Cumbria Accommodation

- 12 Introduction
- 14 Yewfield Vegetarian B&B, Ambleside
- 17 Hall Croft, vegetarian B&B, Appley-in-Westmoreland
- 18 Croft Guest House, Cockermouth
- 19 Lakeland Living, vegetarian B&B, Cockermouth
- 20 Lancrigg vegetarian hotel & restaurant, Grasmere
- 22 Beech Tree Guest House, vegetarian, Coniston
- 23 Old Water View, B&B, Patterdale
- 24 Fox Hall Vegan B&B, Kendal
- 26 The Heights Hotel, vegetarian, Keswick
- 28 Edwardene Hotel, Keswick
- 29 Honister House, guest house, Keswick
- 30 St John's Lodge, guest house, Windermere

- 32 Nab Cottage, Ambleside
- 32 Ardrig Vegetarian B&B, Kendal
- 32 Hazelmere, B&B, Keswick
- 32 Sefton House, vegeatrian B&B, Ulverston
- 32 Kirkdwood Guest House, Windermere
- 44 Upfront Gallery self-catering, near Penrith
- 45 Conishead Priory vegetarian full board, near Ulverston

Cumbria Restaurants & Shops

- **33 Ambleside hot spot**
- 36 Appleby-in-Westmoreland
- 36 Barrow-in-Furness
- 37 Brampton
- 37 Caldbeck
- 37 Cockermouth
- **39 Grasmere hot spot**
- **40 Kendal hot spot**
- **41 Keswick hot spot**
- 43 Milnthorpe
- 43 Penrith area
- **44 Ulverston hot spot**
- 46 Whitehaven
- 47 Wigton
- 47 Windermere
- 47 Workington
- 47 Chain stores

Granny Smiths, Ambleside p.35

The Lake District Cumbria

Cumbria

The Lake District

The Lake District, in the county of Cumbria, is the largest of England's national parks and offers some of the best walking in Britain. It is an extremely beautiful area with high fells, rocky crags, lush green dales, huge peaceful lakes and busy villages. As a vegetarian, it is an excellent place to take a holiday with more 100% vegetarian accommodation than any other county, and there are many more veggie-friendly guesthouses and restaurants in many of its villages. The main bases for the Lakes are **Keswick** in the north and **Windermere & Bowness** in the south.

Windermere and Bowness is the largest tourist centre and is full of bed & breakfasts, restaurants and attractions such as The World of Beatrix Potter. It gets inundated by tourists and can feel like a seaside resort. One of its delights is the vegetarian-owned **St John's Lodge**. If the weather's not so great for walking, visit the Lake District Centre at Brockhole, by Lake Windermere, which has an adventure playground, interactive exhibitions, beautiful gardens, games' lawn and a gift shop.

Keswick, next to Derwent Water is particularly popular with walkers. It's a busy town, but it feels more relaxed than Windermere. A pleasant four mile circular walk from the town centre to the Castlerigg Stone Circle, believed to be around 3000 years old, offers excellent views. Have lunch at the vibrant wholefood veggie café **Lakeland Pedlar**, loved by walkers and cyclists, or take a tasty snack away with you. For a change from walking or cycling, take a boat trip or row a hired boat around the lake. Great places to stay include the new vegetarian **Heights Hotel**.

Ambleside, just north of Windermere & Bowness, is a pretty town, a popular centre for walkers and climbers and a real veggie hotspot. It's a good base to explore the southern Lake District, but although slightly less hectic than Windermere & Bowness, can get very crowded at weekends. **Yewfield Vegetarian B&B** also has self-contained apartments. Eating is more upmarket here. You can feast and take in a film at **Zeffirellis** and the new **Fellinis** vegetarian restaurants, or relax at the new daytime vegetarian **Rattle Gill Cafe** by the waterside. There's even a health food store with take-aways.

Grasmere is a very pretty village. If you love the poetry of Wordsworth then you can visit the Wordsworth Museum and adjoining Dove Cottage, which is where he wrote many of his poems. The luxurious **Lancrigg** vegetarian country house hotel is loved by many readers, who rate it the ultimate UK romantic break for veggies, along with its **Green Valley** organic vegetarian restaurant which is open to non-residents.

Coniston Water and the town are both beautiful. There are some lovely walks in the area, particularly up the Old Man of Coniston. If it's a clear day, the view from the top is breathtaking. Stay at **Beech Tree** vegetarian guest house.

Cockermouth has the famous award-winning **Quince and Medlar** gourmet vegetarian restaurant, rated one of the best in Britain. It is at the very north end of the Lake District, which makes it quieter than many of the other places. Stay at **Lakeland Living**, which can also provide evening meals.

Kendal, on the eastern outskirts of the Lakes, is a busy market town with several interesting museums and galleries. A big selling point has to be **Fox Hall** vegan bed and breakfast serving very imaginative breakfasts and three course dinners, which has moved to a new location closer to the town. There is also **Ardrig** vegetarian B&B. The town has two vegetarian cafes, **Waterside Wholefood** and **Meeting House Cafe**.

Ulverston, at the south end of the Lakes, is at the start of the Cumbria Way and on the Cumbrian Coast Way. Stay at **Sefton House** vegetarian B&B or enjoy a peaceful time with full vegetarian board at the Buddhist Temple and grounds of **Conishead Priory** just outside Ulverston. There are three vegetarian cafes and a cracking wholefood shop. The **Laurel and Hardy Museum** is in Brogden Street.

If you'd prefer to be out of the main hub of the Lake District, consider **Grange-over-Sands** on the southern edge of the park or **Appleby-in-Westmoreland** or **Alston**, close to The Pennines.

The Lake District offers many opportunities for learning about the area and there are many books available on walking or cycling in Cumbria. There are some great cycling routes, particularly the Cumbria Cycle Way which takes five to seven days. It is possible to do navigated walks and bike rides and learn to map read.

If you're tired of walking or it's just not your thing, most of the lakes have boat trips around them, which can be a relaxing way to still see some gorgeous scenery. For pampering, **Review Coffee Bar** vegetarian cafe in Barrow-in-Furness also houses a hairdresser with cruelty-free products, beauty therapies, massage and Indian head massage.

A word of warning: On summer weekends the Lake District is the second most visited area in Britain behind London. Food and accommodation are priced accordingly. If visiting during peak season, ensure you book ahead to avoid disappointment.

www.visitcumbria.com lists over 30 local tourist information centres

www.golakes.co.uk
www.lake-district.gov.uk
www.visiteden.co.uk
ww.explorelakedistrict.co.uk

www.amblesideonline.co.uk
www.cockermouth.org.uk
www.keswick.org
www.laurel-and-hardy.co.uk

Yewfield Vegetarian B&B

Impressive Gothic Victorian house with panoramic views over the Vale of Esthwaite, Lake Winderemere and the fells beyond. There are ten doubles and twins, all ensuite, for £38-£60 per person per night. Single person supplement £25.

Begin the day with a wholefood continental buffet including fresh fruits, vegan muesli, cereals and home baked bread with preserves, followed by a full cooked breakfast. Vegan margarine and soya milk available. Dinner is not offered but Ambleside's veggie restaurants, Zeffirellis and Fellinis, are only four miles away.

Yewfield is ideally situated for walking and enjoying this region of rare natural beauty. A ten minute stroll takes you to a magnificent viewpoint overlooking Tarn Hows and the rugged fells of the central Lakes. The house stands in over thirty acres of private grounds, which include native woodland, rough fell pasture and a small tarn and stream. Areas closer to the house include organic veggie gardens, orchards, a herb patio and a mixed border. A nature trail through the land and gardens is there to guide you.

If you prefer self catering, there are self contained holiday apartments in the former coach house and stables, set 150 yards away from the main house. Please contact Lakeland Hideaways on 015394-42435 with enquiries.

Tea and coffee making facilities, radios and televisions in the rooms. Lounge and library area available for guests' use. Children over nine welcome. Pets accepted by arrangement in the self catering apartments only.

Ambleside

Vegetarian B&B and self-catering

Hawkshead Hill
Ambleside
Cumbria LA22 0PR
England

Tel: 015394-36765

www.yewfield.co.uk

Email: derek.yewfield@btinternet.com

Train Station: Windermere, 6 miles, then taxi

Open: Feb-end Nov

Directions: from Ambleside take the A593 Coniston Road and at Clappersgate (1/2 mile), turn a sharp left at junction signposted B5286 Hawkshead. Proceed for just over one mile, then on the brow of a hill, turn right into an unclassified road signposted Tarn Hows. Follow this road for 2.4 miles (passing the Drunken Duck Inn), before reaching the drive up to Yewfield on the right.

Parking: available

No smoking throughout

No children under 9 years, except in self-catering

No pets except in self-catering

Visa, MC

Yewfield
Tarn Hows / Hawkshead

Vegetarian Bed & Breakfast
PLUS
Luxury Self Catering Accommodation
NON-SMOKING

a peaceful and quiet retreat in the heart

of the English Lake District

Hawkshead Hill, Hawkshead, Ambleside, Cumbria LA22 0PR
Telephone: 015394 36765
www.yewfield.co.uk   email: derek.yewfield@btinternet.com

All you need on the road

Vegetarian London

160 vegetarian restaurants, cafes and take-aways, 25 of them vegan.
200 more with huge veggie menus.
300 shops.
Accommodation.
15 local maps.

"More important than the A-Z."
The Vegetarian Society

Vegetarian Europe

300 entries.
48 tourist destinations.
23 countries.
Includes giant Paris section.

"An ideal springboard for that European holiday you always wanted to take, but were unsure about the food."
The Vegetarian Society

Vegetarian East of England

44 vegetarian restaurants & cafes.
90 more with big veggie menus.
12 city and country pubs.
Vegetarian city and country B&Bs.
160 shops and delis.

Coming soon: Scotland, Wales, South and Vegetarian Britain 4

We also sell vegetarian guides to Spain, Brighton, Bristol & Bath, Lake District, New York, the Vegan Passport and the Scoffer vegan cookbooks.
Read our monthly restaurants page in *Vegetarian Living* magazine.
Visit our /links page for websites covering the whole world.

See the latest guides and print off updates at www.vegetarianguides.co.uk

Hall Croft

Large detached four storey and lovingly restored Victorian villa in the classic English village of Dufton offering quality accommodation: one double with private bathroom, one double ensuite £23-26, one twin ensuite, £30-35 per person per night. Tea and coffee making facilities in rooms as are TV, VCR and hairdryer.

Breakfast is substantial and includes a wide range of cereals, vegan muesli, fresh fruit, homemade wholemeal and speciality breads with homemade marmalade and jam. Orange or grapefruit juice and Fair Trade tea and coffee are also offered. Cooked breakfast is available on request with advance notice such as croissants, veggie/vegan sausages, baked beans, pancakes, homemade muffins, and grapefruit cocktail.

Special diets can be catered for and vegan margarine, soya yoghurt, soya milk and other gluten free foods are all available. The vegetarian owners Ray and Frei pride themselves on their personal service and nothing (almost!) is too much trouble. Also for vegetarians nearby is Little Salkeld Watermill vegetarian organic wholefood tea room and also The Village Bakery organic cafe.

The Eden Valley is a little known part of Cumbria, ideal for a peaceful break - walking, cycling touring or just chilling out. It is ideally placed for touring the Lakes (30 minute drive away), Northumberland, Scotland and the Yorkshire Dales. Carlisle is an interesting city and there are many fascinating small market towns within easy reach. A beautiful, tranquil area in which to relax. Also right on The Pennine Way.

Appleby-in-Westmorland

Vegan/vegetarian bed and breakfast

Hall Croft
Dufton
Appleby-in-Westmorland
Cumbria CA16 6DB

Tel: 01768-352 902

Email: r.walker@leaseholdpartnerships.co.uk

Train station: Appleby 3 miles

Collection available from train station

Open: all year, except Christmas

Directions: A66 to Appleby - Dufton is signposted. The village is 3 miles out of Appleby. Hall Croft is situated at the lower end of the village green.

Parking: available

Children of all ages welcome

Pets by arrangement

Owners more than willing to advise on routes, or occasionally, to lead runs or cycle rides

Packed lunches available on request

Homemade cake and tea/coffee offered each afternoon

No smoking throughout

AA 4 Diamonds

Croft Guest House

Georgian town house, recently renovated and refurbished, with worldwide ethnic influences, on a quiet back street at the edge of a spectacular but quieter part of the Lake District.

5 doubles, 2 twins £35-40 per person, £45 as single. One of the doubles is a large family room with double and bunk beds for well-behaved children, £10 per child. Folding bed on request.

For vegetarian or vegan breakfast you could have tropical fruit salad, cereals, tofu and vegetable kedgeree, Fairtrade tea/coffee. They have soya milk, vegan muesli and sausages and home-made jams and bread. Afternoon teas and packed lunches available on request.

10 minutes drive from Buttermere Falls. Cockermouth is the birthplace of William Wordsworth and Fletcher Christian. You can visit Wordsworth House, the Cumberland Toy Museum, and Bitter End micro-brewery. Kirkgate Arts Centre has film, theatre, music and exhibitions. You can wander the narrow roads, antiques shops and museums, or have an evening stroll along the river or around the parks. Cockermouth has the Quince & Medlar vegetarian restaurant and a wholefood shop. The owners provide an information pack about nearby walks and climbs on the fells or gentler ones around the lakes.

Rooms have tea/coffee making, wall mounted slimline tv, radio/alarm, hairdryer, full length miror. Wifi. Breakfast in room by arrangement. Dining room.

Cockermouth

Omnivorous Guest House

6-8 Challoner St
Cockermouth
Cumbria CA13 9QS
England

Tel: 01900-827533

www.croft-guesthouse.com
info@croft-guesthouse.com

Train: Penrith or Carlisle 25/30 miles then bus/taxi

Open: all year

Directions: M6 junction 40, A66 west 30 mileds, from bypass reach Cockermouth Main St. Challoner St runs up left hand side of Globe Hotel. 3/4 of the way up, big yellow house on left.

Off street parking with CCTV

Children 6+ by arrangement. Room has ample space for travel cot.

No pets

Lockable bike storage

A room to clean and store walkers' boots and waterproofs

No smoking

Visa, MC

Cumbrian Tourist Board four star rating and Silver Award

Lakeland Living

Big family house with a large organic vegetable garden and lots of pets. Country cottage bedroom ensuite £32 per person (single or double occupancy).

Start the day with a selection of fresh and dried fruit, nuts and organic cereals or 7-grain porridge topped with sunflower seeds, dried blueberries, poppy seed tahini and maple syrup. Full cooked breakfast including potato and seaweed cakes. Also toast or bread, homemade marmalade and jams. Choice of milks: soya, rice, almond etc. Home made fruit juice. Vegan margarine available.

The owner Anita is vegan and used to run her own restaurant. There is a fabulous evening menu from £15-20, or supper from £10. Plenty of scrumptious food from around the world including British, European, African and South American recipes. Most of the ingredients are organic and GM free. All served with veggies from the garden. Dessert can be homemade vegan chocolate ice-cream or fruit crumble.

There are several cats in the house and a friendly little dog, and rabbits and guinea pigs in the garden. There are no resident children, but frequent visits from grandchildren.

A few minutes walk from Quince & Medlar vegetarian restaurant and the Granary health food store.

On the edge of the National Park, with mountains and lakes within walking distance. Watersports, walking, swimming and a seaside 6 miles away. Museums such as Wordsworth House and 2 mins away, the Toy and Doll Museum. Brewery with visitor centre close by. The town centre has a theatre and cinema.

Cockermouth

Vegetarian and Vegan B&B

15 Challoner Street
Cockermouth
Cumbria CA13 9QS

Tel: 01900-824 045

www.veggielakelandliving.co.uk
anita@veggielakelandliving.co.uk

Train station: Maryport, 6 miles, then bus or taxi or collection

Open: all year

Directions: Challoner Street is in the centre of town, almost opposite Barclays Bank.

Parking: car parks close by

Children all ages welcome

High chairs and facilities for babies

Dogs welcome if they don't chase cats!

No smoking throughout
Tea and coffee making facilities, radio & CD player, and hairdryer in rooms.

10% discount for Vegan Society, Viva! and people with this book

Gluten, wheat and yeast-free diets catered for. Can also do raw food.

Joint winner Best Vegetarian Breakfast 2007 from the Vegetarian Society

NORTH Cumbria

Lancrigg

Lancrigg, now in its 26th year, is set in 30 acres of idyllic gardens overlooking the serenity of Easedale. You will appreciate the total absence of traffic
noise and the sound of nearby waterfalls and birds, yet Grasmere village and all its amenities is only a short walk away. There is excellent walking right from the doorstep.

There are 11 rooms, with singles, doubles, twins and families, all with ensuite bathrooms. Most have special features such as gorgeous views, 4-poster and whirlpool spa baths. Prices range from £85-£110 per person per night and include breakfast and evening meal. Cheaper rates for stays of three nights or more. Bed & breakfast prices also available. Children under 5 £4 B&B, 5-15 £12 B&B. Dogs in certain rooms £10 per stay.

In the morning help yourself to fruit juices, fruit salads and natural cereals. This is followed by a continental or full cooked breakfast of basil tomatoes, vegetarian burgers, baked beans, potato cakes, fried marinated tofu, mushrooms and toast. Vegan margarine, soya milk, soya yoghurt, vegan muesli and smoothies are all available.

Dinner in the **Green Valley** vegetarian restaurant (open to non-residents 08.30-20.30 last orders, booking recommended, see page 39) could be roasted aubergine and tomato torte with a romesco sauce, followed by carrot and fennel soup. Your main might be provençal mushroom, leek and pine-kernel stuffed pepper, with a tomato and olive sauce and new potaotes, roasted in lemon and fresh herbs, served with salad. They always have vegan desserts available such as chocolate & coffee mousse with homemade coconut sorbet (vegan). Finish off with fresh ground coffee and chocolates. Organic wine available. Special diets catered for. Food is organic where possible and free from artificial additives.

Grasmere

Vegetarian country house hotel & restaurant

Easedale
Grasmere
Cumbria LA22 9QN

Tel: 015394 35317
Fax: 015394 35058

www.lancrigg.co.uk

Email: info@lancrigg.co.uk

Train Station:
Windermere 8 miles
then taxi

Open: all year

Directions: From the M6, take the A591 to Grasmere. In the centre of the village, turn left up Easedale Road. The entrance is 1/2 mile on the right.

Parking: available

Children and pets welcome. They have cots and high chairs.

Breakfast can be served in rooms if requested

10% discount to members of the Vegetarian Society, Vegan Society, Viva! and people presenting this book.

See page 39 for Green Valley Cafe & Restaurant

Champagne, flowers and organic vegan truffle chocolates may be ordered to be in your room on arrival. Tea & coffee making and TV in rooms.

Lancrigg

VEGETARIAN COUNTRY HOUSE HOTEL

THE LAKE DISTRICT

GRASMERE

"Where time stands still"

Idyllic mountain setting, comfy rooms, whirlpool baths, pure food and fine wines provide real inspiration for Romantics and Lakeland Lovers.

✶✶✶✶✶✶

Lancrigg's timeless charm comes from it's unrivalled position overlooking the serenity of Easedale. Whether on foot, car or local transport, you are but half a mile away from the Lakeland village of Grasmere.

One aspect you will really appreciate is the total absence of traffic noise - the silence puctuated only by the sound of nearby waterfalls and birdsong.

Enjoy the relaxed atmosphere of the elegant Georgian dining room where meals are served overlooking Easedale valley. Soft music and candlelit tables add to the setting.

Special Breaks

Tel: 015934 35317
Email: info@lancrigg.co.uk
www.lancrigg.co.uk

Beech Tree Guest House

Beech Tree Guest House is set in its own grounds, at the foot of the Old Man of Coniston, 150 yards from the centre of the village. There are six double rooms, three with ensuites and two twin rooms, one with an ensuite. Rooms with ensuites are £34 per person per night and those without are £28 per person per night.

Begin the day with fruit juice, cereals and grapefruit followed by vegetarian sausage-burgers or vegetarian sausages, mushrooms, beans, tomatoes and toast. Vegan margarine, soya milk and vegan muesli are available. Special diets catered for. Let them know your requirements when you book. No evening meal is offered, but there is a wide range of restaurants and pubs in Coniston and the surrounding villages.

There are walks right from the house to local waterfalls, the lower valleys or to Coniston Old Man and the high fells. Some of the most beautiful scenery in the Lake District is nearby, as well as many famous houses and attractions.

Coniston is an ideal stopover on the Cumbria Way. It is an excellent centre for many activities. There is much to do for people of all interests and abilities, such as walks ranging from gentle strolls to difficult climbs, sailing and canoeing, and of course just sightseeing and relaxing. Coniston makes a good base to explore the Langdale Valleys, Wastwater and the Southern Fells.

Guests are welcome to enjoy the small but interesting garden. Drying facilities are available. Tea and coffee making facilites in rooms. Guest lounge with television.

Coniston

Vegetarian Guest House

Yewdale Road
Coniston
Cumbria LA21 8DX
England

Tel: 01539-441 717

Train Station: Windermere, 12 miles, then bus

Open: all year

Directions: phone for details and map

Parking: ample private parking

Children over 10 only

No pets

No smoking throughout

Old Water View

Victorian house set on the banks of Goldrill Beck river in a charming and peaceful unspoilt Lakeland village nestling at the southern end of Lake Ullswater, away from the busy tourist centres, and yet within easy reach of Ambleside, Windermere, Keswick and Penrith. Vegetarian owned and aiming to go completely veggie when they have enough visitors.

3 double, 1 twin, 1 triple, all ensuite, £35 - 42 per person, or £45 as single. Family room with double and two 2-foot (60cm) children's singles and a travel cot, £35-42 per adult for double occupancy, children 6-17 £25, 0-5 free. Fridays and Saturdays are a minimum of 2 nights and must include both Friday and Saturday night. You can check availability of each room on the website.

Cooked veggie or vegan breakfast includes sausage, potato waffle, tomatoes, mushrooms, baked beans and toast. You may see red squirrels scampering in the trees in the large garden. Packed lunch available. There are vegetarian restaurants within a half hour drive.

Steamers sail on Ullswater year round from Glenridding, 1 mile away, and you can enjoy a leisurely cruise, perhaps with a gentle stroll back by the lake. Helvelyn, Place Fell, Sheffield Pike and St Sunday Crag are all within easy reach along with countless other fells and hills, and there are many low level easy walks along the lakeshore. Garden landing area for if you bring canoes.

Guests can relax at the end of the day and plan the next one with a drink in the garden or their own exclusive lounge with a real log fire, internet, TV and video, a wide selection of maps, guide books and games. Rooms have tea/coffee making, TV, video, CD player, hairdryer, iron and ironing board. Gift vouchers available. Drying facilities and laundry service.

Patterdale

Omnivorous Bed & Breakfast

Old Water View
Patterdale
Cumbria CA11 0NW
England

Tel: 017684-82175
Fax: 017684-82860

www.oldwaterview.co.uk
ask@oldwaterview.co.uk

Train Station: Penrith 15 miles then bus or taxi

Open: all year except Xmas

Directions: **From M6 north** junction 40 take A66 west (signposted Keswick), at first roundabout take A592 to Ullswater. Follow along side of lake to Patterdale. Old Water View is through village, 400 meters past White Lion pub on your left. **From M6 south** junction 36, take A590 then A591 west to Windermere. At mini roundabout turn right onto 592 signposted Penrith and Ullswater. The road takes you over Kirkstone Pass, past Brotherswate rand Hartsop, to Patterdale. Hosue in on right, just after the Youth Hostel and before you enter village. Printable map on website.

Parking available

Children welcome, cot, high chair and baby bath

No pets

No smoking throughout

Credit cards accepted

Fox Hall Vegan B&B

Prizet Stables is a continuation of the successful Vegan B&B established and run by Sylvia and Chris at Fox Hall in Sedgwick for 17 years. The new location is 2 miles nearer to Kendal and continues to offer reliable vegan accommodation, service and food to vegans and vegetarians from all over the world. The town is ideally situated for exploring the lakes and mountains of Cumbria and the North West coast.

2 doubles, 1 twin/double, 1 large family room (for 1 child plus baby), all ensuite, £30-40 per person. Children 5-16 £10, under-5 free.

Breakfast is entirely vegan and is a selection of cereals or porridge with soya milk, soya yoghurt and fresh fruit followed by a choice from several dishes including creamed mushrooms on toast; tofu, onion, mushrooms and dill on toast; home made lemon and sultana pancakes or the Big One- two nut rissoles or bean burgers with scrambled tofu, mushrooms, onions and plum tomatoes. Organic and GMO free foods are used where possible.

There is an extensive evening meal menu £15 for 3 courses, available to residents only, from which you could choose leek and potato soup, wholemeal pancakes layered with fennel, spinach and tomato and for dessert, chocolate and orange gateau. Child's meal £3.50. Packed lunches are available for £4. They can cater for all types of special diet including gluten or sugar free and raw. The dining room caters for 12 diners and there is a guest lounge with sliding doors to a pleasant lawned garden with fine views across the River Kent valley easterly towards The Helm.

A range of home-made preserves, walk leaflets and patchwork shopping bags are on sale. Vegan cookery courses. Gift vouchers. No credit cards.

Kendal

Vegan Bed & Breakfast

Prizet Stables
Helsington
Kendal
Cumbria LA8 8AB

Tel and Fax:
015395 61241

www.fox.hall.btinternet.co.uk
fox.hall@btinternet.com

Train Station: Oxenholme, 3 miles, then bus or taxi.

Open: all year

Detailed directions on webiste: 2 miles south of Kendal on A6 then A591. From M6 junction 36, take A590 then A591towards Kendal. Pass Low Sizergh Barn Shop on right, then immediately turn right across dual carriageway signposted Prizet. After ¼ mile turn left through stone gateposts before first bungalow called South View, Prizet Stables is third house on right.

Parking for 6 cars. Cycle storage. Books and maps to borrow.

Travel cot and high chair

Tea and coffee making and colour tv's in rooms

No smoking inside. No pets

Use of washing machine on request

They no longer have a self-catering cottage

FOX HALL VEGAN B&B
Prizet Stables, Helsington, Kendal, Cumbria, LA8 8AB

Come and stay with a vegan family who care about your holiday in our eco-friendly home 2 miles south of Kendal, South Lakes. Extensive menu - all vegan. Comfortable, well-equipped, happy family home. Children very welcome, travel cot and high chair available. Sorry, no smoking or pets. Good local walks. Ideal base for exploring the English Lake District.

Tel/Fax: Sylvia or Chris on 015395 61241
E-mail: Fox.Hall@btinternet.com or
Visit our Website: www.fox.hall.btinternet.co.uk
for more info and pictures.

The Heights Hotel

Family run hotel in a traditional Victorian Lakeland stone house and grounds overlooking the bustling market town of Keswick, with panoramic views towards Skiddaw, Derwent Water and Bassenthwaite. The bar was converted from the original 17th century Cumbrian cottage, and along with the lounge is a great place to relax after a day's walking, climbing, cycling, touring or sightseeing. Red squirrels visit the garden, there are roe deer in the local woods and various birds of prey in the area.

11 ensuite rooms: 6 doubles, 1 twin, 4 family (3 with bath) - 3 with double & single bed and 1 with double and 2 singles. £30-35 per person per night, and may be higher for any stay that includes part of a Bank Holiday weekend (Fri-Mon). Partial occupancy £5 per room. Children 3-13 half price, babies 0-2 £3. You can check room availability online.

Cooked breakfast includes cereals, veggie/vegan sausages, with vegan margarine and soya milk available. A la carte menu available 7-9pm in dining room or bar. Packed lunches available. **Open to non-residents for dinner.** Lots of restaurants in town.

Outstanding walks and footpaths nearby include to Ashness Bridge, Derwent Water, Castlerigg Stone Circle and Walla Crag. You can take the steamer around Derwent Water, or sail or canoe there or at Bassenthwaite. There is the forest park at Whinlatter to explore or the Cumbrian Myths and Legends experience at Rheged. Further afield, St Bees headland is famous for its breeding puffins and guillemots.

There are plays and concerts at Keswick's modern Theatre by the Lake, a bowls club and several golf courses in the area. Groups of families and friends such as walkers, painters, golfers, bowlers, and those who just want to relax, return to The Heights year after year.

Keswick

Vegetarian hotel & bar

The Heights Hotel
Rakefoot Lane
Castlerigg, Keswick
Cumbria CA12 4TE
England

Tel: 01768-77 22 51

www.theheightshotel.co.uk
info@theheightshotel.co.uk

Open: Feb-Nov & Xmas/NY

Train: Penrith 17 miles Regular buses and taxi. Frequent buses to Keswick from Penrith and the 555 bus from Keswick stops at the end of Rakefoot Lane.

Directions: From the M6 junction 40 take the A66 west. After about 17 miles take the A591 to Keswick and Windermere. After half a mile you will reach a T junction with Chestnut Hill. Turn left up the hill and take the second turning on your right. This is Rakefoot Lane and is marked with a tourist sign indicating The Heights. The hotel is the second property on the right.

Private parking for 24 cars

Children welcome, high chairs

Pets by arrangement £3

Clothes drying facilities

Tea/coffee making, TV and hairdryer in rooms.

No smoking. Visa, MC

The Heights Hotel

Rakefoot Lane, Castlerigg, Keswick
CA12 4TE

Friendly, family run **fully vegetarian** hotel
Vegan and special diets catered for
All rooms en-suite from £34 - Evening meals available
Breathtaking views of surrounding lakes and fells
Cosy bar with open fire and Jennings Real Ale on draft
Residents' lounge with views of Skiddaw
Many walks from hotel. 5 minutes walk to Walla Crag
An ideal base from which to explore the North Lakes.
Pets welcome - Large walled garden

www.theheightshotel.co.uk
info@theheightshotel.co.uk
01768 77 22 51

Edwardene Hotel

The Edwardene is a beautiful three-storey Victorian Lakeland stone property built in 1885, in a quiet position two minutes' walk from Keswick's market square, theatre and lake. 11 ensuite bedrooms with bath and/or shower room: 2 singles £43 per night, 6 doubles and 2 twins £38-44 per person (£46-76 as single), 1 family room £124 (for 2 adults and 2 children, or 3 adults) or £96 as double. Low season midweek Sun-Thu 3 nights £102 per person, excluding half term, Xmas and New Year. Xmas and New Year packages available. There are photos of the rooms on the website.

Full cooked breakfasts cater for vegetarian, vegan, coeliac and special diets, though you should let them know when you book.

The town of Keswick has shops, restaurants, numerous pubs, a theatre, cinema, galleries and museums. Visit the veggie cafe The Lakeland Pedlar in town for lunch.

Keswick is paradise for walkers, set amidst spectacular scenery and overlooked by Skiddaw, the fourth highest mountain in England. The Edwardene serves as an excellent base to explore the central and northern Lake District, whether for a relaxing break away from it all, or for discovering the beauty of the mountains, fells and lakes of this outstanding area, with many excellent varied walks from the doorstep.

In the evenings you can relax by the fireside in the comfortable lounge, chat with friends, plan your next day, or simply enjoy a glass of wine or a game of scrabble.

Keswick

Omnivorous Hotel

26 Southey Street
Keswick
Cumbria CA12 4EF
England

Tel: 017687-73586

www.edwardenehotel.com
Email: info@edwardenehotel.com
Online enquiry form or call

Train Station: Penrith, 16 miles, then bus or taxi

Open: all year

Directions: From the M6 junction 40 follow A66 west towards Keswick, follow sign for Keswick turning left off exit slip road, follow signs for town centre. At the war memorial and just before the pedestrian traffic lights turn left and sharp left into Southey St, we are 150 metres on the right.

Parking: 2 spaces

Children of any age welcome. Cot and high chair

Pets in special circumstances

Secure cycle storage and drying facilities

No smoking throughout

Rooms have direct dial telephone, alarm clock and radio, TV, hairdryer, tea/coffee making. Some rooms contain videos, bars and other luxury upgrades. Credit cards accepted

Honister House

Centrally located 18th century home in the lovely market town of Keswick. There are two doubles and one twin/double, all ensuite, £70-75 per room per night (single rate when available £45). Age 6-15 £10, under 5 free. Under new ownership since our last edition but retaining the same friendly and veggie-friendly approach.

A locally sourced Fairtrade breakfast of fruit juice, fresh fruit and cereal or porridge is offered followed by hash browns, veggie sausages, mushrooms, tomatoes, baked beans, toast and preserves. Soya milk, and vegan margarine are available as is organic vegan bread. Gluten-free bread on request.

Dinner is not offered but there are plenty of restaurants and pubs on the doorstep, and cafes, for example the completely vegetarian Lakeland Pedlar. After dinner you could take in a movie at the cinema or go to the 'Theatre by the Lake', both within 5 minutes' walk.

Keswick is surrounded by beautiful mountains and lake Derwentwater. There are unlimited walks for all abilities, many from the house, as well as cycle routes.

If you want to take it easy, go for a cruise on Derwentwater (all year service) and take in the magnificent views from a different angle.

There are many places of historical and cultural interest within walking distance such as the 4,000 year old Castlerigg Stone Circle. William Wordsworth's home is but a short drive away.

Packed lunches on request. They have bicycle storage, boot storage and a drying area. Facilities for making Fairtrade tea and fresh coffee are available in the rooms with vegan and handmade vegetarian biscuits. Susie and John look forward to meeting you.

Keswick

NORTH / Cumbria

Omnivorous Guest House

1 Borrowdale Road
Keswick
Cumbria CA12 5DD
England

Tel: 01768-773 181

www.honisterhouse.co.uk

Email:
john.stakes@
 btconnect.com

Train station:
Penrith, 20 miles, then bus or taxi

Open: all year

Directions:
From the town centre and tourist information follow the right hand fork, Lake Road. After one minute walk they are on the left hand side.

Parking: available

Discounts to Viva! members

Children welcome.
Cot and high chair available.

Drying area and bicycle storage

MC, Visa accepted

No smoking throughout

Flat screen tv/dvd in rooms

AA 4 star approved, and a best breakfast award

St John's Lodge

Vegetarian owned guest house with a spectacular choice of breakfasts. It's a short walk from Lake Windermere and an excellent base to explore all parts of the Lake District.

All rooms are ensuite, price per person per night: 1 single £35-45, 5 budget doubles £28-39, 2 double/twin £29-39, economy double £25-35, 2 standard doubles £33-44, 1 large double £38-48. Single occupancy supplement.

The large breakfast menu caters for many tastes and diets, with over 14 vegetarian and vegan dishes. All are home made and they do not use processed veggie sausages and burgers. There are 7 gluten-free veggie dishes and the home made bread is suitable for vegans. You might start with a choice of fruit juices, cereals and fresh fruit, followed by for example vegetable patty, bean rissole (both home made), sauté potatoes, mushrooms, baked beans, grilled tomatoes. Fair Trade teas and coffee, herbal teas, soya milk, vegan margarine and muesli are all available. The owners pride themselves on their home made cooking and say there is no such thing as a 'special diet', their menu caters for everyone.

Windermere and Bowness have more restaurants than any other area of the Lake District, many offering veggie dishes. A full local restaurant list is available to all guests.

Nearby are Lake Windermere (cruises, motor and rowing boats), the World of Beatrix Potter attraction, historic houses, gardens, the Steamboat Museum, secluded walks, lots of restaurants, pubs and tea rooms. Minibus tours can be arranged. Free access to a nearby luxury leisure club.

Free 24 hour wireless broadband and free internet access on a dedicated computer. Tea/coffee making, TV and hairdryer in rooms.

Windermere

Omnivorous Guest House (veggie owners)

St John's Lodge
Lake Road
Windermere
Cumbria LA23 2EQ

Tel: 015394 43078
Fax: 015394 88054

www.st-johns-lodge.co.uk
mail@st-johns-lodge.co.uk

Train Station: Windermere, 15 minute downhill walk or 2 minutes in a taxi.

Open: all year except Xmas

Directions: Leave M6 at Junction 36. Follow signs to South Lakes and Kendal on A590/591 then A591 to Windermere. Approaching Windermere turn left at Windermere Hotel. Follow signs for Town Centre. Drive through village towards Bowness and Lake on New Road. After half mile there is a Catholic Church on left. St John's Lodge is 100 yards on left. If you reach police station or lake, go back!

Parking: some on-site. Free parking bay opposite and plenty of unrestricted free street parking.

Children over 12 only.
No pets.
No smoking throughout.

5% discount for Viva! supporters and people presenting this book.

Visa, MC

AA 3 red diamonds;
Tourist Board 3 stars

St John's Lodge
Windermere Guest House

Ideally situated. 10 minutes walk from the lake and secluded woodland. Easy walk to good selection of restaurants, pubs, tea rooms and cinema and close to all amenities.

Vegetarian owners offer daily choice of over 15 vegetarian, vegan and gluten-free home-made breakfasts. Fair-trade tea and coffee. This pretty guest house caters exclusively for non-smokers.

Free access to nearby luxury leisure club
Free internet access including 24-hour wi-fi

St John's Lodge, Lake Road, Windermere LA23 2EQ
Tel 025394 43078 Fax 015394 88054 Email: mail@st-johns-lodge.co.uk
www.st-johns-lodge.co.uk

Accommodation

Nab Cottage

Omnivorous guest house

Rydal, **Ambleside**, Cumbria CA22 9SD
Tel: 01539-435 311
Open: end Sept to end June
www.rydalwater.com

One single, two twin/doubles £30 per person, four twin/double ensuites £34 per person. Children half price in family room with sofa bed, under-4 free. Vegans and special diets catered for with advance notice. Dogs £4 per night. Can do evening meal Fri-Sat for £18. Wifi. Massage, shiatsu and Reiki available. Big barn next door suitable for family gatherings, workshops and events.

Ardrig Vegetarian B&B

Vegetarian bed & breakfast

144 Windermere Road, **Kendal** LA9 5EZ
Tel: 01539-736879
Mobile: 07870 478624
Train: Oxenhome 3 miles then bus
www.ardrigvegetarian.com

Ensuite double, ensuite twin, single with private bathroom, from £28 per person. Lots of organic and Fairtrade. Cycle storage, maps, advice. Website has lots of local links.

Hazelmere

Omnivorous b&b, vegetarian owned

Crosthwaite Road, **Keswick** CA12 5PG
Tel: 017687-72445
www.hazelmerekeswick.co.uk

---

4 doubles (one with 4-poster), one family double/twin with extra single plus put-up bed for second child, 1 single, all ensuite with mountain views, £32-34 per person, add £3 for single night, discounts for 3+ nights, under-14 £18. Single occupancy in double add £18-20. Well-behaved dogs by arrangement. No smoking. Visa, MC. AA 4-star. Off street parking.
Also booking service for independent and individually owned holiday homes in and around Keswick:
www.keswickholidayhomes.co.uk

Sefton House

Vegetarian bed & breakfast

34 Queen Street, **Ulverston** LA12 7AF
Tel: 01229 582190
Open: all year. Train: Ulverston 400m.
www.seftonhouse.co.uk

Georgian town house in the centre of the busy market town of Ulverston. 5 rooms, 1 single, 2 doubles ensuite, 1 double and one 1 twin each with private bathroom, £27.50-30 per person. Single supplement in double £10. Packed lunches are available for walkers if booked in advance. Secure garaging for bicycles. Wifi. Children welcome, travel cot, high chair. No smoking throughout. No pets. No credit cards.

Kirkwood Guest House

Omnivorous bed & breakfast

Princes Road, **Windermere** LA23 2DD
Tel: 015394-43907
Open: all year
www.kirkwood51.co.uk

Midway between Windermere and Bowness on Winderemere, 10 minutes walk from each. Family 4 room, two family 3 rooms, twin and double rooms, all ensuite, £30-38 per person, children half price. Single £39. Winter breaks 3 nights for 2. Lots of 4-poster beds. Children over 5 welcome. No smoking. VisitBritain 4 stars.

Also Upfront Gallery self-catering, p43.
Conishead Priory vegetarian full board, near Ulverston p46.

Ambleside restaurants
Fellinis
Vegeterranean restaurant

Church Street, Ambleside LA22 0BT
Tel: 01539-33845 (extension 1)
Direct line 015394 32487 from 16.30
Restaurant open: Tue-Sun, closed Mon evenings except bank holidays
Cinema open every day
www.fellinisambleside.com

If you like films and you like veggie food then you'll love Ambleside. Zefirrelli's cinema and restaurant complex has added a second modern vegetarian restaurant with a distinct Mediterranean twist. Digital cinema upstairs shows the latest arthouse and niche films. Starters £5.95 such as courgette and potato cakes or veloute d'asperges. Main course £10.95 such as champagne risotto with wild mushrooms and truffle essence; aubergine a la provencal. Desserts £5.95. Vegans and those who don't like cheese note that there are more vegan main courses at Zeffirelli's nearby. 2 courses plus reserved cinema seat £19.95. You can use Zeffirelli's movie vouchers here on payment of a £3 supplement.

Zeffirelli's
Vegetarian Italian restaurant, pizzeria, cinema and jazz bar

Compston Road. Ambleside LA22 9AD
Tel: 01539 433 845
Cafe daily from 10.00, hot food from 12
Jazz bar from 16.00
Evening menu 17.30-22.00 (last orders)
seats 170, but they advise booking ahead.
www.zeffirellis.com

During the day there is a cafe, in the evening it becomes a wholefood gourmet Italian-style restaurant, attached to a jazz bar and a cinema. This place has a lot of fans and is highly regarded. Whilst vegans will be frustrated by the use of dairy in almost every starter and dessert, there are excellent vegan main courses and they do now have one good-looking vegan dessert.

The cafe offers drinks, lunchtime specials, soup £3.75, filled jacket potatoes £4.45, sandwiches £3.40, the full pizza and mains menu (see below), pastries and cakes. Tea and coffees £1.70-2.65, or £3.65 for a large cafetiere. Soft drinks and juices £1.35-1.95.

The **lunch and dinner menu** has 15 starters £3.25-6.15, though just two are vegan, green salad or marinated olives. A whole range of pizzas are available from £7.95-9.65, with familiar and unusual toppings such as red bean chilli, pine kernels, jalapeno peppers, artichokes and capers. They are freshly prepared so cheese can be left off and you can order extra toppings. Main courses £7.95-9.95 include 6 vegan choices such as farmhouse Italian bean casserole; puttanesca; red bean chilli with organic brown rice; puy lentil rissole with salsa; main couse salad with polenta, tapenade and hummus. Gluten-free pasta available.

Lots of desserts from £4.25, all contain cream or yoghurt except the summer berry pudding with Cassis, and sorbets. Beers from £2.50. Extensive wine list from £12.95 bottle, £8.95 carafe, £3.25-5.20 glass.

You can also eat in the **jazz bar** upstairs from 16.00 but note that children under 16 are not permitted in the bar areas after 21.00. Contemporary jazz and world music performances most Fridays and Saturdays. Most live events are free and start around 20.00.

There are 2 cinema screens, and 2 more 100 metres away at Zeffs by the Park. Booking recommended. Gift vouchers available, see online shop.

Ambleside
Rattle Gill Cafe
Vegetarian cafe

2 Bridge Street, Ambleside LA22 9DU
Tel: 015394-34403
Open: Thu–Mon 10-17.00, Tue–Wed closed

Homemade food in a peaceful location opposite a watermill, with tables outside and in. Soups always vegan £4 or £5. Filled jacket potatoes £6. Chilli £6. Salads made to order £5-6. Doorstep sandwiches, toasties and panini £5.50 made to order, with salad. Lots of homemade cakes and scones, vegan and gluten-free options, £2-2.50.

Fairtrade tea small pot £1.50, large £3 (enough for 4 people). Organic Fairtrade coffees, cafetiere, latte, cappuccino all £2, large mug £2.50. Soya milk available.

Dog-friendly inside and out. Takeaway. Kids' menu, high chair. Hungry hiker packed lunches can be pre-ordered for next day £6.95. Cash only, cashpoint nearby.

Doi Intanon
Omnivorous Thai restaurant

Market Place, Ambleside LA22 9BU (in the old market hall)
Tel: 015394-32119
Open: Mon-Thu 18.00-22.00, Fri-Sat 18.00-22.30, Sun usually open 18.00-22.00
www.doiintanon.co.uk

Appropriately for the Lake District, this restaurant is named after Thailand's highest mountain. Now expanded and renovated in 2010, one vegan reader reckons it is the best place to eat in the Lakes apart from Lancrigg, both having gloriously tasty food. No dairy in anything, only coconut milk.

Mushroom lemongrass soup, veg in batter or selection of dim sum £3.50-4.50. Main courses £8 include green or red or hot jungle curry with tofu. Cashew nut salad £7. Stir-fries £5.50-£7. Rice £1.50. Desserts include vegan coconut tapioca. House wine £2.75-4.75 glass, £12.50 bottle. Singha beer. Mango and passionfruit juice. Children welcome. Booking essential in summer. MC, Visa over £10.

Lucy's on a Plate
Omnivorous cafe-restaurant

Church Street, Ambleside LA22 0BU
Tel: 015394-31191
Open every day except Xmas and Boxing Day
Cafe 10.00-18.00
Restaurant 18.00-21.00 last orders
Evening booking advisable
www.lucysofambleside.co.uk

Daytime cafe and candlelit evening international restaurant with a cosy fire and walled garden. Local produce, no GM. Specialists in gluten-free and a huge range of desserts, some vegan. Veggie dishes can be adapted for vegans.

Cafe menu is available all day if you fancy a late full cooked vegetarian breakfast £7.95 tomatoes, mushrooms, fried bread, sausages (but not baked beans - this is Ambleside). They make their own muesli which can be with soya milk, fresh or poached fruit £4.95.

Soups are mainly gluten-free and vegan. Ciabatta or baguette sandwich with hummus & salad plus a side salad £6.50. Main courses £8.50 such as

Doi Intanon

vegan pesto pasta, or munchy mixed seed salad. Potato and onion rostis can be made vegan.

Peckish Pickers snacky things such as hummus with olives and crisps. Some cakes are dairy and gluten-free but not egg-free.

Smoothies £2.25, coffee £1.50, tea £1.20, they have soya milk. House wine £3.75 glass, £13.95 bottle, £16.95 litre.

Evening menu from 6pm changes daily. Starters £6.75 such as asparagus with cherry tomatoes and balsamic herb oil, or plump figs with side salad. 3 veggie mains and specials £10.50-10.95 such as roast Mediterranean veg on linguini pasta with tomato and garlic sauce; or stuffed aubergine with couscous.

Heaps of puddings £4.95 include vegan fruit crumbles or summer pudding. For a party or group they could make a vegan chocolate cake to order.

Children welcome, high chairs. Dogs welcome in the conservatory part of the restaurant. Private dining room upstairs for up to 26. MC, Visa.

Lucy4 Wine Bar & Bistro
Omni Mediterranean bistro/wine bar

St Marys Lane, Ambleside LA22 9DG
Tel: 015394-34666
Open: every day Xmas Day
Mon-Fri 17.00-22.30, Sat-Sun 12.00-22.30
www.lucysofambleside.co.uk

Across the road from Lucy's on a Plate but open later and with a completely different Mediterranean mix and match menu. Starters include 4 kinds of pasta £3.75-4.25, avocado or coucous or green side salad. 4 to 5 main tapas style dishes at £5.95-7.50 each should be enough to fill up 2 vegetarians, such as wild mushroom risotto, tapenade tomatoes, courgette filled with hummus and grilled, Tuscan chargrilled Mediterranean veg with vegan pesto. Fruit platter is the only vegan dessert.

90 different wines. House wine £3.85 glass, £15 bottle. Belgian Trappist beers up to 9% alcohol £3.20. 15 cocktails from £5.95 include 3 kinds of mojito and their own passionfruit martini with a hot of champagne. Continental coffees £2.25, they have soya milk.

Children welcome, high chairs, games, cards, draughts, colouring books placed around the venue. Some outside seating. Dogs allowed on the lower level inside. MC, Visa.

Granny Smiths
Health food shop & greengrocer

Market Place, Ambleside, Cumbria LA22 9BU
Tel: 015394-33145
Open: Mon-Sat 8.00-17.00, Sun 9.00-16.00

The fridge has the new Delphi line of take-aways that come with a spoon £1.49-1.79 such as chickpea salad, couscous and 3-bean salad, mixed salads, mezze dip. No freezer.

Organic English fruit & veg when available. Lots of vegan and gluten-free such as cheeses, protein and gluten-free bars for walkers. Plamil chocolate. Alcohol-free organic wine. Organic baby foods.

A little Aladdin's emporium that crams a lot into a small space, with organic shampoos and creams, Natracare. Ecover cleaning products. They can get things in for you if you order by Tuesday, but homeopathy supplies are in the nearby chemist. 10% discount if you show this book.

Appleby-in-Westmoreland
The Feel Good Factory
Health food shop

3-5 Boroughgate, Appleby CA16 6XF
Tel: 01768-354 129
Open: Mon-Sat 9.30-17.00, Sun closed

Fridge has Delphi falafel mezze dip with hummus, St Delfour French bistro ready meals, vegan cheeses. Freezer with Goodlife nut cutlets, butternut squash roasts, Realeat, Wicken Fen, Swedish Glace, Booja Booja. Snack bars and dairy-free chocolate. Flour from Little Salkeld Watermill. Diabetic and coeliac-friendly jams and preserves from Friendly Food & Drink at Staveley (near Kendal). Ella's Kitchen baby food.

Dr Hauschka, Faith In Nature, Eco Cosmetics, Its Elixir bodycare made in Carlisle, Natracare. Full range of Ecover, refills for washing up liquid, laundry and softener. Full range of A. Vogel and Nature's Aid supplements. Bach remedies. Essential oils. MC, Visa.

Barrow-in-Furness
Review Coffee Bar
Vegetarian cafe + hairdresser/beauty

1A Nelson St, Barrow-in-Furness LA14 1NG
Tel: 01229-820082
Cafe: Tue-Fri 9.00-16.30, Sat 9.00-15.30, Sun-Mon closed.
Hairdresser Tue-Sat 9-18.30;
Beauty salon Thu 16.00-18.30,
Fri 9.00-18.30, Sat 9.00-17.00;
last appointments 17.15.

Quiet, relaxing cafe with mood lighting and no noisy kids.

Homemade soup £3.75 with wholemeal roll. Wholemeal baguette sandwiches £4.35 made to order with crisps and salad. Light bites such £4.40-4.55 as Mediterranean roasted veg with olives, salad in wrap, pitta, flatbread or bagel. Lunch specials £6.25 such as African sweet potato stew with brown rice and organic wholemeal bread; gluten-free African vegetable fruit curry.

Desserts and cakes but currently none vegan. Pot of tea £1.50, coffee £1.60-1.90, latte £1.90, soya milk available.
Freshly made fruit smoothie £2.75. Vitamin waters £1.95.

Children welcome, high chair. Visa, MC. The cafe is on the first floor, over a hairdresser and below a beauty salon which use Aveda, Jane Iredale and Environ cruelty-free products. The beauty therapist and the cafe owner are nutrition consultants and offer the Advanced Nutrition Programme. Also a massage therapist, £15 for 30 minutes, Indian Head Massage 45 mins £35. Environ facial with hand massage £30. Booking recommended for these. Hair-styling £27.50-33.50, also colouring, bridal hair. Manicures, pedicures, waxing, spray tan etc.

Pastures New
Health food shop

64-70 Scott Street, Barrow-in-Furness LA14 1QE. Tel: 01229-833043
Open: Mon-Sat 9.00-17.30, Sun closed
www.pasturesnewhealthfoods.co.uk

Fridge, sometimes pasties delivered on a Thursday, vegan cheeses. Freezer with Realeat sausages and burgers, chicken-style pieces, Swedish Glace, Booja Booja. Lots of snacks for walkers. Bodycare includes Barefoot Botanicals, Trilogy, Weleda, Green People, Jason, Aubrey Organics, Avalon, Natracare, baby products. Big range of supplements. Nelsons and Weleda homeopathy, armomatherapy. Clearspring and Ecover plus refills cleaning. Self-help and relaxation CD's.

Therapy rooms with acupuncture, aromatherapy, Bowen technique, homeopathy, hypnotherapy, CBT, NLP, massage therapy, reflexology.

Brampton
Half Moon Wholefoods
Wholefood shop

14 Front Street, Brampton CA8 1NG
Tel: 016977-3775
Open: Mon–Fri 9.00–17.00. Sat 9.00–16.30,
Sun closed
www.halfmoonwholefoods.co.uk

Fridge has Vegideli and pasties from the Moody Baker at Alston, and they also sell their bread. Freezer with Realeat, Swedish Glace. Geo Organics vegan chocolate.

Bodycare includes Avalon Organics, Faith In Nature, Thursday Plantation tea tree products, Jason, Weleda, Lavera, Natracare. Nature Babycare. Supplements from Nature's Aid, A. Vogel, Solgar. Nelson homeopathy, Bach flower remedies, Amphora Aromatics aromatherapy. Ecover and refills. Allergy testing and herbalist sometimes in the shop.

Caldbeck
The Watermill Cafe
Omnivorous restaurant

Priest's Mill, Caldbeck, south of Wigton, Cumbria CA7 8DR. Tel: 016974-78 267
Open: Mon–Sun 9.00–17.00, 16.30 winter.
Start Jan until mid Feb just Thu–Sun.
Closed Xmas, New Year.

Formerly vegetarian, now under new management and still with lots of vegetarian food. Some tables overlook the river or you can sit outside on the grassy terrace overlooking the village cricket pitch.

Main dishes £7.25–8.15 come with five salads including a tart of the day and a pastie. Filled baked potatoes £4.50–6.50 with 4 salads. Hummus salad sandwich £4.95 with 4 salads and crisps.

Lots of cakes £1.30–1.75 and 3 or 4 puddings £4.15, but none vegan.
Pot of tea £1.30. Coffees, cappuccino £1.70–£2. They have soya milk. Cold drinks £1.15–£2.05.
Children welcome, 3 high chairs, books. Dogs only outside. Disabled access. Free parking. Visa, MC.

Cockermouth
The Granary
Veegetarian wholefood shop

15 Main Street, Cockermouth CA13 9LE
Tel: 01900–822 633
Open: Mon–Fri 9.30–17.00, Sat 9.00–17.00, Sun closed

Fridge with vegan cheese and all the Redwood products. Freezer with fishless fingers, veggie bangers and mince, Swedish Glace. Vegan chocolate. They make up their own bags of spices, big range. They can order in anything you need. (continued next page)

Bodycare includes Jason, Green People, Weleda, Aubrey, Grandma Vines, Faith In Nature, Natracare full range. Specialise in supplements including Nature's Aid, Bioforce (A.Vogel), Quest, Higher Nature, Lifeplan, Solgar, bodybuilding. Full range of Weleda and New Era homeopathy. Full Ecover range and refills.

Upstairs is the Whole Body Centre with a homeopath, acupuncture, remedial massage, reflexology, beauty therapist, allergy testing. MC, Visa.

Quince and Medlar

Gourmet vegetarian food, three times winner of 'vegetarian restaurant of the year' and four times runner up. Situated in a listed Georgian building with a wood panelled candlelit dining room featuring work by local artists. Very swish, recommended for a special occasion.

Starters £3.95-£6.95 such as soup, roast aubergine and sundried tomato paté, and baked French onion tart.

Main courses £13.95 such as parsnip, fennel and basmati rice discs with white truffle oil and Madeira sauce; lentil and apricot strudel in filo pastry on a bed of wilted spinach leaves with tomato and red wine sauce; spiced Moroccan vegetable cone with creamed coconut, lemongrass and tumeric, with a ring of wild rice and chutney.

Home-made garlic bread £1.35.

Desserts £4.95 include chocolate orange pie, lemon tart, and coffee and Tia Maria parfait, some vegan options. Vegan ice cream is available.

The menu changes every 6-8 weeks. Vegan and gluten-free options are marked on the menu. About half the ingredients used are organic.

Organic vegetarian wine list. House wine £11.60-12.60 a bottle, £3-3.20 glass, other wines up to £30. Fruit cordials £2 and nectars £2.10. Coffee £2.25, they have soya milk.

They appreciate advance notice of special diets.

Cockermouth

Vegetarian Restaurant

13 Castlegate
Cockermouth
Cumbria CA13 9EU

Tel: 01900-823 579

www.quinceandmedlar.co.uk

Open:
Tue-Sat from 18.30, last orders 21.30

Free parking on Castlegate Drive or in the marketplace

Booking advisable

Licensed

Children over 5 years welcome

Visa, MC

Grasmere

The Green Valley Organic Cafe & Restaurant at Lancrigg

Vegetarian restaurant

Easedale, Grasmere, Cumbria LA22 9QN
(see Lancrigg entry for directions)
Tel: 015394-35317
Open: every day 08.30-20.30
www.lancrigg.co.uk

International restaurant at luxury vegetarian hotel Lancrigg, now in its 26th year. Open for breakfast, coffee, lunch, teas and evening meals. Most dishes are either vegan or have vegan alternatives and the very experienced chef is also a qualified nutritional therapist.

Start the day with cereals, fruit salad or smoothies, followed by a full cooked breakfast including patties and grilled tofu.

All day menu: soup with wholemeal bread £4.75; pizza £7.95; garlic focaccia, selection of rosemary and olive roll or wholewheat roll sandwiches with salad £5.45; Greek salad £6.95; hot dish of the day £7.75; linguini with roast aubergine and pinenuts £7.50; marinated grilled tofu, lettuce and tomato roll £6.75. Desserts £6.25 include fruit crumble, tofu cheesecake, or fig and almond pudding with orange liqueur syrup.

Evening starters £7.45-7.95, mains £12.80-14.25, desserts £6.95. Sample evening meal could start with courgette parcels filled with "cashew ricotta", olives and pine nuts with gazpacho and capers; root vegetable rosti; chef's salad marinated tofu with chargrilled veg, pesto, olives and seeds. Main courses include brazilnut and mushroom puff pastry roulade, with rich red onion gravy; tofu burger with pesto, char grilled veg, paprika wedges and salad; Cajun spiced aubergine, corn cakes and guacamole with refried beans, salsa and coriander mojo; Swiss chard, roast almond and red wine bake. Desserts include several vegan options such as chocolate tofu "cheesecake" with fruit compote; rich chocolate espresso mousse with coconut sorbet; apricot and banana crumble.

Lots of organic vegetarian (most vegan) wines, beers and unusual spirits.

The Rowan Tree

Vegetarian and fish cafe & restaurant

Church Bridge, Grasmere LA22 9SN
Tel: 01539-435 528
Open: Spring-Autumn Mon-Sun 10-16.30, 17.30-20.30; Jan-Feb just weekend daytime
Closed Xmas and New Year holidays

Mostly veggie cafe by day, restaurant by night, with a terrace by the river Rothay. **Daytime** soups always have a vegan option £4.25 with roll. Hummus, olives, pitta and tortilla chips £5.85. Baked potatoes with fillings including chilli £5.25-6.25. Pizzas day and night made to order £7.50-8.75 (9 inches), can be without cheese, they sometimes have vegan mozzarella.

Lots of cakes £1.60-2.95 includes gluten-free, vegan date slice and fruit scones.

Teas and herb teas £1.60. Coffee, cappuccino, latte £1.95-2.35. Usually they have soya milk. Soft drinks such as pink lemonade, sasparilla, organic lemondae and elderflower £2.25. House wine £3.50 glass, £13.75 bottle. Bottled beers and ciders £2.95-3.50.

Evening there are two veggie main dishes £10.75-13.95 plus 5 veggie pizzas, vegans are best going for a pizza. Desserts £4.25 usually not vegan, but if you let them know you're coming they can have vegan chocolate cake.

Children welcome, high chairs. Visa, MC.

Waterside Wholefood

This vegetarian café and shop has been thriving for over 30 years on the traffic free bank of the river Kent in the heart of this busy market town. They offer a cosmopolitan range of food and strive to be as organic and Fairtrade as possible. Plenty for vegans. Everything made in house.

There is always at least one vegan full meal and on request several others can be made so. Main dishes £6.00-6.75 include pasta and vegetable bakes, mushroom and bean stroganoff, Turkish pilaff, spiced vegetable and chickpea tagine, cauliflower and cashew nut curry, cider lentil and hazel nut loaf, all served with either a choice of three salads or rice, millet, bulgar wheat as appropriate.

Salads include bulgar wheat with mint, cucumber and tomato; pasta with mixed peppers, French dressing and herbs. Salad plate £4.35-6.20, point to what you want.

Tarts and lots of cakes are not vegan, but slices £1.45-1.95 are such as crumble, or apricot, chocolate and date, or flapjacks such as sunflower seed and cherry.

Coffees and teas are largely Fairtrade. Filter £1.40, latte, cappuccino £1.90. Fine organic wines are available from £2.60 per glass. Also organic beers and lager.

Special diets catered for, such as gluten-free, diabetic and raw. They have vegan margarine and soya milk. Everything is available for take-away at 12% less. The 'stock your freezer' menu is particularly well used.

The small wholefood shop sells the things that are in the recipes. Massive selection of spices and herbs. They can order in anything else you need.

Kendal

Vegetarian cafe, restaurant and shop

Kent View
Waterside
Kendal
Cumbria LA9 4DZ

Tel: 01539-729743 shop and restaurant,
01539-733252 office

www.watersidewholefood.co.uk
Toni@watersidewholefood.co.uk

Train: Oxenholme

Open: Mon-Sat 8.30-16.30, Sun closed

Licensed with food

Vegan and vegetarian wholefood 50% organic

MC, Visa

Half portions for children.
High chairs
Baby changing
Feeding mothers welcome

Dogs welcome at outside seating, and at one inside table at the front

Outside catering service is popular for weddings and office parties

Kendal

Meeting House Cafe

Vegetarian cafe

Friends Meeting House, Stramongate, Kendal LA9 4BH. Tel: 01539-722 975
Open: summer Mon-Sat 10.00-16.30; winter Mon-Fri 10.00-15.00 winter, closed Sat-Sun and 24 Dec-10 Jan.
www.quaker-tapestry.co.uk

Part of The Quaker Tapestry Exhibition Centre, with a colourful embroidery in 77 panels of social history, and other displays such as a model railway, films, audio guides, children's activities. Exhibition £6.50, concessions £5.50, children 6-16 £2, under-6 free.
Vegan and gluten-free marked on the menu. Soup and roll £3.80, soup and sandwich £6, panini and soup £6.50. Sandwiches £4.75 made to order, toasted panini £5.25 with chef's salad. Pate and toast with salad from £5.65. Filled baked potato £5.25-5.95, vegans can have hummus or beans. 2 or 3 meal specials £6.25 such as Homity pie with salad and wedges.
Cakes and desserts £1.60-4.15 include vegan sorbet and sticky toffee pudding. Soft drinks and juices 75p-£1.95. Hot drinks are all Fairtrade. Pot of tea £1.85. Coffee £1.60, cafetiere £1.95, cappuccino/latte/choc £2.35. Soya milk.
They can loan you a picnic basket and rug to use on the lawn with their food. High chairs, toys. Outside seating, water bowls for dogs. Gift shop. MC, Visa. Formerly called Tapestry Tearooms.

KAN Health Foods

Vegetarian wholefood shop

9 New Shambles, Kendal LA9 4TS (off the main market square)
Tel: 01539-721190
Open: Mon-Sat 9.00-17.00, Sun closed
www.kanhealthfoods.co.uk

Fridge with pasties, vegan cheese, meat substitutes. Lots of vegan chocolate such as Montezuma, Organica. No freezer. Lots of bodycare such as Jason, Organic Surge, Weleda, Tom's, Aubrey Organics, Urtekram, whole Natracare range. Babycare section. Homebrew kits. Supplements include Higher Nature, Solgar, Nature's Aid, Lifeplan, Pharma-nord, Bioforce, Swiss Herbals organic tinctures, sports nutrition. Ecover, Earth Friendly, Jason and Suma cleaning products, and refills.
Lots of remedies, homeopathy, Lakeland Herbs local organic tinctures. Owner is a medical nutritionist, Ayurvedic practitioner and herbalist and can give advice. Health books and lots of free advice sheets.
They don't sell fruit and veg since the outdoor market is nearby on Wed and Sat, with on Wed the Green Mangle organic fruit and veg stall.

Keswick

The Heights Hotel

Vegetarian restaurant in hotel

Rakefoot Lane, Castlerigg, Keswick CA12 4TE. 01768-77 22 51
Open: 19.00-21.00
www.theheightshotel.co.uk

Open to non-residents for dinner, see page 26.

Mayson's Restaurant

Omnivorous restaurant

33 Lake Road, Keswick CA12 5DQ
Tel: 01768-774 104
Summer: Mon-Sun 10.00-20.30;
Winter: Mon-Thu 10.00-16.30,
         Fri-Sun 10.00-19.30

About 30% of meals are veggie such as Indonesian veg curry £6.75 with coconut milk, but vegans should check for cream or call ahead. Jacket potatoes during they day from £3.50-4.25, the ratatouille filling is vegan. Salad bar £3.25 bowl, £6.50 plate, point to what you want. Desserts from £3.75, not vegan, but strawberries when in season.

The Lakeland Pedlar

Keswick

Vegetarian cafe & bicycle centre

This veggie cafe in central Keswick, popular with cyclists and walkers, has great views of the fells. Decorated in warm deep reds and yellows with the walls festooned with cycling prints and memorabilia, it makes a memorable and relaxing place to pass the time. Most dishes are or can be vegan.

Start the day with a full "Pedlar's" veggie breakfast, served until 11.30am, including veggie sausage or bacon, beans, grilled tomatoes, mushrooms, hash browns for £5.65, add £1 for coffee. Mini-breakfast £3.95 hash brown, sausage and beans. Or try the Bacon or sausage ciabatta buttie £4.90, made with vegan rashers, or child's version £3.50 on wholemeal bread.

Soup of the day with organic bread £4.05, with salad and bread £6.60, or soup and a sandwich £6.35. Hummus and falafel wrap with side salad £6.95. (Toasted) sandwiches with salad garnish £5.65. Filled baked potato with salad £6.25. Vegan garlic bread £2.85. Olives with bread £3.70. Main courses, £7.90, include veggie chilli with pitta bread and side salad; 3 bean burritos with jalapenos. Lunchtime specials change frequently, for example Bengali vegetable curry with rice, noodle and tofu stir-fry, or Moroccan veg and chickpea tagine.

Lots of desserts such as vegan fruit crumble £3.95, at least 5 cakes £2.35 including vegan chocolate cake or fruit cake, vegan fruit scones £1.95. Swedish Glace ice-cream with chocolate sprinkles.

Fairtrade coffee, mocha, cappuccino, tea and herbal teas £1.75-£2.40. They have soya milk. Cold drinks, £1.75-£2.95 include ginger beer, juices, freshly made smoothies and Purdey's.

In summer Thu-Sat the Pedlar is open for the usual cooked food menu, plus pizzas £7.80-8.60, can be without cheese. Vegan wines £3.25 glass, £4.25 large, £12.50 bottle. Bottled beers and ciders £2.95-3.80.

Hendersons Yard
Bell Close Car Park,
Keswick
Cumbria CA12 5JD

Tel: 017687-74492

www.lakelandpedlar.co.uk

Open summer:
Mon-Sun 9.00-17.00
Thu-Sat till 21.00

Open winter:
Mon-Fri 9.00-16.30
Sat-Sun 9.00-17.00

Xmas and summer open later end of the week until 9pm, call to confirm

Licensed for cider, beer and wine. Organic and vegan

Allergies catered for

10% discount to Viva!, Vegetarian Society, Vegan Society and CTC members

Children's menu £2.450-4.50 and half portions

Dog friendly

Private parties catered for.
Outside catering.
Outside seating where you may smoke

Bike shop and expert advice on routes for any ability

Check local press for speciality evenings such as themed, Xmas, slide shows, talks and presentations

Visa, MC

House wine £3.50 glass, half carafe £9.25, litre carafe £18.25. Lots of bottled beers from £3.50. Pot of tea £1.25, coffee from £1.50. No soya milk.

Cash or cheque only. Small portions for children, no high chairs. Outside seating in summer, dogs welcome there.

Milnthorpe

Living Well

Vegetarian wholefood shop

26 The Square, Milnthorpe CA7 7QJ
Tel: 01539-563 870. Open: Mon-Fri 9.15-17.00, Sat 9.15-13.00, Sun closed
www.livingwellhealth.co.uk

Fridge with 3-bean salads, pots of wholegrains with beans, vegan cheeses. Full Provamel range. Freezer with 3 varieties of Swedish Glace, children's ice-pops. Local bread, some organic. Vegan chocolate. Bodycare includes Jason, Faith In Nature, Weleda, Eco Cosmetics, Avalon Organics, some Natracare. Supplements include A.Vogel, Nature's Aid, Nature's Plus, Lambert's, Viridian, Solgar and FSC.

Ecover cleaning, with laundry and washing up refills.

Weleda homeopathy, Bach flower remedies, Kabooshi aromatherapy oils. Rooms for homeopath, allergy testing, massage. MC, Visa.

Penrith area

Upfront Gallery, Coffee Shop & Puppet Theatre

**95% vegetarian cafe
& self-catering accommodation**

Near Hutton-in-the-Forest, **Unthank**, Penrith CA11 9TG (6 miles north of Penrith on b5305 to Wigton)
Tel: 017684-84538
Cafe all year: Tue-Sun 10.30-16.30
also open bank holiday Mondays.
Closed Xmas, Dec 31-mid Jan (call to check)
www.up-front.com

Long established small visitor attraction with something for everyone. The gallery and cafe are open throughout the year, the puppet theatre in summer school holidays, Easter and Christmas.

The **cafe** has tables in the gallery, conservatory and on the outside patio. Plenty for gluten-free and vegans, they use vegan margarine in all their baking. Soup £3.75 is gluten-free, with roll. Sandwiches, toasted sandwiches and panini made to order £3.75-4.75 with salad. They also have rice cakes and oat cakes.

Main courses £6.50-7.25, which come with bread roll or rice and four salads, include mixed bean casserole, Homity Pie, curry, vegetarian chilli, mushroom stroganoff.

Wraps £5.50 such as falafel with hummus and salsa served on a plate with salad. Filled jacket potatoes £4.75-5.75 with 3 salads.

Fruit crumbles (vegan) £3.95. Large slice of cake £2.40, some gluten-free, but none are vegan at the moment, however the tray bakes £1.90 are such as flapjacks and apricot slices.

Pot of tea or cup of filter coffee £1.40. Cappuccino, latte £2. They have soya milk, add 30p. Small bottle of wine £2.75. Bottled Jennings Cumberland ale £2.90.

There are smaller portions for children or they can make whatever you need, high chairs, toy area. Dogs are welcome outside and they can provide a bowl of water. MC, Visa.

The **gallery** has around 12 exhibitions a year by local, national and international artists including painting, sculpture, ceramics and textiles, free admission.

The **puppet theatre** has shows at Christmas, Easter and in the summer, suitable for all ages, £6.

Accommodation: There are three static holiday caravans (sleep 2 to 6 people), an environmentally friendly eco-lodge and a holiday cottage (both sleep 6). From £200 to £600 per week. Pets welcome.

Penrith area

The Watermill

Vegetarian organic tea room

Little Salkeld, Cumbria LA10 1NN
(6 miles NE of Penrith)
Tel: 01768-881 523
Open: every day 10.30-17.00
Closed Xmas to mid Jan
www.organicmill.co.uk

Organic vegetarian cafe using flour from the next door traditional 18th century water-powered mill, which is open to visitors. There is also a mill shop for groceries and books and they run baking and craft courses.

The cafe serves a couple of light meals (not vegan), soups and salads (which are vegan), and sometimes there is hummus or a vegan pate. Cakes are made with their own flour and used to always contain eggs and butter, but now occasionally there is a vegan one.

Teas, coffee, hot chocolate. Bring your own alcohol.

High chairs and children's portions. The shop and tearoom are wheelchair accessible with assistance. Disabled toilet. MC, Visa.

Guided mill tours Mon, Tue, Thu, Fri, Sun at 2pm and 3.30pm, adult £3.50, child £1.50, 2 of each £8. You can view the mill other times as long as a member of staff is in, £2 first person then £1 each, though not Wed or Sat except by prior arrangement.

Nature's Health Store

Wholefood shop

1 King Street, Penrith CA11 7AR
01768-899262
Open: Mon-Sat 9.00-17.00 (Wed from 9.15, Tue & Fri till 17.30), Sun closed
www.natureshealthstore.co.uk

Fridge with Moody Bakery pies, vegan cheeses. Freezer with Swedish Glace, Booja Booja, meat substitutes. Bodycare includes Jason, Weleda, Avalon, Natracare. Earth Friendly and Weleda baby range, Ella's Kitchen. Homeopathy, herbal. Supplements include Solgar, Quest, Nature's Aid, Bioforce. Everything for homebrew. Ecover and some refills, Ecoleaf. Books, Kindred Spirit and free magazines.

Therapy room upstairs with hypnotherapy, medical herbalism, Reiki, homeopathy, counselling and psychotherapy, cranio-sacral therapy, food intolerance testing.

Ulverston

Gillam's Tearoom

Vegetarian organic cafe & tea shop

64 Market Street, Ulverston LA12 7LT
Tel: 01229-587 564
Open: Mon-Sat 9.00-17.00, Sun 10-16.00, also one evening per month
www.gillams-tearoom.co.uk

Opened 2007, this traditional tea room and cafe is a real find with all organic food, local and fair-trade produce where possible. They have a sunny garden in summer and log fires in winter. Great for vegans seeking tea and a choice of cakes or beer.

At least two soups £3.20, gluten-free, of which at least one is vegan. Light meals such as vegan BLT £4.25. 4 or 5 daily specials around £6 such as risotto. Sandwiches made to order such as mushroom pate. Gluten-free bread available.

Cakes £1.95 include 2 vegan ones, plus teacakes and tea bread (like a fruit cake) are also vegan.

30 kinds of loose leaf tea. Pot of house tea £1.60 pot, others up to £2. 8 types of coffee bean ground daily, £1.80 cafetiere (2 cups), cappuccino/latte or vegan hot chocolate £1.95. They have soya milk.

House wine £3.25-4.25 glass, £12.95 bottle. Sam Smith vegan organic Yorkshire bottled beers £3.20.

Children's tea party menu (can be vegan) £3.95 for a sandwich, scone, cake and cordial. High chairs.

One evening a month themed night such as Spanish, sometimes with music. Set 3-course menu £22.95 with two choices per course of which one is vegan and one gluten-free. Phone or visit for details as it gets booked up.

Tea, coffee, cafetieres, jams and chutneys for sale.

Dogs welcome in the garden and in the downstairs area. Disabled access and toilet. MC, Visa.

World Peace Cafe

Vegetarian cafe and meditation centre

5 Cavendish Street, Ulverston LA12 7AD
Tel: 01229-587793
Open: Tue-Sat 10.00-16.00,
Sun-Mon closed
www.worldpeacecafe.org (menu)

Cafe downstairs, meditation centre upstairs. Breakfast till 11.30, lunch 11.30-15.30, cakes and organic drinks all day.

Full cooked breakfast £5.90 with tea or filter coffee, served till 11.30. Beans on toast £2.90. Toast with marmalade £1.40.

Homemade soup of the day £3.50 with bread. Soup and any sandwich £5.50. Sandwiches to order £3.90 such as hummus and olives.

Main meals £5.90 such as curry; falafel in pitta with couscous, hummus, dips and salad; quarter pounder chilli/veggieburger with potato wedges, salad and dips.

Lite bites for a snack or kids: large salad with hummus £4.50, side salad £2.50, bowl of potato wedges and dips £2.50, veggie sausages with wedges and dips £3.50.

Homemade cakes £1.90 include gluten-free and sometimes vegan. Any regular hot drink and cake £3. Pot of tea or herbal tea for one £1.40, for two £2.20. Coffees, mocca, hot choc £1.50-2.30. Cafetiere £1.70-2.90. Hot apple and cinnamon, winter fruit punch £1.70-1.80. Juice and cans £1.40. Smoothies £2.40. Soya milk available.

Garden area. Sofas in front window. No alcohol. Children welcome, kids' meals, high chairs. Dogs welcome outside only. Wifi. MC, Visa.

Meditation room upstairs for private contemplation and meditation. Tuesday and Thursday meditation 12.30-13.00 £3 which entitles you to soup and roll afterwards for £1.50. Classes Thursday 19.30 £5 during term time with guided meditations, talk, discussion and refreshments. *Stop the Week* (advance booking required) Friday night 19.30 guided meditation and three course dinner £12.50. Library of books on Buddhist meditation.

Conservatory Cafe

Vegetarian cafe & accommodation

at Conishead Priory, off A5087 Priory Road / Coast Road, Ulverston LA12 9QQ
Tel: 01229-584029 (lines open Mon-Fri 9.30-17.00, Sat 10.00-12.00)
Open Mar-Oct Mon-Fri 14.00-17.00,
Sat-Sun & BH 11.00-17.00;
Nov Sat-Sun only 12.00-16.00;
Closed Dec-Feb and Buddhist festivals
www.manjushri.org

In the sunny conservatory of Conishead Priory Buddhist Temple for World Peace, with indoor and outdoor seating. 5 minutes drive or 30 minutes walk from Ulverston, or take a bus.

The cafe is run by the same people as World Peace Cafe above. Cakes, scones, coffee. Weekend also light lunches. Children welcome. Dogs welcome on lead. Also gift shop and books on Buddhism and meditation.

Tours of the **temple** and historic house, and 70 acres of grounds and gardens with a beach on Morecambe Bay. Mar-Oct Mon-Fri 14.00-17.00, Sat-Sun & BH 11.00-17.00; Dec-Feb daily 14.00-16.00. Closed during festivals, see website or ask at the World Peace Cafe above.

Vegetarian accommodation: You do not need to take a course to stay at the centre, which is open throughout the year for guests except during their Spring and Summer festivals, New Year retreats and certain weekends. Single, twin and dorm rooms £20-40 includes light breakfast and two meals a day. Bring sleeping bag and towel if in a dorm. Easter break family room twin £180, triple £240, quad £270, quint £300.

Courses, festivals and retreats, £30-50 per day, £80-120 weekend.

Appleseeds

Health food shop

59 Market Street, Ulverston LA12 7LP
Tel: 01229-583 394
Open: Mon-Sat 9.00-17.00, Sun closed

Phenomenal shop for a small town, you will be amazed at the range of stock. Great for picnic supplies. Organic vegetables and fruit, gluten-free products. Fresh bread Thursdays. Fridge and freezer with vegan cheeses, lots of tofu, tempeh, soya yogurts, pates, drinks, Frys, Realeat, ready meals, Clive's pies, Swedish Glace, Booja Booja. They bag up a big range of dried fruit and nuts. Energy bars, flapjacks, vegan chocolate by Plamil and Booja Booja. Lots of Japanese Clearspring, Thai and Indian foods. Loose herbs, spices, and teas.

Lots of bodycare by Faith In Nature, Suma, Jason, Green People, Lavera, Weleda, Avalon Organics, Aubrey, Optima, Dead Sea Magik, House of Mistry, Natracare. Baby stuff by Weleda, Earth Friendly, Green People and Nature Baby.

Cleaning products by Ecover, BioD (including washing up liquid refills), Ecoleaf (and laundry refills), Earth Friendly.

Massive range of supplements including Solgar, Viridian, Quest, A.Vogel, Higher Nature, Nature's Aid, Lifeplan, FSC, New Era tissue salts. Weleda homeopathy, Bach flower. Kobashi essential oils.

Staff are very knowledgeable about products and include a nutritionist Thu-Fri and herbalist. Therapy rooms above the shop with acupuncture, aromatherapy massage, nutrition, herbalist etc.

Books on health, complementary therapies, music tapes. Home brew kits. MC, Visa over £5.

For evening restaurants in Ulverston, Appleseeds recommend **Temple Thai**, **Amigos Mexican**, the Indian restaurants **British Raj** and **Naaz**, and the **Farmers Arms** pub at the top of town.

Whitehaven

Kershaw's Health Foods

Health food shop

127 Queen Street, Whitehaven CA28 7QF
Tel: 01946-66627
Open: Mon-Sat 9.00-17.30 (Wed, Sat 17.00)
Sun closed
www.kershawshealthfoods.co.uk

Fridge and freezer with vegan cheeses, Swedish Glace. Plamil chocolate. Bodycare by Faith In Nature, Jason, Natracare. Supplements by Quest, Solgar, Natures Aid, Viridian, Bioforce. Homeopathy and remedies, essential oils. Ecover and refills. MC, Visa

Wigton
Chrysalis Wholefoods
Wholefood shop

34-36 King Street, Wigton CA7 9EJ
Tel: 016973-49559
Open: Mon-Fri 9.00-16.00, Sat 9.30-12.00
www.chrysalis-cumbria.co.uk

Wholefood, Fairtrade tea, coffee and chocolate, local produce. Run by a registered charity that supports local people with a learning disability.

Winderrmere
Manuka Health Store
Health food store

2 Longlands, Lake Rd, Windermere LA23 3AP. Tel: 01539-448941
Open: Mon-Sat 9.30-17.30, Sun closed

Fridge with lots of vegan cheeses, Vegideli, Taifun. Plamil, Montezuma and Organica vegan chocolate. Lots of supplements including Viridian, Bioforce, Higher Nature. Bodycare includes Weleda, Faith In Nature, Lavera, Natracare. Weleda, Green People and Earth Friendly baby care. Weleda homeopathy, Lakeland Herbs local biodynamic tinctures, Kobashi aromatherapy. Ecover and refills. Kindred Spirit and free magazines. Resource corner for local practitioners.

Workington
Golden Harvest Health Foods
Health food shop

22 Harrington Road, Workington CA14 3ED
Tel: 01900-66132
Open: Mon-Sat 9.30-17.00, Thu till 14.00, Sun closed

Small but well-stocked shop established 30 years. No fridge or freezer. Walkers can find Plamil vegan chocolate, bars, seeds, nuts, dried fruit, mostly organic.
Bodycare by Faith In Nature, Jason, Green People, Weleda, Natracare. homeopathy, iridology. Ecover. Health books. MC, Visa.

Chain stores
Holland & Barrett, Cumbria
Health food shop

2 Market Cross, **Ambleside** LA22 9BT
Tel: 015394-34132
Open: Mon-Sat 9.00-17.30, Sun 10-16.00

206-8 Dalton Rd, **Barrow-in-Furness** LA14 1PR. Tel: 01229-835795
Open: Mon-Sat 9.00-17.30, Sun closed

2 Globe Lane, The Lanes, **Carlisle**
Tel: 01228-530827
Open: Mon-Sat 9.00-17.30, Sun 12-16.00

54 Stricklandgate, **Kendal** LA9 4ND
Tel: 01539-733828
Open: Mon-Sat 9.00-17.30, Sun 10-16.00

33 Main Street, **Keswick** CA12 5BL
(formerly Sundance Wholefoods)
Tel: 01768-780083
Open: Mon-Sat 9.00-17.30, Sun 10-16.00

Unit 15 Angel Square, **Penrith** CA11 7BP
Tel: 01768-892395
Open: Mon-Sat 9.00-17.30, Sun closed

53 Pow Street, **Workington**
Tel: 01900-62214
Open: Mon-Sat 9.00-17.30, Sun 12-16.00

With most independent wholefood stores closed on Sunday, these can be handy for picking up snacks and self-catering supplies, for example the Ambleside shop has a fridge and freezer with take-away pasties, pates, vegan cheeses, Swedish Glace ice-cream.

The Peak District

The Globe vegan pub

Derbyshire is a long, tall county. To the north-west, it borders with Greater Manchester, to the north-east with Yorkshire, and to the south with Leicestershire and Nottinghamshire. It can therefore be thought of as being in the Midlands as well as the North.

Most of the **Peak District National Park** is in Derbyshire. This rugged landscape of the Pennine hills, bogs and wooded valleys is one of the most visited areas in Britain for day trips, as it is within 3 hours drive of around half the population.

The **Dark Peak** area around **Glossop** and **Edale** is the start of the **Pennine Way** long-distance footpath. The scenery round here is beautiful, rugged and rocky, and it is easy to lose the crowds on Kinder Scout or Bleaklow.

The **White Peak** area, south and east of this, has more gentle hills and more general tourist attractions. The busy, pretty villages like **Buxton, Matlock, Matlock Bath** and **Bakewell** have a good selection of pubs and cafes. They can get very crowded on summer weekends.

www.visitderbyshire.co.uk
www.derbyshireuk.net
www.peakdistrict.org
www.visitpeakdistrict.com
www.derbyshire-peakdistrict.co.uk
www.edale-valley.co.uk
www.thepennineway.co.uk
www.nationaltrail.co.uk/PennineWay

Accommodation	50
Ashbourne	52
Bakewell area	52
Buxton	53
Chesterfield	54
DERBY	**55**
Etwall	51
Edale	58
Glossop	58
Hathersage	59
Matlock	59
Scarthin	60
Caterers	60
Chain stores	61
Local groups	61

Derbyshire

Stonecroft

Second generation family run guest house in the historic hamlet of Edale. There are two rooms, one double with private facilities from £40 per person per night and one double ensuite from £45 per person.

Your host is a qualified chef and a vegan on a gluten and wheat-free diet. She caters well for vegans and those on special diets. Organic and locally sourced food is used wherever possible. Start your day with fruit juice and cereal or muesli followed by a continental or cooked breakfast. Continental breakfast could be home made bread rolls, preserves, tahini, soya yoghurt and fruit. Cooked includes veg sausages, baked beans, mushrooms, tomatoes and fried bread. If these choices don't take your fancy, there's more, like mushrooms on toast with garam masala and baked soya bean crunchy balls, scrambled tofu on toast with tomatoes, kitchiri or stuffed pancakes.

For your evening meal, most hotels, pubs and cafes in the area cater for veggies.

Stonecroft is situated at the start of the Pennine Way, in the heart of Derbyshire's Peak District National Park. It is a haven for those seeking peace, beauty and the countryside. There are many attractions within easy reach. It is six miles from Castleton with its show caves and Norman Castle, and twelve miles from Buxton. Chatsworth House and Haddon Hall are only a short drive away.

The owner is a professional photographer and runs courses in the area.
www.highpeakphotography.co.uk

Rooms have tea and coffee making facilities, clock radio, hair dryer and dressing gowns. Iron and drying facilities available. Free wifi.

Edale

Omnivorous guest house

Edale
Hope Valley
Derbyshire S33 7ZA
England

Tel: 01433-670 262

www.stonecroftguesthouse.co.uk

Email: stonecroftedale@btconnect.com

Train Station: Edale, 1/4 mile then collection by arrangement.

Open: all year, except Christmas

Directions: Edale is five miles from the village of Hope. Stonecroft is the third house on the left after the church.

TV lounge

Parking: available

No children or dogs

No smoking throughout (house and grounds)

5% discount for stays of three nights or over (excluding bank holidays)

English Tourist Board four stars gold award and breakfast award

Derbyshire acommodation

Sheldon's Luxury Retreat

Vegetarian guest house

Home Farm, Sheldon, near **Bakewell** DE45 1QS. Tel: 07877 315 216
www.sheldonsluxuryretreat.co.uk
also on Facebook

Recently converted barn house in the quiet and idyllic village of Sheldon in the Peak District National Park, with wonderful walks on its doorstep.
5 individually designed ensuite rooms, 2 kingsize, 2 doubles, 1 twin £80-125 per room. Children welcome, two rooms can be joined as a family room, high chair, travel cot.
Packed lunch £5, dinner £10. Vegan and veggie meals in nearby pub. No smoking. Usually no dogs. Patio areas and 10 acres of farm land. Dry room. Bike lockup. Wifi. Meeting facilities.

The Barn B&B and World Peace Cafe

Vegetarian B&B, Cafe & Peace Centre

Ashe Hall, Ash Lane, **Etwall**, Derbyshire DE65 6HT (6 miles from Derby city centre)
Tel: 07875 250716
Cafe open: every day 10.00-16.30
www.thebarnretreat.co.uk
www.taracentre.org.uk
www.kadampa.com
relax@thebarnretreat.co.uk

Buddhist centre including a B&B set in 38 acres of mature woodlands, lawns, flowerbeds and grounds, surrounded by rolling countryside. Ideal for rest and relaxation. Meditation classes are available in the hall, home of the Tara Buddhist Centre.
There are 18 rooms, 6 within the B&B part: 2 singles £35, 3 ensuite singles £40, 1 twin £30 per person. Children welcome. Rooms have broadband, wifi. No smoking or alcohol.

World Peace Cafe does lunch of the month £5 such as West African peanut stew with rice. Panini or bagel with choice of two fillings and salad £3.50; soup with crusty bread and salad garnish £3.50; meal deal soup with half panini or bagel £5; baked potato with topping and salad £4. Cakes £1.70 but not vegan. Kids' portions £1.75.

Birds Nest Cottage

Omnivorous Guest House

40-42 Primrose Lane, **Glossop** SK13 8EW
Tel: 01457-853478
Train: Glossop less than 1 mile, taxi/walk
www.birdsnestcottage.co.uk

---

2 double, 2 twin, 1 single, all either ensuite or with private facilities, £27.50 per person, £35 single, includes full cooked veggie or vegan breakfast. Two lounges. Pubs and restaurants within 10 minutes walk include the Globe (vegan), Italian, Indian, Thai and Chinese. Owner is a qualified therapist in massage, Reiki, reflexology etc. Children welcome, high chair. No dogs. Wifi. MC, Visa.

Sheriff Lodge

Omnivorous guest house

The Dimple, Dimple Road, **Matlock** DE4 3JX
Tel 01629-760760 Fax 01629-760860
www.sherifflodge.co.uk (to check availability)

Tall veggies will love the 7 foot long beds. Ensuite 2 twins and 2 doubles £35-38.50 per person, £52-57 as single (but full room price weekend or bank holiday). Children 7+ £15, 2-7 £5, additional single bed included; 0-2 no charge, cot, high chair and listener included. Well-behaved dogs £10 flat rate for any length of stay.
Full English cooked veggie, vegan or coeliac breakfast with a big menu. Free wi-fi. Drawing room with newspapers, books, dvd's for the player in your room. Bring your own wine and

champagne and they will chill it and provide an ice bucket.
For evening meals try the **Sycamore Inn** nearby, veggieburger and chips £4.95, 5-bean chilli with rice £5.95.

9 Green Lane

Omnivorous B&B (vegetarian owners)

Green Lane, **Buxton** SK17 9DP
Tel: 01298-73731
Train: 15 mins walk, buses 5 mins walk
www.9greenlane.co.uk

B&B in the Peak District with vegetarian proprietors. 9 ensuite rooms, 7 double or twin £33-37 per person (£45 as single), 2 singles £35-37. Totally non-smoking. Children over 12 welcome. No pets. MC, Visa.

Number 37

Omnivorous B&B (vegetarian owners)

37 Coldwell Street, **Wirksworth** DE4 4FB
Tel: 01629-824258, mobile 07903 501101
www.number37wirksworth.co.uk

1 double, 1 twin/triple, £30-35 per person, or £35-40 as single. 3-course evening meal £12. Owners are vegetarian and can guide you on a walking or cycling holiday. Several kinds of massage, Reiki.
Drying facilities, loan of local maps, hairdryers, ironing boards, alarm clocks, toys, newspapers, free wifi.

Ashbourne

St John Street Gallery & Cafe

Omnivorous cafe in art gallery

50 St John Street, Ashbourne DE6 1GH
Tel: 01335-347 425
Open: Tue-Sat 10.00-17.00 (sometimes also open in the evenings for tapas)
www.sjsg.co.uk

This art and craft gallery is spread over 4 floors of an elegant Victorian building. Their cafe serves light meals and always has sometning vegan, such as the soup of the day, or hummus and roast peppers with bread and olives. They also have vegan fruit cake, which has won awards apparently!

Dog and Partridge Country Inn

Omnivorous hotel / pub / restaurant

Swinscoe, **Ashbourne** DE6 2HS.
Tel: 01335-343 183
Mon-Sun: 12.00-22.00
www.dogandpartridge.co.uk

This is a large old country pub with 30 rooms in a village near Ashbourne and the Staffordshire border. They offer a varied and inclusive menu and get lots of vegetarians and vegans. They have gluten-free and vegan options always available. Most dishes cooked to order so they can do what you like, main courses £8-10 in bar, around £12-13 in restaurant, and could include potato and bean curry served with rice, pickles, onion bhajee and naan bread; or butternut squash strudel with vegetables. Children welcome. Dogs welcome in the bar.
30 rooms including singles and family rooms for up to 6 people, £50-125 for the room including breakfast.

Around Bakewell

Caudwell's Country Parlour

Vegetarian cafe in craft centre

Caudwell's Mill Craft Centre
Rowsley, nr Bakewell DE4 2EB (3 miles from Bakewell, 4 from Matlock)
Tel: 01629-733 185
Centre open year round 10.00-17.30, cafe closed 17.00, closed Dec 24-6
www.caudwellsmillcraftcentre.co.uk

Fairtrade. Everything made daily on site,

even the bread. Always a vegan dish and can cater for special dietary requirements.

Yellow pepper and split pea soup £3.95 with soda roll. Filled baked potatoes £4.95. Miller's £5.75 lunch of salads and open wholemeal roll with various toppings, vegans can have hummus or mushroom pate. Mains at £7.25 such as Homity pie, or Moroccan chickpea and spinach casserole with couscous.

Home made cakes including vegan £1.60-2.95. Tea £1.35, coffee £1.55, they have soya milk. Unlicensed.

Children welcome, high chairs. No credit cards.

The craft centre has jewellery, artist, glass studio, blacksmith, Victorian flour mill and a shop selling crafts, toys, garden decorations, bird boxes, walking books, maps and gadgets. Admission to centre adult £3.50, senior citizens £2.50, children 5-15 £1.25, under-5 free.

Aisseford Tea Rooms

Omnivorous tea rooms

Church Street, Ashford-in-the-Water, Bakewell DE45 1QB. Tel: 01629-812773
Open: Mon-Sun 9.30-17.00, 16.00 winter
www.ashfordtearooms.co.uk

Since the nearby Cottage Tea Room closed, this is a good place to get a vegetarian breakfast or afternoon tea in an exquisite Peak District village. 2 miles north of Bakewell and 8 miles south of Buxton Spa.

Full Derbyshire cooked breakfast £4.95. Always have vegetarian lunch and specials £4.95-6.95 such as Mediterranean veg panini. Lite bites such as beans on toast, soup (may be vegan). Cakes £1.40-2.60, some gluten-free, none vegan but may be on the way.

Pot of tea for one £1.60, £3 for two. Coffees £1.60-2.30, they have soya milk. Children and dogs welcome, garden area, high chair. Cash only.

Buxton
Buddhist Centre Cafe

Vegetarian cafe opening 2011

Samudra Buddhist Centre, 47 High Street, Buxton SK17 6HB
Tel: 01298-79777
Open: call for details
www.samudracentre.org

Buxton's Buddhist centre has moved to a new building which they are busy renovating, and they plan to open a vegetarian cafe there during 2011.

The centre offers classes in meditation and Buddhism, and dharma walks in the Derbyshire and Staffordshire countryside.

Cafe @ Green Pavilion

Omnivorous cafe-bistro

4 Terrace Road, Buxton SK17 6DR
Tel: 01298-77480
Open: Summer Mon-Sun 07.30-17.30, Winter 9.00-17.00; closed 10 days at Xmas

Half their menu is veggie food and homemade. International menu changes every day, for example Homity pie, falafels (from Wild Carrot), around £6.95-7.95 served with salads. Veggie cooked breakfast £4.95.

Lots of home-made cakes but none vegan. Italian Illy coffee £1.70, mug of tea £1.20, no soya milk. Juices, fizzy drinks around £1.50. Glass of wine £3.50, bottle of beer £2.50.

Kids' portions, high chairs. Cash only but there's a cashpoint next door. Daily newspapers. Outside tables.

Simply Thai

Omnivorous Thai restaurant

2-3 Cavendish Circus, Buxton SK17 6AT
Tel: 01298-24471
Open: Mon-Sun 12.00-14.30, 17.00-23.00
www.simplythaibuxton.co.uk

Popular with local vegans for the various veggie dishes including tofu ones. Lunch from £5.50.

A la carte vegetarian soups and starters £4.50-4.95 include tofu, marinated grilled veg, sweet corn cakes, or have a mixture for £10.50. Main dishes £6.95 include (sweet and sour) stir-fried tofu with veg; red curry tofu; mushrooms with cashew; green curry in coconut milk; deep-fried aubergine. Side vegetable dishes £6. Rice £2.20, coconut rice £2.50. Spicy salad £4.75, crispy beancurd and mushroom salad with rice £6.50.

Set meal for two+ people £17.50 each with mixed starters, mild yellow curry, stir-fry mushrooms with roasted cashews, stir-fried mix veg, steamed rice.

Live piano nights on the second and last Wednesday of the month.

The Wild Carrot

Vegetarian wholefood organic shop & deli

4 The Colonnade, Buxton SK17 6AL (at the end of Spring Gardens)
Tel: 01298-22843
Open: Mon-Wed, Fri-Sat 9.00-17.30; Thu 9.00-18.00; Sun 10.00-17.00
www.wild-carrot.co.uk

Entirely vegetarian co-op shop with plenty of vegan stock, all GM-free. Moved April 2011 to bigger premises. They support local producers, including deli foods by Parsnipship such as Indian summer pie, beetroot bombs, Thai green pea and potato cake, Lancashire crumble, roasted parsnip and orange and chili soup, beetroot burger; Natural Fayre daily sandwiches, lasagne, veg crumble, soups such as white onion and herb, dips such as butterbean and garlic, hummus and red peppers, guacamole, curry, cottage pie (all with vegan option); Raw Appetite salads; vegan and gluten-free cakes, puddings, jams, jellies and chutneys by Litton Larder.

Organic fruit and veg. Organic bread. Fridge and freezer with wraps, calzone (can be vegan), vegan cheese, bacon, burgers, tofu, tempeh, Swedish Glace, Tofutti. Vegan chocolate by Montezuma, Organica, Divine and Booja Booja. Organic vegan wine, local beer and cider.

Bodycare by Lavera, Weleda, Faith In Nature, Natracare. One of the part-time staff is a nutritionist and aromatherapist and can supply supplements and free advice Tue-Thu. Essential oils. BioD, Ecover and some refills, Clearspring cleaning.

Organic VegBox scheme for collection or delivery. MC, Visa £10 minimum.

Other good places to eat veggie amongst Buxton's 20+ restaurants are **Ruffi** Indian on the high street, **The Great Panda** Chinese on the market place (lots of tofu), and two Italians on the market place Michelango and Firenze. Also **Flamenco** Spanish tapas.

Chesterfield

Elliotts's for Natural Choice

Vegetarian cafe and health food shop

5 Long Shambles, Chesterfield S40 1PX
Tel: 01246-558 550
Open: Mon-Sat 9.00-17.00, Sun closed

Good size traditional vegetarian cafe with a small wholefood shop, in the old part of town, near the famous church with the crooked spire and handy for the Peak District. Big menu using local and organic produce where possible.

All day cooked breakfast £3.95 includes

a drink. Two home-made gluten-free soups daily £3.30 with granary cob or gluten-free savoury scone. Main meals £5.95 include pizza (can be with vegan cheese), pasty and salad with chips, vegetarian sausage pie with potatoes and carrots, daily specials such as goulash, or risotto with salad and garlic bread which is vegan and gluten-free. Filled jacket potatoes £3.95-4.55. Counter salads £5.30 such as beetroot, cashew and walnut.

An amazing 10 cakes £2 include vegan and gluten-free. Apple pie/crumble £2.20, including a gluten-free version, toppings can include soya cream. Wholemeal scones, but not vegan.

Pot of tea for one £1.20, £2.20 for 2. Coffee £1.40, latte £1.75, cappuccino £1.95. They have soya/ rice milk. Juices and cans 80p-£1.65. Freshly squeezed orange juice in summer £1.20. Outside seating. Children welcome, high chair. MC, Visa.

The **shop** sells wholefoods and has a fridge with vegan cheeses, tofu, hummus etc. Vegan chocolate by Plamil and Booja Booja.

Bodycare by Weleda, Faith In Nature, Jason, Thursday Plantation, Tee Tree, Natracare. Supplements by Nature's Aid, Lifeplan, Quest. Weleda homeopathy. Aqua Oleum essential oils. Ecover.

Organic Kitchen and Home Products

Vegetarian wholefood shop and deli plus omnivorous cafe

4 Theatre Yard, off Low Pavement,
Chesterfield S40 1PF(behind Peak Bookshop)
Tel: 01246-224666
Open Mon-Sat 9.30-17.30, Sun closed

Good-sized wholefood shop, previously called Organic Heaven, under new management since Feb 2011, with a take-away vegetarian deli downstairs with wholefoods and organic fruit and veg, plus from late spring 2011 a small omnivorous cafe area upstairs (plus home and beauty products) and outside.

The **cafe** sells their deli savouries heated up, and also a range of vegan salads to accompany them. Meal deal: any savoury and sweet, tea or coffee £4.25. Small cake £3, slice £1, all vegan.

Pot of tea or herb tea or coffee substitutes such as Barleycup, all £1. Cafetiere of organic Fairtrade coffee £1, £1.50, £2. Soya milk available. Cold drinks from 95p. Children welcome, breakfast bar with books, toys, high chair. MC, Visa over £5.

The **delicatessen** has stacks of vegetarian take-aways (all can be eaten in the cafe), around 16 savoury items including pasties, calzone, burritos, flans, rolls, filos. 10 sweet items including flapjacks and crumbles. Information for those avoiding particular ingredients. Whatever you have in the cafe you can purchase in the shop.

Shop: Organic fruit and veg. Fridge and freezer with meat and dairy substitutes, hummus, Swedish Glace, Tofutti ice-cream, and various tofu. Freshly baked organic bread delivered four times a week. Baking stuff. Range of Japanese foods. Vegan chocolate by Plamil, Organica, Booja Booja.

Bodycare by Faith In Nature, Weleda, Urtekram, Green People, Jason, Dr Bronner, Natracare, baby stuff. Viridian supplements. Ecover and refills. They can order in anything else you want. MC, Visa.

Derby vegetarian

Yaffle Cafe & Bookshop

Vegan cafe, tea room and bookshop

Upstairs from Sound Bites wholefood shop,
11 Morledge, Derby DE1 2AW
Open: Tue 10.00-17.00, Thu 10.00-21.00, Sat 10.00-17.00. Tel: 01332-291369
www.yafflecafe.co.uk
Facebook Yaffle Cafe and Bookshop, also Yaffle Cafe-Bookshop,
twitter.com/Yaffle_Cafe

Derby finally has a veggie, nay vegan, cafe, with social change library. Open any day with a T in it as it's a Tea Shop. Toasties £2.10. Cereals £1.50. Beans on toast with sausage £3.40. Cupcakes £1.50. Wide range of teas £1. Plungey coffee £1.20.

Thursday night 7pm meals approx £5 such as pate starter, stuffed pumpkin with roast potatoes and sweet red cabbage. Book before 5pm on 07799815083. Events with authors, guest readers, storytelling, games nights. Cash only upstairs.

Derby omnivorous

Any Indian restaurant in Derby will do vegetarian food and most Chinese ones. Here are some recommended by local vegetarians and vegans.

New Water Margin

Omni Cantonese/Peking restaurant

72-74 Burton Rd, Derby DE1 1TG
Tel: 01332-290 482
Open: Mon-Sat 12.00-14.30, 18.00-23.30 last order, Sun 12.00-23.30
www.newwatermargin.co.uk

Good choice of vegetarian. A la carte, or eat from the all you can eat menu £12.95, Fri-Sat eve £13.95. Sunday buffet £6.50. House wine £2.50 glass, £9.50 bottle. Children welcome, high chairs. Visa, MC.

Pizza Express, Derby

Omnivorous pizza restaurant

25 Irongate, Little Chester, Derby DE1 3GL (near the cathedral)
Tel: 01332-349 718
Open: every day 11.30-23.00

Level 2 Westfield Centre, Derby DE1 2PP
Tel: 01332-366 406
Open: Sun-Wed 11.00-21.30,
Thu-Sat 11.00-22.00
www.pizzaexpress.com

A chain of restaurants that has some vegetarian and vegan options. See Cheshire section.

The Orange Peel

Omnivorous international cafe

5 Becket Well Lane, Derby DE1 1JW
Tel: 01332-205 600
Open: Mon-Fri 08.00-17.00, also evenings and conferences by arrangement

New international cafe with a vegan owner and an impressive 6 super-healthy vegan main courses £5-7.50 based around wholegrains, pulses, tofu and vegetables. Starters such as vegetable soup £3-3.50. Vegan cheeses, spreads and ice-creams available.
Tea, coffee, shakes and smoothies £1.50-2.50, they use soya milk and can make nut milks.
Children welcome. Can cater for groups of up to 44 in the evenings.

Shahensha

Omni Indian cafe-restaurant & shop

13-15 Pear Tree Rd, Normanton DE23 6PZ
Tel: 01332-362 310
Open: Tue-Sat 10.00-20.00,
Sun 10.00-19.00, Mon closed

Punjabi food and very good value for over 20 years. Starters such as samosa 25p each, spring rolls 40p, aloo tiki potato cakes 25p. Veg curry £2.75, pilau rice 95p eat in. Evenings eat in is 70p starter portion (e.g. 2 samosas), biryani £3.85. Indian sweets and we think the jelabi may be vegan. No alcohol. Children welcome, no high chair. Cash only.

The Shalimar

Omnivorous Indian and Bangladeshi

2-3 Midland Road, Derby DE1 2SN (near the railway station)
Tel: 01332-366 745
Open: Sun-Thu 17.30-24.00,
Fri-Sat 17.30-02.00
www.shalimarderby.co.uk

Vegetable shim, masala, balti, karahi,

jalfrezy plus over 20 curries and starters, a dozen kinds of rice and even more breads. Licensed. Free bottle of wine with deliveries over £25.

Thai Boran

Omnivorous Thai restaurant

56 Green Lane, Derby DE1 1RP
Tel: 01332-343933
Open: Mon-Sat 11.00-15.00, 18.00-23.00; Sun 12.00-15.00, 18.00-22.30
www.thaiboran.co.uk

A local vegan reports there is a huge vegetarian menu, mostly vegan, even vegan dessert including Tofutti ice-cream. Veggies can choose from 7 starters at £3.89 or mixed for 2 people £8.99, 3 soups £3.99, 15 main dishes £5.99-10, desserts £2.99 such as banana in batter. Two drinks, starter and main with rice and noodles less than £20 each. Express lunch £4.29 for a main course, or £6.29 with starter, add £1 for beancurd.
House wine £2.95 glass, bottle from £11.95. Children welcome, high chair. MC, Visa.

Wok 1

Omni Chinese buffet restaurant

55 Woods Lane, Derby DE22 3UD
Restaurant: 01332-224 488
Take-away: 01332-348 998
Open: Tue-Thu 16.30-22.30,
Fri 16.30-23.00, Sat 12.00-14.00, 16.30-23.00, Sun 12.00-22.00, Mon closed
www.wok1.co.uk

Set lunch £4.95, under-10 £2.50. Sun-Thu evening buffet £7.95, U-10 £4.50; Fri-Sat £10.95, £6. A dozen veggie or mushroom take-away dishes £3 such as sweet & sour, curry, satay, Cantonese; rice £1.50, chips £1.30.

Dhesi Sweet Centre

Vegetarian Indian sweet shop

28 Pear Tree, Normanton, Derby. DE23 6PY
Tel: 01332-525 452
Open: Mon-Sun 9.00-20.00, Mon till 22.00
www.dhesisweets.com

Lots of pre-cooked main courses to take away for £3-4, and stacks of sweets. Vegans watch out for dishes that contain cheese and ghee.

Derby shops

Sound Bites

Vegan co-op wholefood shop & deli

11 Morledge, Derby DE1 2AW (between Eagle Centre Market and Guildhall Market, near the new bus station)
Open: Mon-Sat 9.30-18.00, Thu till 21.00, Sun closed
Tel: 01332-291369
www.soundbitesderby.org.uk

A lovely ethical shop, run by a vegan co-op, specialising in local, organic and Fairtrade wholefoods and bread. No animal ingredients or testing.
Great value lunchtime take-aways in the deli such as pasties, homemade soups, salads and sandwiches, most things around £2.50. Great value locally made vegan cakes £1.50. One table for eating in, and they are looking into opening up more space for this.
All organic fruit and veg. Vegan cheeses and yogurts, tofu, meat substitutes, they make their own hummus, reputedly the best in Derby. Vegan ice-cream by Booja Booja and Swedish Glace. They hold the record for the most brands of vegan chocolate in one local shop with Plamil, Organica, Organic Meltdown, Montezuma, Seed & Bean, Divine, and raw Conscious chocolate. Lots of drinks and plant milks.
Organic wines from Vinceremos, and

beers from Marble Brewery in Manchester and Sam Smiths in Yorkshire and Pitfield in Essex. Vegan dog and cat food.

Bodycare includes Faith in Nature, Purely Skincare, Yaoh, Natracare, Urtekram, Weleda, Mooncup, baby stuff. Cleaning by BioD, Clearspring Faith in Nature with some refills, Fairtrade loofas. Essential oils.

First floor meeting and therapies room with EFT/NLP, Bach flower, holistic health for parent and baby, humanistic counselling and psychotherapy, shiatsu, massage, reflexology, Indian head massage, yoga and spiritual healing, life coach, Reiki, you name it they can get it. (You can get homeopathy and remedies from a market stall they know in the Eagle Centre Market)

For those with mobility difficulties they deliver by bicycle locally. Also veg boxes delivered further afield in a van powered by vegetable oil, and they can add on other items to this order. Online shop, home deliveries in Derby area and they are trying out national deliveries. Catering events for 20-500 people.

Upstairs is Yaffle vegan cafe (page 55).

Edale

The Nag's Head

Omnivorous large country pub

Grindsbrook Booth, Edale S33 7ZD
Tel: 01433 670291

Large country pub which marks the start of the long-distance Pennine Way trail. Offers some veggie meals for around £7 such as five-bean chilli with rice, and beanburger with chips. Nothing special, but it'll fill you up if you're a hungry hiker, and there are **two self-catering cottages** at the back.

Glossop

The Globe

Vegan kitchen within a pub

144 High Street West, Glossop, SK13 HJJ
Tel: 01457-852 417
Open for food: Mon, Wed-Sat 17.00-21.00; Sun 13.00 -21.00 closed Tue
foodattheglobe@hotmail.com
www.myspace.com/globeglossop

Vegan kitchen within this old-fashioned real ale pub with a beer garden (below) out the back. An ideal place to crash out after a long walk on Bleaklow or Kinder Scout and fantastic value for money.

Snacks £1-£2 such as samosas, spring rolls, hummus and pitta bread. Mains such as spinach and chickpea curry; Mexican bean chilli with sundried tomatoes £2.90. Luxury smoked tofu chilli £3.90. These prices include the rice! Fry's sausage, chips and gravy £2.50. Small naan bread 60p.

Swedish Glace dairy-free ice cream and sorbet available for £1.50. The menu seldom changes, but the main courses are so good and fillng we don't care! Selection of real ales, most brewed on site.

The Globe is a live music venue with global bands playing upstairs and DJ nights. They attract some impressive and obscure acts, given their size and location. It's 10 mins walk from Glossop train station. Very cheap return fare available to Manchester.

Va Bene
Omnivorous Italian restaurant

12 Norfolk St, Glossop SK13 8BS
(opposite station) Tel: 01457-863 333
Open: Tue-Sat 12.00-2.00, 17.30 - 21.30
(til 22.00 Sat), Sun 16.00-20.00.

A reasonably cheap Italian restaurant with chandelliers and table linen that appeals to both couples and families. Starters £2.75-£5.00 include garlic bread that is made with olive oil. Spaghetti with tomato sauce £7.50; Rustica pizza £7.50 with courgettes, sweet peppers, aubergine, tomato and rocket can be prepared without cheese. Tomato and red onion side salad £2.50. Also serve chips and a range of alcoholic and non-alcoholic drinks. Will cater for gluten-free diets with advance notice.

In the Peak of Health
Wholefood shop

7 Norfolk Square, Glossop SK13 8BP
(by the station). Tel: 01457-865 678
Open: Mon-Fri 9.00-17.30, Sat 9.00-17.00,
Sun closed
www.thepeakofhealth.co.uk

Long established wholefood store under new ownership and now in more spacious new premises.
Organic fruit and veg. Local organic bread and oatcakes. Fridge and freezer with vegan cheeses, meat substitutes, vegan pasties, fruit pies, Swedish Glace. Vegan chocolate Plamil, Organica, Booja Booja occasionally.
Bodycare by Jason, Faith In Nature, Weleda, Toms, Pitrok, Natracare, baby stuff. Supplements by Vogel, Nature's Aid, Lifeplan, Quest, Viridian. Hoemopathic remedies, Bach flower, essential oils. Treatement room for homeopathy, Reiki, sound therapy, aromatherapy.
Ecover and refills, BioD, Clearspring cleaning. Cards of the Peak District by a local photographer. Visa, MC. Formerly called Glossop Wholefoods.

Hathersage
Outside Shop Cafe
Omnivorous cafe within a shop

Main Road, Hathersage S32 1BB
Tel: 01433-651936
Hot food served: Mon-Fri 9.30-17:00 (shop closes at 18.00), Sat-Sun 9.30-17.30
www.outside.co.uk

Outside is a large shop full of walking and climbing gear. Their upstairs cafe has plenty of vegetarian options, including chickpea curry and a modular breakfast with clearly marked vegan options such as fried bread, Linda McCartney sausages, mushrooms, beans, toast and hash browns for £3.50 or £5, served all day weekdays, and until 11.30 weekends. Tea or coffee around £1, soya milk available.

Matlock
Green Way Cafe
Vegetarian cafe

Snitterton House, 3 Snitterton Road
Matlock DE4 3LZ (near Matlock train station)
Open: Mon-Sat 10.00-17.00,
also Wed evening 18.00-22.00 (must book)
Sun and bank holidays closed.
Tel/text: 07502 289273 (evening bookings)
www.greenwaycafe.co.uk

Opened May 2008 by people who used to work at Scarthin (see below), serving home-made food including vegan and gluten-free dishes. They use organic, Fairtrade and local produce where possible. Bread made daily. The front dining room has views down into town and local artists display on the walls. Another family room also has a sofa and a play area with a train set, drawing things, books and toys. At the back is a lovely sunny garden with tables.

Vegan soups with roll include carrot & lentil, or watercress, £4 large, £2.75 snack size. Main meals change regularly and could include cashewnut roast with mustard and herb sauce, or Dragon pie (no dragons were hurt in the making) with salads £7, snack size £5, children £3.

Lots of cakes, desserts and scones, such as yummy date fudge cake £2, or try a hearty slab of vegan choc fudge cake £2.50, date or apricot slices and flapjacks. They have soya cream and ice-cream.

Organic, Fairtrade teas and coffees. Pot of tea £1.50. Cafetiere of coffee £2. Many cold drinks include organic Whole Earth cola, Fentiman's ginger beer and lemonade, Fairtrade juices and organic cordials £1.25-£2.

Daytime outside seating, dogs welcome.

Wednesday evenings they offer a choice of 3 starters, and 3 mains for £13.50, always something vegan and they can adapt dishes. Desserts such as cake heated up with (soya) cream £2.50. Coffee or chocolate £2. Bring your own wine, free corkage. They will open other evenings for groups of 10, and can do a completely vegan menu.

Cash only, cashpoint opposite.

The Cafe in Scarthin Books

Scarthin

The Cafe in Scarthin Books

Vegetarian cafe in a bookshop

Scarthin Books, The Promenade,
Scarthin, Cromford DE4 3QF
Tel: 01629-823 272
Cafe Mon-Sat 10.00-17.15, Sun and New Year's Day 12.00-17.15
Bookshop: Mon-Sat 9.30-18.00, Sun and New Year's Day 12.00-18.00;
25-6 Dec shop and cafe closed
www.scarthinbooks.com

Vegetarian cafe on the middle floor of a new and secondhand bookshop. Plenty for vegans including the rolls, marg, soya milk, soya cream and Swedish Glace.

3 daily changing vegan gluten-free soups with organic wholewheat roll £3.85. Vegan pizzas and flans such as mushroom, leek and spinach; tomato, red bean and brazilnut; lentil, veg and almond; all £5 with side salad, or £6.50 with large salad. Sometimes calzone or burritos.

3 cakes £2-2.50 such as carrot cake, Tunisian orange and lemon polenta gluten-free, vegan chocolate cake, vegan cheesecake. Also smaller items around £1.50 such as muffins, flapjacks, sometimes apple and cinnamon scones from *The Cake Scoffer*, health bars.

Big range of teas and herb teas £1.50 for a pot. All kinds of organic Fairtrade coffees from a cup or cafetiere to a cappuccino £1.95. Organic cordials £1.50.

Children welcome, they have their own book room with toys. Outside seating. Full menu served til 3pm, then soups, drinks and cakes.

Chain stores
Holland & Barrett
Health food shop

Unit 8 Granby Road, **Bakewell** DE45 1ES
Tel: 01629-810207
Open: Mon-Sat 9.00-17.30, Sun 10-16.00

---

19 King Street, **Belper** DE56 1PW
Tel: 01773-824641
Mon-Sat 9.00-17.30, Sun closed

---

17 Spring Garden Centre, **Buxton** SK17 6DF
Tel: 01298- 71021
Open: Mon-Sat 9.00-17.30, Sun 10-16.00

---

11 Vicar Lane, **Chesterfield** S40 1PY
Tel: 01246-558782
Open: Mon-Sat 9.00-17.30, Sun 10-16.00

Dobbies Garden World, **Barlborough**
Chesterfield S43 4XN. Tel: 01246-237678

Unit SU123, Level 1 North Mall, **Derby** DE1 2PG. Tel: 01332-349414
Open: Mon-Wed, Sat 9.00-19.00; Thu 9.00-17.30, Fri 9.00-21.00, Sun 10-16.00

29a Bath Street, **Ilkeston** DE7 8AH
Tel: 0115-9447626
Open: Mon-Sat 9.00-17.00, Sun closed

Unit 1, Crown Centre, **Matlock** DE4 3AT
Tel: 01629-57737
Open: Mon-Sat 9.00-17.30, Sun 10-16.00

Caterers
The Buxton Tram
Vegetarian mobile fast food service

Tel: 01298-72472
thebuxtontram.yolasite.com
Email: buxtram@hotmail.co.uk

Mobile information centre and veg*n fast food services and organic Fairtrade drinks. Edwardian-style "tram" caters at outdoor events within about 25 miles of Buxton. Bookings for animal welfare fundraisers particularly welcome.

Vegan Cake Direct
Vegan cake bakery

115 Northwood Lane, Matlock DE4 2HS
Orders call Julie: 07951 215121
www.babycakesdirect.co.uk
www.vegancakedirect.co.uk
enquiries@babycakesdirect.co.uk

Not a shop or cafe, but a vegan baker who makes wonderful vegan cakes and cupcakes to order in all sorts of flavours from £13.50 to £24 (incl postage) and can even personalise them for you as presents.

Local Groups
Derby Animal Rights
Vegetarian Society affiliated group

www.derbysabs.org and on Facebook

Meets on Wednesday evenings.

Derbyshire Vegetarians
Vegetarian Society affiliated group

Nina Lubman, PO Box 11, Buxton SK17 9FE
Tel/fax: 01298-72472
http://groups.yahoo.com/group/derbyshirevegetarians

Friendly, low volume email list for veggies and vegans living in the Derbyshire area. They don't have official meetings but do catch up with each other at local events posted on the list.

Tourist information:
www.visitderbyshire.co.uk
www.edale-valley.co.uk
www.thepennineway.co.uk
www.nationaltrail.co.uk/PennineWay

Accommodation	**63**
Chester-le-Street	**63**
Darlington	**63**
Durham	**64**
Guisborough	**65**
Middlesbrough	**65**
Stockton-on-Tees	**66**
Chain stores	**67**
Local groups	**67**

County Durham
and Cleveland / Teesside

Accommodation – Barnard Castle
33 Newgate B&B
Omnivorous bed and breakfast

33 Newgate, Barnard Castle,
Co. Durham, DL12 8NJ
Tel: 01833-690208
Train Station: Darlington 20 miles
Open: all year
Email: peter.whittaker@tinyworld.co.uk

Almost in the centre of a small market town, home of the fantastic Bowes Museum which has some amazing art. One family room with private facilities £30-35 per person. 3-course vegetarian or vegan evening meal with coffee £15. Children welcome. No pets. Guest lounge with open fire, books and maps. No smoking throughout. Local farmers market first Saturday of the month.

Accommodation – Durham
Vegge B&B
Vegetarian bed and breakfast

27 Hawthorn Terrace, Durham DH1 4EL
Tel: 0191-3848 071
Email: peter.burdess@btopenworld.com

Vegan owned house in the student city centre viaduct area. Veggie bed and breakfast in the summer £25 per person per night, may also be available at other times of year. Rooms have double bed. Very popular with people visiting students. Durham is a world heritage site with a superb castle and cathedral. It's a small city with everything close together. The surrounding county has beautiful landscapes and friendly locals.

Chester-le-Street
Seasons
Health food shop

Bridge End, Chester-le-Street DH3 3RE
Tel: 0191-388 0050
Open: Mon-Sat 9.00-17.00, Sun closed
www.seasonshealthfoods.co.uk

Focused on supplements (with Sainsbury's and Morrisons 3 miles away having taken a lot of wholefood business) but they still have a fair amount of good stuff such as pulses, grains, Sunnyvale rye and sprouted wheat bread, vegetarian tinned meals and frankfurters, lots of teas and coffees, lots of organic juices. soya and rice milk and cream, Provamel desserts, and their little chocolate, strawberry and banana soya milks. No fridge or freezer. Some bodycare such as Green People. Natracare can order in, baby stuff if requested. They can order in things for their weekly delivery such as Natracare or baby products. Free deliveries. Homeopath and allergy testing weekly

The amazing open air **Beamish Museum** of north-eastern living is 2 miles away, with a 1913 mining village and town and an 1825 manor linked by a tram. The website contains a list of **self-catering cottages** in the area.
www.beamish.org.uk

Darlington
Pizza Express, Darlington
Omnivorous pizza restaurant

1 Skinnergate, Darlington DL3 7NB
Tel: 01325-488 771
Open: Mon-Sun 12.00-23.00
www.pizzaexpress.com

Outside courtyard garden in summer. Children welcome, baby changing facilities. Disabled access. See Cheshire chapter for menu.

Health Warehouse

Health food shop & bakery/take-away

15 Post House Wynd, Darlington DL3 7LU
Tel: 01325-468570
Open: Mon-Sat 9-17.30 (17.00 Wed & Sat)
www.thehealthwarehouse.co.uk

Large independent shop since 1984 with lots of wholefooods, all vegetarian. Take-away savoury pies, pasties, sandwiches, soup, flapjacks and biscuits made on the premises, very handy as Darlington does not have a vegetarian café. In fact they make all kinds of food except bread, and there are always vegan items. They also have samosas, bhajias, veggieburgers, and they can heat up anything for you.

Fridges and freezer with vegan cheeses, meat substitutes, Swedish Glace, Booja Booja. Big range of gluten-free foods and diet products. Vegan chocolate includes Plamil, Divine, Booja Booja.

Lots of bodycare includes Jason, Faith In Nature, Avalon Organics, Earth Friendly baby range, Natratint, Herbatint, full range of Natracare. Full range of Ecover and refills.

Supplements include Nature's Aid, Solgar, Nature's Plus, sports nutrition. Weleda and Nelsons homeopathy, remedies. Food sensitivity testing once a month. Books and magazines.

Durham

Alhana Falafel

Omni Lebanese cafe & take-away

86 Claypath, Durham DH1 1RG
Tel: 0191-383 0607
Open: Mon-Sun 11.00-03.00

By Durham Castle. Luscious falafel with hummus, aubergine, self-serve salad and chili sauce, £3.20 small, £3.80 large. Freshly squeezed orange juice £1.75. Coffee £1.50. Also pizzas made to order, can be without cheese.

Pizza Express, Durham

Omnivorous pizza restaurant

64 Saddler Street, Durham DH1 3PG
Tel: 0191-383 2661
Open: Mon-Sun 12.00-23.00
www.pizzaexpress.com/

Off the market square. Children welcome, baby changing facilities. Sometimes live music. See start of Cheshire chapter for menu.

The Alms Houses

Omnivorous cafe

Palace Green, Durham DH1 3RL
Tel: 0191-386 1054
Open: every day except Christmas Day
Jul-Aug 9.00-20.00, Sep-Jun 9.00-17.00
www.the-almshouses.co.uk

Right outside the cathedral and castle. Always have vegetarian, vegan and gluten-free options. Menu varies daily such as tagine, Italian, Thai, curries for £5 to £7 for a large portion.

Wine £3 glass, £13 bottle, and beer from £2.70 bottle. Children welcome, half portions, high chairs. Disabled access. Daily papers and magazines. May close October 2010 when the university takes back the lease.

Also in Durham there are plenty of Indian and Italian restaurants which are always a good bet. There is a pizza stall in the covered market in Market Place that serves vegan pizza, Mon-Sat 9.00-17.00, and a wholefood stall with lots of Suma products.

Guisborough

For Goodness Sake

Health food shop

28 Westgate, Guisborough TS14 6BA
Tel: 01287-637074
Open: Mon-Sat 9.00-17.30, Sun closed
www.forgoodnesssake.co.uk

See Middlesbrough branches below. This branch also sells lots of health books.

Middlesbrough

Dosa Houze

Omnivorous South Indian restaurant

1 Victoria Road, off Linthorpe Road, Middlesbrough TS1 3QD
Tel: 01642-242441
Open: Wed-Mon 12.00-14.00 lunch deals, 17.00-23.0 a la carte, Tue & BH closed
www.dosa-houze.co.uk

New restaurant with a separate area for preparing vegetarian dishes. Only vegetable oils are used. Lunchtime dosa deals £3.49-3.99 with tea, coffee or a cold drink. Evening dosas, idli, uttapam £3-3.75. Curry and naans £3.99, 2 curries with rice or naans £8.99. Thali £12.99 with 3 curries, rice or naans and dessert. Biryani £8.50. Curry of the day £4.99, rice £2.99-3.99.

Hot and cold drinks £1-2.50. House wine £1.99-2.99 glass, £8.50 bottle. Beers £1.99-2.50. Take-away. MC, Visa. Tees Veg (see later) meet here.

Goodbody's Cafe

Omnivorous cafe & take-away

58 Albert Rd, Middlesbrough TS1 1QD
Tel: 01642-253 503
Open: Mon-Sat 08.30-16.00

Stacks of veggie food here, starting with the full English cooked breakfast £4.50 that includes beans, hash browns, sausages (not vegan), mushrooms, tomato, toast and jam.

Soup of the day £2.95 with baguette or roll, is almost always vegetarian, sometimes vegan. Self-serve vegetarian salad bar includes rice salads, pasta, couscous, roast veg, pulses sometimes. Side salad £2, main course £3.25. Home-made veggieburgers can be made vegan and come in many savoury variations, from £3.15 with salad and crisps. Baked potatoes.

Posh "bomb" sandwiches £3.60-4.50 made to order on baguette or panini, comes with crisps and salad, some unusual fillings such as banana and flaked almonds.

Innocent smoothies, Whole Earth organic cans. Pot of tea £1.75. Coffee from £1.45. No soya milk.

For Goodness Sake

Health food shop

13 Newport Road, Middlesbrough TS1 1LE
Tel: 01642-219249
Open: Mon-Sat 9.00-17.30, Sun closed
www.forgoodnesssake.co.uk

Fridge and freezer with vegan cheese and meat substitutes, soya yogurts, spreads, pates, Swedish Glace, Booja Booja. Tartex spreads. Vegan chocolate by Organica, Plamil, Booja Booja, Blakes, Seeds of Change.

Bodycare by Dr Hauschka, Jason, Green People, Dead Sea Magik, Tom's, Natracare, Weleda and baby.

Supplements include Bioforce (Vogel), Nature's Aid, Solgar, Nature's Plus, Pukka ayurvedic herbs, Weleda homeopathy. Practitioners sometimes in store include nutritionist Gareth Zeal, biochemist Tim Gaunt and herbalist Junnie McGregor, and one of the staff is a holistic therapist in Reiki and Indian head massage.

Earth Friendly, Enviroclean, Ecover. Anything they don't have they can order in for you. MC, Visa.

For Goodness Sake
Health food shop

Parkway Shopping Centre, **Coulby Newham**, Middlesbrough TS8 0TJ
Tel: 01642-599075
Open: Mon-Sat 9.00-17.30, Sun closed
www.forgoodnesssake.co.uk

See above. No freezer in this branch.

Stockton on Tees
The Waiting Room
Vegetarian cafe & restaurant

9 Station Road, Eaglescliffe,
Stockton on Tees TS16 0AB (between Eaglescliffe Station and Yarm Road A135)
Train: Eaglescliffe 2 mins (Darlington to Middlesbrough, Kings Cross to Sunderland)
Tel: 01642-780 465.
Open: Tue-Sat 11.00-14.30, 18.30-22.00, Sun all day 10.00-22.00 (last orders 21.00), Mon closed
Menus and events at
www.the-waiting-room.co.uk
myspace: The Waiting Room - music
Facebook:
Matchbox Cabaret at the Waiting Room

Daytime cafe/coffee shop and award-winning licensed evening restaurant for 25 years. Everything is home-made they don't use meat "replacers", the menu changes with the seasons, lots of organic and gluten-free. They bake their own bread.

Sun morning now opening earlier for papers and board games. Breakfast 10.00-11.30 £3-5 includes crumpet, Marmite soldiers, porridge & syrup, fruit and yogurt, home-made cereal, smoothies, fresh morning rolls.

Sunday high tea 15.00-17.30 with cake tiers, tea cosies, sandwiches and scones.

Daytime there is no set menu but they put on the blackboard what's on, for example:

Light meals £4.25-6.50 such as soup of the day with organic granary roll, pates and dips, antipasti. Daily special £6.90, children £4.95. Other starters £5.50, or £8.50 as a main, such as bean and fresh herb burger with side salad, butternut squash risotto. Sandwiches £4.90 in farmhouse, baguette, flat bread, chappati or pitta.

Puddings £4.45 from the evening menu, and cakes. Vegans would do best to ring ahead so they can sort something out for you. They have vegan ice-cream and custard, sometimes the crumble is vegan or pecan pie, everything is made in small batches daily, so if you let them know you're coming they'll see you right.

Evening menu:
Starters £4.25-6.95 such as soup of the day; lemony hummus; mushroom, cashew and basil pate; 3 pate trio.
11 main courses, made to order so at least 3 can normally be vegan, £8.95-13.25, which might include red pepper and chickpea smoked paprika goulash; butternut squash risotto. Table salad £4.50.

Lots of "proper" home-made **desserts** £5.25 though none of these are vegan they do however have vegan ice-cream and can put nice things in it such as pecans and almonds, and custard.

Drinks: Coffee £2.25, cappuccino/latte £2.65, tea and herbal tea £1.75, no soya milk. House wine £3.45 small glass, £4.45 large, £13.25 bottle. Skinningrove Yorkshire country wines £14.45 bottle (drink in or take-away), typically 8 or 10 from the range of 50, such as raspberry and rose petal, clover, sloe, ginger, blackberry, delicate medium whites, strong dry reds, full bodied and warming mediums. Samuel Smith's organic ale and lager £2.75, cider £3.45 bottle, raspberry, cherry and strawberry beers £2.85. Guest ales.

Music and arts events most Sunday evenings. Vegetarian Society Best UK Restaurant 2008 and in The Observer's top 40 of all UK restaurants. MC, Visa Most Sunday nights **Matchbox Cabaret** with live music or comedy in the back room for 50 people with a cover charge, while food is still available in both rooms. See website for diary and to sign up for their newsletter.

Back room also welcomes private parties and wedding receptions. Outside catering and cakes. Organic wines, beers and Skinningrove fruit wine available to take home.

Children welcome, high chairs. Outside seating, dogs welcome in nice weather. Vegan dishes are not always marked on the menu (they say it deters the non-vegans from ordering) so just ask. MC, Visa.

Local groups
Veg NE
Local vegetarian & vegan group

www.vegne.co.uk
Contact Mark 079410 79 999

Active social group affiliated to the Vegetarian Society, based in Newcastle with members from County Durham, Northumberland and Tyne & Wear. They meet regularly at Bob Trollops and Jack Sprats. Mainly a social group but also puts on exhibitions and stalls.

They run a great value annual week long North East Vegan Gathering in April school holidays in Morpeth, Northumberland.

Tees Veg
Local vegetarian & vegan group

http://groups.google.co.uk/group/tees_veg
and on Facebook: Tees Veg

A friendly group of various ages covering roughly a 20 mile radius of Middlesborough, including Teesside, Hartlepool, Billingham, Darlington, Stockton on Tees, Darlington, Redcar & Cleveland, County Durham and North Yorkshire. Eat out at restaurants across the Tees Valley every month. Meet for coffee, days out by train and also chat on their members-only online forum and Facebook.

Chain stores
Holland & Barrett
Health food shop

31 Market Street, **Barnard Castle** DL12 8NE
Tel: 01833-638 967
Open: Mon-Sat 9.00-17.30, Sun 10-16.00

5 Queen Street, **Darlington** DL3 6SH
Tel: 01325-365 656
Open: Mon-Sat 9.00-17.30, Sun 11-16.00

13 Milburngate, **Durham** DH1 4SL
Tel: 0191-3842 374
Open: Mon-Sat 9.00-17.30, Sun 11-17.00

10 Westgate, **Guisborough** TS14 6BG
Tel: 01287-634 683

184 Middleton Grange Shopping Centre
Hartlepool TS24 7RG
Tel: 01429-860 810

78 Linthorpe Road, The Mall Shopping Centre, **Middlesborough** TS1 2NR
Tel: 01642-242 317
Open: Mon-Sat 9-17.30, Sun 10.30-16.30

4 West Dyke Road, **Redcar** TS10 1DZ
Tel: 01642 490102
Open: Mon-Sat 9.00-17.30, Sun closed

16 Castle Way, **Stockton** TS18 1BG
Tel: 01642-671 127
Open: Mon-Sat 9.00-17.30, Sun 10-16.00

Tourist information:
www.visitcountydurham.com
www.thisisdurham.com
www.visitmiddlesbrough.com
www.thebowesmuseum.org.uk

Lancashire is a large, hilly county with some good walking areas and lots of forests, such as the **Forest of Bowland**. This isn't a National Park, but is a quiet and very underrated area of outstanding natural beauty. The Lancashire/Yorkshire border in particular has several attractive small former mill towns such as Hebden Bridge (see West Yorkshire) and Todmorden which have become tourist attractions in recent years.

Lancaster is a smallish ancient city which has a large university and is used by many as a base for exploring the nearby Lake District.

Blackpool is a popular seaside resort for many families living in the north west, with theme parks, a long beach and the famous illuminations. By night it has a thriving nightclub scene.

The county has over half a dozen unique veggie cafes and restaurants for a day trip or night out.

www.visitlancashire.com
www.citycoastcountryside.co.uk
(Lancaster area)
www.blackpool.com
www.visitblackpool.com
www.visitblackburn.co.uk
www.visittodmorden.co.uk
www.wlct.org (Wigan)

The Whale Tail vegetarian cafe, Lancaster

Accommodation	69
Ashton-under-Lyne	70
Bispham Green	71
Blackburn	71
Blackpool	72
Bolton	72
Burnley	73
Bury	73
Chorley	74
Colne	74
Euxton	75
LANCASTER	**75**
Preston area	77
Rossendale	79
Tarleton	79
Todmordon	79
Wigan	80
Chain stores	82

Lancashire

Crazi Carrots

Vegan or raw bed & breakfast in a quiet semi-detached house in Bolton near a country park, 15 minutes from Manchester. One simple twin room with wooden floor and en suite shower room, £30 sinlge or £50 double.

Breakfast is fresh fruit salad, yoghurts, nuts and seeds, cereals, cooked if required. There is vegan muesli and margarine, soya milk, veggie sausages. There is a small garden frequented by frogs, birds and butterflies where you can have breakfast on the patio.

It is a bright, calm, private space with no nasty chemicals. Food is organic where possible. You can use the diner, sitting room and kitchen. There is a reverse osmosis water filter and juicer and a library.

Packed lunches and simple suppers available. Ten minute walk to shops and pubs – the local does veggie but not vegan meals. There is a new vegan cafe in Bolton, The Kitchen on Moor Street, open 3 days a week, otherwise the nearest veggie places to eat out are in Manchester such as Eighth Day, the Greenhouse and Earth Cafe.

The owner teaches yoga and massage by arrangement and there are therapists nearby including a Life Coach, sports massage, reflexology, aromatherapy.

Bring walking boots (for outside, the house is shoe free) for the many nearby walks including to Entwistle Reservoir by a real ale pub The Strawberry Duck which serves good food. Rivington Pike hill walk is in Horwich with views across to the sea. There is an old fashioned coffee shop in a chapel.

5 minutes from Moses Gate Country Park, with a lake with ducks and geese and a path suitable for prams or wheelchairs. 30 minutes from areas of outstanding beauty: Jumbles, Entwistle, Wayoh, Rivington Pike.

Bolton

Vegan or raw bed & breakfast

113 Aintree Road
Little Lever
Bolton
Lancashire BL3 1ES

Tel: 01204-704600
Mobile 07968 021393

www.wellbeingwork
shopsworldwide.com

Email:
alwynne@wellbeingwork
shopsworldwide.com

Train Station: Bolton, 2 miles, then taxi/bus or owner can collect you

Open: all year

Directions: 15 minutes from Manchester on the A666, exit Farnworth/Kearsley

Parking available

Children welcome

Well behaved pets welcome

No smoking throughout

No credit cards

Disabled access: downstairs bathroom and sofa-bed available

10% discount to members of the Vegetarian Society, Vegan Society, Viva!, PETA, Animal Aid and people presenting this book.

Vegan owner

Hairdryer available

Accommodation Blackpool
Cameo Hotel
Omnivorous hotel

30 Hornby Road, Blackpool FY1 4QG
Tel: 01253-626144
Fax: 01253-296048
Open: all year
www.blackpool-cameo.com
enquiries@blackpool-cameo.com

Vegetarian owned hotel, though not actually vegetarian but they'd love to be if they can get enough of us. 10 rooms, all en suite, including 2 family rooms that sleep 3. £25 per person per night, add £16 for child sharing with two adults. No single supplement. 10% discount senior citizens Oct-June.

4-course evening meal £8, child under 12 £6. Dry lounge and separate bar. Wifi. Close to the Tower, seafront, piers, Winter Gardens and town centre. Completely non-smoking. Children welcome, high chairs. No stag or hen parties. 3-star VisitBritain rating. Park nearby. MC, Visa. The owners can recommend local places to eat.

Ashton-under-Lyne
Topaz Café
Vegetarian cafe/restaurant

at Topaz Well Being Centre, 216-218 Katherine St, Ashton-under-Lyne OL6 7AS
Tel: 0161-330 9223
Open: Mon-Thu 10.00-16.00, Fri 10-15.00, Sat-Sun closed
www.topaz-ashton.org (latest menus)

Opened 2008 in a wellbeing centre for the local community run by Tameside, Oldham & Glossop Mind, with very good prices. They provide healthy food using locally sourced, seasonal and ideally organic produce, all prepared to order. Art exhibitions on the walls.

10 till 12 morning snacks such as organic beans on toast £1.50.

Soups are vegan and change daily such as carrot and butternut squash with crusty bread £1.95. 4-5 seasonal hot dishes plus one or two daily specials from an amazing range such as vegan creamy cashew and coconut curry; spinach pie with hot roasted veg and homemade tomato sauce; layered spinach and hazelnut loaf with wedges and tomato sauce.

Sandwiches £2.75 made to order with Manchester Barbican bakery bread, such as Norlander seedy or Polish rye.

There's always a vegan option or two amongst the cakes £1.25 such as cherry fruitcake or chocolate fudge. Crumbles £2.25 are vegan and come with vegan custard. Vegan ice-cream.

Tea and cofee is Fairtrade, organic hot choc, vegan cappuccinos, from £1.20 up to £1.75 for a pot of tea for 2 people (4 cups). Fruit Juices £1.25. Fizzy Water £1. Filtered water free with other items. Children welcome, high chairs. Free internet access and wifi. Cash or cheque only.

Topaz is a space for everyone, from students looking for a quiet place to study and check emails, or friends looking for a lively yet laid back place for lunch, with a range of activities from art workshops to yoga, wellbeing courses and counselling.

Lily's
Vegetarian Indian restaurant & takeaway

83 Oldham Rd (A635), Ashton-under-Lyne, Lancashire OL6 7DF. Tel: 0161-339 4774
Open: Mon & Wed-Sat 11.00-20.00,
Sun 11.00-19.00, closed Tue.
Last order half an hour before closing

Great value and they have a chef from India Gujarat and two from Kerala in the south, plus they do Punjabi food. Snacks and starters £2-3.50. Curries £4.25-5.25, rice dishes £2-3. No desserts. Latest menu has a separate vegan page.

Mon–Fri 12.00–15.00 is especially good value: sit-down specials £2.50-3.99 meal with soft drink; also Gujarati thali £6.99 with snack, 2 chapatis, dhal, rice, 2 curries, lassi (not vegan) and sweet. Take-away thali £2.99.
Cobra beer is the only alcohol, £1.75. Children welcome, high chairs. Disabled toilet. MC, Visa.

ASM Cash & Carry

Vegetarian Indian grocery

75-83 Oldham Rd (A635), Ashton-Under-Lyne OL6 7DF. Tel: 0161-339 4744
Open: Mon-Sat 10.00-18.30, Sun 10.30-15.30. www.shopspicy.com

Next door to Lily's and round the corner from Topaz. It's huge, 20,000 square feet, they are also a distributor and wholesaler. Load up on beans, lentils, rice, spices, herbs, flour and naans, nuts and dried fruits, exotic fruit and veg, Indian lagers, oil, pickles, chutney and pastes, Indian savouries and sweets, pappadums, cooking utensils, ladies' Indian garments. Recipes to inspire you on the website.

Bispham Green
The Farmers Arms & Southwell's Restaurant

Omnivorous pub & restaurant

Chorley Road, Bispham Green, near Parbold
Lancashire L40 3SL
Tel: 01257-464 640
Pub: Mon-Fri 12.00-14.30, 17.00-23.00;
Sat-Sun 12.00-23.00
Bar food: 12.00-14.30, 17.00-21.00
Sat-Sun 12.00-21.00
Restaurant: Tue-Thu 18.00-21.00,
Fri-Sat 18.00-22.00, Sun 12.00-21.00
www.thefarmersarmsinbishpamgreen.co.uk

Cosy country pub with 4 menu and 4 specials veggie dishes £7.95-9.95, some vegan such as roast veg stir fry in tomato and basil sauce with rice, or vegetable pasta, and they can adapt other dishes. Sandwiches £4.75 with salad, add 75p for fries. Chips £1.75. Wine £3.25-5.50, from £9.95 bottle 9.95. Cask beers. Pool table. Beer garden and play area. No dogs inside.

Blackburn
V-Fresh

Vegetarian cafe & take-away

35 King Street, Blackburn BB2 2DH
Tel: 01254-844 555
Open: Mon-Fri 8.00-16.00,
Sat 10.00-15.00, Sun closed
Also Thu/Sat evening, see below
www.vfresh.org.uk

Relaxing informal vegetarian café in Blackburn town centre, owned by East Lancs Deaf Society, but don't worry they are expert lip readers. Everything is made fresh and they always have vegan versions of dishes. Local artwork on the walls changes every six weeks.
Soup £3 with bread. Falafel £3. Wraps £3.50 such as roast veg, or green and dreamy herbs, garlic, mushrooms and spinach. Swanky sarnie £3.50 with lots of fillings such as spicy roast peppers and tomatoes on ciabatta.
Oven-baked potatoes £3, toppings 40p. Twice baked loaded potato skins £4.50 with chili, salsa, guacamole or mixed veg.
Daily specials £4.50 such as stir-fry, green risotto, aubergine bake, okra curry. Salads £3.50 such as Waldorf (can be vegan) or couscous salad with nuts, seeds, hummus and pitta. Garden salad £2.50.
Desserts £1.50-2.00 such as rhubarb crumble with vegan cream. Cakes £1.30 include vegan carrot cake; all flapjacks are vegan 70p.
Juices 90p. Fruit smoothie of the day £1.50. Pot of tea 90p small, £1 large. Coffee £1.20, (soya) latte/cappuccino/hot choc £1.50 small, £2 large.

They can make anything you ask for if not too busy. Children welcome, small portions, 2 high chairs. Cash or cheque only. A couple of tables outside in summer. Sometimes they have jewellery making classes.

Open for music events approx every 6 weeks Sat night such as jazz band and meal £10 and BYO, phone for details or see visitblackburn.co.uk. From May 2010 themed nights Thursdays, e.g. tapas, Indian, Italian.

Mooreys Health Stores

Health food shop

Mini Shops D+E, Six Day Market, Blackburn, East Lancs BB1 6AS. Tel: 01254-53245
Open: Mon-Sat 9.00-17.00, Sun closed
www.vits4you.com

The biggest of three stores in Lancashire. Wholefoods. Fridge with vegan margarine, dairy-free cheese. Plamil vegan chocolate. Bodycare by Jason (inc Earth's Best baby and kids), Faith In Nature, Natracare. Lots of supplements including Lifeplan, Viridian, Solgar, Vogel, sports and energy drinks. Weleda homeopathy. Ecover and some Envirocare and Faith In Nature cleaning products. MC, Visa.

Blackpool

Bella Italia, Blackpool

Omnivorous Italian restaurant

23/25 Church St, Blackpool FY1 1HJ
Tel: 01253-751 529
Open: Mon-Fri 11.00-23.00, Sat 9.00-23.00, Sun 10.00-23.00

75 Victoria St, Blackpool FY1 4RJ
Tel: 01253 623 952
Open: varies according to time of year
www.bellaitalia.co.uk

Chain of Italian restaurants with some vegetarian and vegan options.

Hellon's Health

Health food shop

84 Highfield Road, South Shore, Blackpool FY4 2JF. Tel: 01253-343 427
Open: Mon-Sat 9.30-17.30;closed Wed, Sun

Independent family run store. Range of wholefoods, and some snacky stuff. Their speciality is bodycare and supplements. Fridge and freezer coming in 2010. Bodycare by Thursday's Plantation, Weleda, Bioforce, Jason, Faith In Nature, Natracare, baby stuff. Absolute Aromas and Tisserand aromatherapy. Ecover cleaning.

Supplements by Nature's Aid, Bioforce, Quest, Floradix, body building. Weleda and New Era homeopathy and remedies. MC, Visa.

Blackpool Nutrition Ctr

Health food shop

22 Deansgate, Blackpool FY1 1BN (town centre). Tel: 01253-749 077
Open: Mon-Sat 9.00-17.00, Sun closed
www.nationalnutrition.co.uk (mail order)

Only a little food, mainly supplements, body building, homeopathy.

Bolton

The Kitchen on Great Moor Street

Vegetarian cafe

Unit 4 Commercial Union House, Great Moor Street, Bolton BL1 1NH
5 mins walk from Bolton train station
Tel: 01204-770881
Open: Tue-Sat 09.00-15.00,
Sun-Mon closed (hours may change)
www.thekitchen.coop and Facebook

New, opened just before we went to press! Good healthy vegetarian food at affordable prices. Lots of organic and local ingredients, and they sell them too. Turkish breakfast £2.50 of olives, hummus, salad, bread. Full English big

breakfast £4 with sausages, scrambled tofu, hash browns, beans, mushrooms, tomatoes, toast.
Main meal such as Moroccan vegetable chickpeas with couscous £3.50. Soup £1.50 with organic bread.
Cakes £1.50 are mainly vegan such as chocolate and cherry. Turkish sweetbreads and spinach bread 90p-£1.
Tea or coffee £1. Cold drinks £1-1.20. Wheelchair access. Children welcome, high chairs. Cash only.

Surya Snack Bar
Indian vegetarian snack bar

98 Derby Street, Bolton BL3 6HG
Tel: 01204-380 679
Open: Mon-Tue 12.00-17.00,
Wed-Thu closed, Fri-Sun 17.00-21.00
vegetarian-indian-caterers-in-bolton.co.uk

Very vegan-friendly with dishes from throughout the sub-continent. Starters, £1.50-£4, with samosas and kachoris, and mains £2-£6.99 with stir-fried aubergines, dosas and spinach mung daal. No longer doing desserts.
Half bottle wine £3.50. Beer £2.40 pint. Coffee/tea 80p, no soya milk. Children welcome, no high chairs. 20% discount to members of Vegetarian or Vegan Society. Outside catering. Visa, MC.

Sokrates
Omnivorous Greek restaurant

80-84 Winter Hey Lane, Horwich,
Bolton BL6 7NZ
Tel: 01204-692100
Open: Sun 15.00-22.00 (last orders 21.00), Mon-Thu 17.00-23.00 (last orders 22.00) Fri-Sat 18.00-24.00 (last orders 22.30)
www.sokratestaverna.co.uk

Lots of vegetarian dishes. Starters £5-6, mains £9.50-11 such as vine leaves, moussaka, oven baked butterbeans. Vegetarian meze platter £8.50. You can pre-order a vegetarian banquet one or two days before, £17.50 minimum two people, with a bit of 25 different dishes. House wine £14.50 bottle, glass £3.60-4.90. Children welcome, high chairs. Visa, MC, Amex. Reservations advised weekends. Another branch in Sale, Cheshire.

Also good in Bolton are **Vedas** Indian www.thevedas.co.uk (branches too in Todmorden and Trafford) who did a £10 vegan buffet for 15 people, and **La Tasca** Spanish tapas www.latasca.co.uk.

Burnley
Red Triangle Cafe
Vegetarian restaurant

160 St James Street, Burnley BB11 1NR (town centre, near the market)
Tel: 01282-832 319
Open: Tue-Sat 10.30-19.00,
Fri-Sat night 19.00-22.30 (you must book, only open for telephone bookings in evenings), Sun-Mon closed

Vegetarian café and restaurant that also has occasional music nights. Mains £4 during the day and £6.95 in evenings such as Moroccan couscous with pumpkin seeds. Big menu that changes all the time. Desserts £1.50 day, £2.50 evening, such as fruit filled oat pancake with soya custard. Coffee and juices £1, tea 90p, they have soya milk. House wine £6.95 for a bottle, £1.80 glass. Children welcome in the day, high chair.

Bury
Paprika
Omnivorous Balti restaurant

21-23 Church Street West, Radcliffe, Manchester M26 9SP (Bury area)
Tel: 0161-725 9910
Open: Tue-Thur & bank holidays 17.30-23.00, Fri-Sat 17.30-00.30, Sun 16.30-22.30, Mon closed except bank holidays.

Technically in Manchester, but along with Rukshmani's, handy for Crazi

Carrots who recommend them for a veggie/vegan meal. £3.75 main course, £1.75 rice. Children welcome, half price veggieburger meals. Bring your own alcohol, free corkage, glassware provided. Free delivery on take-away. MC, Visa. They say they won't be beaten on price on like-for-like meals or you get the difference back.

Bury Natural Health Store

Health food shop

The Mall, 14-15 Bury Markat Hall, Bury BL9 0BD
Tel: 0161-761 2145
Open: Mon-Sat 9.00-17.00, Tue till 16.00
www.buryhealthfoods.co.uk

Over 3,000 products. Yeast-free and gluten-free bread. Fridge with vegan cheeses, meat substitutes, tofu, hummus. No freezer. Big range of teas. Bodycare by Weleda, Dead Sea Magik, Manuka, Jason. Cleaning products by Faith In Nature. Supplements by all the main manufacters. Homeopathy, flower remedies, essential oils. The owner is a homeopath, in every day except Thursday. Nutritionist available for free consultations. MC, Visa.

Earth Mother Health Store

Health/beauty/wellbeing shop

66 Bridge St, Ramsbottom, Bury BL0 9AG
Tel: 01706-828 333
Open: Tue-Sat 10.00-17.00
www.earthmotherstore.co.uk

Run by two sisters, qualified holistic therapists. They don't do food but have lots of bodycare and makeup including Dr Hauschka, Green People, Weleda, Natracare, lots of baby things, soaps. It's great for presents for women.
Supplements include Viridian, Bioforce, Pukka, Terra Nova. Weleda and New Era homeopathy, Australian bush flower. Essential oils. Organic facial treatments. Health, beauty and wellbeing books. Jute shopping bags, aromatherapy candles, organic Fairtrade clothing. MC, Visa.

Chorley

Chorley Health Foods

Health food shop

18 New Market Street, Chorley PR7 1DB
Tel: 01257-277341
Open: Mon-Fri 08.15-17.15,
Sat 08.15-16.00
www.yourhealthfoodstore.co.uk

Gluten-free bread. Fridge and freezer with meat substitutes, vegan cheese, meat substitutes, Swedish Glace and a new vegan ice-cream locally made.
Lots of bodycare including Avalon, Jason, Faith In Nature, Natracare and Organyc, Weleda and Earth Friendly Baby. Homeopathy, essential oils. Ecover cleaning products.
Supplements include Solgar, Nature's Aid, Bioforce, Gemini, Arkopharma, sports nutrition. Lost of books, also magazines. Sometimes a nutritional consultant in the shop, medical herbalist. MC, Visa, Amex. 6,000 products available from their website.

Colne

Jim Skaffy

Vegetarian restaurant

19-21 New Market Street, Colne BB8 9BJ
Tel: 01282-868 828
Open: Fri-Sun 19.00-23.00 or later, sometimes Tue or Thu when music on
www.myspace.com/jimsacousticcafe

Jim's cosy licensed vegetarian restaurant has been attracting regulars since 1978 with world food influences and is renownedfor the friendliness of its waitresses. It is next to the Town Hall in a

Victorian street in an old market town. Sometimes there is live music or an open mic night.

Starters £2-2.95 such as garlic bread, onion bhajias which they are famous for. Specials change weekly and at least one is vegan, such as Polynesian sweet and sour £7.45 with pineapple, deep-fried tofu, green beans, Chinese leaves, peppers, beansprouts, gomasio, brown rice, crispy noodles, nori. Their vegan curries are very popular £7.95.

Desserts £3.25 include a vegan option such as mixed fruit and nuts with sorbet and Grenadine.

House wine large glass £3.45, half litre carafe £6.45, 75cl £8.95, litre £11.20. Organic wine by the bottle from £11.95. Local draft beer £2.25 pint, continental bottled lagers £2-2.95. Fruit juice £1.25. Coffee £1.25, they have soya milk.

Children welcome, high chair. No credit cards, cash machine outside. Best to book ahead Fri-Sat.

The local market hall opens Mon, Wed, Sat 9.00-17.00. Colne is a good base in East Lancs for walking and has some B&B's though nothing specifically vegetarian.

Euxton
The Plough Inn
Omnivorous gastro pub

Runshaw Lane, Euxton PR7 6HB (just the other side of M6 from Chorley, don't confuse with the other Plough Inn in Chorley)
Tel: 01257-266491
Open: Mon-Sun 11.30-23.00 or later (Sun 12.00-)
Food 11.30-21.00 (Sun 20.00)
Facebook Plough Inn Euxton

Spud and Fiona: Country pub that gets a lot of veggie and vegan customers.
4 vegan starters £2.95-4.50 such as garlic bread, garlic mushrooms, salads, barbecue mushrooms.

15 to 18 vegetarian mains including at least 6 vegan ones around £8.95-9.95 which change such as mushroom and bean chili, stir-fry, herby mushroom pasta, vegan stack, vegan bolognaise and other dishes to order. Lots of veggie meals, many containing Quorn products (not vegan). Veggie brunches, burgers, baps and baguettes.

Desserts are vegetarian but not vegan.

Real ales. House wine £2.80 glass, £10.95 bottle.

Large outdoor garden area. Children welcome, half portions from £3.75. Dogs on a lead welcome outside. Sky tv inside and out. MC, Visa, Amex.

Lancaster
The Whale Tail
Vegetarian cafe

78a Penny Street, Lancaster LA1 1XN (above Single Step Wholefoods)
Tel: 01524-845 133
Open: Mon-Fri 10.00-16.00,
Sat 10.00-17.00, Sun 10.00-15.00
www.whaletailcafe.co.uk

Breakfast till 11.30, all day Sunday, with modular options or do the full vegan for £6.75. Soups £3.95. Mains £6-7 include mushroom and walnut burger, spicy beanburger, salad platter, shepherd's pie with salad, chips, potato skins.

Cakes £1.65-2.95 include vegan date and pear slice, chocolate fudge cake, carrot cake. Vegan custard and ice cream available.

Organic wine, beer and cider. House wine £10 for a bottle, £2.95 glass. Juice £1.25. Teas and coffees £1.50. Sofas. Sometimes art exhibitions on the walls. Patio garden. Children's portions, high chairs. Visa, MC.

Gregson Centre

Omnivorous cafe in arts & community centre

33 Moorgate, Lancaster LA1 3PY
Tel: 01524-849959
Food Mon-Fri 12.00-14.30, 16.30-21.00,
Sat 11.00-21.00, Sun 11.00-20.00
www.gregson.co.uk

Cafe and bar, 500 metres up the hill from the Dukes Playhouse. Good community feel and lots of events.
All day veggie/vegan breakfast £7.50 includes burger, beans, tomato, mushrooms, hashbrowns and toast.
Lite bites £4.95 such as veggie chilli. Soup of the day £4.25. Pitta dippers with olives, hummus and salsa £5.95. Garlic mushrooms £5.25. Chips £2.50, hummus £2, olives £2.95, seasonal veg or side salad £2.95.
Main course griled Mediterranean vegetables £8.50 with rice and garlic pitta; pasta or risotto of the day £7.95; chilli non carne with rice and garlic bread £7.95. Veggie burger £7.50 with chips, onion rings, salad and salsa. Nachos with veg chilli £7.95. Sunday nut roast. Also specials board. Veggie buffet £8 includes salads, hummus, salsa, nachos, etc, or £12 also gets you samosas, curry and rice. Party buffet £5. Puddings £3.95, cakes 95p. House wine £10.75 bottle. Draught beer £3.30 pint, vegan local bottled beer £2.80. Children's menu with veggie sausages, pasta, high chairs. MC, Visa.

Bella Italia, Lancaster

Omnivorous Italian restaurant

26/28 Church Street, Lancaster LA1 1LH
Tel: 01524-36340
Open: Mon-Fri 11-23.00, Sat 10.00-11.00, Sun 11.00-22.00
www.bellaitalia.co.uk

Near the city centre and university.

Pizza Margherita

Omnivorous pizza restaurant

2 Moor Lane, Lancaster LA1 1QD
Tel: 01524-36333
Open: Mon-Sun 10.30-22.30
www.pizza-margherita.co.uk

Founded in 1979 by the sister of the founder of Pizza Express. Vegan pizza bases. Vegans can take your own non-dairy cheese. Regular pizza £5.30-7.95. House wine £3.30-4.50 glass, £12.50 bottle. Children welcome. MC, Visa.

The Sultan of Lancaster

Indian omnivorous restaurant

The Old Church, Brock Street, Lancaster LA1 1UR (opposite Whale Tail)
Tel 01524-61188
Open: every day 17.00-23.00
www.sultanoflancaster.com

Amazing atmospheric place in an old chapel. Veggie dishes cooked separately and they can customise them. Starters £3.25. Vegetarian mains £9.95 include vegetable or spinach and mushroom rogan josh, madras, vindaloo or masala, or biryani. RIce or fries £1.75. Side dishes £5.95. Thali for 2 £24.95. Also some World dishes such as lentil soup £3.75, hummus with pitta £3.95, main course veg sitr-fry with nuts £11.95.
Juices and soft drinks £1.75-1.85 glass, £4.75 jug. No alcohol. Children welcome, high chairs. MC, Visa.

Sultan Food Court

Mediterranean & Middle Eastern cafe, delicatessen and art gallery

The Old Church, Brock Street, Lancaster LA1 1UR (opposite Whale Tail)
Tel 01524-849 494
Open: Mon-Sun 10.00-17.00
www.sultanoflancaster.com

Downstairs from Sultan restaurant is

this daytime Mediterranean and Middle Eastern cafe, delicatessen and art gallery with meals, snacks and coffees.

Samosas, pakoras, patra or falafel with salad £3.75. Selection of 3 dips £3.75, choose from aubergine baba ghanouj, marinated aubergine, hummus, exotic tomato etc, served with pitta or popadoms, carrot and cucumber sticks. Soup with bread £3.25. Fries or wedges £2. Falafel or soya bean burger with salad and kettle chips or curly fries £4.95.

Veg masala panini £4.95 Veg biryani with side salad £5.95. Platters £6.95, either Indian samosas, spring roll, bombay potatoes and pakoras; or Middle East tabouleh, baba ghanouj, hummus, falafel, vine leaves and pitta; also Greek or Mexican.

Juices and smoothies £1.95. Single pot of tea or cafetiere of coffee £1.95, large £3.95. No soya milk.

Children welcome, high chairs. MC, Visa. On nice days in summer tables outside.

All the other Indian restaurants in Lancaster are vegan aware and friendly such as **Moguls**.

Single Step

Vegetarian co-op wholefood shop

78a Penny Street, Lancaster LA1 1XN
Tel: 01524-63021
Open: Mon-Sat 9.30-17.30
www.singlestep.org.uk ✓

Loose food in hoppers. Organic fruit and veg. Organic bread baked daily. Lots of Fairtrade. Gluten-free foods. Vegan cheese, milk, yoghurt, ice-cream. Vegan chocolate heaven with Plamil, Booja Booja, Organica, Divine, Montezuma and others, flapjacks, snack bars. Loose herbs and spices. Organic wines and beers.

Bodycare includes Suma, Faith In Nature, Green People, Weleda, Pitrok, Natracare, baby stuff, vegan condoms. Ecover, BioD, Clearspring and refills for most of them.

Supplements by Nature's Own, Viridian, Vega. Vogel remedies. Essential oils. Books and magazines. Postcards and greetings cards. Locally made vegan candles. 10% discount for senior citizens. Cash or cheque only.

Preston and nearby

RK Sweets

Vegetarian Indian deli & take-away

169 St. Pauls Road, Preston PR1 1PX
Tel: 01772-200 505
Open: Mon-Sat 10.00-20.00, Sun 10.00-19.00
www.rksweets.com

This is an authentic Indian delicatessen since 1986 that sells much more than sweets at very reasonable prices, including a variety of snacks and a selection of Indian dishes (much more than a usual Indian takeaway). Friendly and helpful staff will let you try before you buy in some instances. Veg curries £2. Biryani, pulao or plain rice £1-2. Cold drinks, sometimes at weekends they serve tea. Some seats to eat in. Outside catering and dinner parties.

Preston Health Food Store

Health food shop

✓ Good for seeds

26 Guildhall Street, Preston PR1 3NU
Tel: 01772-257 617
Open: Mon-Sat 9.00-17.00, Sun closed
www.jandevrieshealth.co.uk

Fridge with vegan cheese, tofu. Vegan chocolate by Plamil, Montezuma, Blakes, Booja Booja. Fruit and veg box scheme dropoff point.

Bodycare by Dr Hauschka, Barefoot Botanicals, Jason, Desert Essence, Aubrey. Ecover and refills.

Supplements by Nature's Plus, Kordels, Nature's Aid, Solgar, Viridian, Quest, Bioforce. Allergy testing monthly, and naturopath Jan de Vries who owns the store visits bi-monthly and they sell his books. MC, Visa.

Mooreys Health Stores

Health food shop

36-37 Market Hall, Market St, Preston
PR1 2JD Tel: 01772-254015
Open: Mon-Sat 9.00-17.00, Sun closed
www.vits4you.com

Wholefoods. Fridge with vegan margarine, dairy-free cheese. Plamil vegan chocolate. Bodycare by Jason (inc Earth's Best baby and kids), Faith In Nature. Lots of supplements including Lifeplan, Viridian, Solgar, Vogel. Weleda homeopathy. Ecover and some Envirocare and Faith In Nature cleaning products. MC, Visa.

Garstang Natural Health

Health food store & natural health clinic

High Street, **Garstang**, near Preston PR3 1FA
Tel: 01995-602 833
Open: Mon-Sat 9.00-17.00, Wed 13.00
www.garstang-natural-health.co.uk

Wide range of gluten free products and organic foods. Fridge and freezer with vegan cheese, meat substitutes, Swedish Glace and the new local Worthenshaws Cocoa Nice vegan diabetic ice-cream. Plamil and Montezuma vegan chocolate. Some Ecover.
Supplements by Solgar, Quest, FSC, Nature's Aid. Bioforce herbal products. Bodycare by Barefoot Botanicals, Aubreys, Dr Hauschka, Natracare. Essential oils, burners, candles, books, crystals and gem jewellery. Homeopathy, essential oils. Allergy testing, Alexander technique, aromatherapy, Bowen, Dr Hauschka treatments, channelled healing and emotional freedom technique, massage, lymphatic drainage, osteopath, reflexology, crystal healing. MC, Visa. Postal deliveries. Gift vouchers.

Aphrodite Health Foods

Health food shop & homeopathic pharmacy

1a Priory Lane, **Penwortham**, Preston PR1 0AR (outskirts of Preston)
Tel: 01772-746 555
Open: Mon-Fri 9.30-17.30, Sat 9.30-17.00

Fridge and freezer with vegan cheeses, meat substitutes, tofu, hummus, take-away tabouleh, salads, chickpeas, local Worthenshaws vegan ice-cream. Plamil vegan chocolate.
Ecover and all the refills.
Bodycare by Aubrey, Green People, Jason, Faith In Nature, Natracare. Supplements by Viridian, Pukka, Vogel, Nature's Plus, Nature's Aid, Solary, Quest, Lifeplan, Weleda. Weleda, Nelsons homeopathy and resident homeopath. Complementary health clinic round the corner. A few books. MC, Visa.

The Greenhouse Natural Healthstore

Health food shop

76 Bury Lane, **Longridge**, Preston PR3 3WH
Tel: 01772-780 562
Open: Mon- Fri 9.30-17.30, Thu 18.00, Sat 16.30, Sun closed
www.yourhealthfoodshop.co.uk

Organic wholefoods and they can order in anything you need. Montezuma chocolate. Small fridge so if you want chilled goods you need to collect as soon as they arrive. Lots of bodycare such as Akin, Dr Hauschka, Jason, Earthline, Faith In Nature, Natracare.

Supplements by Solgar, Viridian, Nature's Plus, Nature's Aid etc. New Era, Weleda and Nelson homeopathy, Bach Flower. Natural By Nature essential oils. MC, Visa.

Simply Natural
Health food shop.

26 Poulton St, **Kirkham**, Preston PR4 2AB (between Preston and Blackpool)
Tel: 01772-671 489
Open: Mon-Fri 9.00-17.00, Sat 9.00-16.30
www.simplynatural.org.uk

Fridge and freezer with vegan cheese, meat sustitutes. Vegan chocolate by Plamil, sometimes others. Homebrew wine and beer. supplies.
Bodycare by Faith In Nature, Weleda, Health Aid, Dead Sea Magik, Jason, Natracare. Supplements by Solgar, Nature's Plus, Nature's Aid, Lifeplan and others. Homeopathy, essential oils. Ecover. Books. MC, Visa.

Rossendale
Mooreys Health Stores
Health food shop

54 Bank Street, Rawtenstall, Rossendale, East Lancs BB4 8DY. Tel: 01706 -260 060
Open: Mon-Sat 9.30-17.00, Sun closed
www.vits4you.com

Wholefoods. Fridge with vegan margarine, dairy-free cheese. Plamil vegan chocolate. Bodycare by Jason (inc Earth's Best baby and kids), Faith In Nature, Green People kids, Natracare. Lots of supplements and homeopathy. Ecover and some Envirocare and Faith In Nature cleaning products. MC, Visa.

Southport

See Merseyside for *Edendale* accommodation.

Tarleton
Libra
Health food shop

98 Church Road, Tarleton, Preston PR4 6UP (village half way between Preston and Southport, about 9 miles outside Preston)
Tel: 01772-816 100
Open: Mon-Fri 10.00-17.00, Sat 16.00, Sun closed

Regular health food shop, no take-aways. Fridge with vegan cheeses, freezer out back with Swedish Glace, and the new Worthenshaws vegan diabetic ice-cream. Vegan chocolate by Plamil, sometimes Divine.
Bodycare by Green People, Nature Knows Best, Avalon, Faith In Nature, Natracare, some Weleda baby.
Supplements by Nature's Plus, Viridian, FSC and many more. Weleda and Nelsons homeopathy, Bach Flower, Ainsworth, essential oils. Hypnotherapist and intolerance testing. Greetings cards, magnetic bracelets. MC, Visa, Amex. Big car park opposite.

Todmorden
The Bear Cafe-Bar
Licensed vegetarian eatery & deli

29 Rochdale Road, Todmorden OL14 7LA (direct train or slightly cheaper bus from Manchester)
Tel: 07714 333 230
Open: Mon-Sat 9.00-17.00, Sun 10-17.00, last food orders 16.30
www.bearco-op.com/cafe

Food from around the world. Newly refurbished since our last edition, now all open-plan, with a deli counter with take-away options. They make everything themselves and source most ingredients locally, and have homemade preserves and chutneys. All soups are vegan, so is at least one special and they always have vegan cake and soya milk.

Breakfast panini, homemade beans on toast etc. Sunday brunch all day £6.95 includes drink. Sandwiches and paninis, such as hummus, carrot and olive £3.75. Snacks such as tomatoes on miso toast, and soups for around £3.50. Main courses £5.95-6.50 such as African groundnut stew with coconut rice and salad; deluxe bean burger with salads; daily specials. Tapas/meze style platters such as Indian, Mexican or Middle Eastern £6.95.

Cakes include vegan chocolate cake £2.50, vegan cream available. Hot drinks, pots of tea, £1.40-2.40. Freshly made juices and smoothies £2.20-£3. Organic sparkling elderflower £1.70.

Now licensed to sell alcohol. Organic local beers such as Little Valley Brewery including Tod's Blonde and Withens IPA, ginger pale ale served with fresh lime. Vegetarian and vegan wines from £10 bottle, £2.60 glass.

Deli does take-away panini, salads etc, point to what you want. Child portions and options, high chairs, baby changing. Outside seating in summer. Student and Viva! discount. Free wifi. MC, Visa, Amex. Outside catering for private functions, with buffets typically £6.50 per head.

Hanuman Thai

Omnivorous Thai restaurant

15 Water Street, Todmorden OL14 5AB
Tel: 01706-817 010
Open: Wed-Sun 17.30-23.00 or later, Mon-Tue closed
www.hanumanthai.com

Pulse cafe has closed and is now a new Thai restaurant with 5 vegetarian starters and 5 Thai tapas £3.50, 20 mains around £5.50, rice £1.50. Desserts £2.50 can be made vegan with banana and coconut milk. House wine £10 bottle, £2.50 glass. Big range of European and Thai beer £2.50. Families welcome, high chairs. No disabled access.

Bear Healthfoods

Vegetarian wholefood shop

29 Rochdale Road, Todmorden OL14 7LA
Tel: 01706-813 737
Open Mon-Sat 9.00-17.30, Sun 10-17.00
www.bearco-op.com/shop

Well-stocked wholefood shop. Local, organic and Fairtrade. Organic fruit and veg, 80% local. Fresh local bread every day from Saker bakery. Fridge and freezer with vegan cheeses, pasties, sos rolls, hummus, tofu, meat substitutes, sprouts, Booja Booja and Swedish Glace vegan ice-cream. Vegan chocolate by Plamil, Montezuma, Divine, Organica, Booja Booja. Enormous range of herbs and spices. Baby foods. Own range of preserves, sauces and fine foods. They can order in anything you want.

Bodycare includes Faith In Nature, Australian Organics, Lavera, Visage cosmetics, Fikkerts handmade soaps, Natracare, baby products.

Complementary medicines include Weleda, Biohealth and Bach flower. Aromatherapy. Mail order service. Aromatherapist, homeopath available. BioD and refills, Clearspring cleaning.

Local organic beers, cider, vegetarian and vegan wines and spirits. Magazines. Veg box deliveries. MC, Visa.

Wigan

The Coven Delicatessen

Omnivorous deli-cafe & take-away

45 Hallgate, Wigan WN1 1LR
(next to the bus station)
Tel: 01942-237801
Train: Wigan either station 2 minutes, half hour from Manchester or Liverpool
Open: Mon-Sat 08.00-17.00
www.thecoven.biz
also on Facebook and Twitter

Opened 2007 and moved in 2010 into bigger premises with a large outdoor garden terrace eating area, bigger menu and kitchen garden that they pick fresh herbs, salad and veg from. They give preference to local, organic and Fairtrade. Everything is made on the premises, most of it vegetarian and much of that vegan including cakes and gluten-free.

Cooked breakfast £4.45. Mushrooms, tomatoes or beans on toast £2.50, or two toppings for £3.25. Snacks such as linseed toast or crumpets £1.30. Soup of the day £2.50-3.50. Vegan naan-bread pizza £2.50. Hummus and toast or pitta £3.95.

Vegan noodles or couscous with chickpeas £3.50, both come with stir-fry. Range of home-made burgers and falafels £3.50-5.95.

Lots of new specials in the new premises £3.95-5.95 such as falafel with chunky Coven chips; or nutburger salad with soya yogurt, syrup and peanut butter dressing. Roast jacket potatoes with lots of fillings or anything else they sell from £1.95. Pies such as tomato and onion or Mediterranean veg from £2 slice, or with jacket or chips and/or salad. Fresh baked daily baguette sandwiches £2.45-3.50 made to order.

Lots of desserts £3.50 include fruit salad with orange rosewater or coconut milk, or stewed apple with cinnamon and raisins. Lots of cakes £2.25, mostly vegan and change all the time such as matcha Japanese tea, lemon drizzle, chocolate orange, peanut butter.

20 kinds of tea and lots of coffees £1.30-2.50. Teas are served in Japanese glass teapots. Soya milk available.

Children's portions and variations, you can bring in buggies, breast-feeding friendly. Dogs welcome. Cash only, cashpoints nearby.

Look out for tea tasting events with vegan cake made from tea, a cracking alternative to a wine and cheese evening. Vegan and vegetarian ready meals, cooking classes.

Nature's Best
Health food shop

74a Bryn St, Ashton-in-Makerfield, Wigan WN4 9AU (5 miles from Wigan centre)
Tel: 01942-204038
Open: Mon-Sat 9.00-16.30, Wed till 14.00

Some wholefoods. Fridge and freezer with vegan cheeses, meat substitutes. Plamil vegan chocolate.
Bodycare by Faith In Nature, Dead Sea Magik, Aloe Vera, Natracare.
Supplements by Lifeplan, Optima, Quest, Nature's Aid. Weleda homeopathy. New Era salts. Aqua Olea essential oils. Allergy testing. MC, Visa. They can order in anything you need.

Only Natural
Health food shop

64 Standishgate, Wigan WN1 1UW
Tel: 01942-236 239
Open: Mon-Sat 9.00-17.30, Sun closed

Gluten-free bread. Fridge with Tofutti cheeses, tofu, sprouts. No freezer. Plamil vegan chocolate. Herbs and spices.
Bodycare by Avalon, Weleda, Healthaid, Eco, Natracare and they can order in others.
Lots of supplements include Vogel, Higher Nature, FSC, Healthaid, Savant, Nature's Aid, Lifeplan, Biohealth. Homeopathy, essential oils.
Ecover, Clearspring cleaning products. Some books. MC, Visa.

Julian Graves
Health food shop

14-16 Makinson Arcade, Wigan WN1 1PL
Tel: 01942-824 789
Open: Mon-Sat 9.30-17.00, Sun closed

Good for snacks and bags of nuts.

Lancashire chain stores
Holland & Barrett
Health food shop

Unit 12, Arndale Centre, **Accrington** BB5 1EX
Tel: 01254-235 114
Open: Mon-Sat 9.00-17.30, Sun closed

Unit 22, Staveleigh Walk, Lady Smith Centre
Ashton under Lyne OL6 7JQ
Tel: 0161-339 6552
Open: Mon-Sat 9.00-17.30, Sun 11-16.00

3 Cobden Court, **Blackburn** BB1 7JG
Tel: 01254-693 010
Open: Mon-Sat 9.00-17.30, Sun 11-16.00

33 Corporation Street, **Blackpool** FY1 1EJ
Tel: 01253-299 393
Open: Mon-Sat 9.30-17.30, Sun 10-16.00

26 Newport Street, **Bolton** BL1 1EA
Tel: 01204-385 954
Open: Mon-Sat 9.00-17.30, Sun 10-16.00

33 The Mall, **Burnley** BB10 4PX
Tel: 01282-459 833
Open: Mon-Sat 9.00-17.30, Sun 10-16.00

25 Haymarket, Millgate Centre, **Bury**
BL9 OBX. Tel: 0161-7617663. Open: Mon-Sat 9.00-17.30, Sun 10.30-16.30

Unit 27 Market Walk, Shopping Centre
Chorley PR7 1DE. Tel: 01257-271414
Open: Mon-Sat 9.00-17.30, Sun 10-16.00

44 Victoria Road West, Thornton, **Cleveleys**
FY5 1BU. Tel: 01253-864 030
Open: Mon-Sat 9.00-17.30, Sun 10-16.00

326 Penny Street, **Lancaster** LA1 1UA
Tel: 01524-848 633
Open: Mon-Sat 9.00-17.30, Sun 10-16.00

Unit 26, Spinning Gate Shopping Centre,
Ellesmere Street, **Leigh** WN7 4PG
Tel: 01942-674901
Open: Mon-Sat 9.00-17.30, Sun 10-16.00

Unit F10, Arndale Centre, **Middleton**
M24 4EL. Tel: 0161-643 3180
Open: Mon-Sat 9.00-17.30, Sun closed

24 Euston Road, **Morecambe** LA4 5DD
Tel: 01524-401 383
Open: Mon-Sat 9.00-17.30, Sun closed

Lower Mall, 37 The Spindles Shopping
Centre, **Oldham** OL1 1HE
Tel: 0161-622 0180
Open: Mon-Sat 9.00-17.30, Sun 11-16.00

33 Moor Street, **Ormskirk** L39 2AA
Tel: 01695-578 686
Open: Mon-Sun 9.00-17.00

Unit 1, 13 Friargate Walk, St Georges
Shopping Centre, **Preston** PR1 2NG
Tel: 01772-259 357
Open: Mon-Sat 9.00-17.30, Sun 11-17.00

Unit 51 Market Way, Rochdale Exchange,
Rochdale OL16 1EA. Tel: 01706-353 445
Open: Mon-Sat 9.00-17.30,
Sun 10.30-16.30

39 Raven Way, Salford Shopping Centre
Salford M6 5HT. Tel: 0161-736 6524
Open: Mon-Sat 9.00-17.30, Sun 10-16.00

51 St. Annes Road West, **St Annes** FY8 1SB
Tel: 01253-712 022. Open: Mon-Sat 9.00-17.30, Sun 10.30-16.30

8 Hardshaw Centre, **St Helens** WA10 1DN
Tel: 01744-208 211
Open: Mon-Sat 9.30-17.30, Sun closed

Unit 66 Arndale Centre, **Stretford** M32 9BD
Tel: 0161-865 5229
Open: Mon-Sat 9.00-17.30, Sun 10-16.00

Unit 33-34, The Galleries, **Wigan** WN1 1PX
Tel: 01942-8264 25
Open: Mon-Sat 9.30-17.30, Sun closed

NORTH
Lincolnshire

Accommodation	**84**
Boston	**84**
Bourne	**84**
Grimsby & Cleethorpes	**85**
Holbeach	**85**
LINCOLN	**85**
Louth	**87**
Tealby	**87**
Chain stores	**88**
Local groups	**88**

Lincolnshire

Lincoln accommodation
Pyewipe Inn
Omnivorous B&B, pub & restaurant

Fossebank Saxilby Road (A57), Lincoln LN1 2BG (20 mins walk NW of the centre)
Tel: 01522-528 708
Open: Sun-Thu 12.00-21.00, Fri-Sat 21.30
www.pyewipeinnlincoln.co.uk

21 room lodge for B&B, within the grounds of a riverside inn and restaurant, offering four vegetarian meals and cooked breakfast. The location is fantastic with views of the city, 20 minutes walk from the centre along the ancient Fossdyke Canal. Bridal suite with 4-poster bed £90; single £60; 7 twins, 13 doubles, disabled double, £70 for the room; family triple £80, family quad £90, but no special facilities for children.

Vegetarian mains £9.50 such as risotto; leek, mushroom and spinach pie. Everything is made to order so they can cater for anyone with dishes that are not on the menu, such as vegan baked aubergine or pan-fried gnocchi, with fruit salad or agar agar jelly for dessert. Dogs welcome, also in the pub. No smoking throughout. Lots of car parking, and for boats. Visa, MC.

Skegness accommodation
The Monsell
Omnivorous guest house

2 Firbeck Avenue, Skegness PE25 3JY
Tel: 01754-898374
Open: all year
www.monsell-hotel.co.uk

Family-friendly, caters for vegetarians and vegans and the chef is a veggie. All rooms ensuite. £22-25 per person bed and breakfast, 5-10 years half price, under-5 free. Add £7-8 for 4-course evening meals. Discounts for weekly stays, or 3+ nights low season. Chair lift to first floor bedrooms. Pets by arrangement. Bar. Wifi. Car park. Function room. No smoking. MC, Visa.

Boston
Maud's Tearoom
Omnivorous cafe

Maud Foster Windmill, Willoughby Road, Boston PE21 9EG. Tel: 01205-352 188
Open: all year Sat 10.00-17.00,
Wed-Sat 10.00-17.00 Easter and school summer holidays, see website for exact dates or phone.
www.maudfoster.co.uk

Previously vegetarian cafe in a working windmill serving 2 or 3 vegetarian meals around £5, such as soups, salads, vegetable fajitas, but vegans please ask, they can do something for you. MC, Visa. Children welcome, one high chair. 10% discount to members of the Vegetarian Society. You can go into the mill which is a separate business, £2.50 adults, £2 senior, £1.50 children, family (2+2) £6.50. Organic flour for sale.

Bourne
Spice of Life
Wholefood shop

4 Burghley Centre, Bourne PE10 9EG
Tel: 01778-394 735
Open: Mon-Sat 9.00-17.30 (Sat from 08.30)

Sister shop to Holbeach Wholefoods (next page) with similar stock.

Grimsby & Cleethorpes

The Sonargaon

Omnivorous Indian restaurant

45 Market Place, Cleethorpes DN35 8LY
Tel: 01472-600082 / 690468
Open: Sun-Thu 17.00-24.00,
Fri-Sat 17.00-02.00
www.thesonargaon.co.uk

The local vegetarian group eat out here. Starters £2.50. Veg or mushroom biriani £4.95. Veg bhuna, dupiaza, Madras, vindaloo, korma, rogan josh, dhansak all £3.95, balti £4.50. Side curries £2.40, rice £1.50-2.50, chips £1.25, nan £1.50-2.25. Set meal for 2 £1.50, for 4 £35, with starter, main and sides. Children welcome. Free local delivery, 20% discount if you collect.

Little China

Omnivorous Chinese take-away

2 Lynton Parade, Cromwell Road, Grimsby DN31 2BD. Tel: 01472-250088
Open: every day including bank holidays 17.30-23.30, Fri-Sat till 24.00

Grimsby has stacks of Chinese take-aways but this one is recommended by the local veggie group. Vegetarian section of menu with over a dozen dishes around £2. Big portions. Four course set meal £5.50. Sweets such as banana fritters with syrup £1.30-1.80. Delivery £1 within 3 miles.

Holbeach

Holbeach Wholefoods

Wholefood shop

32 High Street, Holbeach PE12 7DY
Tel: 01406-422149
Open: Mon-Sat 9.00-17.30

Lots of loose things to help yourself to including herbs and spices. Some veggie take-away food such as pasties, slices, much of it vegan. Vegan chocolate by Divine, Montezuma, Plamil, Booja Booja. Fresh tomatoes in the summer and they can sort out organic veg boxes for you. Fridge and freezer, vegan ice-cream. Remedies, vitamins, bodycare including Natracare, cleaning products. Health books. MC, Visa.

Lincoln eating out

Pimento Tearooms

Vegetarian cafe & tearoom

27 Steep Hill, Lincoln LN2 1LU
Tel: 01522-544 880
Open: every day 10-17.00 (Sun from 10.30)

On the steep hill between the high street and the cathedral, near the cathedral end. You go through women's fashion shop to enter. Main meal £5.95-6.95 such as veg and bean casserole with speciality breads; spring veg curry; salads. Sandwiches £3.95 made to order served with salad.
Home made cakes £2.25-2.50, always at least one vegan but usually more, and they offer soya cream.
20 leaf teas and 20 coffees £1.95 for an infuser pot of tea, £2.10 cafetiere of coffee. Organic fruit juice £1.85.
Two tables in the outside courtyard. Children welcome, one high chair. MC, Visa.

Thailand Number One

Omnivorous Thai restaurant

80-81 Bailgate, Lincoln. Tel: 01522-537000
Open: Mon-Sat 12-14.30, 18.00-23.00;
Sun 18-22.30 (not lunch)
www.lincoln.thailandnumber1.co.uk

Extensive vegetarian section on their menu. Special lunch of starter and main course with rice £7.50. A la carte starters £4.95, mains £7.95, rice and noodles £2.50-

2.95. Desserts include vegan Thai coconut pancake roll or banana fritters £3. House wine £2.25 glass, £11.50 bottle. Beers £2.75. Soft drinks and coffee £1.35-1.75. Children welcome, high chair. 10% discount on take-away. MC, Visa.

JD Wetherspoon
Omnivorous pubs

Ritz, 143-147 High Street, Lincoln LN5 7PJ Tel: 01522-512103

The Square Sail, Brayford Wharf North, Lincoln LN1 1YW. Tel: 01522 559920

The Forum, 13-14 Silver Street, Lincoln LN2 1DY. Tel: 01522 518630

Open: Mon-Thu 07.00-24.00, Fri-Sat 07.00-01.00, Sun 10.00-24.00
www.jdwetherspoon.co.uk

Three central JD Wetherspoon pubs (see page 3) about 10 minutes walk from each other, all with the usual sweet potato, spinach and chickpea vegan curry available all the time, but also on Thursday they have a curry night with an additional aubergine dhansak, you can have either curry with rice, popadom and a pint for a superb £4.99. Children welcome. They do bargain early morning veggie cooked breakfasts £2.79, and can modify for vegans though it will be mainly beans on toast!

The central **Tower Hotel** at 38 Westgatre LN1 3BD does a good vegetarian and vegan menu says the local group, one of them even had her wedding reception there. Rooms £45-65 per person. Tel 01522-529999.
www.lincolntowerhotel.co.uk

Lincoln shops
Bailgate Health Store
Health food shop

4 Gordon Road, Lincoln LN1 3AJ (near Pimento). Tel: 01522-526453
Open: Mon-Sat 08.30-16.30,
Sun often open summer afternoons

Fridge and freezer with vegan cheese, sausages, tofu, hummus, Swedish Glace. Sometimes gluten-free bread. Lots of high energy snacks such as nuts, seeds, dried fruit, vegan chocolate by Plamil and Montezuma. Herbs and spices.
Bodycare by Dead Sea Magik and others. Supplements by Nature's Aid, Quest, Higher Nature, Lifeplan etc. Homeopathy. Essential oils. Ecover. MC, Visa.

Greens
Health food shop

175 High Street, Lincoln LN5 7AF (city centre). Tel: 01522-524874
Open: Mon-Sat 9.00-17.30, Sun closed
www.greenshealthfoodshop.co.uk

Organic fruit and veg. Fridge and freezer with salad pots such as cous-couscous, vegan cheese, meat substitutes, hummus, tofu, vegan ice-cream. Vegan chocolate by Plamil, Montezuma, Holex, Siesta.
Bodycare by Faith In Nature, Jason, Weleda, Akin, Dead Sea Magik, Natracare. Earth Friendly baby.
Supplements by Solgar, Quest, Bioforce, Nature's Aid, Lifeplan etc, sports nutrition. Weleda and New Era homeopathy. Essential oils. Kinesiology, massage, food sensitivity testing. Ecover and some refills. MC, Visa.

Gaia Wholefoods
Organic Fairtrade market stall

Units 17/18, Lincoln Central Market, Sincil Street, Lincoln LN5 7ET
Open Mon–Sat 08.30–16.00
www.lincolncentralmarket.co.uk

Wide range or vegetarian and vegan wholefoods, many gluten-free, on a stall run by a medical herbalist. Fridge with soya yogurt, hummus, olives, tofu, vegan cheeses, burgers. Plamil chocolate. Herbs, spices and medicinal herbs. They can order in anything you need. Ecover and Ecoleaf washing products. Cash only.

Louth
Perkins' Pantry
Omnivorous restaurant & tea room

7 Mercer Row, Louth LN11 9JG
Tel: 01507-609 709
Open:
Summer Mon–Sat 8.30–16.00, Sun closed.
Winter Mon–Tue, Wed, Fri 8.30–14.30, Sat 8.30–16.00, closed Sun and possibly Thu.
Sometimes extra days if market in town, oprn evening for private parties.
www.lincsuk.com/perkinspantry.htm

Popular with local veggies and vegans, one of the chefs is a veggie, they cook chips separately and even have vegan spread and gravy. Several vegetarian dishes and at least four vegan options around £7.60 available at any time, (vegans can call ahead for a bigger range) such as vegan bangers and mash, spelt pasta with roast veg, falafel with chips and salad. Sometimes vegan cake or other desserts if they know you're coming. They can do gluten-free and diabetic. Tea or cofee £1.50, latte/cappuccino £2.20, they have soya milk. Wheelchair access. Children and nursing mothers welcome, 2 high chairs and baby equipment. MC, Visa.

Wholefood Co-op
Wholefood shop

7-9 Eastgate, Louth LN11 9NB
Tel: 01507-602411
Open: Mon–Fri 9.00–17.30, Sat 9.00–17.00, Sun closed
www.louthwholefoodcoop.co.uk

Fridge and freezer with take-away pasties and flans, some vegan. tofu, vegan cheeses, meat substitutes, Swedish Glace, Tofutti. Organic fruit and veg. Bread. Vegan chocolate by Plamil, Montezuma, Booja Booja. Japanese foods.
Organic vegetarian (most vegan) wines, spirits, cider and beer.
Bodycare by Neal's Yard, Faith In Nature, Aubrey Organics, BWC vegan makeup, Natracare. Neal's Yard organic and Aqua Oleum essential oils. Homeopathy, Bach flower, and herbal remedies. Herbalist in the shop on Wednesdays. Supplements by Nature's Own, Nature's Aid, Queste, Weleda, Lifeplan etc.
Ecover and refills, Clearspring cleaning products. MC, Visa.

Tealby
The Olde Barn
Omnivorous pub & restaurant

Cow Lane, Tealby LN8 3YB
Tel: 01673-838304
Open: Tue–Sat 12.00–15.00, 17.30–23.00, last food orders 14.00, 21.00;
Sun 12.00–16.00, last food orders 14.30
Closed Sun evening and all day Mon.
www.theoldebarninn.co.uk

400 year old stone-built pub with gardens in summer, a real fire in winter, and real ale. There is a 9-dish vegetarian menu that includes penne, risotto, balti, pasta, veggie sausages. Lunch £7.95, dinner £10.95. Kids welcome, baby change unit. Baby grand piano for music nights. Licensed for weddings and civil partnerships.

The Kings Head

Omnivorous pub & restaurant

Kingsway, Tealby LN8 3YA
Tel: 01673-838347
Open: every day 12.00-15.00, 18.00-23.00 (Fri-Sat 23.30)
Food served 12.00-14.00, Sun till 15.00;
evening every day 18.30-21.00,
Mon closed
Food: every day lunch and evening
www.woldviewhouse.co.uk/tealby_outer.pdf
www.woldviewhouse.co.uk/tealby_inner.pdf

14th century thatched pub with a large pub garden, big on ales and wine. 4 vegetarian dishes £7-11 such as vegetable tart, veg Wellington, and if you call ahead the chef can do something for you or on the day. Disabled access.

Tealby village is a Conservation Area of Outsanding Natural Beauty with over 20 listed buildings and stone cottages, Norman church, post office with tourist info, though the eating is a bit on the meaty-gamey-dairy side apart from the two pubs. It's on the Viking Way ramblers' route along the Wolds, lots of marked trails for cycling and walkers.

Local Groups
Grimsby Vegetarians

Edward Hawkins, Tel: 01472-870738
email: gy.vegetarians@btinternet.com
www.grimsby.veggroup.org

For vegetarians in north Lincolnshire. Meet for meals locally and at Hitchcock's in Hull, East Yorks.

Vegan Lincs

Linda Wardale 01522-851915 after 8pm
www.veganlincs.co.uk

Veggies and non-veggies welcome. Meet 1st Saturday of the month from 8.30pm at Widow Cullen's Well, Steep Hill, Lincoln, a pub with a great selection of vegan beers. Every second Saturday at Pimento 12.00-14.00. Monthly Supper Club bring and share.

Louth Vegetarian Group

www.louthveggiegroup.org.uk

Pot luck suppers, walks and community outreach.

Lincolnshire chain stores
Holland & Barrett

Health Food shop

47 Market Place, **Boston** PE21 6NF
Tel: 01205-359712

Unit 16, Marshalls Yard, **Gainsborough** DN21 2NA. Tel: 01427 678981

Unit 35 Isaac Newton Centre, **Grantham** NG31 6EE. Tel: 01476 579334

61 Friargate, Freshney Place Shopping Centre, **Grimsby** DN31 1ED
Tel: 01472-344 115

319 High Street, **Lincoln** LN5 7DW
Tel: 01522-567 615. Open: Mon-Sat 9.00-17.30, Sun 10.30-16.30

18 Market Place, **Louth** LN11 9PD
Tel: 01507-607202

37 High Street, **Scunthorpe** DN15 6SB
Tel: 01724-278 157

37 Lumley Road, **Skegness** PE25 3LL
Tel: 01754-764412

35 Hall Place, **Spalding** PE11 1SQ
Tel: 01775-724220

57 High Street, **Stamford** PE9 2AW
Tel: 01780-480387

Tourist information:
www.visitlincolnshire.com
www.visitnorthlincolnshire.com
www.lincolncathedralquarter.co.uk
www.lincoln.gov.uk

Manchester is a large, hectic city, famous for its nightclub culture. There is a strong gay scene, and a massive population of students, so the city has had a cosmopolitan feel for a long time and really comes alive at night. There's a thriving live music scene, especially if you like guitar stuff. There are also good cinemas and lots of art galleries and museums.

The **shopping centre** has all the chain and department stores and some great little independent shops and cafes. These are mainly found in the **Northern Quarter**, a block of streets running northwards from Piccadilly Gardens.

Vegetarians are well catered for in Manchester, with excellent daytime cafes such as **Earth Cafe**, **Eighth Day**, **Oklahoma** and a food pub that in 2010 went vegetarian **The Thirsty Scholar. Bistro 1847** is the first city centre evening vegetarian restaurant, also a bar, otherwise hop on a bus to **The Greenhouse**, or further out to **Greens** or **Fuel**. Alternatively, we have listed a selection of omnivorous restaurants and bars recommended by local veggies. See the veggie map of central Manchester on page 103.

Manchester has some excellent independent wholefood shops, including an entirely vegan supermarket **Unicorn** in Chorlton, a suburb full of character that is about 3 miles south-west of the city centre.

Rusholme is the curry mile, great for vegetarian-friendly Indian restaurants.

Manchester Visitor Information Centre is now at Piccadilly Plaza, Portland Street, Manchester M1 4BT. Open Mon-Sat 9.30-17.30, Sun 10.30-16.30.
www.visitmanchester.com

If you want to venture even further afield, Manchester serves as an excellent base for day trips to the Peak District, North Wales, Lancashire, the Lake District and the Yorkshire Dales.

For Bolton, Bury and surrounding areas see Lancashire.

Manchester

Places to visit in Manchester

Museum of Science and Industry
Manchester was the first industrial city, as it grew on the back of the cotton spinning trade. This museum contains many functioning examples of steam-driven machinery.

People's History Museum
A small, friendly museum dedicated to charting the history of events such as the Peterloo Massacre, women's suffrage and the birth of the Trade Union movement. Inspiring and thought-provoking.

Walks and Tours
There's a wide range of organised walks and tours happening throughout the year along with open top bus trips and guided tours of the City and United football grounds. Most do not require pre-booking. For an up to date list, call into the Manchester Visitor Information Centre (previous page).

Chorlton
Or Chorlton-cum-Hardy to give the suburb its full title, is a fairly affluent part of south Manchester characterised by small shops, pubs, cafes and delis. Organic food is everywhere, and the most interesting destination for vegetarians is the huge all-vegan Unicorn Grocery, winner of many awards for the quality and sustainability of its produce. You won't find lard butties in Chorlton.

The Northern Quarter
A series of parallel streets running northwards from Piccadilly. The Northern Quarter contains comic and book shops, antique and curios shops, stylish hairdressers, music venues and independent cafes, and the Buddhist Centre, with the vegan Earth Cafe in the basement.

Parks and open spaces
The city centre is disappointingly lacking in pleasant open spaces, but if you venture further afield by train or tram, you'll find the huge Heaton Park to the north and Dunham Massey Hall grounds to the south. Both are free entry to those not arriving in vehicles.

www.mosi.org.uk
www.phm.org.uk
www.chorlton.co.uk
www.northernqtr.co.uk
www.heatonpark.org.uk

Manchester's new veggie pub, P.95

Earth Café

Central vegetarian café near the Arndale shopping complex, housed in the same building as the Manchester Buddhist centre, downstairs. Recently they started opening Sundays and introduced a platter service from their hot buffet. They chop, mix, cook and bake daily almost everything they sell. In line with the Buddhist principle of not harming living beings versus the cruelty of all versions of the dairy and egg industries, everything is vegan, except cow's milk option for hot drinks for people who don't like soya milk. Lots of Fairtrade and local seasonal produce.

Weekdays food served from 11.30. Soups of the day £3. Spicy beanburger £2.80. Tofu and vegetable quiche £2.40. Mushroom and cranberry roulade £3.20.

There are at least two mains such as Indonesian stew, sweet vegetable curry, Shepherd's pie. 3-4 side dishes and 7 salads: hummus, coleslaw, green beans, beansprouts, rice-noodle, lettuce, carrot salad. Main course with rice or veg and generous side salad costs about £8.

£5 platter gives you 4 items from their hot and cold buffet, of which up to 2 can be main course portions such as mushroom and cranberry roulade, the rest side dishes such as rice, millet, potatoes, roast vegetables, greens, 6 or 7 mixed salads. £2 gets you one large portion. Dahl and rice £3.50, though at the end of the day you might get curry and rice. Salad plates £5, £3, £2.

10 fabulous vegan cakes and desserts £2.40-2.60 including dark chocolate (wheat-free) or mixed berry cheesecake, apple strudel, sugar-free date and pecan loaf, ice-cream.

Tea, coffee, cappuccino £1.15-2.20. Cold drinks £1.50. Organic juice bar with juices and soya smoothies £2.20-3.20.

Northern Quarter

99% vegan cafe and take-away

16-20 Turner Street
Northern Quarter
Manchester M4 1DZ

Tel: 0161-834 1996

www.earthcafe.co.uk

www.manchesterbuddhistcentre.co.uk

Open:
Mon-Fri 11.00-16.00,
Sat-Sun 10.00-17.00

Also evening events, see website

Can cater for special diets, i.e. wheat and nut-free

High chairs

Bring your own reusable containers for 10% discount on take-away.

10% discount for students spending over £10

No credit cards

Eighth Day Café

Oxford Road

Excellent basement cafe under the Eighth Day wholefood shop, with an international wholefood menu and space for 80 diners. About 75% vegan and much is wheat-free.

Full cooked breakfast £4.95 until 11.00 weekdays, 12.00 weekends. Beans on toast, sausage sandwich, muesli all around £3.

Two soups daily £2.55. Self-serve salad bar £2.40 small, £3.60 large, with a choice of mixed salads which are a meal in themselves, plus vegan wheat-free dressings. Brown rice and dahl £4.30. 2 bakes daily, one always vegan, £5.50 with a side. Daily stew is always vegan £5.30, such as mushroom stroganoff or Thai curry, with organic brown rice.

Hot desserts £3 are often vegan such as fruit crumbles and sticky toffee pudding, with sticky toffee sauce and custard. Cakes and flapjacks £1.25-3.50 are often vegan such as chocolate or carrot cake, chocolate and rum torte, and always have a gluten-free and a sugar-free. No charge for vegan cream with any cake.

Tea, coffee £1.50. Latte, cappuccino, hot choc £1.90. Soya milk available. Juices and smoothies £3.10, 50p for superfood boosts.

Licensed for vegan beer and wine.

Children welcome, half portions, high chairs, baby changing, breast-feeding friendly. Lift from ground floor.

Vegetarian cafe and wholefood shop

111 Oxford Road
Manchester M1 7DU

Tel: 0161-273 1850

www.eighth-day.co.uk
Events on Facebook and Twitter

Open: Mon-Fri 9.00-19.00 Sat 9.30-17.30, Sun and bank holiday closed

Visa, MC, Amex over £4

5% discount to Vegetarian Society and Vegan Society members. 10% for students spending over £5.

10% take-away discount for bringing your own container

Live music Fri 5-7pm term times and other events. Available for hire.

Catered events, cakes, see website for menu

Vegetarian Restaurants

The Greenhouse

Vegetarian restaurant

331 Great Western St, **Rusholme** M14 4AN (170 yards from Wilmslow Rd at junction with Heald Grove; 2 miles south from city centre)
Tel: 0161-224 0730
UK Freephone booking: 0800 092 2733 or through their website www.dineveggie.com
greenhouse@dineveggie.com
Open: Mon-Sun 12.00-18.30 for advance bookings;
Mon-Thu 18.30-23.00, Fri-Sat till 23.30 (last bookings 21.30), Sun till 22.30 (last booking 21.00). Can open slightly earlier for advance bookings.
Last entry for casual diners half hour before last booking time.
Some years closes end July to early September and Christmas to mid January
www.dineveggie.com and on Facebook

Long-established vegetarian restaurant with over 150 a la carte and specials dishes, half of them vegan, all listed on the website. Noted for its unique atmosphere and relaxed service.

47 starters £2.95-4.95 such soup, samosas, various sausages, falafel, Spanish chickpeas with tortilla chips and salad, stuffed aubergine, pasta with (vegan) cheese, vegan haggis, vegan herb and galic cheese and sour cream dip, spicy garlic mushrooms, falafel. Mixed mezze £7.95.

54 mains £7.65-£10.45 such as tamarind vegetable chilli with brown rice and salad; aduki bean and oyster mushroom bake; Szechuan style aubergine; pies and veg; fishless fish or scampi, chips and mushy peas; butternut squash and mixed nut roast. Choice of Sunday roasts £11.85 with onion gravy, roast veg, cranberry and apple sauces.

A stunning 30 desserts £2.95-4.95, of which just under half are vegan, such as cheesecake, topped with blackcurrant, lingonberry (from Sweden), apricot, raspberry, strawberry or even chocolate or fresh chopped chillies; ice-cream;l crumbles; chocolate fudge cake; Christmas pudding.
House wine £1.95 glass, £6.95 half litre.
Coffee £1.70, latte/cappuccino £2.25, tea £1.50. Soya milk available.
10% service charge. 10% discount for Vegetarian or Vegan Society members (except Sat, Xmas, New Year and Valentine's). Sometimes special 2 for 1 early booking offer via website Mon-Thu. Children welcome, one high chair. Disabled access. Gift vouchers. Visa, MC.

Greens Restaurant

International vegetarian restaurant

43 Lapwing Lane, **West Didsbury**, South Manchester M20 2NT (between Burton Rd and Palatine Rd, about 5 miles out of town)
Tel: 0161-434 4259
Lunch: Tue-Fri 12-14.00,
Sat 11-15.00, Sun 12.30-15.30;
Dinner: Mon-Sun 17.30-22.30
Bus 43 or 143 from town
www.greensdidsbury.co.uk and on Facebook

Modern international vegetarian restaurant, extremely popular with vegetarians and meat eaters, and for vegans there are always at least two starters, two mains and one "proper" vegan dessert. They can cater for nut and gluten-free. They have grown rapidly from the original 28 seats in 1990 to 48 seats in 2005 and now 90. Best value is their **Short Menu** £15.95 for starter, main, dessert and small glass of wine or soft drink or beer, available Sun 12.30-15.30, all night Sunday and Monday, and Tue-Fri 17.30-18.45.

Tasters and nibbles £1.50-2.95 such as bread with olive oil and balsamic, marinated olives, garlic bread, deep-fried black pudding with mustard mayo. **Starters** and small dishes £4.50-5.95 such as soup; deep-fried oyster mushrooms with Chinese pancakes and

plum sauce; puy lentil, wild rice and aubergine salad.
Lunchtime soup and a sandwich £6.50.
Main courses lunch £8.50-9.50, dinner £10.95-11.95, such as griddled aubergine and red Thai curry with sticky rice; Moroccan spiced koftas with spicy tomato sauce and tabouleh; three bean chilli with mushrooms and rice. Extra side veg £3.50.
Desserts are around £5.50, most contain dairy but there is always something vegan such as apple and blueberry crumble.
Lots of wine, house £3.75-4.95 glass, from £13.50 bottle. Beer £1.90 half, £3.70 pint, botled £2.50. Spirits and liqueurs from £3.95. Champagne from £7.50. Dessert wine £4.50-5.95.
Juices and soft drinks £1-£1.90. Teas £1.50, fresh peppermint £2.50. Coffee, cappuccino, latte £1.50-2.50. Liqueur coffee £4.50. Hot chocolate £2.75. Vegans note they don't have soya milk. Kids menu £3.95. 10% service charge for tables of 6+. Booking recommended weekends. You can book all or part of the restaurant for parties or weddings. Outside catering. Visa, MC.

Fuel Café Bar

Vegetarian café & music venue

448 Wilmslow Road, **Withington**
M20 3BW (about 5 miles out of town)
Tel: 0161-448 9702
Open: Mon-Thu 11.00-24.00, Fri 11.00-02.00, Sat 10.00-02.00, Sun 10.00-24.00
twitter.com/fuelcafebar
myspace.com/fuelcafebar

Cafe by day, plus free independent music and arts venue upstairs by night with music, craft and comedy events. Tuesday night quiz
Full breakfast £5.30. Cafe meals £2.20-£6 include ciabattas, stuff in pitta, soup, salads, burritos and specials. Falafel burger with chips and hummus £6. Mixed lentil casserole £5.50. Mezze with dips, olives and pitta £5, or full mezze £9 adds falafel, wedges, tabbouleh. Side dishes £2.70-3.20 include olives, tabouleh, spicy potato and sweet potato wedges, chips with salsa.
Desserts £1.50-3.50, including vegan banana loaf.
Lots of teas £1.20. Coffee, latte, cappuccino, mocha, chai £1.20-£2. Hot spicy apple juice £1.50. Juice and sodas £1.20 half pint, £2 pint. Squash 70p half pint, £1 pint. Fruit smoothies and shakes to order £2.90.
House wine £2.80-3.20 glass, £10-12.50 bottle. Draught beers from £1.40 half pint. Bottled ales, beers and cider £2.80-3.30. Spirits £2.20, double with mixer £3.30.
Children welcome during the day, no high chair. WiFi. Visa, MC.

Oklahoma

99% vegetarian cafe and gift shop

74-76 High Street (Turner St), **Northern Quarter**, Manchester M4 1ES
Tel: 0161-834 1136
Open: Mon-Sat 10.00-19.00

Friendly cafe with speedy service attached to a kitsch homewares and gift shop, opposite Earth Cafe. Everything is veggie apart from one sandwich. Lots of vegan dishes. Noted for their baked potato or sweet potato £5.20 with a range of amazing toppings such as beetroot, apple, mint and hummus; lentils and marmalade; hummus and roast veg;.
Cakes £2.60, some vegan such as coconut, or toffee cake. Vegan cornettos £1.80. (Vegan option) ice-cream milkshakes £2.80-3.50.
Tea £1.60, coffees £1.50-2.50, they have soya milk. Freshly squeezed juices £2.60-3.10.
Outside seating, dogs welcome inside and out. High chairs. MC, Visa.

Vegan Hot Dog Stall

Fast food stall in front of Unicorn

In front of Unicorn Grocery, 89 Albany Road, **Chorlton**, Manchester M21 0BN.
Open: Saturdays late morning till they run out mid-afternoon 3-4pm

Scoff while you do your shopping. £2.50 for a vegan hotdog in a white or wholemeal roll with fried onions, mustard and ketchup. See also Unicorn listing in shops page 102.

Vegetarian Pubs

Bistro 1847

Vegetarian bistro restaurant and bar

58 Mosley Street (corner Booth St), Manchester M2 3HZ
Tel: 0161-236 1811
Tram: St Peter's Square
Open: Wed-Sun 12.00-22.00, Mon-Tue closed
www.bistro1847.co.uk

Brand new, opposite Manchester art gallery, with vegetarian cocktails, spirits, wines and bottled beers. It opened under as detoxretox, but changed name April 2011, 1847 being the year the Vegetarian Society was founded.

The bar always has a small tapas style menu. £4.50 for one plate, £6.95 two, then £3 per plate, most dishes vegan including edamame soya beans with salt and lemon, Thai sweetcorn fritters and salsa, sweet potato wedges with herb dip, lemon and sundried tomato pate with warm rosemary flatbread.

A la carte starters £3.95-4.95 include soup and some of the tapas dishes. Mains £9.95-12.95 such as roast cauliflower and barley risotto, Malay curry laksa with tofu and noodles, bangers and mash with peas and gravy. Desserts £4.50 such as vegan sticky toffee pudding with thyme custard, or pears poached in vanilla syrup with ginger sponge and cream.

Sunday lunch main £9.95, two courses £13.95, three £16.95. Sunday mains include a different pie every week, roast veg and all the trimmings. Always a vegan option such as breadcrumbed spiced swede patty.

Wine from £12 bottle, £4.75 glass. Tea £1.50, coffee from £1.50, soya milk.
Children welcome, high chairs. Outside tables, dogs welcome there. Vegan options marked on menu. Booking advised. MC, Visa.

The Thirsty Scholar

Vegetarian food pub

50 New Wakefield St, Manchester M1 5NP (on Oxford Road opposite the Palace Hotel, under Oxford Road station, between Piccadilly Gardens bus stops and 8th Day)
Tel:: 0161-236 6071
Pub open: Sun-Thu 12.00-24.00, Fri-Sat 12.00-02.00
Food Mon-Sat 12.00-19.00, may do longer hours in future and for special events
www.thirstyscholar.co.uk

Manchester now has an all vegetarian city centre pub! The chef from the much missed Mod Pop cafe is now the chef here and veggie and vegan food has completely taken over the menu with a meat-free kitchen, they don't even sell beef crisps anymore.

Classic British pub grub and world food from ciabatta toasties to Jamaican curry and Tex Mex. From £2.50 bar snacks, £3.50 bowl food such as chili or curry, rice and bread, up to £5.95 for specials. The Pop Cafe all day breakfast £3.95 regular, £5.95 double size brunch with spicy wedges. Vegan cakes. Cup of tea £1.20. House wine £7.50 bottle, £2.60 glass.

Children welcome during the day, no high chair. Large sheltered outdoor drinking area where smoking is permitted and dogs welcome during the day. Cash only. Outside catering.

The pub is also a live music venue that is very popular with students. Mon-Thu free live music, weekends DJ's. Manchester Vegan Society meet here.

Omnivorous Pubs

Kro Piccadilly

Omnivorous Danish-style pub

1 Piccadilly Gardens, Unit A and B,
Manchester M1 1RG
Tel: 0161-244 5765
Open: Mon-Fri from 08.00, Sat-Sun from 09.00, food served until late.
www.kro.co.uk

also at **Kro2** Oxford House, Oxford Road Manchester M1 7ED. Tel: 0161-236 1048

Kro Trafford Centre Unit R28 Great Hall, Manchester M17 8AA (by main entrance) Tel: 0161-747 2801

Kro Bar 325 Oxford Road,
Chorlton on Medlock M13 9PG
Tel: 0161-274 3100

Kro Old Abbey Inn Manchester Science Park, 61 Pencroft Way M15 6AY
Tel: 0161 232 9796

A light, airy bar right in the heart of Manchester with a range of continental drinks. Has a large menu with a number of mainly cheesy vegetarian options and some bar snacks for £2.50-£4.00 that are a cut above what other pubs and bars in the area have to offer, such as spicy potato wedges; pitta with hummus, tapenade and salsa; and marinated olives. Vegetarian cooked breakfast £6.50. Plate of meze £8.50. Children welcome.

The Bar (Marble Brewery)

Omnivorous pub with vegan real ale.

553 Wilbraham Road, **Chorlton** M21 0UE
Tel: 0161-861 7565
Open: pub hours

The Bar is a huge pub with some vegan dishes, including Sunday roast, baked aubergine, and falafel platter.
They have another pub half a mile away on Manchester Road, Chorlton which is smaller and doesn't do food.
Their own 'Marble' beers are all vegan and organic. Their brewery pub on Rochdale Road, just north of the city centre has their full selection of ales, but suprisingly no vegan options on the menu.

Odd Bar

Omnivorous food pub

30-32 Thomas Street, **Northern Quarter**, Manchester M4 1ER
Tel: 0161-833 0070
Open: Mon-Wed 11.00-24.00
Thu 11.00-01.00, Fri-Sat: 11.00-01.30
Sun 12.00-24.00
Midnightwww.oddbar.co.uk (menus)

Chain of three bars with gigantic drinks menu and a good selection of veggie food, some of it vegan (though more could be). DJ's Thu-Sun, ad hoc events, monthly acoustic night, juke box. Giant cinema screen, free wifi, free newspapers, even free brollies. Gallery wall with Manchester artists. Vegan full English breakfast £5.95 till 4pm. Falafel £5.75. Draught beers £3.10-4.30 including European lagers, British ciders, award winning ales from Manchester microbreweries and some bonkers bottled beers from around the globe £3.20-£4 such as Fruli Strawberry. House wine £3.20-4.20 glass, £11.99 bottle, happy hour 5-7pm Mon-Fri £7 bottle. More spirits than Ghostbusters 2, most £2.50-2.80. Soft drinks £1.60-£2. Tea £1.50, herb tea £1.60, coffee £1.50-2.50.

Odder Bar

Omnivorous food pub

14 Oxford Rd, **Southern Quarter**, Manchester M1 5QA (opposite the BBC)
Tel: 0161-238 9132
Open: Sun-Wed 12.00-24.00,
Thu-Sat 12.00-02.00
www.oddbar.co.uk/odder (menus & events)

Sister venue to nearby Odd and Oddest, which have a very similar menu. This lives up to its name, with fake buffalo heads on the wall and confusingly-placed mirrors. Ever changing gallery wall featuring Manchester's up and coming artists. Not the cheapest joint in town, but a really chilled out and comfortable place to enjoy a pint with a full vegan cooked breakfast £5.95 (until 4pm) or a vegan cheese pizza £5.99 with olives and charred peppers.

Free internet, free umbrellas when raining. There is something on most evenings including DJ's Thu-Sun evenings, Quizimodo Tue, free film and live music Sundays. Conference venue, private parties.

Oddest Bar

Omnivorous food pub

414-416 Wilbraham Road (junction Buckingham Rd), **Chorlton**, Manchester M21 0SD
Tel: 0161-860 7515
Open: Mon-Thu 11.00-24.00, Fri 11.00-00.30, Sat 10.00-00.30, Sun 10.00-24.00
www.oddbar.co.uk/oddest

Attempting to out-odderer Odd and Odder, by day this is a mild-mannered space to do some work with free wifi and enjoy food and bring the kids to draw on the paper table cloth with the crayons provided, by night a vibrant place to hang out with friends and drink and dance the night away. Vegan full English breakfast £5.95 till 3pm.

Wednesday quiz, Friday music, Saturday DJ. Children welcome till 7pm, bottle warmers, tots chairs, baby changing.

Omnivorous Restaurants

Dough

Omnivorous pizza restaurant

75-77 High St, **Northern Quarter**, Manchester M4 1FS (10 mins walk from both Piccadilly and Victoria stations)
Tel: 0161-834 9411
Open: Mon-Sun 12.00-23.00
www.doughpizzakitchen.co.uk

The veggie pizzas are really nice, taste fresh and just the right size, about 9-10 inches, £5.75-£7.75, though if you have a big appetite you might find them small. They have vegan mozzarella cheese (really, really nice and it melts too). Side salads include the unusual tomato, mango and red onion £3.95 with basil infused olive oil and balsamic. Pasta around £7. Nibbles like olives, bruschetta etc £2.35-£2.95. Gluten-free pizza and pasta available.

Hallelujah, a mainstream restaurant with vegan dessert, ok it's only fruit salad but they also have lots of flavours of Swedish Glace vegan ice-cream £3.25-4.25.

Bottled beer and cider £3.20-3.95, alcohol free £2.50. Wine from £3.55-4.95 glass, £13.45 bottle. Bellinis £5.45. Soft drinks £1.95-2.25. Hot drinks £1.60-2.65. They have rice milk. Liqueurs from £3.75.

They are very child-friendly before 6pm and give kids a drawing and crayons so they can design their own pizza! High chairs. Outside seating in summer, dogs welcome. MC, Visa, Amex.

Barburrito

Omnivorous Mexican cafe

1 **Piccadilly Gardens**, Manchester M1 1RG
Tel: 0161-228 6479
Open: Mon-Wed 11.00-21.00,
Thu-Sat 11.00-22.00, Sun 12-19.00
www.barburrito.co.uk

also at 68 **Deansgate**, Manchester M3 2BW
Tel: 0161-839 1311
Open: Fri-Sat 11.30-03.00,
Sun-Thu 11.30-21.00

134 The Orient, **Trafford Centre** M17 8EH
Tel: 0161-747 6165
Open: Mon-Fri 11.30-23.00, Sat 11.00-23.00, Sun 12-22.00

Fast food burrito bar which provides well for vegetarians. You can either choose the chilli mushrooms veggie option listed on the menu, or create your own filling combo by simply pointing to what you want. Vegan options include rice, black beans or pinto beans, peppers and onions, guacamole, lettuce and salsa. Expect to pay around £4-6. Hot and cold drinks, wine and bottled Mexican beers £1.50-3.25.

Ning

Omni Malaysian/Thai restaurant

92-94 Oldham Street, **Northern Quarter**
Manchester M4 1LJ
Tel: 0161-238 9088
Open: Tue-Thu 18.00-23.00,
Fri-Sun 17.00-23.00, Mon closed
www.ningcatering.com

Ning has become so popular you usually have to book. This is mostly due to their off-peak special offer of £12.95 for a starter, main course and rice or noodles (anytime except Fri-Sat after7pm). The portions are generous, fresh and no MSG.

A la carte there are around 3 vegetarian starters £5.25-6.50, such as spring rolls with sweet chilli sauce; Gado gado salad with tofu; and Tom Yam (hot and sour) soup.

Main courses are around £9, including Musamman curry (the vegan option simply has tofu instead of chicken); stir-fried mushrooms, noodles and spinach; or green or red Thai vegetable curry (veggie on request).

Sorbets £2.75, such as mango and ginger, are the only vegan desserts on the menu, but others such as banana fritters £4.50 can be adapted though they don't sell a lot of desserts as people are usually pretty full from the earlier big portions.

Wines from £3.55 glass, £14.50 bottle. Thai and other Oriental beers £3.75. Coffee from £2, they have soya milk. Children welcome, high chairs. Take-away available. They sometimes run vegetarian cookery classes. MC, Visa.

Pizza Express, Manchester

Pizza restaurant chain

The Triangle, Exchange Square M4 3TR
(Next to Victoria Stn) Tel: 0161-834 6130
Mon-Sat 11.30 -23.00, Sun 11.30-22.30

Old Colony House, South King St M2 6DQ
Tel: 0161-834 0145. Open as above.

1 Piccadilly Gardens, Manchester M1 1RG
Tel: 0161-237 1811. Open as above.

56 Peter St, Manchester M2 3NQ
Tel: 0161-839 9300. Open as above.

95 Lapwing Lane, **West Didsbury** M20 6UR
Tel: 0161-438 0838. Open as above.

130 Bury New Road, **Prestwich** M25 0AA
Tel: 0161-798 4794. Open as above.

Unit R8a, **The Trafford Centre** M17 8EQ
Tel: 0161-747 2121
Mon-Sat 11.30023.00, Sun 11.30-22.00

G38 Lowry Designer Outlet, **Salford Quays**, M50 3AG. Tel: 0161-877 3585
Open: Mon-Sun 11.30-23.00
www.pizzaexpress.com

A national chain with 8 branches in and around Manchester.
Pizzas have vegan bases and can be made without cheese. In some branches you can bring your own vegan cheese. See **Cheshire** entry for full details.

Sweet Tooth Cupcakery

Omnivorous cafe

9a Oswald Road, **Chorlton** M21 9LP
Tel: 07855 765355
Open: Wed-Sat 10.00-16.30, Sun 11-16.00, Mon-Tue closed

34-36 Oldham St, **Northern Quarter**
Manchester M1 1JN
Tel: 0161-236 3877
Open: Mon-Sat 10.00-18.00, Sun 11-16.00
www.sweettoothcupcakery.co.uk

New, friendly and retro old-fashioned style milk bar and shop full of exquisite cupcakes. Everything is vegetarian apart from marshmallows and some sweets. At least one vegan cupcake £1.75, one dozen £19.

Illy coffee £1.60. Cappuccino/latte £1.90, mocha £2.20, soya milk add 30p. Sherberts and (soya) milkshakes with (vegan) ice-cream £3-3.3.50. Teas £1.40, Chinese flowering teas £2.50 for a glass pot. Organic orange juice £1.50. Chegworth Valley juices £1.50. Fentimans ginger beer and others £1.95.

Children welcome. Outside tables at both, and bike stands. Cash only, cashpoint near both branches. Catering.

Tampopo, Manchester

S.E. Asian omnivorous restaurants

16 Albert Square, **City Centre** M2 5PF
Tel: 0161-819 1966

Triangle Shopping Centre, Unit 2,
38 Exchange Square, Manchester M4 3TR
Tel: 0161-839 6484

The Orient, **Trafford Centre** M17 8EH
Tel: 0161-747 8878
All open: Mon-Sat 12-23.00, Sun 12-22.00
www.tampopo.co.uk

Eastern and fusion dishes with a strong Thai and Vietnamese slant. Like Wagamama, only a larger menu. Canteen-style layout and very fast service. Veggie items clearly marked. Some delicious vegan dishes and others can be adapted as everything is made to order.

Starters such as miso soup from £1.50. Typical main course around £6.50, such as Xio Po tofu with coriander and black bean sauce. Vegan desserts such as fried bananas in sesame and caramel sauce. Beers and sake around £3. Juices and green teas. Children welcome, high chairs and colouring packs provided.

Wagamama, Manchester

Omnivorous Japanese Restaurant

1 The Printworks, **Corporation Street**, Manchester M4 4DG
Tel: 0161-839 5916
Open: Mon-Sat 12.00-23.00,
Sun 12.30-22.00

Also new branch at **1 Spinningfields Square** Hardman Street (off Deansgate), M3 3AP
Tel: 0161-833 9883. Open as above
www.wagamama.com

This is the main Wagamama listing for this book, referred to in listings for other branches. The food is GMO-free and offers something for vegans, but watch out for egg in some and noodles. All branches have a similar menu and opening hours. Vegans go for rice noodles or thick udon wheat noodles which are egg-free, and speak to your server. All dishes listed below are either vegan or can be modified. Yasai means vegetables in Japanese.

Miso soup with Japanese pickles £1.40. Steamed edamame green soybeans £3.70. Raw salad £3. Mains course noodle dishes £6.65-8.10 come in a big bowl and will really fill you up, such as saien soba whole wheat noodles in a vegetable soup topped with fried tofu, beansprouts, courgettes, asparagus, red onion, leeks, mushrooms, mangetout and garlic, garnished with spring onion; yasai cha han stir-fried rice with mangetout, sweetcorn, butternut squash, fried tofu, spring onions, shiitake and white mushrooms, accompanied by a bowl of miso soup and pickles; yasai yaki soba teppan-fried whole wheat noodles with lots of veg; yasai chilli men stir-fried whole wheat noodles with tofu and veg in a spicy chilli men sauce.

Desserts all contain dairy products which is a real let-down after so many vegan mains, but we've always been totally stuffed anyway after their massive soup-noodle dishes.

Kids menu includes mini veg cha han £2.85, or veg ramen £3.60 with noodles in a vegetable soup topped with deep-fried tofu, seasonal greens, carrot and sweetcorn.

Green tea free with meals on request. Various raw, fresh and very healthy juices £3-4. Soft drinks £2. Peach iced tea £1.70. Japanese beer £3.45-£6.10. Wine from £3.65 glass £12.95 bottle. Sake for one £5.20, to share £8.10. Plum wine £3.40 with ice and water.

Manchester shops

Eighth Day

Vegetarian wholefood shop

111 Oxford Road, **Manchester** M1 7DU
Tel: 0161-273 4878
Open: Tue, Sat 9.30-17.30,
Mon, Fri 9.00-17.30,
Wed-Thu 9.00-19.00,
Sun and bank holidays closed
www.eighth-day.co.uk

Huge, well-stocked wholefood shop with organic veg, fruit and bread, a fridge and freezer and a large, popular deli take-away section with separate and vegetarian and vegan areas, and a take-away olive and pesto counter. Pasties, pizzas, tortilla wraps, cakes including vegan and sugar-free. Vegan options clearly marked and lots of gluten-free. Japanese and macrobiotic foods. Organic wine (mostly vegan), beer, cider, spirits. Huge range of Fairtrade, over 300 products.

Gigantic and ever-changing and expanding range of bodycare by over 70 manufacturers including Akin, Aubrey Organics, Avalon, Barefoot Botanicals, Dr Bronner, Earth Friendly Baby and Kids, Elysambre, Faith In Nature, Giovanni, Green People, Jason, Lavera, Natracare, Ren, Suma, Thursday Plantation, Weleda and Yaoh. Free makeovers by their instore beauty expert once a month.

Supplements by Solgar, Lamberts, BioCare, Viridian, Higher Nature, Kordels, Planetary Formulas, Nature's Own. Helios and Weleda homeopathy. Lots of herbal remedies. Two qualified nutritionists to advise.

Vegetable seeds and FSC gardening sundries. Local crafts and Fairtrade gifts. 5% discount to Vegan Society and Vegetarian Society members on any amount. 10% for students spending over £8. MC, Visa, Amex over £4.

Health and Vegetarian Store

Health and wholefood shop

33 Old Church Street, **Newton Heath**, Manchester M40 2JN (10 mins by bus from city centre towards Oldham)
Tel: 0161-683 4456
Open: Mon, Wed-Thur 10.00-17.00;
Fri-Sat 10.00-15.00; closed Tue, Sun
Website on the way in 2010

Organic fruit & veg with local deliveries. Soda bread and muffins on Saturdays. Fridge and freezer with vegan cheeses, lots of meat substitutes, Swedish Glace, Tofutti. All the Provamel products. Vegan chocolate by Organica and Divine. Wine at Christmas or special order. Bodycare by Faith In Nature, Weleda, Natratint, Suma soaps, Natracare. Supplements by Nature's Aid, Pharmanord, Solgar, Alfred Vogel, Lamberts. Weleda homeopathy, essential oils. Room for homeopathy, Bowen technique, kinesiology, aromatherapy, reflexology, nutrition.

Ecover and Ecoleaf cleaning products. Mobile phone and computer antiradiation domes. Bamboo socks. Fusion vegan condoms. Water bottle with built in filter, ideal for cyclists, campers and walkers. They can order in anything else you need. MC, Visa.

The Laughing Lentil
Vegetarian health food shop

10 King Edwards Buildings, Bury Old Road, **Salford** M7 4QJ
Tel: 0161-740 5766
Open: Mon-Tue, Thu-Fri 10.30-17.30;
Wed 10.30-16.00, Sat 11.00-17.00,
Sun closed

Established 1956. Wholefoods including lots of vegan items such as breakfast cereals, biscuits, milks, soya dessert. Fridge and freezer with tofu, vegan cheeses, Frys burgers and sausages, Swedish Glace, Tofutti. Plamil vegan chocolate.
Bodycare by Faith In Nature and others. Supplements by Quest, Nature's Aid, Lifeplan. Homeopathy, essential oils. Visiting allergy tester. Ecover. MC, Visa, Amex.

Lush
Vegetarian cosmetics

Unit L4, **Arndale Centre**, Corporation Street, Manchester M4 3QA
Tel: 0161-832 3294
Open: Mon-Fri 9.30-20.00, Sat 9.30-19.30, Sun 10.00-17.00

---

113 Regent Crescent, **Trafford Centre**, Manchester M17 8AR
Tel: 0161-746 9644
Open: Mon-Sat 10.00-17.00, Sun 11.00-16.00

---

10 Market Street, **Royal Exchange**
Manchester M1 1PT
Tel: 0161-839 7848
Open: Mon-Sat 9.30-18.00, Sun 110-17.00
www.lush.co.uk

100% vegetarian hand-made cosmetics, the majority vegan.

Olive Deli
Omni deli, take-away & grocery

36-38 Regency House, Whitworth Street, **Manchester** M1 3WF (by Sackville Park, above Bannatyne's gym, near the gay village)
Tel: 0161-236 2360
Open Mon-Fri 08.00-22.00,
Sat 09.00-23.00, Sun 09.00-22.30
on Facebook

Much more than a deli, you can get all your groceries here plus fruit and veg. Barbican bread. Fresh olives, sundried tomatoes, gherkins. Lots of wine and beer. Vegan selection in the deli such as burritos, pesto, and made to order salads, sandwiche and their famous and very filling panini £3-4 (enough for a meal). Separate grill for vegetarian food. Cakes though not vegan.

Swinton Health Foods
Health food shop & clinic

177 Moorside Road, **Swinton**, Manchester M27 9LD
Tel: 0161-793 0091
Open: Mon-Tue, Thu-Fri 9.30-17.30;
Sat 9.30-16.00; Wed, Sun closed
www.swintonhealthfoods.com

Lots of dairy, wheat and gluten-free. Fridge and freezer with vegan cheese, soya ice-cream, tofu.
Bodycare by Faith In Nature, Optima, Pharmanord, Natracare, some kids stuff.
Supplements by Viridian, Solgar, Quest, Lamberts, Optima, Lanes, Bioforce. Homeopathy, flower remedies, essential oils. Clinic upstairs with homeopath, acupuncturist, allergy testing, counselling, Indian head massage, reflexologist, nutritional therapist, hypnotherapy, EFT. Ecover. Books. Crystal jewellery. Home deliveries, mail order. MC, Visa.

Unicorn Grocery
Vegan supermarket

89 Albany Road, **Chorlton**,
Manchester M21 0BN.
Open: Tue-Fri 9.30-19.00, Sat 9.00-18.00,
Sun 11-17.00, Mon closed
Tel: 0161-861 0010
www.unicorn-grocery.co.uk

Co-operatively run all vegan supermarket on the 86 bus route out of town. Has an impressive range of wholesome and organic fruit and veg, beer and wine, bread and other groceries. A deli counter selling olives, hummus, salad, pasties, home-cooked foods, cheesecake. Ethical household products.
Specialists in gluten-free food. They have a sugar-free policy, which means you won't find some of the usual wholefood shop staples such as 'Redwood rashers' and organic dairy-free chocolate. However, you'll find unusual European stuff, like blueberry tarts and hazlenut waffles sweetened with corn syrup. Bulk-buying enables them to sell quality organic food at competitive prices. Their carob fridge cake comes highly recommended.
They recently acquired some farmland and are growing some of the produce in the store. MC, Visa over £5.
See page 95 for Saturday hot dog stall.

Caterer
Something Fishy

PO Box 293, Manchester M12 0AD
Tel: 0777 395 0468
www.something-fishy.org.uk
email: something-fishy@live.com

Voluntary, fund-raising caterers, running the worlds first mobile, 100% vegan, 'fish' 'n' chip shop. All proceeds go to groups like Coalition to Abolish the Fur Trade and Manchester Animal Protection or to animal sanctuaries to help fund neutering schemes etc. As they say, there's never been a more ethical reason to stuff your face with delicious vegan lard.

Chain stores
Holland & Barrett
Health food shop

102 **Market Street**, Manchester M1 1PB
Tel: 0161-819 5561
Open: Mon-Sat 08.00-19.00, Sun 11-17.00

22 **St Anns Square**, Manchester M2 7JB
Tel: 0161 834 9483
Open: Mon-Sat 08.30-18.00, Sun 11-17.00

Unit 34, Lower Mall, **Trafford Park** M17 2BL
Tel: 0161-747 2699. Open: Mon-Fri 10.00-22.00, Sat 10-21.00, Sun 11.00-18.00

607 Wilbraham Road, **Chorlton cum Hardy**
M21 1AN. Tel: 0161-881 1539
Open: Mon-Sat 9.00-17.30, Sun closed

Local groups
Manchester Vegan Society

www.manchester.vegangroup.co.uk
http://groups.yahoo.com/group/manchester-vegan-society
also on Facebook
Lynnmarie 07595 568168

Food and cake stalls, restaurant meals, walks, outings. Meets regularly at the Thirsty Scholar.

Manchester Vegetarian & Vegan Group

www.mvvg.co.uk
http://groups.yahoo.com/group/mvvg/
on FacebookMVVG
Mike Coulton 01204-654401
mike@mvvg.co.uk

Meet for lunch on the first Saturday at Eighth Day. Parties, walks.

VEGETARIAN
1 Earth Cafe p.91
2 Eighth Day p.92
3 Greenhouse p.93
4 Greens p.93
5 Fuel p.94
6 Thirsty Scholar p.95
B Bistro 1847 p.95

OMNIVOROUS
7 Kro pub p.96
8 Odd Bar p.96
9 Barburrito p.97
10 Dough p.97
11 Ning p.98
12 Tampopo Albert Sq p.99
13 Tampopo Triangle p.99
14 Wagamama p.99
15 Sweet Tooth p.98
16 Odder Bar p.96
17 Oklahoma p.94

Central Manchester

Liverpool attracts a lot of tourists due to the worldwide success of the band the Beatles who put it firmly on the map in the 1960's. Today's fans can visit a museum, a shop and can even see the houses where the "fab four" grew up. The city celebrated its 800th birthday in 2008.

There is some splendid Victorian architecture including many unspoiled city centre pubs. Most of the docks are still in operation but Albert Dock has now been turned into a tourist attraction with lots of little shops and cafes and the impressive Tate Modern art gallery. There are lots of museums to visit, including ones with certain historical themes, such as the Maritime Museum and the Museum of Liverpool Life.

Liverpool is a very compact city and it is easy to walk around the city centre. If you want all the usual high street shops, leave Central Station and walk straight up Church Street. The Beatles attractions and the Tourist Information Centre are also off this and the Docks are at the far end.

The most interesting area for vegetarians is Bold Street, which runs to the left of the station in the opposite direction. The small streets running parallel to and branching off Bold Street are full of pubs, clubs and cafes and are very lively in the evenings. The **Green Fish** and **Egg** cafes are long-established vegetarian cafes in this area and there is also the **Food From Nowhere** weekend vegan cafe on Saturdays. **Studio2** at Parr Street has an amazing vegan breakfast by Ian Cook, winner of tv's *Come Dine With Me*, and has started doing occasional vegan buffet nights. **Dragon Indulgence** is a new wholefood store with stacks of vegan chocolate, and over on the Wirral is a new vegan shop **Honest to Goodness**.

With the Egg cafe being the only veggie place open evenings, we list some ethnic restaurants recommended by the local group Scouseveg, and you can find even more on their amazing website.

Liverpool is well served by railways and motorways and is a good base for exploring North Wales and the North West. The coast to the north has stretches of sand dunes and woodlands noted for their wild birds and red squirrels.

www.visitliverpool.com
www.visitsouthport.com

www.scouseveg.co.uk

Liverpool & Merseyside

1. Egg Cafe
2. Green Fish
3. Food From Nowhere
4. Studio2 @Parr St
5. Ego
6. Green Days
7. Gusto
8. Host
9. Maharajah
10. The Quarter
11. Sabai
12. Yuet Ben
13. Dragon Indulgence
14. Holland & Barrett
15. Holland & Barrett
16. Mattas
17. Windmill Wholefoods

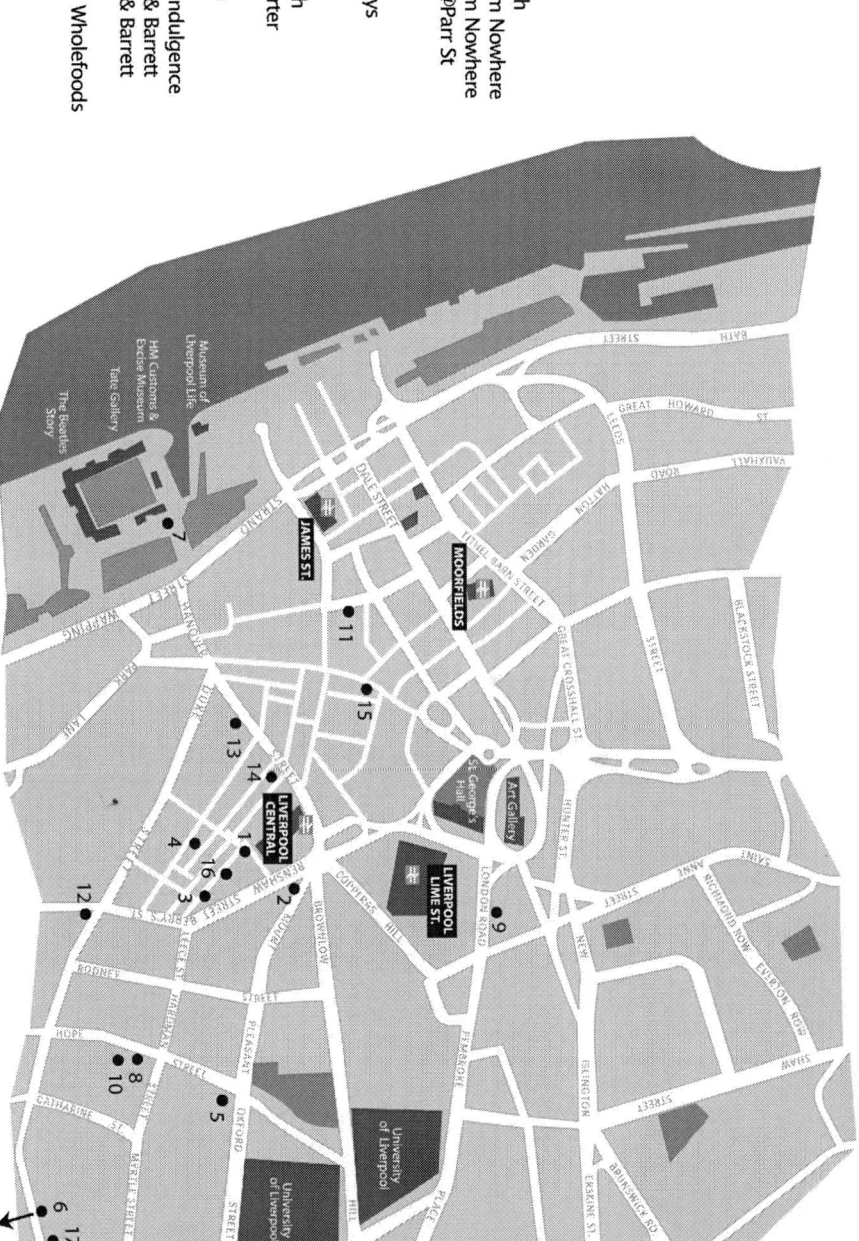

Merseyside accommodation
Studio2@Parr Steet
Omnivorous hotel & breakfast bar

33–45 Parr Street, **Liverpool** L1 4JN
Tel: 0151-707 1050 hotel
0151-707 3727 cafe
Breakfast: Mon–Fri 08.00–12.00, Sat–Sun 9.00–14.00.
www.parrstreet.co.uk/STUDIO2/Home.htm
www.parrstreet.co.uk/Hotel.html

Food: This central complex has a breakfast and snacks bar with **vegan brekkie** for £6 on the menu and it is the best in Liverpool according to the local Scouseveg group, with Redwood's bacon, griddled potato, grilled tomato, mushrooms, Fry's sausages, Heinz beans, chunky toast and tea or coffee. You don't have to stay at the hotel to eat here.

Chef Ian Cook won the tv show *Come Dine With Me* with the highest ever score of 39 out of 40, with a mostly vegan menu. Look out for Ian's new **vegan buffet nights** organised in conjunction with Scouseveg (see end of this chapter). The first in 2010 have attracted 60 people, with Thai red curry, yellow curry with mango and pineapple, coriander basmati rice, quinoa with peas and mint and butterbeans, coleslaw with toasted pecan nuts, leaf salad. Ian is also planning a vegan catering business.
www.cookscatering.net

Hotel: The eating area is on the ground floor of Parr Street's historic recording studios and 12-bedroomed 4-star Parr Street boutique hotel and apartment annexe. £69-110 for double or twin room, triple £145, penthouse £150 sleeps 4. Rooms have plates, bowls, cups, cutlery, cooler fridge, mini-bar, kettle, iron, hairdryer. Wifi.

Edendale House
Omnivorous guest house

83 Avondale Road North, **Southport** PR9 0NE
Tel: 01704-530718
Open: all year
www.edendalehouse.co.uk
email: edendalehouse@aol.com

In a peaceful residential area between the centre and the sea. 2 single (one ensuite) £27.50-40 depending on time of year, 2 twins and 2 twins/doubles £27.50-45 per person or £25-32.50 sharing for over 60's. 2 family rooms sleeping 4, £75 triple or £80-85 quad, cot, high chair. Full cooked vegetarian breakfast. Licensed for drinks to take to your room. Armchairs in rooms. Non smoking throughout. Off-road parking.

Liverpool – vegetarian
The Egg Café
Vegetarian café

Top Floor, Newington Buildings, Newington, Liverpool L1 4ED (Walk up Bold Street turn right at the big Oxfam shop onto Newington and about half way along look out for a tall old building on your right. Climb stairs to top (2nd) floor)
Tel: 0151-707 2755
Train: between Liverpool Central and Lime Street (main railway station)
Open: Mon–Fri 09.00–22.30, Sat–Sun 10–22.30
www.comestrutyourstuff.co.uk

Cheap vegetarian café on the top floor, open long hours and brilliant for vegans. Not the most upmarket of cafes, but if you like traditional veggie fare and down-at-heel-charm then you'll love it.

Full cooked vegetarian or vegan breakfasts £4.20 every day till 12.00 and all day Sunday, can include scrambled tofu, sausages, coffee or tea. Pancakes £2.75.

Soup with bread and spread £2.50. Mains £4.95-5.95 such as spaghetti bolognaise; potato and pea Madras with rice and/or salad; spinach dal; Morrocan veg; hummus with salads and pitta; spicy beanburger with pitta and salad; tandoori mushrooms with salads etc.

The best place in Merseyside for vegan desserts with banana cake £2.25, wheat-free apple crumble £2.60; chocolate crunch cake £1.75, muffins £1.50.

At night it's more restaurant style and relaxed with candles. It's split level and you can go up to the mezzanine floor which is good for parties. Bring your own wine, £1 corkage per bottle. Children welcome, high chairs. No credit cards.

Walls are used as a gallery space for local and national artists, exhibition changes every 6 weeks. Poetry night 1st Mondays of the month from 20.00. Events listed at www.comestrutyourstuff.co.uk

Food From Nowhere

Weekend vegan cafe

Basement of News From Nowhere bookshop (see below), 96 Bold Street, Liverpool L1 4HY
Bookshop: 0151-708 7270
Basement: 0151-703 6806
Train: Liverpool Central
Cafe Sat 12.00-17.00,
Alternate Sun evenings
www.liverpoolsocialcentre.org

Liverpool's only vegan cafe (previously known as The Basement) is run by volunteers. Food depends on who is working that day and you can usually get something hot for no more than £3 such as curry, veggieburger, soup. Cakes around £1-1.50. Hot drinks around 50p. Kids welcome, toys, high chair. Cash only.

Fortnightly Sunday free film screening with vegan soup & cakes from 5pm, donations for food appreciated, film starts at 6.

Green Fish Café

Vegetarian café & tea house

11 Upper Newington, Off Renshaw Street
Liverpool, Merseyside L1 2SR (Directions: turn left out of Lime Street station)
Tel: 0151-707 8592
Train: Liverpool Central
Open: Mon-Sat 11-16.30, Sun closed
www.greenfishcafe.com

Cheap, modern-looking vegetarian café with at least two vegan meals per day. Smaller and more up-market in appearance than The Egg.

Starters £1.90 upwards include soup and salads. Main courses or combos £4.50 change daily and can include curry, burritos, potato bake, pasta, roasted Mediterranean veg. Desserts from £1.40 which normally includes vegan flapjakes. Big range of pots of tea £1.10 regular, herbals from £1.20, green or jasmine £1.40, green leaf teas £2-2.30. Filter coffee £1. They always have soya milk and spread.

Children welcome, high chairs. Unlicensed. No credit cards. Resident harpist Wed and Sat from about 12.00 till closing.

Liverpool - omnivorous
Ego, Liverpool

Omnivorous Mediterranean restaurant

Hope Street, Liverpool L1 9BW
Tel: 0151-706 0707
Open: Mon-Sun 12.00-22.30
www.egorestaurants.co.uk

The restaurant sits in the heart of Liverpool's "foodie" district, and because it's right next to the Philharmonic Hall it's possible to combine an evening of music with eating out. In the summertime, sit outside and just soak up the atmosphere in Europe's 2008 Capital of Culture. See Bramhall, Cheshire, for menu.

Green Days

90% vegetarian cafe

13a Lark Lane, **Aigburth**, Liverpool L17 8UW
Tel: 0151-727-0783
Open: Mon-Sun 10.00-17.00, Thu till 20.00
Mersey rail train to Aigburth/St Michaels, or bus from centre

Upstairs cafe on two floors with great music, art and photography exhibited on walls. Everything made in house. No additives or preservatives, not even in the bread which they get bread from the famous Kolos Ukrainian bakery in Bradford, and the Liverpool German bakery, plus their own fruit and walnut Irish tea bread.

All day cooked veggie/vegan breakfast with tea or coffee and refill £4.90. Soups £3.10 with bread. Filled jacket potato £3.90 with hummus, avocado and pesto; beans; or Mexican sauce. Baguettes and sandwiches £3.90 made to order. Chimichangas £3.90 with salad. Spaghetti £4.60 with pesto or tomato sauce, plus salad and bread. Specials Thu-Fri £5 such as tortillas, Mediterranean mezze platter, curries.

Home-made cakes £2.80 but none vegan. Fruit salad £2.50.
Own lemonade £1.30, freshly squeezed orange juice £1.80. Cartons and water £1. Cup of tea 80p, pot £1.10. Cafetiere of coffee £1.90 small, £3 large for up to 4 people. Cappuccino or latte £1.60-1.80. They have soya milk.
Thursday night starter, main and dessert for £10. You can bring your own wine, £2 corkage, off-licence nearby.
Children welcome, 2 high chairs, books. A couple of chairs outside, good for people with dogs. Book group meets here weekly. Cash only.
Lark Lane runs from Aigburth Road to the lovely Sefton Park, 2-3 miles from the centre, and is the Bohemian part of the city full of arty types. There are galleries, a bookshop, antiques and at night it is buzzing with restaurants and wine bars. Keith's Wine Bar at 107 has some vegetarian food. Farmers' Market nearby every fourth week.

Gusto, Liverpool

Omnivorous Italian restaurant

Edward Pavilion, Albert Dock, Liverpool, Merseyside L3 4AF (near Tate Gallery)
Tel: 0151-708 6969
Open: Mon-Sun 12.00-23.00
www.gustorestaurants.uk.com

See Aderley Edge, Cheshire. Also in Heswall, Wirral (see below).

Host Restaurant

Omnivorous Asian fusion restaurant

31 Hope Street, Liverpool L1 9HX
Tel: 0151-708 5831
Open: Every day 11.00-23.00
www.ho-st.co.uk

Stylish new restaurant with lots of vegetarian options from Japan, China, Vietnam, Thailand and India, a cocktail bar and a juice bar. Starters £3.25-£3.50 include vegetable spring rolls; onion bhajias, and corn fritters with chili caramel. Typical mains £7.50-8.25 include miso soup with udon flat wheat noodles, tofu, seaweed and greens; udon noodles with pumpkin, courgette, spinach and oyster mushrooms; crispy salt and pepper tofu with wok-fried shitake mushrooms and Asian greens; tomato and lentil curry with aubergine and roast pumpkin. Rice £1.50. They make to order so can adapt dishes for you, and unlike Wagamama where everything comes at once, you'll get your starters first.

Desserts may include vegan rhubarb crumble £4.50.

Kids menu has veg fried rice or veg noodles £2.95 and main dishes are available in smaller portions.

House wine £12.95 bottle, £3.35 glass. Freshly squeezed juices £2.50. Tea and coffee £1.80-2.50.

Full disabled access. Some outside seating. Reservations recommended Friday and Saturday night.

Maharajah Restaurant

Omnivorous Keralan Indian restaurant

34-36 London Road L3 5NF (junction Hotham St, city centre, near Lime St train station and Natoinal Express coach station)
Tel: 0151-709 2006
Open: Mon-Sun 12.00-14.30, 17.30-23.00 (Fri-Sat till 23.30)
www.maharajaliverpool.co.uk

Keralan food (like Rasa in London) that is good for veggies and vegans, with each dish prepared individually with different spices instead of the pre-mixed curry sauces that many Indian restaurants use. Vegetarian banquet £17.50. Business lunch 12-14.00 £6.95 with 3 curries, side, rice, bread, dessert. Starters £3.95, curries £6.95, side dishes £3.50, dosas £7.95-8.95, rice £2.45, exotic rice such as tamarind and nuts or coconut and urid dal £2.,60. Coffee and tea £1.20. Deliveries 18.00-22.30. Function room. Outside catering.

The Quarter

Omnivorous Mediterranean bistro

7 Falkner Street, Liverpool L8 7PY
(off Hope Street, behind Philharmonic)
Tel: 0151-707 1965
Open: Mon-Fri 08.00-23.00,
Sat 10.00-23.00, Sun 10.00-22.30
www.thequarteruk.com

Spanish, Italian, Greek dishes. Different specials each week and they customise dishes for you, you could even bring your own ingredients if you call ahead to check. Mezze plate £5.95. Roast veg pasta or arrabiata £5.99. Vegan stone-baked pizza bases with tons of stuff on top £4.85-6.65, extra toppings 85p. Huge dessert menu but unfortunately none of it vegan. House wine £3.50 glass, £11.95 bottle. Beer and cider £3-3.95. Sangria £11.95 litre jug. Soft drinks £1-1.40. Innocent smoothie s£2.25. Pot of tea £1.50-1.80, coffee £1.30-1.85. You can sit outside in good weather. Children welcome, several high chairs. Wifi. Visa, MC.

Sabai

Omnivorous Thai restaurant

26 North John Street (opposite the Cavern Club), Liverpool L2 9RU
Tel: 0151-236 7655
Open: Mon-Sat 12.00-23.30,
Sun 12.00-22.00
www.sabairestaurant.co.uk

Almost everything on the menu has a vegetarian option. They do a very good offer before 5pm, £9.50 a head for a 3 course lunch with drink.

Sultan's Palace
Omni Indian Tandoori restaurant

73-79 Victoria Street (Queens Sq end, opp Millenium House), Liverpool L1 6DE
Tel: 0151 227 9020
Open: Mon-Fri 12.00-14.30, 17.00-late; Sat-Sun 17.00-late
www.sultans-palace.co.uk

A favourite with Scouseveg. Starters £4.50-5.50 include chaat, pakoras, samosas. Mains £7.95 (£5.50 as side) include rogan josh; black lentils with ginger; korma veg in coconut cream sauce; and Bengan Bhartha baked aubergine mashed and cooked with tomatoes and onions. Biryani £10.95. Thali £15.95. Rice £2.50. Chips £2. Vegetarian multi-course banquet £18.95 each for at least two people.
Wine from £13.95 bottle. Draught and bottled beers. Take-away menu online, delivery over £15. Vegans be sure to let them know and they'll take care of you. Private dining room available.

Valparaiso
Omnivorous Chilean restaurant

4 Hardman Street, Liverpool L1 9AX
Tel: 0151-708 6036
Open: Tue-Sat 17.30-22.30
www.valparaisorestaurant.com

Veggie and vegan dishes are marked on the menu and use South American staples. Starters and tapas dishes £4-5.95 such as soup, avocado salad, sauteed mushrooms, or cannellini beans with linguini, corn, pumpkin and peppers. Mains around £12 such as quinoa paella; cannellini beans with corn, pumpkin, peppers, linguini, with basil salsa, tortilla chips and rice; or roast peppers stuffed with ratatouille.
House wine £2.95-£4 glass, £11.95 bottle.

Some of the vegan chocolates at Dragon Indulgence

Yuet Ben Restaurant
Omnivorous Chinese restaurant

1 Upper Duke Street, Liverpool, L1 9DU
(corner of Berry Street)
Tel: 0151 709 5772
Open: Tues-Sat 17.00-23.00
www.yuetben.co.uk/vegetarian.html

Long-established Chinese restaurant with a huge vegetarian menu, most of it vegan.
There are 5 veggie soups £2.50-£3, including sweetcorn, tofu and pickled veg, or hot and sour. 21 starters, stir-fry and steamed/braised veg £3-5.50 such as shredded tofu and pancakes, deep-fried aubergine, or steamed vegetables in black bean sauce. Rice £1.70. 4 vegetarian set menus per person £9.50, £12, £14, £16.50. Jasmine tea 50p, coffee £1. Reservations advised for evenings as they get quite busy.

Liverpool - shops
Dragon Indulgence
Vegetarian wholefood / new age shop

Gostins Shopping Arcade,
32-36 Hanover Street, Liverpool L1 4LN
(next to Paradise Street bus station)
Tel: 07906 743849
Open: Mon-Sat 9.30-17.00, Sun closed
www.dragonindulgence.co.uk
Also on Facebook with product reviews

Liverpool's central vegetarian shop (run by two vegans) has moved from Grand Central Hall to bigger premises and gradually adding more and more products. Lots of Fairtrade.
Groceries. Fridge with Redwood cheezley, soya yogurts, Clearspot tofu, seacake. Vegan chocolate heaven, they say people even come from London to buy their vegan praline chocolate hearts. Cherry filled chocolate hearts, Carmel cups, vegan equivalents of Mars, Snickers and Milky Way. Carob flowers and eggs, Easter eggs and Christmas Booja Booja etc in season.
Some vegan soap, toothpaste and creams.
Spells, Tarot, Anna Riva products and magical oils. New Age clothes, T-shirts, jewellery and bags. Candles, oils and incense. Pagan and Buddhist statues. Crystals and minerals. Crystal therapist. New age and veggie books. Kindred Spirit magazine. Organic cotton Blue Mountain T-shirts. Local art which can be customised.
Cash or cheque only.

Mattas International Foods
International food shop

51 Bold Street, Liverpool L1 4EU
Train : Liverpool Central
Tel: 151-709 3031
Open: Mon-Sat 9-18.00 (Thu till 19.00),
Sun 10.30-16.00

Cheap international food shop, selling some meat but also very well stocked with vegan products. Cheapest soya milk, tofu and take away vegan pasties and samosas in town. Delivery of vegan Turkish Delight every Thursday, ask at the counter! Walk up Bold street and it's on the left, near the top.

News From Nowhere
Bookshop & Saturday vegan cafe

96 Bold Street (almost right at the top)
Liverpool L1 4HY
Bookshop: 0151-708 7270
Basement: 0151-703 6806
Train: Liverpool Central
Open: Mon-Sat 10.00-17.45, Sun closed
www.newsfromnowhere.org.uk
www.liverpoolsocialcentre.org

Radical bookshop which only stocks vegetarian and vegan cookbooks. Very knowledgeable and helpful staff. Huge noticeboard by the door packed with events and contacts in Liverpool, or see the website.

Down in the basement is **Next to Nowhere** social centre. On Saturdays 12.00-17.00 they have Liverpool's only vegan cafe **Food From Nowhere** (under vegetarian restaurants above). Fortnightly Sunday free film screening with vegan soup and cakes from 5pm, donations for food appreciated, film starts at 6.

Windmill Wholefoods

Organic wholefood shop

337 Smithdown Road, Wavertree, Liverpool L15 3JJ (corner Gainsborough Rd, south of the station, bus 60 & 86)
Tel: 0151-734 1919
Open: Mon-Wed, Fri 9.30-18.00,
Thu 9.30-19.30, Sat 9.30-17.30,
Sun closed
www.windmillorganic.co.uk

Workers coop since 1991 in the student area, a little out of the city centre but well worth a trip. Vegetarian wholefoods, organic fruit and veg, bodycare, cleaning products. Diabetic, gluten-free. Take-away vegan pasties, Sojasun yogurt jars, bottled juices. They deliver vegebags.

Holland & Barrett

Health food shop

17 **Whitechapel**, Liverpool L1 6DS
Tel: 0151-236 8911

3a **Bold Stret**, Liverpool L1 4DJ
Tel: 0151-708 9343
Open: Mon-Sat 9.00-17.30 (Thu 19.00), Sun 11.00-17.00

Southport
Holland & Barrett

Health food shop

Unit 12 Station Arcade, Southport PR8 1BH
Tel: 01704-530734
Open: Mon-Sat 9.00-17.30, Sun 11-17.00

Wirral restaurants

Kerala Kitchen

Omnivorous South Indian restaurant

342 Woodchurch Road, **Prenton** CH42 8PQ
(Leave the M53 at J3 and straight ahead onto direction Birkenhead, A552. Continue 1.1 miles. It's on the left after Sainsburys.)
Tel: 0151-201 1121
Open: Tue-Sun 17.00-23.00, Mon closed
www.keralakitchen.co.uk

Very vegan-friendly. The manager pointed out to one Scouseveg member that "animals who don't eat meat live longer – much more healthy!" The food is Indian, but quite different from normal "curry house" food – although they do that too.
Lentil soup £2.25. Bajias, pakodas, dal vada, £1.75-2.90. Curries £3.80-4.90. Veg biryani or balti £5.90. Veg vindaloo, korma, jalfrezi, tikka masala, Madras, rogan josh £5.50. 10 kinds of rice £1.90-3.25. Indian breads, 3 idlies or 3 dosas £1.30-3.90. Masala dosa £4.90. Chips £1.50.
Multi-dish set meals for 2 people: Traditional Kerala £18.90, North Indian £20.90, Kerala Special £21.90.
Juices £1.75. Tea £1.50, coffee £1.90. Discount on take-away.

Ego, Heswall

Omnivorous Mediterranean restaurant

166 Telegraph Road A540, Heswall CH60 0AH(near junction Downham Rd South)
Tel: 0151-342 4224
Open: Mon-Sun 12.00-22.30
www.egorestaurants.co.uk

For menu see Bramhall, Cheshire.

Gusto, Heswall

Omnivorous Italian restaurant

146-148 Telegraph Road, Heswall CH60 0AH
Tel: 0151-348 4538
Open: Mon-Sun 12.00-23.00
www.gustorestaurants.uk.com

See Alderley Edge, Cheshire. Also in Liverpool Albert Dock.

Mezze

Omnivorous Turkish/Med restaurant

233 Liscard Road (A551), **Wallasey** CH44 5TH (NE corner of Wirral)
Tel: 0151-638 3222
Open: Mon-Sun 17.00-22.30
www.mezze.co.uk

Have a selection of a mezze starters or a mixed platter, a veggie main such as imam bayildi (baked veg stuffed aubergine) with rice and chunky chips, or get stuck into a Vegetarian (or Vegan) Banquet for 2 or more people including houmous, cevizli biber (red chili puree with walnuts), soslu patlican, borek, olives, dolmades, falafel, salad, veg moussaka, rice, chips and home-made pide bread, served slowly so you can eat at your own pace. Mon-Thu 2 courses £10.95, 3 courses £12.95. 15% discount on take-away. For parties of 20+ they can organize a Turkish night with belly dancer and mezze banquet for £17.95 each (not Saturday night).

Ming Vase

Omnivorous Chinese restaurant

385 Woodchurch Rd, Prenton, **Birkenhead**, CH42 8PF. Tel: 0151-608 2306
Open: Tue-Sun 17.30-23.00, closed Mon

Starters from £3.50, main courses £6.50 for veggie main course with lots of choice including veg, curries, noodles. Vegetarian banquet £15 per head. House wine £9.50 bottle, glass £2.30. Children welcome, high chairs. MC, Visa. Wirral Veggies sometimes meet here.

www.Honest-to-Goodness.org.uk
Ethical - Organic - Vegan
t: 0151 632 6516

A Grocery store with a difference

Our products are ethically sourced and many are organic
Vegetable Boxes - Small: £7.00, Medium: £10.00, Large: £15.00

FREE delivery all over North Wirral

Organic & Natural Foods
Grains & Cereals • Nuts & Dried Fruits
Baking Supplies • Pasta
Herbs & Spices
Bread Flours

Fine Foods
Teas & Coffees • Jams & Spreads
Chutneys & Pickles
Confectionery
Soft Drinks

Vitamins & Supplements

Japanese Food

Eco-Friendly Cleaning Range
Household Cleaners
Refill Service

Cruelty Free Bodycare
Handmade Soap
Organic Hair Care
Organic Skin Care
Toothcare

Vegetarian/Vegan Groceries
Meat Substitutes
Dairy-Free Milk & Cheese
Iced Desserts

Gluten Free Food

Special Offer 10% Discount
*excludes other promotions

Ethical Grocery Store • 33 Market Street, Hoylake, Wirral CH47 2BG
www.honest-to-goodness.org.uk

Wirral shops
Honest to Goodness
Vegan ethical grocery store

10 Market Street, Hoylake, Wirral CH47 2AE
Tel: 0151-632 6516
Open: Mon-Sat 9.00-18.00,
Sun 12.00-18.00
www.honest-to-goodness.org.uk

If you like Unicorn vegan grocery in Manchester, you'll like this, and they have lots of sugar, ice-cream, chocolate. Over 1600 vegan products.
All the usual wholefoods. Organic fruit and veg, and box scheme. Organic bread. Fridge with Sheese and Tofutti vegan cheeses, tofu, VegiDeli and Viana and Dragonfly sausages, pasties, burgers. Freezer includes Swedish Glace, Booja Booja, vegan cheesecake. Japanese foods. Lazy Day shortbread, chocolate tiffin slices. Hawkshead Relish preserves.
Chocolate by Booja Booja, Organica, vegan equivalents of Mars, Snickers and Milky Way, Lyme Regis marzipan bars.
Bodycare by Trilogy, Essential Care, Faith In Nature, Organic Blue, Green People, Suma, Yaoh lip balm, Organyc women's stuff, Mooncup.
Supplements by Solgar, Viridian, Vega, Floradix, A.Vogel. Essential oils.
Cleaning by Simply Washing, Earth Friendly, BioD and all five main refills, Ecoleaf, Method, Eco balls, soap pods. The Vegan magazine. They have an online shop. MC, Visa.

Heswall Health
Health food shop

16 Pensby Road, Heswall CH60 7RE
Tel: 0151-342 9994
Open: Mon-Sat 9.00-17.00, Sun closed
On Facebook

Fridge and freezer with vegan cheese and meat substitutes, Swedish Glace. Vegan chocolate by Plamil, Booja Booja and Organica.
Bodycare by Avalon, Faith in Nature, Jason, Olive, Dead Sea Magik etc, Natracare, Organic Baby and Earth Friendly Baby.
Supplements by Solgar, Lifeplan, Nature's Aid, Vogel, Pharmanord. Weleda homeopathy, New Era and Bach flower, essential oils. Sometimes nutritoinist Gareth Zeal is in store.
Cleaning by Ecover and refills, Citrus Magic, Faith In Nature.
MC, Visa.

Wirral chain stores
Holland & Barrett
Health food shop

6 Borough Pavement, **Birkenhead** L41 2XX
Tel: 0151-647 7327
Open: Mon-Sat 9.00-17.30, Sun 10-16.00

10 The Palatine, New Strand Shopping Centre, **Bootle** L20 45N
Tel: 0151-922 9157
Open: Mon-Sat 9.00-17.30, Sun closed

Unit 114 The Designer Outlet Centre, **Cheshire Oaks**, Ellesmere Port CH65 9JJ
Tel: 0151-3571306
Open: Mon-Fri 10.00-20.00,
Sat 10.00-19.00, Sun 10.00-17.00

28 Marina Walk, **Ellesmere Port** CH65 0BN
Tel: 0151-355 9228
Open: Mon-Sat 9.00-17.30, Sun 11-16.00

23 Chapel Lane, **Formby** L37 4DL
Tel: 01704-879 071

4 Cherry Square Shopping Centre, **Wallasey** CH44 5XU
Tel: 0151-639 7707
Open: Mon-Sat 9.00-17.30, Sun closed

Delivery services
Nature's Boutique
Vegan cosmetics & fashion

www.naturesboutique.com
Tel: 0845 045 1505

Vegan organic mail order business based in Merseyside. Body and hair care, cosmetics, bags, wallets, fragrances, mother and baby, men's stuff, soy wax candles, gifts.

Organic Direct
Fruit & veg boxes and wholefoods

57 Blundell Street, Liverpool L1 OAJ
Tel: 0151-707 6949
http://organicdirect.look4local.co.uk

Deliver organic vegetables and fruit box to your home for £10 in Liverpool, Wirral or St Helens, weekly or fortnightly. All produce sourced as locally as possible (except bananas). Also organic wholefoods and bread.

Local groups
Scouseveg
Vegetarian Society affiliated group

www.scouseveg.co.uk
and on Facebook

Social and campaigning group for vegetarians and vegans in and around Liverpool, Merseyside and the Wirral. Regular meetings, pub evenings, meals out, parties, pot luck suppers and other activities and events. Open to everyone all ages, singles, couples, and families. Or you can just join the email list, great for aspiring veggies.
For the latest news on eating out:
www.scouseveg.co.uk/
eating-out-in-liverpool

Wirral Veggies
Vegetarian Society affiliated group

Tel. 0151-678 1487
www.wirralveggies.org.uk

Local social group for vegetarians and vegans who meet twice a month for an evening restaurant meal, walk and talk, picnics and occasional pub drink. They try to make the outside events as family friendly as possible.

Northumberland is most famous for Hadrian's Wall – the Roman barrier against the marauding Scottish Picts, which is extremely well-preserved in some parts of the county.

The county has stunning coastline and lots of ancient castles and ruins to visit, and is relatively unspoilt by tourism.

Tourist information:
www.visitnorthumberland.com
www.northumberland-coast.co.uk
www.northumberlandnationalpark.org.uk
www.visitnortheastengland.com
www.www.alnwickcastle.com
www.exploreberwick.co.uk

Photos of the region:
www.northumberland-cam.com

Coast to coast cycle route:
www.reivers-guide.co.uk

Introduction	**117**
Accommodation	**118**
Amble	**120**
Berwick upon Tweed	**120**
Falstone	**121**
Hexham	**122**
Headley on the Hill	**122**
Morpeth	**123**
Thropton	**123**
West Woodburn	**123**
Chain stores	**123**
Local groups	**123**

Northumberland

Accommodation
The Long View
Vegan bed & breakfast

Laurel Bank Cottage, Main Street East End, Chirnside, Berwickshire TD11 3XR, **Scotland** (just over the border from Berwick, which you can see in the distance)
Tel: 01890-818102
Open: all year
Train: Berwick-upon-Tweed (on London-Edinburgh East Coast Main Line) + bus/taxi
Directions: By car the most direct route is to take the A1 to Berwick-upon-Tweed then follow the A6105 for approx 9 miles to Chirnside. Entering the Main Street at the east end, Laurel Bank Cottage is approx 500 yards along on the left, just after bus stop on the opposite side. Entrance is at the rear, down drive next to adjoining property.
Email: karendpage@live.com

Opened summer 2010, vegan B&B on a sporadic basis by an organic vegan gardener, 10 minutes drive from Berwick. The area offers excellent cycling, walking, sightseeing, and running routes, with dramatic coast, countryside and castles. Enjoy vegan-organic fruit and vegetables from the garden; sample home-made bread, pies, cakes and pastries; and relax in front of a blazing log fire. A peaceful haven for vegans.

2 double rooms £26-30 per person. No single supplement. Huge vegan cooked breakfast. Evening meal with dessert £15. Picnics, packed lunches. Afternoon teas in garden or guest louge with log fire, books and music but no tv.

Pick your own veganic fruit and veg boxes to take away. Well-behaved children over 6. No pets. No smoking. Wifi. Secure cycle storage. 5% discount to Vegetarian Society, Vegan Society, Viva!, PETA, Animal Aid, Dr Hadwen, BUAV, people presenting this book.

This is also a great stopping-off point on the way to Edinburgh or the Highlands.

Bay Horse Inn
Omnivorous bed & breakfast

West Woodburn, near Hexham NE48 2RX
Tel: 01434-270 218
www.bayhorseinn.org

7 rooms, 5 ensuite: 4 twins, 3 doubles, one with 4-poster bed. £42-45 per person b&b, single supplement £8, children under 12 sharing half price (Z-bed), cot £4.50. 5% online booking discount. Vegetarian or vegan breakfast. Dogs welcome. English Tourist Council 3 stars. For food see page 123.

The Coach House
Omnivorous guest house

Crookham, **Cornhill-on-Tweed** TD12 4TD. (on A697, 1 hour drive from Edinburgh or Newcastle)
Tel: 01890-820293
Open: Feb-Nov
www.coachhousecrookham.com

A complex of renovated old farm buildings, including a 1680s cottage and an old smithy, surrounding a sun-trap courtyard. 3 traditional and 7 modern rooms including disabled, all en suite or with own bathroom, £39-52 per person, single occupancy £15-28 extra. Beware of leather furniture in most rooms. Vegetarian and vegan cooked breakfasts. Dinner £22.95. Dogs welcome in certain rooms. Visa, MC +2%, no charge for debit cards.

Kielder Youth Hostel

4 star youth hostel

YHA Kielder, Butteryhaugh, **Kielder Village**, Hexham NE48 1HQ
Tel: 01434-250 195
Open: all year, 24 hour access
Reception 09.00-10.00, 17.00-21.00
www.yha.org.uk
Email: kielder@yha.org.uk

Kielder is the most remote village in England, great for cycling, walking, wildlife and watersports. There is a village store with banking facilities open normal shop hours. Secure bike storage. Laundry. The nearest supermarket and bank is 17 miles away.

May-Oct adult £20 each in a twin bed room (two of those), £14 winter. Single-sex dorm £18 summer, winter £16, under-18 £13.50/£12. Non-YHA members pay £3 extra (U-18 £1.50), and two people at the same address can join for £22.95 so if you stay at more than 3 hostels a year it is worth it. Buffet breakfast £4.95 with plenty of hot and cold choices, good for vegetarians, vegan check when booking.

Evening meal starters £2.50-3.50, mains £5.50-6.95, always has a vegetarian choice, vegan if you warn them, such as courgette curry with coconut milk with rice and popadoms; lots of bean dishes such as 3-bean casserole or chilli. Kids' portions. Beer (Wylan Brewery, vegan) and wine available. No dogs. Children welcome, 2 carrycots. MC, Visa.

Noah's Place

Omnivorous organic B&B

31 Main Street, Spittal, **Berwick upon Tweed**, Northumberland TD15 1QY
Tel: 01289-332 141
Open mainly Easter and summer
www.noahsplace.co.uk

Family-run B&B in a house built in 1792 on a Georgian high street, near sandy Spittal beach in the historic fortified border town of Berwick-upon-Tweed. Small double £20 per person; big double/twin/family with kingsize double and bunks, adult £22.50, under-13 £12, U-4 free. Extra Z-bed £10. Free cot. Single occupant £25-27.50. Cotton pillows and duvets but vegans note they have duck/goose feather filling. Bicycle storage. Mainly open Easter and summer because of long-term residents, check website. No dogs. Cash or cheque only.

Ravensdowne Guest House

Omnivorous guest house

40 Ravensdowne, **Berwick-upon-Tweed**, Northumberland TD15 1DQ
Tel: 01289-306 992
Open: all year except 24-27 Dec
Station: Berwick 7mins walk
www.40ravensdowne.co.uk

1760 townhouse in the centre of Berwick near the Elizabethan fortified walls. 2 double (one with 4-poster), 1 twin, £30-40 per person, 1 single £35-50, all ensuite. Full English veggie breakfast. The owners have a vegan sister and vegetarian daughter. 3-course evening meals £10-15 include veggie pie, Indian, Indonesian style Thai, vegan, coeliac and nut-free on request. They can recommend cafes for lunch. Free on street parking. Secure covered bike storage. Free wifi. Totally non-smoking. No pets or children under 12. MC, Visa.

Amble

Marina Arms

Omnivorous pub & restaurant

The Wynd, Amble, Morpeth, NE65 0HH (on the coast, 10 miles from Morpeth)
Tel: 01665-710094
Drinks: Mon-Sat 12.00-15.00, 17.00-late; Sun 12.00-23.30;
may close early in bad weather.
Food 12.00-14.15 last order,
winter 17.00-20.30 last order,
summer 17.00- 21.00 or a bit later, phone to check
Early bird menu till 18.45, main menu from 19.00
www.amble.co.uk

Family pub, oriented for diners rather than drinkers, in sight of Warkworth castle (2 miles) and 5 miles from Alnwich castle. The Greek chef says they get a lot of vegetarians here.

Early bird menu 5.00-6.45pm has two main courses for £8.99-11.99 but for vegetarians it might be just the lasagne, however you may be able to order off the main menu if not too busy, otherwise wait till 7pm.

Main menu from 7pm has vegan starters that include crunchy garlic mushrooms £3.95, melon with Grand Marnier, crispy garlic bread £1.45. Main courses around £8 such as moussaka, lemon and thyme risotto, wild mushroom stroganoff, vegan stir-fry. House wine £11.70 bottle, £2.60-3.60 glass.

Being near the marina there is quite a bit of fish on the menu, but you can avoid the aroma by eating outside, which is a good idea anyway if you have a dog with you. Children welcome, high chairs, and there is a climbing apparatus in the garden. MC, Visa.

Berwick upon Tweed

Cafe Curio

Omnivorous French bistro-cafe

52 Bridge St, Berwick TD15 1AQ
Tel: 01289-302666
Open: Mon-Sat 10.00-16.00 or later,
Fri-Sat dinners by reservation, Sun closed

Eating out in Berwick can seem grim but this very unusual cafe has regular local vegan and vegetarian customers and knows what we like and also understands gluten-free. The American chef uses local ingredients with a French colonial twist, such as potato and butterbean soup. Always a vegetarian option £5.95-8.95 on the menu and they try to avoid basing it on cheese, e.g. stuffed peppers with couscous and pinenuts, rice noodles with veg stock, poached Asian veg with mirin glaze, and for dessert they could make you poached plums with almonds. Sometimes open Fri-Sat night if you book, £25 for 4 courses, either a fixed menu or as a taster menu.

Pot of tea or bottomless cup of coffee tea £2. House wine £3.50 glass, bottles from £15. Bottled beer £3.

They also sell antiques and in fact everything that isn't nailed down is for sale including the furniture and cutlery, though you might have to wait for someone to finish using it first. Children welcome, high chairs. No dogs. Cash or cheque only, cashpoints nearby.

Sinners Cafe

Omnivorous cafe

1 Sidey Court, Berwick upon Tweed
TD15 1DR. Tel: 01289-302621
Winter: Mon-Sat 10.00-15.00, Sun closed.
Summer Mon-Sat 10.00-16.00,
Sun 10.00-15.00.
www.berwickbedandbreakfast.co.uk
/sinners-cafe-bar.htm

Local vegans come here for a cooked

breakfast £4.50 including orange juice or a hot drink. Panini and toasties £3.70-4.00, filled jacket potatoes £3-4.70, veggie burger £4.50 with chips and salad. They keep a supply of frozen home-cooked vegetarian and vegan specials ready, such as goulash, chilli, curry £4.50 each with chips or rice. Soup £2.70. Cakes and scones, usually not vegan. Tea and coffee £1.10, they have soya milk. Children welcome, high chair, no big prams inside. Dogs welcome in the courtyard seating. Car park nearby. MC, Visa.

Caffe Nero at 77-79 Marygate is the only other cafe we know of to do soya milk, though it's 30p extra. Open: Mon-Sat 9.00-18.00, Sun 9.00-18.00.

The Green Shop

Omnivorous organic food & eco shop

30 Bridge Street, Berwick upon Tweed
TD15 1AQ. Tel: 01289-305 566
Open: Mon-Sat 9.00-17.30, Sun closed
www.berwickholidaycottages.co.uk/green-shop.htm
www.exploreberwick.co.uk/Stores/Green.htm

Family-run business with nothing tested on animals and locally produced where possible. Organic fruit and veg, vegan and veggie foods, beers, wines, spirits, frozen fruit, seeds, non-dairy yoghurt. Fairtrade snacks. Clothing, cards and crafts. Toiletries, make-up, sun cream, essential oils.

The Market Shop

Vegetarian health food shop & art gallery

48 Bridge St, Berwick-upon-Tweed
TD15 1AQ. Tel: 01289-307749
Open: Mon-Sat 9.30-17..00, closed Sun
www.exploreberwick.co.uk/Stores/Sallyport.htm

Fuill range of wholefoods. Lots of gluten-free. Fridge (but no freezer) with vegan yogurt and cheeses, hummus. Huge range of herbs and spices. Lots of teas. Good for walkers with bars, Plamil vegan chocolate, nuts, seeds and dried fruit.

Bodycare by Avalon, full Weleda range and baby, Thursday Plantation, Dead Sea Magik. Supplements by Solgar, Bioforce, Viridian, Weleda. Homeopathy and remedies, Absolute Aromas essential oils. Food allergy testing by appointment. Ecover cleaning. Books.

Also nautical gifts, art supplies and a gallery. MC, Visa.

Falstone

Falstone Tearoom

Omnivorous cafe

Falstone Old School, Falstone NE48 1AA (near Kielder), Tel: 01434-240 459
Winter: Thu-Mon 10.30-16.00, call ahead if bad weather as they may close and the answering machine will have hours.
Easter-Oct: every day 10.30-17.00 later if busy.
Open weekend evenings if they have bookings for at least 10 people
www.falstonetearoom.co.uk

Based in the former Victorian School at Falstone, a small village between Bellingham and Kielder, is a tearoom, local crafts gallery, community shop and National Park information point. There are photovoltaic cells on the roof, a biomass wood pellet heating boiler, rainwater tank for flushing toilets.

Veggie options including jacket potatoes (can be vegan), sandwiches, salads, soups. Always a veggie main meal, usually a pasta bake (not vegan), £4.75 with salad, £5.95 with jacket potato or chips and veg. If there's something you want and they have the ingredients they will have a go for you. Cakes and cookies 85p-£1.75 not vegan. Pot of tea £1.30, coffee £1.50-2.15, no soya milk. Children welcome, high chair. Dogs welcome in conservatory area but not in the garden. Outside seating in the garden. Wifi. Free car park. Visa, MC.

Hexham
The Garden Station
Vegetarian organic cafe

Langley on Tyne, Hexham NE47 5LA
Tel: 01434-684391
Garden Station Cafe open:
Summer May-Aug: Mon-Sun 10.00-17.00.
Spring Mar-Apr, Autumn Sep-Oct:
 Fri-Mon 10.00-17.00, Tue-Fri closed.
www.thegardenstation.co.uk

New vegetarian cafe in a restored Victorian railway station in a woodland garden, with garden, woodland walk and art exhibitions. A place of beauty and tranquility. Cordon Vert chef is Mike Winstanley of Veg NE. You can enjoy courses on gardening, environment, wildlife, art, sculpture, textiles, poetry and food & drink. Vegan dishes marked on menu which you can see on the website.

Lunch 12.00-16.00. Vegan soup with homemade organic bread £3.95, plus salads £5.15. Baked potato with salads £4.05, add 90p for filling. Hummus with olives, bread, oatcakes or ricecakes £6.05. Main meal specials of the day such as shepherd's pie £6.90. Dessert of the day £3.55.

Cakes £1.55. Pot of tea for one £1.50, for two £1.85. Fair Trade coffee £1.55-1.75, latte/cappuccino or hot choc £1.90, mochaccino £2. Fair Trade juices £1.55.

There is a second little self-service cafe **The Learning Shed** with just drinks and snacks which is open every day Mar-Dec.

Hexham Tans
Vegetarian cafe

11 St Mary's Chare, Hexham NE46 1NQ
Tel: 01434-656 284
Open: Tue-Sat 08.30-16.00,
Sun-Mon closed

Cheap, friendly veggie and fish cafe, part of the NHS Opus Employment Project, and from 2010 they have dropped fish to make it all vegetarian. All specials £5.50 such as veg curry, chilli are vegan. Sandwiches and toasties made to order £3.10. Cakes £1.40 and scones £1 are not vegan. Pot of tea £1, filter coffee £1.20, latte £1.40, no soya milk. Very child friendly, high chairs. No dogs. No credit cards.

Hedley on the Hill
The Feathers Inn
Omnivorous real ale pub and B&B

Hedley on the Hill, Stocksfield NE43 7SW
(near Prudhoe, 15 minute drive west of Newcastle). Tel: 01661-843607
Pub open: Tue-Sat 12.00-23.00;
Sun 12.00-14.30; Mon 18.00-23.00.
Food: Tue-Sun 12.00-14.00,
Tue-Sat 18.00-20.30, Mon 18.00-20.00
www.thefeathers.net

18th century pub. Menu changes every day and always has vegetarian starters and mains made in house so lots of unusual dishes, and they can cater for vegans. See sample daily menu on the website. For example curried carrot and parsnip soup £4, (in autumn) local hedgehog and pixie stool mushrooms on toast £6; casserole of local wild mushrooms, baby violet artichokes and heritage potatoes, cider and herb £10. House wine £2.30 small glass, bottle £12.60. Children welcome, high chairs and changing facilities. Visa, MC. Outside seating on village green. No dogs inside.

Winners of the Good Pub Guide Northumbria 2008, 2009, 2010.

Morpeth
The Chantry Tea Room
Omnivorous restaurant

9 Chantry Place, Morpeth NE61 1PJ
Tel: 01670-514 414
Open: Mon-Sat 9.00-16.00, Sun closed

Several vegetarian choices on menu, jacket potatoes, sandwiches, various pies and hot dishes, from £3.10-5.50. Soup £3.10 is always vegan, baked potato with beans £4.10. Tea or coffee £1.50. No soya milk. Children welcome, high chairs. Visa, MC.

Manzil Tandoori
Omnivorous Indian restaurant

2b Oldgate, Morpeth NE61 1LX (in the Market Place). Tel: 01670-515405
Open: Mon-Sat 12.00-14.00, 17.30-23.30, Sun closed lunch, 18.00-23.30

There are lots of cafes and restaurants in Morpeth that have something veggie, but locals recommend this one. Starters around £2.50, curries £5.95, rice £2.35. House wine £9.95 bottle, £2.50 glass. Children welcome, high chairs. MC, Visa.

Advanced Nutrition
Health food shop

14 Sanderson's Arcade, Bridge Street, Morpeth NE61 1NS (at entrance to new arcade being built in 2009)
Tel: 01670-514 212
Open: Mon-Sun 08.45-17.45, from Nov 2009 also on Sundays 11.00-16.00 when the rest of the new shopping arcade opens

Small shop with 80% supplements and 20% food, including dairy-free, wheat-free, nuts, snacks. Allergy testing.

Thropton
The Three Wheat Heads
Omnivorous country inn & restaurant

Thropton NE65 7LR
(From A697 take B6344, 2 miles after Rothbury, in village centre next to church)
Tel: 01669-620262
Open: all year
www.threewheatheads.com

300 year old restored inn with summer beer garden and 2 bars. Real ale and guest ales. 6 rooms, 5 en suite and 1 with private bathroom, double £60 or £70 with main course dinner for two, single £49. TV, tea/coffee makers and room service. Vegetarian and vegan evening meals. £8-9 such as veg curry, nut roast, tortilla wraps, homemade spicy lentil veg rissoles, cauliflower and lentil bake. Desserts £3.75 but not vegan. House wine £9.95 bottle, £3.80 large glass. Children welcome, high chair. Dogs welcome in rooms or garden. Visa, MC.

West Woodburn
Bay Horse Inn
Omnivorous pub & restaurant

West Woodburn, near Hexham NE48 2RX
Tel: 01434-270 218
Open: Mon-Sun 11-23.00
Food served 12-14.30, and 18.30-21.00
www.bayhorseinn.org

Separate vegetarian menu. Soup £3.95. 4 veggie mains from £7.95-8.95 such as bean and cider casserole. House wine £3 (125ml), bottle £12.45. Some outside seating in summer. Children welcome, high chairs. Dogs welcome in the bar. Visa, MC.
For rooms see page 118.

NORTH Northumberland

Chain Stores
Holland & Barrett
Health food shop

23 Station Road, **Ashington** NE63 9UZ
Tel: 01665-579225
Open: Mon-Sat 9.00-17.30, Sun closed

Chiller with vegan cheese and meat substitutes but no take-aways. Freezer with Tofutti, veggie ready meals.

---

74 Marygate, **Berwick** TD15 1BN
Tel: 01289-309262
Open: Mon-Sat 9.00-17.30, Sun 12-16.00

---

5 Keel Row Shopping Centre, **Blyth**
NE24 1AH. Tel: 01670-360411

Chiller with vegetarian pasties but not vegan.

31-33 Fore Street, **Hexham** NE46 1LU.
Tel: 01434-609067
Open: 9-17.30 Mon-Sat Sun 10.00-16.00

Chiller with pasties and pies

Julian Graves
Health food shop

36 Bridge Street, **Morpeth** NE61 1NL
Tel: 01670-511 758
Open: Mon-Sat 9.00-17.30
www.juliangraves.com

Lots of nuts, dried fruit and trail mix for hungry veggie hikers and cyclists.

Local Groups
Veg NE
Local vegetarian & vegan group

www.vegne.co.uk
Contact Mark 079410 79 999

Active social group affiliated to the Vegetarian Society, based in Newcastle with members from County Durham, Northumberland and Tyne & Wear. They meet regularly at Bob Trollops and Jack Sprats in Newcastle. Mainly a social group but also puts on exhibitions and stalls.

They run an annual week long vegan gathering during April school holidays in Morpeth, Northumberland.

Northumbria Veg*ns
Local social group

Gordon Forrest, 9 Seymour St, N. Shields,
Tyne & Wear NE29 6SN.
Tel: 0191-258 6793
gmforrest@tiscali.co.uk

Monthly picnic or bring and share.

Nottingham is famous worldwide due to the legend of Robin Hood. It is a small city, but has some lovely old pubs and buildings, and is very easy to get to by road and rail. If you want to see what remains of Sherwood Forest, you'll need to head north on the A60 to Edwinstowe, where you'll find a visitor centre and the ancient Noble Oak.

The 700 year old *Goose Fair* still takes place in Nottingham during the first weekend in October, though these days it is mostly a huge funfair. In December there is usually the East Midlands Vegan Festival, though in 2010 the Council were being awkward about the venue as the festival has grown so big and successful.

Nottingham has stacks of vegetarian places, but only one is in the city centre. For others head for the student area of Lenton, or north up Mansfield Road to Forest Fields and Carrington / Sherwood.

Unfortunately on Sundays veggie places tend to be closed, but there are lots of good curry houses. The local Veggies crew highly recommend Kayal south Indian in the city centre, and Royal Thai on Mansfield Road, as knowing exactly what vegetarians and vegans like.

www.visitnottingham.com
www.nottinghamgoosefair.co.uk
www.vegan-nottingham.co.uk
www.veggies.org.uk/veganfestival

NOTTINGHAM	**125**
Vegetarian restaurants	**126**
Omnivorous restaurants	130
Chain stores	134
Caterer	134
Local groups	135

Notinghamshire **Nottingham**

Nottingham - vegetarian
Crocus Cafe
Fair Trade vegetarian cafe

Unit 2 Church Square,
Lenton, Nottingham, NG7 1SL
Tel: 0115-950 5080
Open: Mon-Fri 9.00-16.00, Sat 10-16.00
(last hot food orders 15.00), Sun closed
Now also Thu eve 19.00-22.00

Some of the best value veggie food in Nottingham, gastro-pub style food but at cafe prices. Crocus is a community project in the student area of Lenton, which offers Fair Trade and locally-sourced food. Plenty of vegan options.
As well as daily specials, there are always light meals such as soup for £2. Pastries, salads and main meals such as Thai green curry, pizza (can be vegan), pasta, sausage mash and veg, for £3.80-4.20. Their own speciality veg pakora 90p.
Cakes £1-2 include at least one vegan, crumbles £1.50-2.50 are occasionally vegan.
Juices £1.10, squashes 60p-£1, Whole Earth cans £1. Tea 80p, herb or fruit tea £1, pot of tea £1.10 small, £1.60 large, coffee £1.30, latte/cappuccino/mocha £1.60, hot choc £1.70, they have soya milk.
Now also open Thursday nights with the normal menu, except second Thursdays of the month 2-course restaurant meal £6, 3-course £8, themed menu such as Thai.
They sell to take away things used in the cafe such as drinks, and eco washing up liquid and refills, Fairtrade jam and organic peanut butter. Good links with other community focused initiatives promoted through their leaflet display.
Outside catering, and buffets in the associated gallery next door. Book exchange shelf. Cash only, cashpoints nearby.

The Flying Goose & Roya's at Flying Goose
Vegetarian cafe

33 Chilwell Road, **Beeston**, Nottingham
NG9 1EH. Tel: 0115-925 2323
Open: Tue-Sat 08.30-22.00,
Sun-Mon closed

Daytime: Eat for under a fiver. Sandwiches made to order with good sized side salad £4.75, baguettes £4.95, seeded pitta with falafel and hummus £5.50. Soups £3.95 with bread, vegan spread always in. Tapas bowls such as hummus, marinated olives, salted almonds, salsa, bread, salad, £1.50 per portion, mix and match to make a meal. Cakes £1.95-2.50, including a vegan one such as carrot cake. Coffee from £1.80, tea £1.60, soya milk available. Alcohol, see below. Children welcome, toy box, high chair. MC, Visa.
New from September 2010 in the **evenings** the cafe transforms into a gourmet vegetarian restaurant **Roya's at The Flying Goose** Tue-Sat 17.30 till 22.00 with fusion food from around the world 3 options for each course, change regularly, usually 2 of each are vegan.
Starters £3.95 such as spicy carrot pancake with roasted carrot and cumin hummus; spicy beetroot and coconut soup. Mains £8.25 such as vegan aubergine parmesana with pinenuts; baby stuffed aubergine curry; mixed mushroom stroganoff with Italian rice and garlic ciabatta.
Desserts £3.95 feature vegan delights such as Viennese chocolate tart with ice-cream, toffee apple crumble with custard, or cheesecake with cream.
Now fully licensed all day with a good selection of organic vegetarian and vegan wines. House wine £2.45, £3.45, £4.90 glass, £11.95 bottle, up to £17.95 bottle. Organic lager £2.75 bottle, cider £3.60 large bottle. Coffee from £1.80, tea £1.60.
Occasional poetry evenings, usually third Tuesday of the month. MC, Visa.

Alley Café

Nottingham

Vegetarian and vegan cafe-bar

Vegetarian café-bar in the centre of Nottingham, located in a courtyard near the market square.

All day breakfast £4.50 with Baconesque, sausage, hash browns, grilled tomatoes, mushrooms, organic baked beans, scrambled tofu, or have a colossal version £6.50. BLT £4.10. Sausage sandwich £4.10.

Starters and light meals £3.65-6.50 include soup with bread or garlic bread, falafel, burrito, pizza (can be with vegan cheese), tempeh or hemp burger with organic potato wedges, organic marinated tofu steak with root mash patties. Main course salads around £6. There is a daily special £7.25 such as spicy enchilada, or Allotment Gratin - slow-baked pumpkin, courgette, sweet peppers and leeks in creamy tomato sauce. Sunday roast £6.95.

Large selection of sandwiches, choice of 5 breads (bagel, granary, ciabatta, tortilla wrap or rye) all £4.45 with names. Mildred is smoked tofu, vegan pesto and artichoke heart; Winston is roast veg and hummus.

Desserts £2.65-3.10 are usually vegan and hugely popular. Cheesecakes include raspberry and mango, blueberry and cranberry, or mango and banana. Cakes include blueberry and banana, chocolate and nut brownie (both gluten-free), chocolate biscuit cake, courgette and lime cake, all come with vegan ice-cream.

Organic Fairtrade tea and coffee, latte, cappuccino, mocha, iced coffee/mocha £1.10-£2.20. Coffee and cake £3. Juices and soya shakes £1.50-2.50, fresh fruit cocktails £2.65, soft drinks £1.20-1.80.

All wine is organic vegan, £2.70-3.15 glass, £14-20 bottle. Organic champagne £20. World beers £1.50-3.40. Westons organic cider £3.60. Spirits and shots from £2.20. Cocktails £6, 2 for 1 Mon-Fri 5-8pm.

1A Cannon Court
Longrow West
Nottingham NG1 6JE
(opposite the main library)

Tel: 0115-955 1013

www.alleycafe.co.uk

Open:
Mon-Tue 11.00-21.00
(food till 20.00),
Wed-Sat 11.00-00.30
(food served till 21.30)
Sun 12.00-17.00
(food till 16.00)

Kids welcome till 8 or 9pm

Outside seating, dogs welcome outside

There is a DJ Thu-Fri evenings with a mellow funky sound

90% of menu vegan or vegan option. Mayonnaise and margarine are vegan and you can ask for vegan cheese.

They cater for special diets and there are wheat-free options

They try to have environmentally sound initiatives using eco products and recycling waste wherever possible

Outside catering

Visa, MC

Mm... Deli
Veggieterranean cafe & deli

610 Mansfield Rd, **Sherwood**, Nottingham, NG5 2FS. Tel: 0115-910 1601
Open: Mon-Sat 9.00-17.00, Sun closed
www.mmdeli.co.uk

Hey hey, a vegetarian Mediterranean delicatessen. Eat-in filled bespoke (design your own) focaccia, panini, sandwiches £2.50-4.50 include breakfast variations, with veggie bacon, roast veg, pine nuts, basil, sun-dried tomato, aubergine, hummus, avocado, jalapeno pepper, olives, spicy tomato, onion chutney, pate, cranberry, real ale chutney, peanut butter, jam etc.

Also salads they make up as you go along £3.50, soups £1.50, sweet and savoury snacks.

Cookies and cakes 80p include vegan, both their own and from Screaming Carrot.

Tea £1, coffee £1.30, they have soya milk. Smoothies £2.50 include coffee delight with free coffee, banana, hazelnut syrup and soya milk. Organic chili hot choc £1.30. Firefly, Fentimans, Purdeys, Bundenbug root beer, Ubuntu cola, juices 60p-£1.50.

They also sell some wholefoods, gluten-free flour, polenta, pasta sauces, chutneys, their own hummus, sauces, jams, olives, spice mixes, stuff that goes in the sandwiches, Willie's cacao vegan chocolate, chai, coffee.

Seating for about 12. Children welcome, little chairs. Dog and bike parking rail outside. MC, Visa.

Cafe Nomad
Vegetarian restaurant

118 Hucknall Road, **Carrington**, Nottingham NG5 1AD. Tel: 0115-969 2239
Open: Wed-Sat 17.00-22.00,
Sun-Tue closed
Booking recommended in the evening
www.cafenomad.co.uk

Laid-back veggie world food cafe with lots of vegan options. They also do take-away. Everything made on the premises.

Typical starters and light meals are from £3, and include soup, or hummus with rosemary crackers. Main courses plus several specials daily include plenty for vegans, £9.50-12.00, such as Moroccan tagine; stuffed nut roast with roast veg and red wine sauce; Moroccan kufta with couscous and salad.

Several desserts £2.75-£3 include for vegans fruit pie, or chocolate pancake layer cake filled with pears cooked in vodka and red wine with chocolate. Coffee and tea £1.50. Bring your own alcohol, free corkage.

Will open lunchtime for parties of 10 or more. Cash or cheque only. Children welcome, no high chairs.

Squeek
Gourmet vegetarian restaurant

23-25 Heathcote Street
Hockley, Nottingham NG1 3AG
Tel: 0115-955 5560
Open: Thu-Sat 18.00-22.00 (last orders),
Sun-Wed closed

Really friendly vegetarian restaurant noted for its imaginative world food that's also popular with meat eaters. Most things on the menu can be made vegan. Menus change all the time depending on what organic veg are in season.

All starters £4.95, such as caponata with grilled smoked tofu. Mains £11.95, such as tandoori roast veg tart with spinach and coriander mash.
Desserts £4.95, such as banoffi pie with chocolate ice cream sundae (and yes, that's vegan!). 2 courses for £15.45 or 3 for £18.50
All wines and beers and most soft drinks are vegan organic.
House wine from £13.95 bottle, £3.70 glass. Children welcome, high chair. Visa, MC.

Sumac Centre
Vegan bar, cafe & campaigns centre

245 Gladstone Street, **Forest Fields**, Nottingham NG7 6HX.
Tel: 0845-458 9595
Bar open Thur-Sat 19.30-23.00
Occasional Sunday brunch 11.00 - 15.00
Cafe food sometimes on Sat early evening and at special events, see website or call
www.veggies.org.uk/sumac

Campaigning resource centre for animals, humans and the environment. Vegan bar Thu-Sat night with occasional vegan food for events, call or check website for events, and sometimes Sunday brunch.

When there is a cafe it's around £3 for a meal made from fresh local produce. A typical meal could be three salads with couscous, salsa, chutney and butterbean curry. It's a very cheap way to get a very healthy meal! When the Sunday breakfasts are available, it costs around £3.50 for a fry-up plus cuppa.

Social club/bar selling a range of local vegan real ales for around £2 a pint, and continental lagers for around £2.20. 'Samosas for Social Change' are available for 50p donation on the bar.

They also host gatherings, meetings and films. The centre can close for this 4 times a year, so check if travelling any distance.

Internet access, library, lots of magazines on green issues to read. Home of Veggies Catering Campaign, volunteers always needed.

World Peace Cafe & Shop
Vegetarian cafe and shop

Akshobya Buddhist Meditation Centre,
Pelham Road, off Sherwood Rise,
Nottingham, NG5 1AP (15 minutes walk from centre)
Tel: 0115-985 7356
Cafe open: Mon-Sun 12.00-15.00
www.akshobya.com

Soup and roll £2, hot filled paninis £3, vegan wraps £2.50, cakes and vegan flapjacks £1-1.50. Fairtrade tea £1, coffee £1.60, they have soya milk. In summer you can eat outside in the peace garden.

The shop sells Buddha statues, books, cards, meditation CD's, Fairtrade handmade gifts.

See website for meditation classese and retreats, including the Friday lunchtime meditation. Monthly Stop the Week evening guided relaxation meditation followed by a lovely 3-course meal, see website.

Nottinghamshire — NORTH

Nottingham – omnivorous
Balti House
Omnivorous Indian restaurant

35 Heathcoat St, **Hockley**, Nottingham
NG1 3AG. Tel: 0115-947 2871
Open: Mon-Thu 17.30–24.00,
Fri-Sat 17.30– 01.30
www.thebaltihouse.com

Traditional curry house in trendy Hockley in he heart of Nottingham, with separate veggie menus on their website. Starters £2.85–3.65, or have a mixed platter for 4+ people for £2.95 each. Over a dozen mains such as veg balti or biryani £6.65–7.35. Breads, rice and side dishes 55p–£2.95. Wine £1.95 glass, from £5.95 bottle. Soft drinks £1.30. Tea and coffee from 1.10. Takeaway cheaper.

Broadway Media Centre
Omnivorous cafe / bar in cinema

14–18 Broad Street, Nottingham NG1 3AL
Tel: 0151-952 6611
Open: Mon-Fri 9.00–23.00,
Sat 11.00–23.00, Sun 12.00–22.30
www.broadway.org.uk

The café within the Broadway cinema serves drinks, snacks and light meals such as mixed mezze, pizza, tapas. Meals are typically around £6.95. There's always a vegan option, such as stir-fry with tofu and sesame noodles. Vegan beers around £3, vegan wines marked on the menu, juices around £2. Locals recommend ordering food downstairs then sitting in the nicer Mezz Bar upstairs. Meal and film combo £12.45, concessions £10.45. Monday night curry, film and beer £13.45.
Opposite is Screen Room, the world's smallest cinema with just 21 seats, which has vegan carrot cake and chocolate cake. Best to reserve!

Encounters
Omnivorous European restaurant

59 Mansfield Road, Nottingham NG1 3FH
Tel: 0115-947 6841
Open: Tue-Fri 12.00–14.00,
Tue-Sat 18.30–22.00, Sun-Mon closed
Bookings outside of these times available
www.encountersrestaurant.co.uk

They have a vegetarian and vegan menu and everything is made to order, mains are £6.50–7.95 such as vegetable chilli, stir-fry veg with pineapple and cashews, peppers stuffed with korma style mild curried veg, Mediterranean veg bake, vegetable Stroganoff, vegetable strudel, vegetarian haggis (kidney beans, lentil, mixed veg and nuts, oatmeal, onions and seasoning). All meals served with rice, veg and potatoes or chips. Desserts £3.95 include a vegan batter for banana fritters etc. House wine £3.50 glass, £11.50 litre, cheapest bottle £9.95. Gay-friendly. Visa, MC.

Kayal
Omnivorous South Indian restaurant

8 Broad Street, Nottingham, NG1 3AL
Tel: 0115-941 4733
Open: Mon-Fri 12.00–15.00, 18.00–23.00,
Sat & BH 12.00–23.00, Sun 12.00–22.00
www.kayalrestaurant.com

Keralan cuisine highly recommended by local vegans. Their speciality is Sadya (thali) served as 3 courses. Express lunch stuffed aubergine with curry sauce, lemon rice and salad £4.95, Business lunch £5.95 three curries, side, rise and dosa. Wine from £3.25–4.25 glass, £11.95 bottle. Juices £1.75–3.25. Tea and herb tea £1.50, coffee from £1.50.

Langtong Thai

Omnivorous Thai restaurant

32 Lower Parliament Street, Nottingham
NG1 3DA. Tel: 0115-924 3011
Open: Mon-Sat 18.00-23.00, Sun 18.00-22.00. Last order 1 hour before closing.
www.lantongthairestaurant.com

The only onivorous restaurant in Nottingham to have a separate full vegan menu, all of which is authentic and delicious. For those sick of tofu, Langtong also offers mock duck and mock chicken as a substitute. Very good value and friendly. Starters £3.50-4.95, or four mixed for £11. Mains £6.50-8.50. Rice £2. 9-dish set menu for 2+ £14.95 each includes coffee.

The Palm Tree

Omnivorous Lebanese restaurant

7/11 Arkwright Street, Nottingham NG2 2JR
(next to train station)
Tel. 0115 986 97 97
Open: Every day 18.00 – 23.00
ww.palmtreerestaurant.com

This is one of the few places in Nottingham where you can get decent vegetarian food on a Sunday, though it's recommended any day of the week. Starters cost £4-5, and about two thirds of them are vegetarian, including Moutabal grilled aubergines, and falafel. Mains have 3 veggie options £8 or £10. Great for couples or large groups, especially if you order a big array of starters and share. No dairy-free desserts. Licensed. Belly dancers perform on Saturdays. House wine £8.95 bottle. Coffee £1.50.

Red Hot World, Nottingham

Omnivorous buffet restaurant & bar

38-46 Goosegate, **Hockley** NG1 1FF
Tel: 0115-958 9899
Open: daily Mon-Sat 12.00-16.45, 18-22.30 (Fri-Sat 23.00);
Sun 12.30-17.00, 18.00-21.00
www.redhot-worldbuffet.com

Eat as much as you like buffet with many vegetarian options. Lunch Mon-Sat £6.99, Sun £8.99. Dinner Mon-Thu £9.99, Fri £11.99, Sun £13.99. Under-10 half price. Gigantic buffet with Chinese, Indian, Italian, Mexican, Thai, salad and desserts, though vegans can only finish with fruit salad.
Wine from £11.95 bottle, £2.95 glass. Cocktails £4.45-5.20, pitcher £12.95-14.95, mocktails £2.75. Spirits £1.95-2.50. Beers £2.60-4.95 for a 660ml Cobra. Soft drinks from £1.50. Coffee and tea £1.60. Student 15% discount Sun-Thu.

Royal Thai

Omnivorous Thai restaurant

189 Mansfield Road, Nottingham NG1 3FS
Tel: 0115-948 3001
Open: Mon-Sat 12-14.30, 17.30-22.30, Sun closed. www.royalthairestaurant.co.uk

Thai restaurant popular with local vegans. 12 main courses on vegetarian menu, 7 suitable for vegans, around £6. Set lunch £6.95, set dinners £15-18. Wine £2.50 small glass, £10.95 bottle. Thai beer £2.50. Soft drinks £1.50. Tea and coffee £1.20. 20% off take-away.

Thailand No.1
Omnivorous Thai restaurant

16 Carlton St, Hockley, Nottingham NG1 1NN. Tel: 0115-958 2222
Open: Mon-Sat 12-14.30, 18-23.00; Sun 12.00-15.00, 18.00-22.30
nottingham.thailandnumber1.co.uk

Upmarket Thai with separate vegetarian menu most of which is vegan. 2-course lunch £7.50. Starters £4.95, 10 mains £7.95. Wine £2.25 small glass, £4.50 large, £11.50 bottle. Thai beer £2.75. Soft drinks £1.50, juices £1.75, tea and coffee £1.65. 10% off take-away. Previously Siam Thani at this address.

Tamatanga
Omnivorous Indian restaurant

The Cornerhouse, Trinity Square, Nottingham NG1 4DB
Tel: 0115-958 4848
Open: Mon-Sat 12.00-23.00, Sun 12-22.00
www.tamatanga.com

Recommended by a local vegan as like an Indian version of Wagamama though not a huge number of veggie dishes. Curry bowl with rice or naan £7.75, vegans watch out for paneer cheese inserted at every opportunity. Thali £10.95-12.95 with one or two curries of your choice. Weekday £6 before 6pm meal deal with soft drink. Wine from £3.65-4.65 glass, £14.95 bottle. Beer from £2.95. Juices and soft drinks £1.95.

Victoria Hotel
Omnivorous pub-restaurant

Dovecote Lane, **Beeston**, Nottingham NG9 1JG. Tel 0115-925 4049
Open: Mon-Sat 10.30-23.00, Sun 12.00-23.00; Food Wed-Sat 12.00-21.30, Sun-Tue 12.00-20.45; no U-18s after 20.00
www.victoriabeeston.co.uk

40% vegetarian menu. 7 or 8 vegetarian dishes with their own half of the menu, including hummus, olives and warm pitta with salad £4.95; spicy veg and bean chilli burritos £8.95; roast sweet peppers stuffed with Mediterranean veg couscous £8.50; Goan veg curry £8.95. Beer monster ale heaven with 12 to 14 at any time, three regular ones from £2.50 a pint listed on the website, and half a dozen more that change frequently. House wine starts at £1.75-4.10 glass, £12 bottle.

No in your face mobiles or laptops inside – this is a pub not an office. Under-18 till 8pm, no high chairs. Dogs in bar and outside tables. No smoking throughout. MC, Visa, cashback.

Wagamama
Omnivorous Japanese Restaurant

The Cornerhouse, Burton Street, Nottingham NG1 4DB
Tel: 0115 924 1797
Open: Mon-Sat 12.00-23.00, Sun 12.30-22.00
www.wagamama.com

See Manchester entry for menu

Nottingham - shops
The Health Store
Health food shop

29-31 Central Avenue, **West Bridgford**, Nottingham NG2 5GQ
Tel: 0115-981 4080
Open: Mon-Sat 8.45-17.30, Sun closed

Fridge and freezer with vegan cheeses, meat substitutes, Swedish Glace. Gluten-free bread and other foods.
Bodycare includes Jason, Dr Hauschka, Faith In Nature, Avalon, Weleda, Dead Sea Magik, Natracare. Baby bodycare and Kee-ka organic clothes.
Ecover refills and the new.
Wide range of supplements including Solgar and Viridian. Bach remedies, Weleda homeopathy, essential oils. Homebrew kits. Complementary therapies room being installed as we go to press.
5% discount for senior citizens Thursday.

Natural Food Company
Vegetarian wholefood shop

37a Mansfield Road, Nottingham NG1 3FB
Tel: 0115-955 9914
Open: Mon-Fri 9.00-18.00, Sat 9.00-17.30, Sun closed

Spelt and gluten-free bread. Fridge and freezer with vegan cheese, meat substitutes, hummus, pies, pasties, wraps, Swedish Glace, Tofutti, Booja Booja. Vegan chocolate by Plamil, Montezuma, Booja Booja.
Bodycare by Faith In Nature and Jason in particular, Natracare, Weleda and Earth Friendly baby.
Supplements by Nature's Aid, Vogel. Cleaning by BioD, Ecover and refills.
MC, Visa over £5.

Roots Natural Foods
Wholefood & Organic shop

526 Mansfield Road, **Sherwood**, Nottingham NG5 2FR. Tel: 0115-960 9014
Open: Mon-Fri 9.00-18.00 (Wed 18.45), Sat 9.00-17.00, Sun closed
Website on the way

Small, packed shop. Organic fruit and veg, bread. Fridge and freezer with rolls, pies, crumbles, vegan cheeses and yogurts, Veggies burgers and sosages, hummus, Swedish Glace, Booja Booja. Very good range of chocolate including Montezuma and Booja Booja.
Bodycare by Jason, Weleda, Faith In Nature, Natracare, Weleda Baby.
Supplements by Solgar, Lamberts and Higher Nature, only the best as the owner is a qualified nutritionist and herbalist and sells their own tinctures, teas, creams, bath mixes, hair rinses practitioners, loose herbs, available for consultation.
Cleaning by BioD, Ecover. MC, Visa.

Rosemary's
Health food shop

6 Lincoln St., Nottingham NG1 3DJ (off Clumber Street)
Tel: 0115-950 5072
Open: Mon-Sat 9.00-17.30, Sun 11-.16.00
www.rosemaryshealthfoods.co.uk

The most central health food shop, and also the largest and cheapest in Nottingham. Lots of vegan and organic foods. Wholefoods include pick and mix. Fridges with pasties, minipies, hummus, vegan cheeses and yogurts, lots of tofu, sprouts. Vegan chocolate by Montezuma, Plamil, Divine, Booja Booja. Bodycare by Jason, Faith In Nature, Bentley, Avalon, Green People and they can order anything you need. Supplements by Solgar, Viridian, Terra Nova, Quest, Nature's Aid, Vogel, own brand,

Natracare. Sports nutrition. Ecover cleaning. MC, Visa, Amex. 15% discount when you buy two of any identical item. Also in Worcester and Wolverhampton.

Screaming Carrot

Vegan bakery and wholefood shop

42 Foxhall Road, **Forest Fields**, Nottingham NG7 6LJ. Tel: 0115-910 3013
Open: Mon-Fri 08.00-17.30 (Wed 18.00), Sat 10.00-16.00, Sun & bank holiday closed
www.screamingcarrot.co.uk

Entirely vegan bakery stocking a range of health foods and snacks. They have organic bread, vegetable boxes, chocolate, frozen foods, soya milk, etc. Take-away pasties, wraps and cakes range from 50p to £2. The selection on offer is very variable, as some days the counter is bursting with choice and other days it's almost empty. Their Eccles cake is especially recommended.

Caterer

Veggies Catering Campaign

Vegan catering for any event

www.veggies.org.uk

Workers' co-operative based at the Sumac Centre (above), backed by a team of volunteers, providing vegan food at local and national events including campaign rallies, community festivals, family celebrations and green gatherings. Vegan buffets for meetings, birthdays and weddings.
Also speakers for talks at schools, info stalls and occasional free vegan food give-aways in Nottingham City Centre in conjunction with Nottingham Animal Rights.

Nottinghamshire Chain Stores

Holland & Barrett

Health food shop

95c **Victoria Centre, Nottingham** NG1 3QE
Tel: 0115-958 0753
Open: Mon-Sat 9.00-17.30, Sat 9.00-18.30, Sun 10.30-16.30

Unit 37 Listergate, **Broadmarsh Centre, Nottingham** NG1 7LE..Tel: 0115-941 3163.
Open: Mon-Sat 9-17.30, Sun 10.30-16.30

Unit 2, Co-op Development, High Rd, **Beeston** NG9 2JP. Tel: 0115 922 4302
Open: Mon-Sat 9-17.30, Sun 10.30-16.30

7 Carolgate, **East Retford** DN22 6BZ
Tel: 01777-711963
Mon-Sat 9.00-17.30, Sun closed

36 High Street, **Hucknall** NG15 7HQ
Tel: 0115 -9638683
Mon-Sat 9.00-17.30, Sun closed

63-65 High Street, **Long Eaton**, Nottingham NG10 1HZ. Tel: 0115-9725561
Mon-Sat 9.00-17.30, Sun closed

Unit 55, Four Seasons Centre, **Mansfield** NG18 1SX. Tel: 01623-634543
Open: Mon-Sat 9-17.30, Sun 10.30-16.30

1 St. Marks Place, **Newark** NG24 1XS
Tel: 01636-605025
Open: Mon-Sat 9.00-17.30, Sun closed

617 Mansfield Road, **Sherwood** NG5 2PW
Tel: 0115-962 4527
Open: Mon-Sat 9.00-17.30

4 The Idle Wells Shopping Centre, **Sutton in Ashfield** NG17 1BJ. Tel: 01623-515842
Open: Mon-Sat 9.00-17.30, Sun closed

17 Bridge Street, **Worksop** S80 1DP
Tel: 01909-476185
Open: Mon-Sat 9.00-17.30, Sun closed

Local Groups
Nottingham Animal Rights
Local campaigning group

Based at the Sumac Centre (above)
www.veggies.org.uk/nar
Email: nar@veggies.org.uk
Tel: 0845 458 9595

Co-ordinate the activities of many of the groups and individuals campaigning for animal rights and welfare in Nottingham. Monthly meetings also act as a social gathering.

On Saturdays, whenever not at another event, they aim to hold a street information stall, just down from St Peters Church, opposite Marks and Spencer or near the Council House on the Old Market Square.

East Midlands Vegan Festival
Annual vegan festival

www.veggies.org.uk/veganfestival

A regional vegan festival is held each December at the Council House, Old Market Square, Nottingham, though in 2010 the Council decided it was too busy and should move to a new location. Organised by Veggies. Check website for latest.

Vegan Nottingham Guide
Online guide

www.vegan-nottingham.co.uk
twitter.com/VeganNottingham

One of the best local guide sites ever, packed with all the restaurants, cafes and shops. Particularly useful is the list of places that have closed down.

NORTH — Nottinghamshire

VEGGIES
CATERING CAMPAIGN
245 Gladstone Street, Nottingham NG7 6HX
0845 458 9595 email: info@veggies.org.uk
www.veggies.org.uk

Providing catering services, using no animal ingredients whatsoever, and giving practical suppport, to the animal rights movement.

Resources for local groups and individuals, campaigning for human and animal rights, on environmental issues, and for peace, co-operation and social justice worldwide.

CATERERS TO THE SOCIAL JUSTICE MOVEMENT

Gosforth	**137**
Heaton	**137**
NEWCASTLE UPON TYNE	**140**
Whitley Bay	**144**
Chain stores	**145**
Local groups	**145**
Caterer	**145**

Tyne and Wear

Gosforth

Pizza Express, Gosforth
Omnivorous pizza restaurant

125 High Street, Gosforth NE3 1NA
Tel: 0191 285 9799
Open: Sun-Thu 11.30-22.30,
Fri - Sat 10.30-23.00

Happy to make vegan pizzas without cheese. Full disabled access. See Cheshire for more details.

World Peace Shop
Wholefood shop in meditation centre

Compassion Centre, 2 Station Road, South Gosforth, Newcastle Upon Tyne NE3 1QD
Tel: 0191-284 3501
Open: Mon-Fri 10.00-18.00,
Sat 11.00-17.00, Sun closed
www.meditation-newcastle.org

Range of staples such as oats, quinoa, rice, various pulses and beans. They order from Suma wholesalers and are happy to take personal orders.
Organic whole foods and Fairtraded gifts. Organic chocolate, healthy snacks, cards, little treasures and gifts from around the world such as bags, jewellery and ornaments.
Organic baby foods and products.
Ecover cleaning products and refills.
Drop-off point for North East Organic Growers veg box scheme weekly and fortnightly deliveries. For further information about the scheme contact Compassion Centre.
If you're interested in meditation and sprirtual practice they sell a range of Buddhist products such as books, statues, pictures postcards and guided meditation CD's.
Compassion Centre is a place where anyone can learn to meditate, discover how to apply Buddha's teachings to solve their daily problems, and find lasting peace and happiness. Compassion Centre is part of the New Kadampa Tradition - International Kadampa Buddhist Union.
Also classes in Whickham, Wylam, Whitley Bay and Sunderland.

Heaton

Jack Sprats
Vegetarian cafe & take-away

413 Chillingham Rd, Heaton, Newcastle upon Tyne. NE6 5QU. (end of the road, near the coast road) Tel: 0191-265 7708
Open: Mon-Fri 11.00-21.00,
Sat-Sun 10.00-22.00
Bus 62 or 63 from Newcastle
www.jacksprats.co.uk

Relaxed, spacious cafe with comfy chairs and couches, local art and photos on the walls. The extensive menu has many vegan and wheat-free options and everything is made from scratch. Fairtrade where possible.
The all-day breakfasts are fantastic and huge. £4.95 gets you tomatoes, wholemeal toast, mushrooms, baked beans, vegan sausages, fried potatoes, £5.95 large, add £1 for wheat-free bread (bread is quite expensive). Or have veggie rashers, sausage sandwich. 2 or 3 soups £3-4 with a big wedge of bread. Wraps, sandwiches, panini, £4.95 served with 2 salads and tortilla chips (£2.50 take out).
Main meals £5-£8.95 include curries,

salads, toad in the hole with vegan Yorkshire pudding, vegan fish and chips, fajitas. Two specials daily £8.95, normally vegan and wheat-free, such as tofu surprise, stir-fry, Harvest pie. Sunday nut roast, toad in the hole £8.95. Evening menu has a few more dishes on it at the same prices. They do special offers such as three courses for £10.

Desserts £2.50-3.50 include plenty of vegan and wheat-free such as Bakewell tart, chocolate fudge cake, coffee fudge cake, white chocolate cake, cheesecake, crumble, truffles.

Pot of tea £1.50, mug of coffee, latte etc £2-2.50. Big smoothies and juices £3.50. Bring your own alcohol, £1 corkage charge. Off-licence nearby.

Outside seating. Wifi. Children very welcome, high chairs, they have toys. Computer. MC, Visa, and cashpoint. Outside catering.

Butterfly Cabinet

Omnivorous cafe

200 Heaton Road, Heaton, Newcastle upon Tyne NE6 5HP (bus number 1, 62 or 63 from town)
Tel: 0191-265 9920
Open: Mon-Sat 9.00-17.00, Sun 10-16.30, planning to open evenings mid 2010
www.butterflycabinet.com and on Facebook

Formerly Belle & Herbs cafe and still with the same staff. The head chef is Greek so there are lots of healthy Mediterranean veggie options. Everything is made in house, even the breads. A cut above a greasy spoon and therefore more expensive but massive portions. It's quite small and packed at weekends. Sofas, and local artists' work on the walls, more always welcome.

All-day cooked veggie breakfasts £5 made to order so ask for what you want. Triple decker toasted club sandwiches and panini £5.50, such as avocado with roast red peppers marinated in oregano olive oil, salsa, coriander and sunblushed tomatoes, served with side salads.

Main course soup £4.50 such as roast butternut squash with olive oil to make it creamy with rustic bread. Main course salads £6.50 can be customized for vegans. Large beanburger £6.50 comes with dipping sauce and portion of chips. Daily specials £7 such as stuffed peppers with white bean stew.

Homemade cakes and desserts are not vegan, but there is a fruit bowl.

Fruit smoothies £3 can be with soya milk. Tea £1.70, coffee £1.90.

Kids welcome, high chairs. Newly licensed for alcohol. MC, Visa. Live music, cinema licence and longer hours on the way.

Khan's Restaurant

Omnivorous Indian restaurant

178 Heaton Rd, Newcastle upon Tyne NE6 5HP (next door to Sky Apple)
Tel: 0191-276 0400
Open: Mon-Sun 17.00-22.30
www.khans-restaurant.co.uk

Recommended to us by Jack Sprats. Starters £2.90 such as mushroom or veg pakora, samosa, bhaji. Veg or mushroom dansak, korma, masala, balti, Punjabi or jalfrezi £6.50, made to order so they can adjust strength. Veg curry £5.90. 9 non-cheese mains £5.90 such as mixed veg, dal, sag or gobi aloo, brinjal. 14 side dishes £3.50 include chana bhaji (chick peas). Veg biryani £7.90. 12 kinds of rice from plain £2.30. nut or veg pilau £2.80, to special pilau £3.90. Chips £1.50. Lots of nan and paratha £2.30-2.80.

Bring your own alcohol, which is a big selling point with local students. Soft drinks £1. Tea, coffee £1.80. Parties and outside catering. Children welcome, high chair. MC Visa

The Sky Apple

Vegetarian cafe, in the style of a coffee bar, cloudscape walls and crystal chandeliers. Lots of vegan options as well as home-made cakes. Wednesday to Saturday evenings from 6pm it transforms into a popular vegetarian restaurant with a menu that changes every 6 weeks. Booking advised. Candles on the tables in the evening. Now that the chef has become the manager, they are trying new opening hours, with breakfast and afternoon cream teas every day, plus more take-aways, but closed on Sundays rather than Mondays.

Full cooked breakfast till 12.30 £4.90 includes rashers, sausages, tomatoes, mushrooms, toast, hash browns. Also now potato pancakes, muffin toastie, toast and spreads, vegan cereal crunch with (soya) milk, fresh fruit, toasted nuts and a dollop of soya yogurt. Half size portions for kids.

Daytime: Soup of the day £3. Sandwiches with salad £4.80. Mains £5.50-7.50 include spinach and chickpea masala, mixed mezze, tortillas, burritos, pasta, vegeburger, mixed salad. Felafel salad £5. Proper chips £2.20. Chip butty £3.50 with curry gravy, salsa or garlic mayo. Olives £1.90.
Brownies £1.50 and mostly vegan cakes around £2 such as carrot cake.

International evening menu from all over the world changes every 6 weeks and has 4-5 starters £3.90-4.80 such as soup, green tea sushi, Chinese dim sum with spring rolls and dumplings, Thai baked aubergine, or crispy pancakes. 5 mains around £8-9 such as Asian sweetcorn and veg pancakes with Thai coconut and lime sauce; yam and pepper stew; wild mushroom pie, green risotto cakes; stir-fried Thai noodles.
Desserts (always one vegan) £4.60 such as summer pudding, or brandy cherry choc steamed pudding, with vegan ice-cream.

Organic Fentimans drinks £2.20, cans £2. Coffee, cappuccino, latte £1.50-2, they have soya milk.

Heaton

Vegetarian cafe and evening restaurant

182 Heaton Road, Heaton, Newcastle-upon-Tyne
NE6 5HP

Tel: 0191-209 2571

Metro: Chillingham Rd or Byker
Number 1 bus from centre, also bus 16 or 18

Menus at www.skyapple.co.uk

Open:
Mon-Sat 10.00-16.30;
Wed-Sat evening menu 18.00-22.00 (last orders);
Sun closed

BYO alcohol evening, £1.50 per person, off licence 2 doors down

Children welcome, high chairs

Evening booking advised

No credit cards

Outside buffet catering

NORTH — Tyne and Wear

Heaton
The Honey Tree
Omnivorous organic food store

68 Heaton Road, Newcastle upon Tyne NE6 5HL Tel: 0191-240 2589
Open: Mon-Sat 10.00-17.00, Sun closed
www.thehoneytree.org

Greengrocer and organic farm shop with the largest range of organic food in the region. It's mostly veggie but they do sell organic meat. Seasonal fruit and veg from local organic farms. They make organic sandwiches in the shop, muffins, cakes including vegan. Full range of wholefoods from Suma. Vegan cheeses, sausages and meat substitutes including Beanies, cream, yogurt, tofu. Bodycare. Essential oils. Baby products and environmentally-friendly disposal bags. Women's things.

The Honey Tree recommends a couple of places in the student suburb of Heaton: **The Grocers** on Chillingham (locally known as Chilli) Road, which is really good for both chilled and non chilled vegan food, has fresh fruit & veg too. And in the **Grainger Market** there is a wholefood stall Mon-Sat.

Newcastle upon Tyne
Gekko, Newcastle
Omnivorous international buffet

The Gate, Newgate St, Newcastle NE1 5TG
Tel: 0191-260 5005
Open: Mon-Sat 12.00-22.00, Sun 12-21.00
www.lovegekko.com/newcastle.html

Huge international buffet with plenty of vegetarian food. 12.00-16.30 £6.99, 16.30-18.30 £9.99, 18.30 onwards £12.99. Sunday £9.99 all day. Under-10 £2.99 anytime.

8+ Indian veggie dishes include kormas, curries, dal, bhajias; Chinese spring rolls and samosas, mixed veg stir-fry, chow mein, garlic mushrooms; Thai/Malaysian curry, stir-fry aubergine, pineapple fried rice, Oriental potatoes, Asian pumpkin curry, hot Thai red veg curry; pizzas cooked to order and pastas; Mexican nachos, hot 3-bean chilli, corn on the cob; Japanese sushi.
Selection of desserts include vegan fruit fritters, fruit salads, dairy-free trifle.
Wine £2.50 glass, £7 bottle. £2.30 for refillable soft drinks. Coffee £1 to up £5 for Irish coffee, no soya milk. High chairs. Visa, MC. Also in Brighton. Previously called Wokmania.

Pizza Express, Newcastle
Omnivorous pizza restaurant

10 Dean Street, Newcastle NE1 1PG
Tel: 0191-221 0120
Open: Sun-Thu 11.30-22.30,
Fri-Sat 11.30am -23.30
www.pizzaexpress.co.uk

A beautiful, listed, building in the heart of the city, close to the quay side underneath the Tyne Bridge. Elegantly presented, offering a welcoming atmosphere for families and private room for large bookings or business meetings. See Cheshire for menu.

Bob Trollop's Pub

100% vegetarian pub with a terrific British and international veggie food menu and good value. Everything is home-made and the many vegan and vegan-option dishes are marked on the menu.

Starters £2.50-3.50 include soup of the day with warm crusty bread, pan fried garlic mushrooms, bruschetta, jacket wedges with salsa, baked mushrooms.

All day brunch £4.95 or mega £5.95 include sausage, veggieburger, mushrooms, beans, tomato and hash browns. Bean & cashewnut or lentil & vegetable burger £3.50 with fries and salad. Create your own lite bite tortilla wrap, jacket potato or toasted panini with your choice of filling such as salsa and jalapenos £3.25. Daily specials starting autumn 2010.

10 main courses, half vegan, £3.95-4.75 include chilli non carne with rice and tortilla chips, chilli burrito, vegetable nut roast with potatoes and veg, curry with rice or chips, vegetable hot pot with warm crusty baguette, stuffed peppers with spicy couscous and salad. Extra fries, garlic bread, wedges £1.25-1.50.

Desserts £1.95 such as apple crumble or selection of vegan ice-creams.

Under-14 kids' meals £2.75 are all vegan such as chilli non carne, mini brunch, veg curry, bangers and mash, lasagne, and come with a soft drink and one scoop of ice-cream.

Tea, herb teas, filter coffee, mug of hot chocolate all 95p. Soya milk available.

House wine £8 per bottle, glass from £2.50. All bottles, pints and cocktails £2.25 except Fri-Sat after 20.00.

Newcastle-upon-Tyne

Vegetarian pub

32-40 Sandhill
Quayside
Newcastle
Tyne & Wear NE1 3JF

Tel: 0191-261 1037

Directions: right by Tyne Bridge and opposite the Guildhall

Pub open:
Mon-Sun 11-24.00 or later.
Food:
Mon-Thu 12-19.00, or later if prebooked;
Fri-Sat 11-19.00
Sun 12.00-18.00.

Children having a meal welcome until 7.30pm, Sun 6.30pm

Vegan and vegan-option dishes are marked on the menu and they have a magic vegan button on the till to remind the chefs not to put butter in your sandwich or cheese on your burrito etc.

Visa, MC, Switch, Amex and they do cashback if you spend over £5, up to £50

The local group VegNE meet here: www.vegne.co.uk

Function room available with buffets catered to meet your needs. Please phone the manager.

Monday is open mic night
Tuesday Irish folk till 1am

Scrumpy Willow and the Singing Kettle

Omnivorous organic restaurant

89 Clayton Street Newcastle NE1 5PZ
Tel: 0191-221 2323
Open: Mon-Sat 10.00-21.00 (last orders),
Sun 11.00-16.00
scrumpywillowandthesingingkettle.co.uk

Over 90% organic, and they have the best labelled online menu we've seen in an omnivorous restaurant, with bright green v, blue vg and red g next to veggie, vegan and gluten-free dishes. And they have vegan cake!

Brunch available until 5pm has vegan porridge £2.50, smoothies £2.50, and full vegan breakfast £5 with potato cake, puy lentils, tomato, mushrooms, spincah baked beans and toast.

Sandwiches £2.20-4.25 made to order until 5pm, such as hummus with salad, pinenuts and chutney ; falafels with red cabbage salad; dahl, spinach and artichoke.

Soup £3.75. Choice of 3 mezze with bread and crudites £4.95 small (1 person), £7.95 large (2-3 people) include Indian, Mediterranean and vegan fondue dishes; add grain of the day £2.50 to make a light meal. Mains £4.95-6.95 such as chickpea dish of the day with greens and pitta; dahl with broccoli, pine nuts, toasted coconut and bread.

Specials after 6pm £6.95-9.95 such as ginger, orange and veg medley with sesame rice and pak choi dumplings.

Hooray an omnivorous place that has proper vegan desserts and not a boring fruit salad or sorbet in sight: organic homemade cakes £2.50, cookies £1, elderflower jelly with mixed berries topped with rosehip syrup and Swedish Glace ice-cream £3.50, house crumble with Swedish Glace £3.50. SWSK we love you.

They even label which booze is vegan including organic ales £3.65 such as Ginger Pale Ale, Studley Stout and Cragg Vale Bitter; Oafarm cider. £6.50 litre; Sedlescombe organic wine £14 bottle, £3.60 glass.

Smoothies £2.50. Cold drinks £1.75 such as dandelion & burdock, grape juice.

Last sitting 8pm. They regularly exhibit and sell arts and crafts. Cakes for special occasions. You can hire the cafe. Cash or cheque, no cards.

Wagamama, Newcastle

Omnivorous Japanese restaurant

6 Eldon Square, Newcastle NE1 6JG
(500m from Newcastle United ground)
Tel: 0191-233 0663
Open: Sun-Wed 12.00-22.00,
Thu-Sat 12.00-23.00
www.wagamama.com

See Manchester for menu or online. Lift, disabled toilets.

Newcastle upon Tyne shops

Almonds & Raisins

Health food shop

2 Upper Princess Square, Newcastle NE1 8ER (behind the new library)
Tel: 0191-261 5959
Open: Mon-Sat 8.30-17.00, Sun closed

An organic and wholefood supermarket with all the usual health foods, flapjacks, supplements, vitamins, bodycare and household products.

Bread and savouries from Mistletoe Bakery in Jesmond. They can warm up vegan pasties and rolls. Vegan chocolate cake 99p slice, or buy a whole cake. Vegan chocolate includes Organica and Plamil.

3 fridges and freezer with drinks, lots of tofu, spreads, Redwood Cheatin,

Vegideli sausages and burgers, rashers, Tofutti vegan cheese, Bute Island Sheese, tempeh, Tofutti cones and Swedish Glace,
Bodycare by Faith in Nature, Avalon, Weleda, Green People, Jason, Natracare. Supplements include Solgar, Quest, Higher Nature, FSC, Vogel. Small range of homeopathy and remedies.
Ecover with hand soap refills, BioD, Earth Friendly.
Kindred Spirit, The Vegan and other magazines. A few gifts. MC, Visa over £5. They can order things in for you.

Alternative Stores

Vegan wholefood shop & lots more

Brunswick Industrial Estate, Wideopen, Newcastle upon Tyne NE13 7BA (bus 45 from city centre or from Regent Centre metro station)
Tel 0191-236 8519
Open: Wed-Thu 10.30-16.00, can be later on request; Fri 10.30-16.00;
Sat by appointment only;
Sun-Tue closed, they may open up specially if you are desperate!
www.alternativestores.com

After many requests from customers, this vegan mail order company has opened a vegan shop, and what a shop it is. They sell everything they do on the website including wholefoods and health foods, vegetarian shoes, ethical gifts, green products, sosmix to make your own burgers, frozen and chilled food, health and beauty.

Fridge with vegan cheeses, spreads, sausages, burgers. Freezer with sausages, mince, fishless fingers, lots of Redwood and Fry's, Auntie Jees curries, Great Nineveh curries, Get Real Tuscan style ready meal bakes, Linda McCartney, Swedish Glace, Smooze coconut and other flavour vegan ices.

St Dalfour vegan tinned ready meals such as bean salad, couscous and raisins, 3-bean mix. Huge range of vegan chocolate including Plamil, Organica, Blake's, Cocoa Loco, Booja Booja, Montezuma, Divine, Dove Farm organic bars. Vegan sweets such as Whizzers, Biona, cola and pineapple chews.

Big range of health and beauty include Faith In Nature, Ecoleaf, Suma, Organic Blue, Weleda, Lavera, Green People, Beauty Without Cruelty, Suncote, Bentley Organics, Natracare. Baby stuff includes Maltex and Earth Friendly. Cleaning products from BioD, Ecoleaf, Earth Friendly with the big 5 litre packs.

Supplemements include the full range of Veganicity, Vega, Nature's Own, Higher Nature, Viridian, Bio-Health, Essential Care. Homeopathy and remedies. Essential oils. They can refer you to local practitioners.

Lots of eco and recycled household products like sponges, scourers, long life lightbulbs, toilet fresheners, Magnaball. Vegetable oil candles.

400 different styles of vegetarian shoes from safety boots to ballet and dance shoes (which they are the only place in the UK to do) and they do mail order too.

Animal rights and recipe books, magazines. MC, Visa.

Fenwick's Food Hall
Department store

Ground floor, Fenwick Dept Store, 39 Northumberland Street, Newcastle upon Tyne NE99 1AR. Tel: 0191-232 5100
Open: Mon-Sat 9.00-18.00, Thu till 20.00, Sun 11.00-17.00 (from 10.30 for browsing)
www.fenwick.co.uk

In the chilled section near the checkouts of the ground floor food hall of this department store are Redwoods vegan cheeses including melting Cheezely, seitan slices, Alpro soya yogurt, and Booja Booja non-dairy ice-cream. The own brand ciabatta is also vegan.
The Yo! sushi bar can make you a vegan sushi takeaway, ask for veggie box no tamago and crunchy tofu salad.

Newcastle has a large Asian community and there are a few Chinese and Pakistani supermarkets which are excellent for vegan basics. Particularly in the NE1 centre and NE4 Fenham areas.

Panni's cafe on High Bridge in the city centre also does some nice vegan food if you ask them to tweak the ingredients.
And **Solomon's Dharbar** in Fenham will do special vegan requests if you ask nicely. It's at the west end of Newcastle, a mile from the centre, and the area has an Asian/Chinese community and big student population.

Whitley Bay
The Barnacle
Omnivorous cafe & bistro

7-8 Lower Promenade, Whitley Bay NE26 1AN (near North Shields)
Tel: 0191-253 3876
Open: Mon-Sat 10.00-21.30, Sun 10-17.00 (hours subject to change)

Seaside place that is a cafe by day and bistro by night, previously called Down Under which specialised in veggie food, and the new owner promises two veggie starters and mains such as wild mushroom risotto £9.95.

Chain stores
Holland & Barrett
Health food shop

5 Cameron Walk, Metro Centre, **Gateshead** NE11 9YR. Tel: 0191-460 2546
Open: Mon-Fri 10.00-21.00,
Open: Sat 9.00-19.00, Sun 11-17.00

---

11 Bigg Market, **Newcastle** NE1 1UN
Tel: 0191-232 7540
Open: Mon-Sat 9.00-17.30, Sun 11-17.00

Unit E3 Blackettbridge, **Eldon Square** Shopping Centre, Newcastle NE1 7XJ
Tel: 0191-261 4259. Open: Mon-Sat 9.00-18.00, Thu -20.00, Sun 11-17.00

Unit 17, 1 Bedford Way, The Beacon Shopping Centre, **North Shields** NE29 6RX
Tel: 0191-296 0244
Open: Mon-Sat 9.00-17.30, Sun 11-16.00

---

4 Denmark Centre, Fowler Street
South Shields NE33 2LR
Tel: 0191-455 9724
Open: Mon-Sat 9.00-17.30, Sun closed

---

21 Blandford Street, **Sunderland** SR1 3JP
Tel: 0191-565 6249
Open: Mon-Sat 9-17.30, Sun 10.30-16.30

---

27 Albany Mail, **Washington** NE38 7SA
Tel: 0191-417 8451
Open: Mon-Sat 9-17.30, Sun 10.00-16.00

287-289 Whitley Rd, **Whitley Bay** NE26 2FN
Tel: 0191-251 6107
Open: Mon-Sat 9-17.30, Sun 10.30-16.30

Local Groups
Veg NE
Local vegetarian & vegan group

www.vegne.co.uk
Contact Mark 079410 79 999

Active social group affiliated to the Vegetarian Society, based in Newcastle with members from County Durham, Northumberland and Tyne & Wear. They meet regularly at Bob Trollops and Jack Sprats. Mainly a social group but also puts on exhibitions and stalls.
They run a great value annual week long North East Vegan Gathering in April school holidays in Morpeth, Northumberland.

Northumbria Veg*ns
Local social group

Gordon Forrest, 9 Seymour St, N. Shields, Tyne & Wear NE29 6SN.
Tel: 0191-258 6793
gmforrest@tiscali.co.uk

Monthly picnic or bring and share.

Caterer
The All Good Catering Co.
Vegan catering company

07931 943459
www.allgoodcateringco.co.uk

Newcastle based catering business events, weddings, festivals and private parties. They provide cold and hot buffets, canapes and onsite BBQs, hot drinks, fresh smoothies and juices.

Vegetarian North Yorks

Rugged Moors to windswept beaches on the coast are enough to take your breath away. The **Yorkshire Dales National Park** has fine walking, with rivers and waterfalls, from gentle trails to full-on fell walks and 240km of cycle way. Or take the scenic Settle-Carlisle railway. The **Cleveland Way** is a walk of just over 100 miles from Filey along the coast to Saltburn then along the edge of the North Yorkshire Moors to Helmsley. Most of Yorkshire's 100% vegetarian accommodation is concentrated in North Yorkshire and the number of veggie cafes in rising.

Whitby was the setting for *Dracula* and attracts lots of goths and other tourists who are into vampires. Stay at **Falcon Guest House, Shepherd's Purse** or **Sanders Yard**. For a totally relaxing holiday away from it all, try **Fountains Court** in **Scarborough** which is perfect for a seaside holiday with pampering, or the Buddhist run **Wolds Retreat** with its own vegetarian cafe in Pocklington, 15 miles east of York. In summer, gardners and horticulturalists will love the five-acre **Helmsley Walled Garden** with its **Vinehouse** vegetarian cafe that uses produce from the garden.

Tourists flock to **York** for its wonderfully preserved Roman walls and rambling streets, with handsome Tudor-style buildings. Come in early July and you'll have a chance to see the York Early Music Festival, if you can fight off the crowds. **Blake Head** vegetarian world cafe and **El Piano** tapas bar are joined by the new **Goji** cafe and plenty more places cater for us, plus several central wholefood stores.

North Yorkshire tourist information:
www.visityorkshire.com
www.yorkshiredales.org.uk
www.northyorkmoors.org.uk
www.discoveryorkshirecoast.com
www.clevelandway.co.uk
www.scarborough.co.uk
www.whitby.co.uk
www.thewhitbyguide.co.uk
www.dracula-in-whitby.com
www.draculaexperience.co.uk

Yorkshire tourist information:
www.visityorkshire.co.uk
www.yorkshire.com
www.yorkshirenet.co.uk
www.iknow-yorkshire.co.uk
www.thepennineway.co.uk

Accommodation	147
Grassington	150
Harrogate	151
Helmsley	151
Knaresborough	152
Northallerton	152
Pocklington	153
Ripon	153
Saltburn by the Sea	153
Scarborough	154
Skipton	156
Whitby	156
Chain stores	157
YORK	**158**

North Yorkshire

Accommodation - vegetarian

Lidmoor Farm

Vegetarian guest house

Lidmoor Farm, **Bransdale**, York, North Yorkshire YO62 7JL (40 miles north of York)
Tel: 01751-432 214
Open: May-September
e-mail juleswatson62@yahoo.co.uk
www.lidmoor.co.uk

An isolated sheep farm in the heart of the North Yorkshire Moors, surrounded by heather moorland, ancient oak-wooded valleys and your very own lake to swim in.

Two double rooms, one with an extra bed £30 per person with continental breakfast including home-made bread and fresh fruit, children 12 and under half price, babies free if you bring bedding, they have a travel cot. Vegans catered for. No dogs. No credit cards. Ideal base for walkers. Pubs and restaurants with veggie menus 15 minutes drive. Owner runs a natural health centre in Kirkbymoorside, 8 miles away, with 20 practitioners offering from aromatherapy to yoga and classes.

The Women's Holiday Centre

Vegetarian holiday centre

The Old Vicarage, **Horton-in-Ribblesdale**, Settle, N Yorks BD24 0HD
Tel: 01729-860 207
Train: Horton-in-Ribblesdalde 10 mins, Leeds to Carlisle line
www.hortonwhc.org.uk

Only veggie and vegan food at this centre for women and girls, and boy children up to 10 (up to 16 for 4 weeks per year) in the Three Peaks part of the Yorkshire Dales.

Very inexpensive sliding scale, from £8.50 per night depending on income, half price for children, £2 under-5, cots available. Two dorms for up to 5 (single beds) or 11(large platform bed, 2 doubles, 1 single), two double rooms. £2 discount for camping. Open fires. Large garden with play area, dining/sitting room with open fire, sitting room with open fire and tv, communal kitchen with Aga and electric cooker, playroom. Winter themed weekends. Groups can book the whole house for minimum 2 nights from £180 per night. Bring your own towel to save laundry costs. No smoking in house. Themed weekends include writing, drumming, art, belly dancing, crafts, bridge, spirituality. No dogs except support dogs.

The Wolds Retreat

Vegetarian bed & breakfast

Kilnwick Percy Hall, **Pocklington** YO42 1UF (15 miles east of York on A1079 to Hull)
Tel: 01759-305 968
UK Freephone: 0800 0283 104
www.thewoldsretreat.co.uk
www.madhyamaka.org

Affordable new 4-star B&B set in 42 acres of parkland at the heart of the beautiful Yorkshire Wolds. Run by the Madhyamaka Buddhist Centre which has a vegetarian cafe (see Pocklington below).

2 doubles and 1 double/twin all ensuite, plus 2 singles with shared bathroom, all £30 per person, or £40 for a double/twin for one person. Continental or cooked breakfast. Check in 3-7pm.

Free wifi, hairdryer. No alcohol or smoking. MC, Visa.

Accommodation - vegetarian

The Orange Tree

Vegetarian B&B and relaxation centre

The Orange Tree, **Rosedale** East,
Pickering YO18 8RH (just outside the village of Rosedale Abbey)
Tel: 01751-417 219
www.theorangetree.com

---

6 twins, 1 triple, 1 double/single, all ensuite or with private bathroom. Group relaxation sessions, sauna, jacuzzi hot tub for up to 8, massage, reflexology, beauty treatments. £189 weekend 2 nights full board, treatments £19.50. Yoga weekend £200. Spa day with lunch and two treatments £85. Wine around £10 a bottle. Living room. MC, Visa +2%.

Falcon Guest House

Vegetarian bed & breakfast

29 Falcon Terrace, **Whitby** YO21 1EH
Tel: 01947-603 507
Train: Whitby, 7 minutes walk

In a quiet part of Whitby, with a two mile beach and by the North Yorkshire Moors national park. Two rooms, each with a double and a single bed, interchangeable as singles at £30 per night, double or twin £25 per person, or a family at £50-60. Huge vegetarian or vegan breakfast, much of it organic. No evening meals, but wholefood restaurant Sanders Yard is nearby (page 156). Tea making facilities in the rooms. TV in the lounge. Children welcome. No animals. Parking on street. No credit cards.

The Shepherd's Purse

Bed & no breakfast with veggie wholefood shop

95 Church Street, **Whitby** YO22 4BH
Tel: 01947-820228
www.theshepherdspurse.com

In the heart of the old town, a perfect base to explore the ancient seaport. Accommodation behind the wholefood shop (see below) in a choice of galleried rooms overlooking the courtyard. 7 rooms, 5 ensuite, some have 4-poster or brass bedsteads and country furniture, £55-70 per room, singles sometimes available off peak £30. One room has a double and 2 singles, add £25 per extra adult or £12.50 for children, under-3 free. They have travel cots, games and toys.

They do not provide breakfast but there are lots of places nearby that do such as Sanders Yard restaurant next door (see below). They can arrange flowers, wine, champagne or chocolates. No smoking throughout. Baggage storage. MC, Visa.

Accommodation - omnivorous

Airedale Guest House

Omnivorous guest house

23 Trafalgar Square, **Scarborough** YO12 7PZ
(off North Marine Road)
Tel: 01723-366809
Open: all year
www.airedaleguesthouse.com

Vegetarian owners. 1 family, 1 twin, 4 doubles, 1 single, £20-25 per person, discounts for children. Cooked breakfasts use Quorn or soya alternatives with a separate oven and grill. Rooms have Freeview and wifi. 3 rooms overlook the cricket ground. Dogs by prior arrangement. MC, Visa.

Burnley House

Omnivorous bed and breakfast

Hutton-le-Hole, North Yorkshire YO62 6UA
Tel: 01751-417 548
www.burnleyhouse.co.uk

There are three double ensuites and two twin ensuites at £75-95 double occupancy, or £65 for single occupancy.
Breakfast could be muesli or cereal with fresh fruit followed by tomatoes, mushrooms, baked beans. Soya milk and vegan muesli are available. Local, organic and home made ingredients are used when possible.
Rooms have TV and tea and coffee making faciltes. One has a four poster bed. Ground floor rooms so some disabled access. Children welcome, cots and high chairs. Dogs welcome. No smoking throughout.
Previously called "Moorlands".

North Cliff

Omnivorous bed & breakfast

Mount Pleasant North, **Robin Hood's Bay** near Whitby, North Yorkshire YO22 4RE
Tel: 01947-880481
Train: Whitby, 6 miles, then bus
www.north-cliff.co.uk
Email: northcliff@rhbay.co.uk

Beautiful Victorian villa still retaining many original features. Two double rooms and one twin, all ensuite, £30 per person or £35 as single. Full cooked English veggie breakfast, vegan no problem. Evening meal or packed lunch may be available and there is a health food shop in Whitby. The rear rooms have views over the bay. No smoking. No pets.

Fountains Court

Omnivorous holistic health hotel with almost entirely vegetarian food

120 Columbus Ravine, **Scarborough** YO12 7QZ
Tel: 01723-381 118
Fax: 01723-381 181
www.fountainscourt.com

A haven of peace in North Bay (no children or nightclubbers) specialising in healing holidays, personal retreats, or just a relaxing base to explore the North York moors and this ancient coast town, walks, sandy beaches, history, theatre and traditional shops. They can cater for any diet. 7 ensuite single, twin, double and triple rooms, £40 per person B&B. Light lunch £5, vegetarian 3-course or buffet dinner £12. Bring your own wine.
35 treatments and therapies from acupuncture to Thai massage by practitioners with a minimum of 5 years practice. 7-seat hot tub, sauna, zen garden, lounge, conservatory, workshops studio. No children. Mobiles on silent. Open to non-residents by apointment. MC, Visa.

Phoenix Court

Omnivorous hotel

Phoenix Court, 8/9 Rutland Terrace
Scarborough YO12 7JB
Tel: 01723-501150
www.hotel-phoenix.co.uk

14 ensuite single, double, twin and family roms, many with views of North Bay, £27-35 per person, £36-40 single, family £68 (2+1) to £80 (2+2). Vegetarian cooked breakfast includes their own vegan tofu and mushroom sausages.
One ground floor accessbile room. No smoking throughout. Free wifi. Wine, champagne, flowers and chocolates can be in your room on arrival. VisitBri-

tain 4 stars. No dogs except guide/hearing dogs. MC, Visa.
For vegetarian dinner try the nearby **Tikka Tikka** Indian restaurant on Castle Rd or **Gianni's** Italian on Victoria Road and they can suggest others.

Oast Guest House
Omnivorous bed & breakfast

5 Pen-y-Ghent View, **Settle** BD24 9JJ
Tel: 01729-822989
Train: Settle 8 minutes walk
www.oastguesthouse.co.uk

Edwardian house in the Yorkshire Dales market town. 5 ensuite rooms, 1 double, 4 twins, 2 can be used as a family suite, from £30 per person, children sharing reduced prices, under-5 free, cots and travel cots. Vegetarian or vegan breakfast. No dogs. Indoor cycle store, drying room. VisitBritain 3 stars, should be 4 stars in 2011.

There are plenty of places to eat in Settle for vegetarians including 2 Indians Ruchee and The Royal Spice, Italian Gusto, English/global Ravenous, and food pubs.

Weekend package for up to 5 couples or 10 persons includes Fri-Sat dinner and Sun brunch. Bring your own alcohol.

Sanders Yard
Guest house & holiday cottages with omnivorous restaurant

95 Church Street, **Whitby** YO22 4BH
Tel: 01947-825010
www.sandersyard.co.uk

4 double rooms, 3 of them ensuite, £70-90 with breakfast. Two holiday cottages, normally rented by the week but can be by the day, one over 3 floors sleeps 4 adults and 2 children, the other for 2 to 4 people, around £90/day or £300/week. Note that both have leather sofas. Out of season and last minute discounts. Sky+ and playstation.

Rooms have dvd and selection of films, ensuite, include full breakfast. Babies and children welcome, qualified sitting service available. Huge toy box, bottle warming. Well behaved pets welcome.

Breakfast in Sanders Yard restaurant (see listing later) includes juices, fruit salad, muesli or cereals, or full cooked. Endless pots of tea or fresh coffee. They have soya milk.

Grassington
The Retreat Cafe & Tea Rooms
Vegetarian cafe and tea-room

14-16 Main Street, Grassington, nr Skipton BD23 5AA. Tel: 01756-751887
Open: every day except Wed 10.30-17.00
www.theretreatcafe.co.uk

Very chilled and good value vegetarian cafe in old market town a few steps from the cobbled square in grade 2 listed buildings. The whole of July is a music festival from folk to rock to classical.

Soup, usually vegan, £3.50. Sandwiches £3-3.50, large panini served with salad or chips £6.

Main meals 12.00-16.30 £4.50-£6 served with salad and chips, such as Brazil nut and mushroom pie, chilli, curry, roast veg with Yorkshire pudding.

Hot puddings and fruit pies £3.50. Lots of cakes £2.50 including gluten and dairy-free.

Pot of all sorts of teas £1-1.30, latte £1.50, cappuccino £1.90, soya milk available. Soft drinks £1. House wine £2.50 glass. Bottle of lager or Yorkshire bitter £2-2.50. Children's menu £2-2.50, high chair. Dogs welcome. No credit cards.

Harrogate

ABC of Health

Health food shop

34 Beulah St, Harrogate HG1 1QH
Tel: 01423-568852
Open: Mon-Sat 9.00-17.30, Thu-Fri 18.00,
Sun 12.00-16.00 (not Jan-Feb)
www.abc-health.co.uk

Lots of Suma wholefoods. Chiller with vegan cheeses, meat substitutes. Bodycare includes Faith In Nature, Aubrey Organics, Jason, Elysambre organic mineral makeup, Natracare. Oganic wines, almost all vegan, and at Christmas local beers.

Supplements include Nature's Aid, Pharmanord, Nature's Answer, Viridian. Weleda and Nelsons homeopathy and remedies. Homeopath in store. Lots of other practitioners available by appointment. They sell *Get Fresh!* raw food magazine.

Quality Health Foods

Health food shop

3 Westminster Arcade, Harrogate HG1 2RN
Tel: 01423-541154
Open: Mon-Sat 9.00-17.30
email shop@qualityhealthfoods.co.uk

Wholefoods, but no take-away or freezer. They specialise in supplements and herbal remedies.

Wild Ginger vegetarian restaurant in Harrogate has closed.

Helmsley

Vinehouse Cafe

Vegetarian cafe

within the Helmsley Walled Garden,
Cleveland Way, Helmsley YO62 5AH
Garden office: 01439-771 427
Cafe 01439-771 194
Open: April-Oct every day 10.30-17.00
www.helmsleywalledgarden.org.uk

The café is situated in the newly restored Victorian Vinery, sit beneath the vine arches or out on the terrace. Lots of organic. Very open to different requirements such as vegan, gluten-free.

Amazing salad plates are their speciality, £7.95 with as much as possible picked from the garden, with selection of bread, some made with wholemeal organic local flour, and homemade pates.

Soup £3.95 is nearly always vegan with selection of bread.

2 hot dishes of the day £7.95, such as Walled Garden veggieburger made with locally made tofu; falafelburger; served with salad and bread.

Sandwiches made to order £3.95 with salad garnish.

Lots of fruit pies and crumbles £3.95, some vegan.

Cakes and flapjacks £1.75-2.50 including Tassajara vegan fruit cake (using fruit from the garden), usually a vegan chocolate cake.

Fairtrade organic coffee, tea and hot chocolate £1.50-£2. No soya milk.

Bottled soft drinks and juices £1.75, £3.50 750ml bottle, including organic local applejuice.

Children and dogs welcome, covered area. Cash or cheque only, cashpoint 5 minutes walk in the town.

The Helmsley Walled Garden is a tourist attraction, a beautiful five acre walled garden dating from 1758 set against the spectacular backdrop of Helmsley

Castle in the grounds of Duncombe Park. There are dozens of varieties of fruit trees, vines, 250 clematis varieties, an orchid house, vegetables, herbs and a wide range of plants including many rare species, all for sale. Or just picnic and relax. Open April-Oct 10.30-17.00, Nov Mon-Fri 10.30-16.00, Dec Mon-Sun 10.30-16.00, Jan-Mar Mon-Fri 10.30-16.00. Adults £4, concessions £3, U-17 free, dogs on leads welcome. Shop with plants, herbs, seeds and garden related products.

Knaresborough
Mungo Deli Wholefoods
Vegetarian organic grocery

11 Castlegate, Knaresborough HG5 8AR
Tel: 01423-862351
Open: Mon-Sat 9.00-17.00, Sun closed
www.mungodeli.co.uk

Over 2,000 products in stock with lots of Fairtrade and special diets and unusual brands like Seggiano vegan pesto. Fridge and freezer with pasties, porkless pies, meat and cheese substitutes by Redwood, Tofutti, Realeat, Vegetarian Choice, Dragonfly; vegan ice-cream by Swedish Glace and Booja Booja. Vegan chocolate by Plamil, Booja Booja, Montezuma, Infinity, Organica, Divine.
Organic local fruit and veg and box scheme, with many small producers. Organic vegan wines, beers and spirits.
Bodycare including Weleda, BWC, Faith In Nature, Lavera, local Bentley Organics, lots of Natracare.
Clearning by BioD, Clearspring, Earth Friendly, Ecover and refills.
Viridian and Lifeplan supplements.
Books, magazines including *The Vegan*. Dogs welcome in the shop, they can order in veggie cat and dog food for you.

McQueens cafe on the High Street has vegan options for sandwiches, main meals, cakes. Soya milk. 6 days. 01423-861668.
Also in the evening, **Carriages Wine Bar** on High Street has a tapas menu with unusual tapas, five of them vegan and you can fill up with olives and bread.

Natural Choice
Health food shop

4 Market Place, Knaresborough HG5 8AG
Tel: 01423-867705
Open: Mon-Sat 8.45-17.00, Sun closed

Local wholemeal bread Wed-Sat. Fridge with soya yogurt, milks, non-dairy cheeses, spreads. No freezer. Loose herbs and spices. Valor sugar-free diabetic chocolate, some vegan, and lots of other snacky things and bars. Lots of teas and bottled drinks.
Full range of Dr Hauschka skincare and cosmetics, Elysambre cosmetics, Jason, Faith In Nature, Natracare. Ella's Kitchen baby food, bodycare and nappy stuff. Ecover cleaning products.
Supplements include Solgar, Pharmanord, FSC, Lifeplan, Viridian. Homeopathy, Bach flower, Floradix, Biostrath, essential oils. Therapy room upstairs includes Reiki. MC, Visa.

Northallerton
The Peppermill
Omnivorous bistro & wine bar

227a & 228 High St, Northallerton DL7 8LU
Tel: 01609-779 805
Food Tue-Sat 12.00-14.00 (last orders), 17.00-21.00 (last orders);
Bar Tue-Sat 12.00-14.00, 17.00-22.30/23.00, Fri-Sat 17.00-02.00.
Sun-Mon closed except for private parties
www.peppermillwinepress.co.uk

As well as veggie dishes, there is a separate vegan menu with 3 starters

£3.65: tomato and basil soup, miso soup or mushroom bruschetta; 3 mains £7.95 are spicy chickpea stew with couscous, butternut squash risotto with white wine, and mushroom and nut pie, all with veg, salad or fries; 3 vegan desserts £4.25 are fruit crumble, baked coconut banana, or fresh fruit platter with red berry coulis.

Kids' menu, high chairs. Courtyard seating area, dogs welcome. Beers and real ales. Lots of wines from £3.80 glass, £13 bottle. Pot of tea or cup of cofffee £1.30, no soya milk. MC, Visa.

Pocklington

World Peace Cafe

Vegetarian organic cafe & retreat

Madhyamaka Buddhist Centre, Kilnwick Percy, near Pocklington YO42 1UF
(15 miles east of York on the A1079 to Hull).
Tel: 01759-304832
Open: Wed-Sun 10.30-16.30,
Mon-Tue closed (check website for possibly extended hours or days)
www.madhyamaka.org

Set in lots of gorgeous woodland and gardens where you can relax or explore. Vegan options. Home baked light meals £4.95 such as veggieburger with side salad and kettle crisps, chilli, filled jacket potatoes. Hot special of the day £5.95. Cakes £1.70-2.10. Fairtrade organic tea £1.20, freshly ground Americano coffee £1.40. Smoothies £2. Soya and rice milk available.

Terrace and wood burning stove. Space for kids to play and dogs kept on a lead welcome in outside area with tables, Summer barbecue. As part of a Buddhist complex, they also offer accommodation and retreats, with full vegetarian catering. Gift shop with Fairtrade goods. For B&B see the Wolds Retreat at the start of this chapter.

Ripon

Prima

Omnivorous Italian restaurant

33 Kirkgate, Ripon (on the road between market and the cathedral)
Tel: 01765-602034
Open: Mon-Sun 17.00-22.45
www.prima-ripon.co.uk

Veggie dishes are marked on the menu and for vegans they're happy to leave cheese off pizzas £7.20-8.50.

Fountains Health Store

Health food shop

7 North Street, Ripon HG4 1JY
Tel: 01765-604 726
Open: Mon-Sat 9.00-17.00, Sun closed

Fridge and freezer with vegan cheese, meat substitutes, fruit, vegetables, Booja Booja ice-cream. Vegan chocolate by Booja Booja.

Lots of bodycare and cosmetics by Faith In Nature, Tom's, Weleda, Natracare. Whole Weleda baby range. Supplements by New Era, Quest, Solgar, Vogel, Blohealth, Floradix. Weleda homeopathy, Ainsworth Bach flowers. Julia Lawless Aqua Oleum aromatherapy. Ecover cleaning. MC, Visa.

Saltburn by the Sea

Saltburn Health Foods

Health food shop

5 Station Buildings, Station Square, Saltburn by the Sea TS12 1AQ
Tel: 01287-624622
Open: Mon-Fri 9.00-17.30, Sun closed

Fridge and freezer with tofu, pates, lentil salads, hummus, Provamel yogurts, Redwood vegan cheese and meat subsitutes, Vegideli, Swedish Glace and vegan gluten-free choc ices. Local Larchfield Bakery bread. Taylors of Lots of teas, including Harrogate teas and

coffees and they grind them, lots of juices.
Bodycare by Thursday's Plantation, Suma, Weleda, Dead Sea Magik, Faith In Nature, Eco Cosmetics. Supplements by Solgar, Nature's Aid, Bioforce, Weleda homeopathy. They give physiotherapy advice. Ecover and refills. Books, especially by Jan de Vries. MC, Visa.

Saltburn by the Sea is between Whitby and Middlebrough, a seaside town with pier, cliffs, beach, gardens and woods. There are lots of restaurants though nothing specifically veggie.

Scarborough

Nutmeg Cafe

Vegetarian organic Fairtrade cafe

93 Victoria Road, Scarborough YO11 1SP
(a few minutes walk from railway station)
Tel: 01723-503867
Open: Tue-Sat 10.00-16.30,
Sun-Mon closed
www.nutmegcafe.co.uk

Modern vegetarian cuisine, global flavours, organic vegetables. Lots of vegan and gluten-free options. Often has local art on the walls.
Soups £2.80. Main course salad £4.80. Jacket potato £3.50 with fillings including chilli bean. Bagel sandwiches made to order £2.50. Two daily specials £4.80 such as marinated tofu with shitake mushrooms, miso gravy, kale and roasted squash; carrot falafel with aubergine and tomato salsa and herby tabouleh; butterbean and butternut squash stew; tofu cashew fritters; sausages and veg cider casserole.
5 or 6 cakes daily, most vegan and/or gluten-free, £1.50-2.20, such as orange Cointreau, raspberry chocolate, Hawaiian carrot, can be with dairy-free ice-cream. Usually one or two vegan, gluten-free desserts £1.80 such as berry crumble. Toasted teacakes £1.20.
Loose leaf and green herbal teas in glass teapots, coffee, cappuccino, chai latte £1.40-1.90. latte. Soya milk available. Bottled organic juices and smoothies £2.20. Vegan organic wine with meals 12.00-14.00, £3 glass.
Children welcome but no high chairs. You can park a well-behaving dog in the yard at the back and they'll leave the back door open so you can see each other. As we go to press the cafe is up for sale as a going concern.

Cafe Venus

Vegetarian cafe

29 Ramshill Rd, South Cliff, Scarborough YO11 2LW (start of the A165 to Filey, opposte Sainsbury Local)
Tel: 07950 163160
Open: Mon-Wed, Fri-Sat 10.30-16.30; Thu, Sun closed. Also first Sat 19.00-22.00.
www.facebook.com/pages/
Cafe-Venus/149111271780318
www.facebook.com/acousticbistrolive

Opened 2010. Vegan and gluten-free options. Food changes every day.
Soup of the day with bread £3. Two main dishes daily £4.50-4.95, one usually vegan, including butternut squash Thai curry with basmati rice and naan bread, red lentil shepherd's pie, Homity pie, Cornish pasties, homemade pizzas, chilli, lasagne, bognaise.
Sandwiches and toasties £2.50 made to order with salad garnish.
Desserts £1.50 include cakes, scones, vegan flapjacks and apple crumble (not necessarily every day).
Mug of tea £1.30, pot £1.50, for two £2.40, lots of speciality teas. Mug of coffee £1.50, small cafetiere £1.75, large £2.60. Juices, fizzy drinks £1, milkshakes £1.50. They have soya milk.
Children's section of menu, high chair, toys. First Saturday of the month they have an alliance with the local acoustic music promoter, live music 7-10pm with a meal and drink for around £10. Alcohol licence applied for.

Eat Me
Omnivorous cafe

7 Hanover Road, Scarborough YO11 1LS
Tel: 07595 596518
Open: Mon–Sun 08.00–16.00, also Thu–Sat 17.30–21.00
www.eatmecafe.com

Opened October 2010, near the train station and Stephen Joseph Theatre. Produce is locally sourced where possible. Menu changes weekly. Full cooked breakfast £4.

Two soups are normally vegetarian and sometimes vegan, £3 day, £3.50 evening. At least one vegetarian starter such as tempura veg. Main dishes £5 vary weekly, such as the very popular fennel and potato gratin (can be vegan cheese), bean casserole, and Thai green, red and Penang curries – one owner has lived in Thailand!

Pear tart (gluten-free and vegan) £3. Swedish Glace vegan ice-cream.

Sundays unlimited organic bread and jam for £3 while you read the papers.

Fairtrade tea £1 pot. Fairtrade organic coffee and cappuccino £1.40–1.60. They have soya milk. Bring your own wine evening, off licence nearby, or organic vegan wine from Fairchild's nearby.

Mojo's Music Cafe
Omnivorous cafe

55 Victoria Road, Scarborough YO11 1SH
Tel: 01723-503 666
Open: Tue–Sat 10–18.00, closed Sun–Mon
www.mojosmusiccafe.com

This Anglo-American diner has a big menu that includes veggie breakfast, jacket potatoes, toasties, salads, burgers and even their "Suzanne" vegan pizza with pan-fried veg. And they have soya milk.

Children welcome, toys, 3 high chairs. Dogs welcome outside. MC, Visa.

Fairchild's at the Cheeseboard
Vegetarian deli, wholefood shop and Fairtrade products

21 Victoria Rd, Scarborough YO11 1SB
Tel: 01723-381000
Open: Tue–Sat 9.00–17.30, Sun–Mon closed
www.fairchildsgreenshop.co.uk

Wholefoods, organic and Fairtrade, with everything vegetarian except dog food. Organic fruit and veg and deliveries. Local organic bread delivered Thursday afternoon. Fridge with tofu, vegan cheeses, yogurts. Vegan chocolate by Organica, Divine. Organic and Fairtrade wines, local beers. Loose tea and coffee. Bodycare by Lavera, Suma, Faith In Nature, Natracare. Cleaning products by BioD, Ecover and Faith In Nature. Can order in anything you need.

Adult, children and baby mainly organic and Fairtrade clothes, bedding and bags, by Black Yak, Gossypium and Bishopston. Jewellery, candles. MC, Visa.

Well Bean
Health food shop

11 St. Thomas St, Scarborough YO11 1DY
Tel: 01723 500 319
Open: Mon–Sat 9.30–17.00, Sun closed

Opened summer 2010. All the usual wholefoods, dried fruit, seeds by weight if you want to make your own muesli, plant milks and supplements. No fridge or freezer.

Small amount of bodycare by Manuka. Lots of supplements by Lifeplan and Nature's Aid. Vogel remedies.

Ecover washing up liquid and refills. Cash only, cashpoints nearby.

Skipton
Wild Oats
Vegetarian cafe

190 High St, Skipton BD23 1JZ
(above Healthy Life wholefood shop)
Tel 01756-790619
Cafe: Mon-Sat 9.00-16.30, Sun 10.30-15.30

50% of the food here is vegan. Soup £3.95 with wholemeal bread. Lots of main courses £6.25 with two salads, such as stuffed pancakes or nut roast. Sandwiches made to order £4.50. Cakes £2.50-2.95, some vegan and gluten-free.
Freshly squeezed orange juice £2.20. Pot of tea £1.80, cafetiere of coffee £1.95, (soya) cappuccino £1.80.
Children welcome, high chairs. Organic beer £1.95, small bottle of organic wine £3.75. MC, Visa.

Healthy Life
Wholefood shop

190 High St, Skipton BD23 1JZ
(beneath Wild Oats vegetarian cafe)
Tel 01756-790619
Shop: Mon-Sat 9-17.30, Sun 10.30-15.30

They sell take-away sandwiches, soup and salad from the vegetarian cafe upstairs. Fridge and freezer with vegan cheese and meat substitutes, Swedish Glace ice-cream. Local bread. Vegan organic wine.
Bodycare by Dr Hauschka, Faith In Nature, Natracare. Baby stuff. Supplements by Higher Nature, Solgar and lots of others. Homeopathy and remedies. Ecover cleaning. Magazines. MC, Visa.

Whitby
Sanders Yard
Omnivorous restaurant

95 Church Street, Whitby YO22 4BH
Tel: 01947-825010
Open: Mon-Sun 9.00-18.00, summer evenings
www.sandersyard.co.uk

This is the place to come for breakfast when staying in their rooms or at Shepherd's Purse (earlier in this chapter).
Lunch £7.95 for a meal such as filled baked potatoes with salad. Sandwiches made to order £4.99. They can get vegan ingredients in as necessary.
Huge cake counter and they always have some frozen vegan desserts from Suma such as ginger or lemon drizzle cake. Coffee £1.20, pot of tea around £1.20. Licensed.
Summer evenings there is an a la carte restaurant where you can get a main course for around £10.

If eating after 6pm, try Whitby's Indian or Italian restaurants.

First Season
Vegetarian wholefood shop

1 St. Ann's Lane, Whitby YO21 3PF (at the bottom of Flowergate near Swing Bridge)
Tel: 01947-601 608
Open: Mon-Sat 9.00-17.00, Sun closed
www.firstseason.co.uk

Local organic breads. Gluten and dairy-free products. Fridge and freezer with pasties, salads, hummus and dips, sausages, vegan cheeses, yogurts, Swedish Glace and Booja Booja ice-cream. Local jams. Herbs and spices. Vegan chocolate by Plamil and Organica.
Bodycare by Organic Botanics, Aubrey,

Faith in Nature, Suma, Weleda, Natracare.

Supplements include Solgar, Vogel (Bioforce), Quest, Kordels and Weleda. Herbal medicine, homeopathy. Essential oils. Staff can advise on health needs, homeopath sometimes in shop. Books and magazines. Young's wine-making and home brew.

They say if they don't stock it, they will do their best to get it asap. Large noticeboard with local events. MC, Visa.

Shepherd's Purse Wholefoods

Vegetarian wholefood shop & deli

95 Church Street, Whitby YO22 4BH
Tel: 01947-820228
Open: Mon-Sun 10.00-17.00
www.theshepherdspurse.com

Wholefoods are organic and Fairtrade where possible. Bread fresh every morning from a local Moorland bakery. Deli sells everything you need for a picnic, Mediterranean foods, with hummus. Middle and far eastern ingredients such as saffron, tamarind, poppadoms, chutneys, pastes and pickles. Over 60 spices and herbs. Nuts and dried fruit, flapjacks, Trek and other bars.

Lots of local organic beers such as Cropton and Black Dog, ciders and Lindisfarne fruit wines.

Bodycare by Ficketts, Suma, Faith In Nature, Labyrinth soap, Weleda.

BioD cleaning. A few cookbooks and other books. MC, Visa over £5.

Suma cotton carrier bags and recycled carriers bags. Also a dress shop. MC, Visa.

Chain stores North Yorks

Holland & Barrett

Health food shop

11a James Street, **Harrogate** HG1 1QF
Tel: 01423-503 469
Open: Mon-Sat 9-17.30, Sun 10.30-16.30

177 High Street, **Northallerton** DL7 8JZ
Tel: 01609-771 505

Brunswick Pavillion, Westborough
Scarborough YO11 2PA
Tel: 01723-501 369
Open: Mon-Sat 9-17.30, Sun 10.30-16.30

Unit 5, Market Cross, **Selby** YO8 4JS
Tel: 01757-707 389
Open: Mon-Sat 9.00-17.30, Sun closed

30 Sheep Street, **Skipton** BD23 1HX

30 Market Place, **Thirsk** YO7 1LB.
Tel: 01845-526868

1-2 Sandgate, **Whitby** YO22 4DB
Tel: 01947 602828

Julian Graves

Health food shop

76 Newborough, **Scarborough** YO11 1ET

Founded by the Romans, the historic city of York is one of the most popular tourist and weekend desinations in England, with York Minster cathedral, York Museum, castle, art gallery and many more attractions. Cornmill Lodge vegetarian guest house has recently closed, but we have found some excellent central guest houses that cater well for us. Be sure to book well ahead for weekends as York is *very* popular. Alternatively, to the east of York is the new very tranquil Buddhist vegetarian B&B **The Wolds Retreat**, with its own vegetarian cafe, see North Yorkshire chapter (page 147,153).

Top places to eat out are **El Piano** vegan restaurant and the new **Goji** vegetarian cafe. (The Blake Head cafe has recently closed.) There are also Italian, Indian, Chinese and other Asian restaurants which you will need Sunday evening when the vegetarian places are closed. With several central wholefood stores, this is one trip you won't need to pack supplies for.

Tourist information **www.visityork.org**, 1 Museum St YO1 7DT

These websites are recommended by Dairy Guest House:

All about York	www.york-united-kingdom.co.uk
	www.insideyork.co.uk
Brief history of York	www.localhistories.org/york.html
Air Museum	www.yorkshireairmuseum.co.uk
Art Gallery	www.yorkartgallery.org.uk
Bar Convent	www.bar-convent.org.uk
Barley Hall	www.barleyhall.org.uk
Jorvik Viking Centre	www.vikingjorvik.com
Merchant Adventures Hall	www.theyorkcompany.co.uk
Murton Park	www.murtonpark.co.uk
National Railway Museum	www.nrm.org.uk
York Castle Museum	www.yorkcastlemuseum.org.uk
York Dungeons	www.thedungeons.com
York Minster	www.yorkminster.org
Yorkshire Museum	www.yorkshiremuseum.org.uk

Accommodation **160**
Vegetarian **161**
Omnivorous **164**
Shops **165**

York

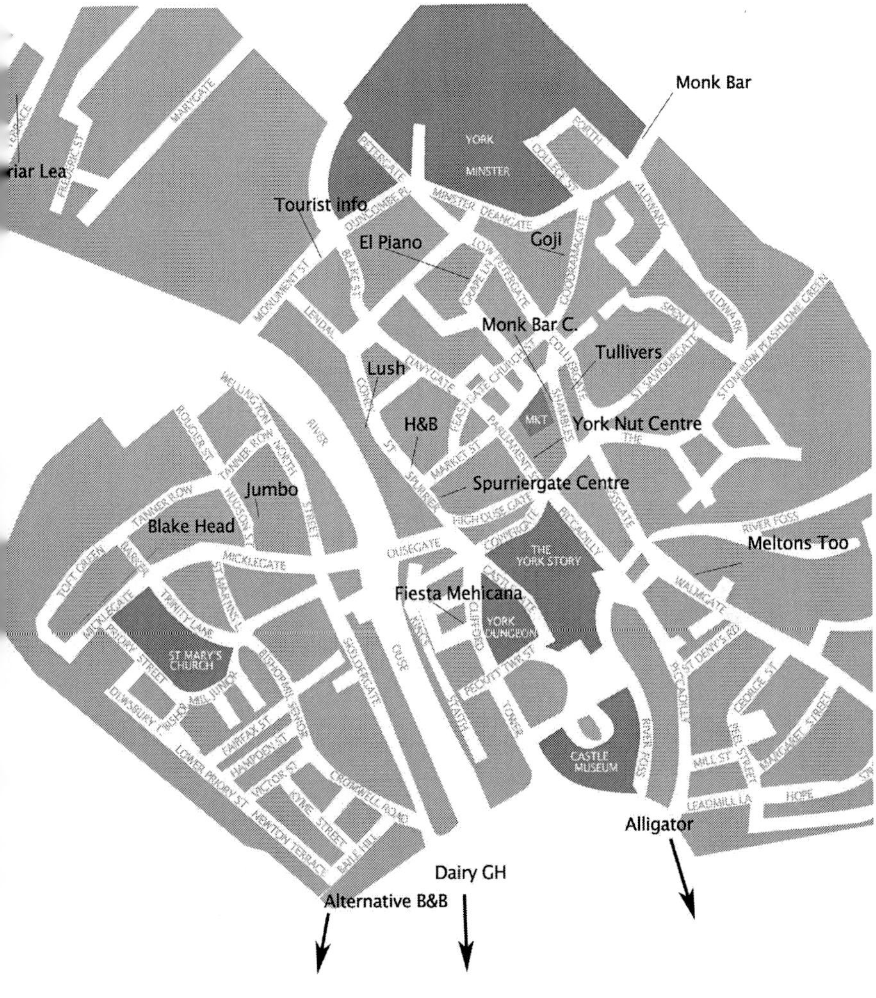
Monk Bar
YORK
MINSTER
riar Lea
Tourist info
El Piano
Goji
Monk Bar C.
Tullivers
Lush
H&B
MKT
York Nut Centre
Spurriergate Centre
Jumbo
Blake Head
Meltons Too
THE
YORK STORY
Fiesta Mehicana
YORK
DUNGEON
ST MARY'S
CHURCH
CASTLE
MUSEUM
Alligator
Dairy GH
Alternative B&B

York accommodation
Briar Lea Guest House
Omnivorous Guest House

8 Longfield Terrace, York YO30 7DJ (5 mins walk from town centre)
Train and bus stations: 10 mins walk
Tel: 01904-635061
Open: all year
www.briarlea.co.uk

All 6 rooms have ensuite shower. Double or twin £31 per person, four-poster £33, single £37, family with double and 2 singles price according to occupancy, U-5 free, children under 12 half price. Winter 3 nights £70. One of the owners is veggie and cooks the breakfast; vegan or gluten-free let them know and they'll get stuff in. Free wifi. Parking. Rooms have colour TV, refreshment tray, hair dryer, towels. Ironing facilities. Visa, MC. Min 2 nights at weekend. No pets.

Dairy Guest House
Omnivorous Guest House

3 Scarcroft Road York, YO23 1ND
Train: 15 mins walk or 5 mins taxi
Tel: 01904-639 367
Open: all year
www.dairyguesthouse.co.uk

6 ensuite room: 1 twin, 3 doubles, £60-£75 per room; king size 4-poster £70-85; family with double and 2 singles £90-105. Cooked veggie or vegan breakfast. Travel cot. Disabled access. No pets. No smoking throughout. Rooms have TV with dvd player, drink facilities, hairdryer and alarm clock. MC, Visa.

York Alternative B&B
Omnivorous Guest House

82 Scarcroft Road, York YO24 1DD (central)
Tel: 01904-625931
Train: 10 mins walk
Open: almost all year
www.yorkalternativebandb.co.uk

1 double, 1 twin, £30 per person, no single supplement. Cooked veggie or vegan breakfast, organic or local where possible. Toiletries not animal tested. Rooms have TV, tea/coffee making, hair dryer. Iron available. Secluded garden. Lock up garage for bikes. No young children. No dogs, they have a cat. No stag or hen parties. No credit cards. But veggies very welcome and they specialise in special diets.

El Piano

York

99% vegan Spanish and international restaurant

This brightly decorated restaurant is one of the latest opening in the heart of the city. All food is vegan and gluten-free, and where possible organic. Menus show which drinks are vegetarian or vegan and dairy milk is available for hot drinks. The cuisine is Hispanic and internationally influenced and presented in individual tapas dishes.

6 starters, £3.95 tapas size or £5.95 ración size, include corn basket, lentil and rice tabuleh, hummus, salsa, mushroom and basil salad, mixed salad. Soup £4.50.

12 mains each come in a pine boat, all £3.95 tapas or £5.95 ración, such as dhal, berenjena Bankok aubergines toasted with potato in their own Thai curry paste, coconut kofta with spicy soya mincemeat balls, Bolivian Tinas carrots and spring onions fried in rice flour, egg-free Spanish omlette, deep-fried sushi. Share 6 tapas or racions for £19.50 or £29.50, or 12 for £39.50 or £59.50.

Combos until 7pm include breakfast £6.95 with tapas fry-up or mezze; Cheap Chow for single diners £6.95 which gets you lentil and rice tabuleh, dhal and tinas, or salads with fried sushi; soup and corn bread with 2 salads £7.50; any tapas and 2 salads with pate and corn chips £9.95. Tapas selection tray £7.50, or £10 with wine. Burger with salad and corn chips £6.95.

Desserts £4.50, or £5.50 with a pot of tea or jug of coffee, include brownie, carrot cake, coconut and banana Pacific poké, sticky toffee pudding, scheezecake with seasonal fruits.

Big bottle of juice to share £5.50, other soft drinks £1.90. Bottled Spanish beer £2.50, organic cider £3.50. Large glass vegan house wine £3.75. Jug of sangria £9.95 jug, mulled wine £10.50. 3 litres of juice, beer, sangria or wine £15-35. Pot of tea £1.90 per person. Coffee, hot choc, chai £2.25.

15/17 Grape Lane,
The Quarter, York
Y01 7HU

Tel: 01904-610 676

www.elpiano.co.uk

Open all year
Mon-Sat 11.00-23.00;
Sun 12-17.00, maybe later in summer, call to check

Wheelchair and pushchair access, disabled toilets

Live music sometimes on Fridays and Saturdays

Booking recommended weekend as they get busy and have to turn people away.

Customers can use their own musical instruments or the restaurant's piano in the upstairs room, good for parties

Special diets catered for Include gluten-free, raw, macrobiotic, diabetic, candida and sugar-free

No nuts except for coconut, pine kernels, sesame, tahini

Wrapido take-away has lower prices, open till 11pm

2 function rooms, terrace, buffet £15 per head

Outside catering

MC, Visa

goji
Vegetarian Cafe & Deli
STUDENT SPECIAL
FREE DRINK + FREE TRIMMINGS WITH GOJI'S DELICIOUS VEGAN HOTDOGS
TAKEAWAY

Vegetarian restaurants
Goji Vegetarian Cafe
Vegetarian cafe & deli/take-away

36 Goodramgate, York YO1 7LF
Tel: 01904-622 614
Open: Sun-Fri 11.00-16.00, Sat 9.30-17.00;
also Thu-Sat 18.30-23.00, last orders 21.30
www.gojicafe.co.uk (menus)

New cafe using local suppliers and organic produce, but no microwaves or aluminium pans. Vegan and gluten-free options. Local art and photography on display for sale.

Daytime menu: Soup of the day is almost always vegan, with speciality fresh bread £4.60. Soup with speciality wrap £7.50. Goji's famous mushroom burger £7.65. Goji hot dog £5.25. Home-made quiches with roast potatoes and salad £7.50. Mixed deli salad plate £7.25. All dishes can be vegan.

A range of daily specials a£7.50, like aubergine and feta mixed nut filo parcel served with vine tomatoes and salad.; wild mushroom hotpot served with roast potatoes.

Daily dessert specialities £1.95-4.60, such as chocolate and cherry roulade, apple and rhubarb crumble, chocolate and chestnut cake. Various vegan/gluten-free cakes such as lemon and poppy seed cake, chocolate cake, carrot cake, banana and walnut coffee muffins.

Evening menu: Starters £5 to £7 such as spring nettle soup, island black bean salad, palm tree heart salads with lemongrass mayonnaise. Main courses £11.50-13.00 include Indian potato pie, or Italian barley and mushroom risotto.

Desserts around £5.95 such as Bailey's and dark chocolate cheesecake, cinnamon and apple strudel served with a berry compote.

Goji serves a wide range of speciality teas and coffees which include a pot of Pollard's loose leaf teas £1.90, or flowering teas £2.95. Pot of Wellness tea £2.50 such as Gojiberry tea. Pollard's cafetiere coffees £2.35. Latte or cappuccino £2.25. Juices, smoothies, milkshakes (with vegan ice-cream) £2.95.

A huge range of organic wines, beers, ciders, vintage speciality wines (mostly vegan) £3.50 glass, from £14.95 to £50 a bottle.

Children welcome, outside courtyard. No dogs except guide dogs. MC, Visa from £5.

The take-away and deli has a wide range of salads, wraps, cakes, speciality bread and hot take-away food. Swedish Glace ice-cream cones £1.50 1 scoop, £2.50 for two scoops.

Omnivorous restaurants
Fiesta Mehicana
Omnivorous Mexican restaurant

4 Clifford St., York YO1 9RD
Tel: 01904-610243
Open: Mon-Sun from 17.30 till late
www.fiestamehicana.com

Andale arriba, a colourful Mexican themed restaurant with lots of vegetarian options marked on the menu. While Mexican places generally smother everything with cheese, the vegan owner of one of the other Yorkshire listings says they can make good chimichangas for vegan amigos. Platter of starters with bean dip, salsa picante, guacamole, stuffed jalapenos, onion rings and chilli empanadas served with corn chips. Chimichangas filled with refried beans and deep fried, come with rice, beans, corn, mushrooms, peppers, tomato, courgettes and coriander. Burritos, enchiladas, tacos, fajitas.

Tequila, cocktails, beers, spirits and wines.

Children's portions with salad or fries but not chilis. Gluten-free menu. Party menu £14.95, or £16.95 with pre-dinner cocktail, organiser eats free with bookings of 10+, served buffet style down the centre of the table, book 24 hours ahead.

Jumbo Buffet
Omnivorous Chinese restaurant

4 George Hudson Street, York YO1 6LP
Tel: 01904-623656.
Open every day 12-22.30.

Omnivorous Chinese all-you-want buffet with lots for veggies and vegans including mounds of fresh fruit. Rice contains egg or ham but they always have plain boiled rice though you may have to ask for it. Afternoons £5.99 till 16.30, then it goes up to £7.99; after 18.30 Mon-Fri £8.99, Sat £9.99; Sun after 18.00 £7.99.

Meltons Too
Omnivorous cafe-bistro

25 Walmgate, York YO1 9TX
Tel: 01904-629 222
Open: Mon-Sat 10.30-24.00, Sun 10.30-23.00; last orders 90 minutes before closing
www.meltonstoo.co.uk (menus)

Large cafe, bar and bistro in a 17th century building. Menu changes seasonally around every 6 weeks. Cooked vegetarian breakfast tray with hot or cold drink £5.90. Starters £3.95-4.50 such as organic carrot and turnip soup, or mushroom stuffed with caramelised red onion and pine nuts. Mains £8.20-9.00 such as imam bialdi (stuffed aubergine) with couscous, or haricot bean and veg fritters with broccoli. Small tapas and mezze dishes to share £3-4 include marinated olives, capers and nuts; falafel and red pepper dip; potato, onion and tomato tortilla; stuffed piquillo peppers with watercress salad; Express lunch until 5pm £6.90 such as falfel and hummus with a piquillo pepper and chips. 2-course lunch and early dinner (before 7pm, vacate table by 8pm) £12.50. Desserts £4.50 are not vegan. Wine from £14.50 bottle, £10.95 half litre, £3.60 glass (175ml). Prices do not include service.

The Spurriergate Centre
Omnivorous cafe & Fairtrade shop

St. Michael's Church, Spurriergate, York YO1 9QR. Tel: 01904 629 393
Open: Mon–Fri 10-16.00, Sat 9.30-17.00, Sun (seasonal, call to check) 11.00-15.00
www.thespurriergatecentre.com

12th century church offers a place to meet, shop and eat. Two shops with cards, books, Fairtrade coffees, teas, and third world crafts. Child friendly. Food is fairly basic soups, salads and cakes.

Shops
Alligator Wholefoods
Organic vegetarian wholefood grocer & greengrocer

104 Fishergate, York YO1 4BB
Tel: 01904-654525
Open: Mon-Sat 9.00-18.00, Sun closed
www.alligatorwholefoods.com

Since 1972, 10 minutes walk along the river south of the centre. Lots of vegan options.

Local organic fruit and veg. Lots of baked goods including speciality breads from The Village, Kolos, Jordan Valley Wholefoods and local bakeries, snacks, pasties, samosas, bhajias and vegan cakes and flapjacks. Saker Bakery pasties such as chickpea, Mexican, Mediterranean, and sosmix rolls. Chilled and frozen burgers, Redwood and Tofutti cheese, sausages, Clearspot local tofu, Provamel an Sojasun yoghurts, dairy-free ice-cream by Swedish Glace, Tofutti cones. Booja Booja, Organica, Divine, Montezuma and Plamil vegan chocolate plus Zotters and Vivani, some vegan.

Bodycare by Faith In Nature, Suma, Natracare. Maltex nappies and Weleda cream. They don't do supplements or remedies. No pills or potions.

BioD and refills for laundry, conditioner and washing-up.
Delivery service within York outer ring road. They can order in anything you want. MC, Visa.

Holland & Barrett
Health food shop

28-30 Coney Street, York YO7 1LB
Tel: 01904-627 257
Open: Mon-Wed 9.00-17.30, Thu-Sat 8.30-18.00, Sun 11.00-17.00

Fridge and freezer with pasties etc.

Lush
Cruelty-free cosmetics

3 Coney Street, YO1 9QL
Tel: 01904-541 927
Open: Mon-Fri 9.30-18.00, Sat 9.00-18.00, Sun 11.00-17.00
www.lush.co.uk

Sweet-smelling soaps, shampoos, fizzing bath balls and other treats, most of them vegan and clearly labelled.

Monk Bar Chocolatiers
Chocolate shops

7 **The Shambles**, York YO1 7LZ
Tel: 01904-634 999
Open: Mon-Sat 10.00-17.30, Sun 11.00-16.30

1 **Goodramgate**, York YO1 7LJ
Tel: 01904-672963
Open: Mon-Tue, Fri-Sat 10.00-17.15; Sun 11.00-16.00, Wed-Thu closed
www.monkbar.com

Two identical shops with 60 kinds of luxury handmade sugar-free chocolates, with plenty of choice for vegans, though obviously not cheap.

Tullivers Herbs & Wholefoods
Health food shop

1-2 Colliergate, York YO1 8BP
Tel: 01904-636437
Open: Mon-Sat 9.30-17.30, Sun closed
www.tullivers.co.uk

Since 1983 in the centre of York. They can cater for any sensitivities and give nutrition advice. Local organic wholemeal Fred's Bakery bread. Fridge with vegan cheese, meat substitutes, local tofu. No freezer. 200 herbs and spices by weight. Plamil, Montezuma and Booja Booja vegan chocolates and Vivani, some of it vegan.

Bodycare includes Green People, Akin, Faith In Nature, Barefoot Notanicals, Elysambre, Brown Earth, Kneipp, Weleda, Natracare, Mooncup. Baby care. Supplements by A.Vogel, Solgar, Quest, Nature's Plus, Tullivers own label, Floradix. Weleda and Nelson homeopathy and remedies. Natural by Nature (essential) Oils. Practioner consultations in store. BioD and Ecover cleaning products. Sprouters and seeds. Turtle Bags old-fashioned string shopping bags. A few books. MC, Visa over £10. Mail order by phone, postage at cost.

The York Nut Centre
Wholefood and health food shop

21 Market Street, York YO1 8FL
Tel: 01904-641205
Open: Mon-Sat 9.00-17.30, Sun closed

Owned by the same people as Millies in Leeds, small but very well stocked shop. Specialists in nuts and dried fruit loose, but the full range of wholefoods too. No fridge of freezer.
Bodycare by Jason, Natracare.
Supplements include Solgar, Nature's Aid, Health Aid, Lifeplan, Higher Nature, Vogel, Viridian. Sports nutrition. Some homeopathy and essential oils.
Ecover. MC, Visa.

Newgate Market
Street market

Newgate, York YO1 7LA (between The Shambles and Parliament Street)
Tel: 01904-551 355
Open: daily 9.00-16.00, Sat-Sun till 16.30

Huge market with 110 stalls including fruit and veg.

Quick, hide, the Vikings are coming!

Hull

Kingston upon Hull is on the up as a tourist destination. Attractions include the Hull Maritime Museum, William Wilberforce Museum about the abolition of slavery (and some would say there are parallels with working to end farmed animal slavery), the Streetlife Museum, Ferens Art Gallery, Hull and East Riding Museum and the Guildhall Collection. You can find links to all of these on the menu page of the veggie-friendly **Acorn Guest House**.

Everyone who watches British tv knows ebullient local MP and former Deputy Prime Minister Two Jabs/Jags/whatever John (now Lord) Prescott and his chip butties. Indeed Hull used to be appalling for veggies. But these days **Hitchcocks** is renowned as one of the best vegetarian restaurants in Britain, attracting visitors from all over the country with a buffet themed on a different country each night. **The Zoo** vegetarian cafe is now joined by **Green Ginger Cafe**. **Mimosa** Turkish and **Thai House** are fine examples of mainstream restaurants that go out of their way to attract vegetarians and vegans.

There are cinemas, sports arenas and an ice rink. Shop until you drop at the Princess Quay centre (on the river) which is built almost entirely of glass. Check out the markets on Sunday. There is plenty of night life including lots of olde worldly pubs, restaurants and clubs.

North of Hull is the seaside town of Bridlington, well worth a trip for the long-established **Bean There** and the new **Seasalt & Passion** vegetarian cafes. North of Brid is the UK's best seabird-watching site at **Bempton** with its own vegetarian cafe. If travelling the A1079 road to York, you can stop off for luxury vegan chocolates at the **White Rabbit** chocolate shop in Beverley.

www.realyorkshire.co.uk
www.hullcc.gov.uk
www.acornguesthousehull.com

Accommodation	**168**
Beverley	**168**
Bridlington	**168**
Goole	**170**
Kingston upon **HULL**	**170**
Local group	**173**
Chain stores	**173**

East Yorkshire

Hull Accommodation
Acorn Guest House
Omnivorous guest house & apartment

719 Beverley High Road, Hull HU6 7JN
(2 miles north of centre and station on
A1079 Beverley to York road)
Tel: 01482-853 248
Fax: 01482-853 148
Open: all year
www.acornguesthousehull.co.uk

One of the owners is vegetarian. Full veggie or vegan breakfast. 7 ensuite rooms: single £40, twin £50, double with kitchenette for long stays £60, 2 king size doubles £60 (one with balcony, good for smokers), triple £75 (3 singles), very spacious family room £75-100 for 3 to 5 persons. Single occupancy £40 in twin room £40, £50 in double. They also own a city centre penthouse **self-catering apartment** with 2 double bedrooms, 2 bathrooms, living room and kitchen/diner, £600 per week, ideal for long corporate lets.

2 ground floor twins/triple suitable for people with mobility problems. All rooms have satellite HD tv, tea and coffee making, fridge, microwave, hairdryer, ironing board and iron. Parking. Children welcome. Animals welcome. No smoking throughout. Free wifi.

Beverley
White Rabbit Chocolate Company
Chocolate shop

16 Dyer Lane, Beverley HU17 8AE (north of Hull). Tel: 01482-679325
Open: Mon-Sat 10.00-17.00, Sun closed
www.white-rabbit-chocolate.co.uk

The perfect treat during a romantic weekend and heaps of dairy-free chocolates. They make their own organic vegan dark chocolate, 55% or 74% chocolate, with flavours including hot chilli; ginger; orange and mango; pecan, date, walnut and cocoa nib; crystallized violet petal. Chocolate dipped ginger, orange, prunes. Scorched almonds dusted with cocoa. Several types of vegan truffles by Montezuma.

Bespoke service for weddings, corporate, chocolate pizza, edible chocolate boxes, even chocolate vegab slab cake that you break with a hammer.

Bridlington
Bean There
Vegetarian cafe

10 Wellington Rd, Bridlington YO15 2BL
(near the war memorial)
Tel: 01262-679 800
Open: Mon-Sat 9.00-16.00, closed Sun

An oasis in the centre of town, now under new Yorkshire ownership since 2008 with value and generous portions to match and hence very busy. 95% of ingredients are organic. Everything home-made by the proprietors, seasonal local veg and they have Fairtrade. Sunny rear courtyard.

Starters £2-3 such as soup (always vegan) with homemade bread. Mains £4.50-5.50 such as burgers with salad and home-made bread; up to six different pies with mushy peas, mint sauce and onion gravy.

Desserts include lots of cakes from 50p to £2, but not vegan.

Fairtrade coffee with free refills £1.20. Pot of tea £1.20. Big glass of juice £1.50. Cordials, ginger beer 80p.

Children welcome, high chairs and baby changing. No credit cards, cashpoints nearby.

Also an art gallery selling arts and crafts.

East Yorkshire — NORTH

Seasalt & Passion
Vegetarian cafe, restaurant & gallery

22 West Street, Bridlington YO15 3DX (1 min walk from Brid Harbour and Spa Theatre, across the road from Spotlight Theatre)
Tel: 01262-671 117
Open: Tue-Fri 9.00-16.00, Sat 9.00-16.00, Sun-Mon closed; open peak summer Sun
www.seasaltandpassion.co.uk
vegetarian-vegan-catering.moonfruit.com
seasaltgigs.moonfruit.com

In an eclectic, up and coming street. Food is pan-European, 50% organic, with gluten-free and many vegan options. Art on walls for sale by local, national and international artists. World music is played, with live acoustic food and music events every 6 to 8 weeks.

Menus change seasonally, plus several daily specials, £4.95-6.95, such as 5-bean chilli with spiced couscous; chestnut and cashew fritters; Thai tofu cakes with hot chilli dip; all served with something such as couscous salads, roast veg. Winter soup £3 with bread. Tapenade or hummus in sandwich from £2.25 or on a plate with salad and bread. Beanburger £3.95, falafel etc.

Cream teas can be vegan (without cream) as they include vegan scones. They aim to have at least one vegan dessert around £2.80 such as fruitcake, carrot cake, raspberry pie. Alpro soya dessert always available.

Pot of tea £1.40, lots of speciality teas. Coffee £1.60. Juices £1.40.

Children's portions, high chairs. No dogs except guide dogs, but you can park one outside. Disabled toilet. 5% discount Vegan or Vegetarian Society and people presenting this book. No credit cards. Also sells hand-made pickles and relishes, bread, infused oils and vinegars, spice mixes, sometimes bakery goods and chocolates. Cookery demos. Private hire, outside catering, whole cakes and dishes for your own dinner parties. Product catalogue available.

Bempton Cafe
Vegetarian cafe

at RSPB Bempton Cliffs Reserve, Cliff Lane, Bempton, Bridlington YO15 1JF
Train: Bempton (45 mins walk), East Coast linefrom Hull, Bridlington, and Scarborough
Visitor Centre: 01262-851179
Trailer: 07853 303049
Reserve open 24/7, part of national coastal pathway. Visitor Centre open every day except Xmas 10.00-16.00 winter, 10.00-17.00 summer
www.rspb.org.uk/reserves/guide/b/bemptoncliffs
Facebook: ECO (Ethical Catering Outdoors)

Vegetarian catering caravan with picnic tables at the RSPB's Bempton Cliffs nature reserve. As it's hard to manoeuvre up the trail in these suddenly fierce winters, it may be closed until spring, call to check until they move into a new permanent building. Organic, Fairtrade handmade food.

Savoury board has many vegan options £1-3.50 such as spicy beanburgers with mayo, pasties, falafels, scones, soup, homemade bread, sandwiches to order, casserole, mushroom lattice tart. Puddings 80p-£1.80 include has scones, nut & raisin flapjack, date oaty slice, chocolate crunch, brownie or lemon cake. Proper coffee machine, teas, herb teas, juices, Whole Earth cans, local apple juice, Fentimans.

The reserve has 400 foot high chalk cliffs, the most northerly in the UK, with gannets, puffins, kittiwakes, guillemots, razorbills. Shop with educational stuff, toys, bird food, cards, gifts. Gift pack if you join the RSPB and free passes, well worth joining if you come regularly.

The reserve is on the cliff road from Bempton village, on B1229 Filey to Flamborough. In Bempton, turn northwards at White Horse public house and reserve is at the end of the road after 1 mile (follow the brown tourist signs).

Walk in. £3.50 car, free for RSPB members.

Goole

Peppercorn

Health food shop

77-79 Pasture Road, Goole DN14 6BP
(midway between Hull and Leeds)
Tel: 01405-769 875
Open: Mon-Fri 9.30-17.00,
Sat 10.00-16.00, Sun closed
www.mbsfestivals.co.uk

Moved in summer 2010 to bigger premises, adding a deli counter with Mediterranean foods, cakes, nice things to make a picnic and there's a baker nearby.

Lots of wholefoods and organic products. Fridge and freezer with Tofutti vegan cheeses, Redwood, Taifun, Fry's, Vegetarian's Choice, Provamel, Linda McCartney, Booja Booja ice-cream. Vegan chocolate by Montezuma, Plamil, Organic Meltdown and others at Christmas. Loose herbs, spices. They have a coffee grinder.

Bodycare by Aubrey, Weleda, Akin, Natracare, some baby products.

Supplements by Nature's Plus, Vogel, Nature's Aid, Biohealth, Pharma Nord, Swiss Herbal Formula, Lifeplan, Arkopharma, Salus, sports nutrition including vegan pea protein and hemp. Weleda and some Nelsons homeopathy, Bach flower remedies, essential oils. Jewellery, crystals, hand-made gifts, books, candles. Now also 2 therapy rooms with acupuncture, hypnotherapy, reflexology, crystal healing, massage.

BioD and Ecover cleaning products. Some books, Namaste and free magazines. Discounts for buying in bulk. They can order in anything else you need. MC, Visa.

The proprietors organise the large Harrogate (end September), Buxton (end June) and Bridlington (early May) Health & Healing Festivals.

(Kingston upon) Hull vegetarian

The Zoo Cafe

Vegetarian cafe

80B Newland Avenue, Hull HU5 3AB
Tel: 01482-494 352
Open: Mon-Sat 10.00-17.00,
Sun 12.00-14.00

Friendly community cafe between the centre and the university on a popular shopping street. Large open doors onto courtyard with some outside tables, lovely in summer. Local groups such as Amnesty meet here, meditation classes Tuesday evening. The menu varies during the year. Four daily main course options for vegans, usually two gluten-free, and a stunning choice of vegan desserts.

All-day full cooked breakfast £4.25 includes 2 sausages, beans, mushrooms, tomatoes, toast. Soup £2.25 with bread. Salad platter £4 with hummus, olives, bread. Main meals are all under £5 such as burritos, casseroles, veggieburgers with salad, jacket potatoes, bangers and mash with peas and gravy.

Scones £1 with jam and spread, can be vegan. Vegan dessert heaven all £2 such as chocolate brownies, banana cake, orange and lemon cake, chocolate fudge cake, banana and fig cake, with cream or custard or ice-cream.

Fresh fruit shakes and smoothies £2.50. Tea £1, coffee £1.20, large cappuccino £1.70. Soya milk available.

Children welcome, high chair, large collection of toys and books, small play area downstairs. Dogs welcome outside. Cheques ok if spending over £10, no cards.

Hitchcock's

Superb vegetarian all-you-can-eat buffet restaurant in the Museum Quarter. Hitchcock's attracts lots of meat eaters and is worth stopping in Hull for. One price £15 (£12 concessions Tue-Thu) for three courses and coffee, with one sitting starting from 8.15pm.

Being in a quiet area of the Old Town, they only open when enough people book, usually 15-20 are sufficient, either as a single group or several separate bookings.

The menu is chosen by the first person to book and is based around a particular country, such as Italian, Chinese, Mexican, Thai, Cajun, Indian, Afro-Caribbean, Russian. But they could do Nepalese, Patagonian, Israeli, Tibetan, German and even English. Or a mixture.

Almost all food is vegan, for example the Cajun menu starts with salsa red bean, dips with crudites and toasted bread. The awesome main course buffet includes okra gumbo, red beans and rice, banana bread, Jamaican curry, fried plantain bananas and sweet potatoes, lemon spinach, sweetcorn, hot salsa, salads, chillies.

Several desserts such as pecan pie, crumble and (vegan) ice cream.

House wines from £2 glass, £9 bottle. Beer £2-3 for a pint or a bottle. Spirits from £2. Or bring your own wine and pay £1 per bottle corkage.

Caters for coeliacs, nut-free and other diets on request.

This is one of the best vegetarian restaurants ever, anywhere.

Hull

Vegetarian Restaurant

1-2 Bishop Lane
Hull
East Yorkshire HU1 1PA
(on corner of Bishop Lane and High Street)

Tel: 01482-320 233

Open:
Tue-Sat 20.00-24.00,
Sun-Mon closed

Best to arrive 8-9pm as food is served in one sitting between these times

www.hitchcocksrestaurant.co.uk

Children welcome, prices to suit as they like haggling.

No dogs except guide dogs

Licensed

Outside catering

MC, Visa

£2 discount for members of the Vegetarian or Vegan Society
Advance bookings required. Deposit of £5 per head for groups of 8+.

MC, Visa

NORTH East Yorkshire

Green Ginger

Vegetarian cafe

8a Bowlalley Lane, Land of Green Ginger, Hull HU1 1XR (in the Old Town)
No telephone
Open: Mon–Sat morning and afternoons
www.greengingercafe.com

New central cafe, great for a fast take-away lunch or a quick coffee. Menu changes daily. Locally sourced where possible.

Hot and cold sandwiches £3 on bread, ciabatta, wrap, pitta or multigrain slice, include crunchy pepper and hummus; sausage and mushroom; BLT. Tray with your choice of 4 salads £3.50, take-out £3. Cooked breakfast £3.95 includes sausages, rashers, hash browns, tomatoes, mushrooms, beans and toast. Soups £3. Hot mains £3.95 include chicken curry, chilli, chickpea/lentil curry, chicken and mushroom pie, burritos, sausage casserole and mash, shepherd's pie.

Cakes £1.50. Flapjack 80p. Muffins £1.20.

Fresh fruit and veg juices £2.50. Soft drinks £1. Tea £1.20, coffee £1.20-1.70, cafetiere to share with friends £4.70.

Hull omnivorous

Ask, Hull

Omnivorous Italian restaurant

Warehouse 6, Princes Dock St, Hull HU1 2PQ
Tel: 01482-210 565
Open: Mon–Thu 12.00–23.00, Fri–Sat 23.30, Sun 22.30
www.askrestaurants.com

Good standby for when the veggie places are closed. Salads and pizza can be made vegan. Outside seating in nice weather.

Mimosa

Omnivorous Turkish & Mediterranean restaurant

406–408 Beverley Road, Hull HU5 1LW
Tel: 01482-474748
Open: Tue–Sun 17.00–22.30 (last orders), Mon closed for private parties
www.mimosahull.com (menus)

Handy for when Hitchcocks is closed and they know what vegans like. Usual mezze dishes £3.40-3.80 or have a platter for two £9.50 cold, £11.50 hot. Mains £8.50-9.50 include stuffed peppers, pasta, vegetarian kebabs served with salad and Turkish rice. Side veg, olives, chips £1.50-2.50. Set menu £18.50 for 2+ people with platter of 8 starters, any main, dessert. 3 vegan-option desserts £3.50 such as Armut pears in wine syrup with cinnamon, sun-dried figs with nuts, Kemalpasa sweet bread balls with nuts. House wine £12.50 bottle, £3.25 glass. MC, Visa.

Thai House Restaurant

Omnivorous Thai restaurant

51 Princes Av, Hull HU5 3QY (near Zoo Cafe)
Tel: 01482-473 473
Open: every day 17.30–23.00, Fri–Sat 23.30

Almost every dish has veggie option £7.45-9.50, such as curries, stir-fries, mixed veg or bean curd. Rice £1.95, coconut rice £2.60. 2 courses and drink around £15. House wine £9.95 bottle, £2.50 glass. Children welcome, high chair. MC, Visa, Amex.

Hull shops
Arthur Street Trading

Organic vegetarian wholefood delivery service

Unit 2, 23 Arthur Street, Hull HU3 6BH
Tel: 07949 805695
www.arthursorganics.com
info@arthursorganics.karoo.co.uk

Workers' cooperative since 1999. Home delivery service for organic fruit, veg, groceries, organic hummus they make themselves, BioD cleaning products in Hull and surrounding villages. In Hull they use a solar-powered milkfloat.

Grain Wholefoods

Wholefood shop

25 Newland Avenue, Hull HU5 3BE
Tel: 01482-448680
Open: Mon-Sat 9.30-17.30, Sun closed
www.lovelocal.org.uk/grainwholefood

Seasonal local organic fruit and veg. Fridges and freezer with pasties, tubs of salad, falafel, hummus, vegan cheeses and meat substitutes, vegan black cherry and lemon crumble, raw chocolate, tofu, sprouts, frozen vegan cheesecake, Tofutti, Swedish Glace, Booja Booja. Local breads delivered Wed-Sat.
Lots of bodycare by Lavera, Weleda, Faith In Nature, Trilogy, Suma, Tom's, Urtekram, Sarakan, Vicco ayurvedic, Optima, Natracare. Earth Friendly, Weleda and Lavera baby stuff.
Supplements by Nature's Own, Higher Nature, Nature's Aid, Floradix. Weleda homeopathy, A.Vogel tinctures. Sometimes a nutritionist in store.
BioD (which is based in Hull), Clearspring, Ecoleaf, Ecover and some refills. Free magazines. MC, Visa.

Chain stores
Holland & Barrett

Health food shop

60 Toll Gravel, **Beverley** HU17 9BN
Tel: 01482-871 346
Open: Mon-Sat 9.00-17.30, Sun 10-16.00

Unit 1, 47/49 Kings St, **Bridlington** YO15 2DN. Tel: 01262-676 006
Open: Mon-Sat 9.00-17.30, Sun 10-16.00

3 Finkle Street, **Cottingham** HU16 4AU
Tel: 01482-841 107
Open: Mon-Sat 9.00-17.30, Sun closed

9 Jameson Street, **Hull** HU1 3EN
Tel: 01482-326 597
Open: Mon-Sat 9.00-17.30, Sun 10-16.00

21 Whitefriargate, **Hull** HU1 2EX
Tel: 01482-225 829
pen: Mon-Sat 9.00-17.30, Sun 10-16.00

Julian Graves

Health food shop

22 Toll Gavel, **Beverley** HU17 9AR
Tel: 01482-880866

Unit 18, The Promenades Shopping Centre, **Bridlington** YO15 2DX
Tel: 01262-608058

Unit 55, Hornsea Freeport, Rolston Rd, **Hornsea** HU18 1UT
Tel: 01964-537 220

Local group
East Riding Vegans

Local group

Mark Evans, 140 Victoria Avenue, Hull HU5 3DT. Tel 01482-471119
www.merrydowncontrolware.co.uk/ervegans
(includes a vegan map of Hull)
ervegans@merrydowncontrolware.co.uk

Local group organising events and providing support for vegans and supporters in Hull and the surrounding area.

NORTH East Yorkshire

Sheffield

Sheffield has seven very different vegetarian cafes including Blue Moon (also good for an early dinner), Airy Fairy, Heeley City Farm and Homemade Cafe, which also does a Friday night bistro and in summer a Wednesday night burger bash.

For eating out at night there is also a superb range of omnivorous restaurants that have lots of veggie and vegan food, from the Bohemian Cafe through Indian and Italian to the African UK Mama, and even a real ale pub specialising in vegetarian dishes.

Round this off with a big choice of proper wholefood stores, and it's no surprise that one lass from the veggie paradise of Glastonbury told us she moved to friendly Sheffield because it's the only other place in the UK for her.

Sheffield is on the doorstep of the Peak District National Park which offers an abundance of walking and climbing.

www.yorkshiresouth.com

Bawtrey	**175**
Doncaster	**176**
SHEFFIELD	**176**
Chain stores	**185**
Local groups	**185**

South Yorkshire

Bawtrey

Bawtry Natural Health & Therapy Centre

Health food shop

David House, 2 South Parade, Bawtry DN10 6JH (south of Doncaster, 15 miles from Sheffield). Tel: 01302-719917
Open: Mon-Fri 10.00-17.30, Sat 10-17.00

Gluten-free breads. Fridge with vegan cheeses but not meat substitutes. They don't do takeaway food but do have snack bars. Vegan chocolate by Montezuma.
Bodycare by Jason, Barefoot Botanicals, Dr Bronner, Faith In Nature, Dr Hauschka, Green People, Weleda, Eco Cosmetics, Lavera, Natracare, kids' stuff.
BioD, Ecover and Earth Friendly cleaning products.
Supplements by Solgar, Viridian, Vogel, Nature's Plus. Homeopathy, flower essences, Pukka herbs, essential oils. Lemon Detox. Practitioner rooms with homeopath, chiropodist, Bowen Technique, osteopath, colonic irrigation, EST, life coaching, holistic therapist, acupuncturist, and the owner does food intolerance testing. Health and diet books. MC, Visa.

Bawtry Deli & Cafe

Omnivorous cafe and delicatessen

11 Dower House Square, Bawtry, Doncaster DN10 6LS (9 miles south of Doncaster on the Notts border, 9 miles north of Retford)
Tel: 01302-711 114
Open: Tue-Sat 10.00-17.00 (Tue from 10.30), Sun-Mon closed except in Dec

Soup £3.95 with bread. Bowl of salad £3 such as pasta salad, tabouleh, pearl barley salad with sundried tomato and apricot dressing. Jacket potato with roast veg or anything else they sell in the shop such as artichokes, £5.95 eat in with salad, £2-3.75 take-out. Sandwiches made to order with whatever you fancy from the shop, eat-in from £3, or £5.50 with salads, take-away from £2.
Cakes but not as yet vegan. Pot of tea £1.50, coffee or cappuccino/latte £1.90-2.20, no soya milk. Chegworth apple juice, ginger beer, juices, soft drinks £1.50-£2. Freshly made fruit smoothies £2.
Children welcome though no special facilities, can do smaller portions.
Shop and deli has antipasti such as 3 kinds of sundried tomatoes, artichoke hearts, chillis, lots of olives, garlic cloves, vegan pesto. Hummus, vegan pates, chutneys and jams from around the world. Scottish country wines, unusual English liqueurs. Yorkshire made sloe gin, brandy and vodka.
The cafe is on the first floor and also has outside seating where dogs are welcome. Formerly called The Bay Tree. MC, Visa.

Doncaster
Eating Whole
Vegetarian cafe-restaurant

25 Copley Road, Doncaster DN1 2PE
Open: Mon-Sat 09.00-16.00,
also Thu-Sat 19.30-22.30. Closed Sun.
Tel: 01302-738 730

Small, friendly cafe during the day, restaurant at night, near the market. Always a vegan option in each course and they have vegan cheese. Menu changes every few days. Good range of vegetarian alcohol from Vinceremos.

Pate, soups £2.50. Light meals £2.60-2.80 such as jacket potato, wedges. Mains £4.50 such as spicy lentil rissole with chilli sauce; lentil and spinach bake. Cakes, pies £2.50, some vegan such as chocolate and pear tart and wholewheat teacakes.

Juices £1.20. Huge range of teas £1-1.20. Cafetiere of fresh ground coffee £1.30.

All wines and bottled beers are vegetarian or vegan. House wine £2 glass, from £7.50 bottle, right up to £20 for the top stuff. Bottle of Dunkerton's organic cider £2.10. Little Valley Brewery vegan organic stout from Hebden Bridge £2.50. Border Gold organic 6% real ale £2.30. Caledonian organic ale Golden Promise £2.30.

Children's portions, high chair. Xmas and New Year dinners. MC, Visa. Vegetarian and Vegan Society members 10% discount.

Planning to close end Feb 2011 when the lease expires unless someone wants to buy it as a going concern.

Sheffield - vegetarian
Airy Fairy
Vegetarian coffee shop

239 London Road, Sheffield S2 4NF
Tel: 0114-249 2090
Open: Mon, Sat 11-17.00; Tue-Fri 11.00-17.30; Sun closed.
www.airyfairy.org

Cafe at the back of a gift shop with wood-burning stove in winter and garden.

Homemade soup and bread £2.95, always a vegan option. Homemade hummus, mushrooms and (vegan option) pesto, or organic beans on toast £1.85-2.75. Mains include tomato, olive and basil vegan calzone with salad £3.90.

Sandwiches made to order on their homemade bread £2.40-3.25.

Homemade and mostly organic cakes £1-2.50 include at least 4 vegan ones, mincemeat crumble cake, seasonal fruit crumble cake, fruitcake, and a Parkin. Dark chocolate, cherry and coconut flapjack £1. Vegan choc ices and cornets 90p-£1.15.

Pot of tea, herb tea, or loose fruit teas £1.15-1.25. Cafetiere of coffee £1.35. Cappuccino, mocha, latte £1.50-1.90. Soya milk available. Banana smoothie £1.55, large orange juice £1.15, elderflower cordial 90p, organic sparkling drinks £1.15.

Children welcome, high chair, breastfeeders welcome, free drinks for under 5. Outside seating in the garden but warn them if bringing a dog so they can hide the free-range rabbit. The shop has handmade and local crafts with pagan influences, and Fairtrade items from around the world including vegan chocolate, flapjacks, chocolate coated orange marzipan. Cruelty-free bodycare products. Hand-made jewellery. Lots of cards for all occasions. MC, Visa.

Blue Moon Cafe

Vegetarian cafe

2 St James's Street, Sheffield S1 2EW (city opposite west end of the cathedral)
Tel: 0114-276 3443
Open: Mon-Sat 8.00-20.00, Sun closed
www.facebook.com/group.php?gid=665267 77769

Big cafe with counter service by the Anglican cathedral. Half the food is vegan, some gluten-free. Soup £3.35 with bread. 3 hot mains £6.05 daily, 2 of them vegan, with rice or salads such as lentil bake with red pepper, courgette and coconut; imam bayaldi; squash, courgette and mushroom pie. Pasties, burritos and tortilla wraps £2.05-3.35. Cakes £2.15 include their famous vegan chocolate one; banana; date and cashewnut slice; Crunchie Munchie slice. Vegan muffins £1.55, vegan scones 95p, add 5p for jam. Soya cream available. Swedish Glace ice-cream £1.55 for a bowl.

Pot of tea £1.70, cafetiere of coffee £2.15. (Soya) latte or cappuccino, hot chocolate, £2.25. Fruit smoothies £2.95. Cold drinks £1.60. Fentimans Victorian lemonade £2.05.

Organic wines and beers are all vegan. House wine £2.75 small glass, £3.05 large, £10.70 bottle. Lots of local beers such as Tadcaster Yorkshire brewery Samuel Smiths best ale and lager £2.60 bottle. Westons cider £3.45. Sheffield Kelham Island brewery beers Pale Rider and Grande Pale £3.45 (500ml).

Children welcome, baby seats. Visa, MC over £5. Outside catering.

The cafe is for sale as a going concern to interested veggies.

Homemade Cafe

Vegetarian daytime cafe, deli, mostly vegetarian evening restaurant

4 Nether Edge Road, **Nether Edge**, Sheffield S7 1RU (opposite Zed Wholefoods, 1.5 miles from centre. Bus 22 to Nether Edge from centre of town, also 75, 76, 97)
Tel: 0777 4013 438
Cafe: Tue-Thu 9.30-15.30, Fri 9.30-14.30, Sat 9.30-15.00, Sun-Mon closed
Fri bistro evening 19.00-22.30 BYO
Wed burger & shakes May-Oct 17.00-21.00
www.homemade-sheffield.co.uk

A huge entry because it's really 4 places in one. Firstly a small but excellent **daytime vegetarian cafe**, previously Green Edge vegetarian cafe, now under new ownership and much expanded. Also **Wednesday night for burgers** (4 vegan, one meat) and shakes, and candlelit **Friday night bistro** when there is one fish dish. Plus a new **deli** updstairs. Clean cut 1950's style decoration, with a nostalgic feel with lots of old recipes on the wall. The menu changes every day. Lots of coeliacs and vegans eat here, and it also attracts a high proportion of non-veggies.

Saturday all day breakfast from toast and marmalade £1.20 up to the massive cooked

Blue Moon Cafe, Sheffield

breakfast for £7.50-8.00 which includes roasted tomatoes, mushrooms, sausage, baked beans, sauteed potatoes and toast with tea or coffee.

Daytime cafe: Vegan gluten-free soup £4 with bread. 5 or 6 mains such as quesadilla of the day with roasted veg in tortilla with 2 salads £5.25; in winter a hearty special £5.25-£6 such as veggie stew or cottage pie; chili; curry; falafel; all served with veg or salads. At least 4 salads daily, 3 vegan and these include Moroccan chickpea, Waldorf with apple, walnut and celery in cider vinegar and wholegrain mustard dressing; carrot, red cabbage, orange and cumin; Italian mixed bean salsa verde.

Homemade cakes £1.25-£3 include cupcakes, vegan choc brownie, gluten-free polenta cake. Crumpets or cinnamon and raisin bagel with pot of tea/coffee £2.50/£3. Pot of tea £1.40. Coffees and latte/cappuccino £1.40-£2. Their speciality is noisette coffee cocktail with hazelnut syrup in a glass £2.20. Soya milk available. Lots of organic cordials, sparkling drinks, traditional lemonade, ginger beer, juices £1.20-1.60.

Wednesday evening May-Oct is burger & shakes night and of 7 burgers, 1 is veggie and 4 vegan (some gluten-free) in griddled ciabatta £5.95-7.95 (regular vegan burger, double sos burger, spicy bean, or chickpea) with potato wedges or 2 salads such as vegan coleslaw, and relish tray. Double hot dog £5.50 with wedges. Coleslaw or green salad £1, wedges £1.50. Dessert muffins £1.50, coke float £2. Kids' burgers with wedges £3.75-£4. Large shake £2, soya 50p extra.

Friday bistro evening has one fish dish on the menu. 2 courses £15, 3 for £18.50. 3 starters such as soup; griddled bread with asparagus topped with homemade salsa verde; quinoa with roasted butternut squash and pumpkin seeds. Mains such as Sicilian stew made with aubergines, olives and toasted almonds served with homemade bread; sausage meatballs with tomato sauce, mash and veg; tagine with couscous; mezze platter with falafel, dolmades, roasted peppers, toasted nut and cinnamon pilaf. Lots of desserts, most not vegan, but when booking tell them your dietary needs and they design the menu around them, so vegans could have a choice of desserts such as summer pudding, crumble, chocolate pudding.

Children welcome, high chairs, book box, breastfeeding friendly. Cash or cheque only, cashpoint next door. Bring your own alcohol evenings, no corkage charge, off-licence opposite. Booking advised evening, essential well in advance Friday.

Outside catering onsite, or food-to-go that you pick up, for corporate events, dinner and birthday parties, weddings, bbq, picnic food, birthday cakes. See website for menu. Private evening events for 15+. Local vegan and veggie groups have meals here and some of them work in the Oxfam shop next door.

Summer 2010 they opened a small **deli** selling olives, antipasti, handmade pates, jams, jellies, chutneys, relishes, sauces and dressings, crisps, nuts, spicy broadbeans, biscuits and crackers, loose leaf teas and coffee beans ground how you like.

Cafe Number 9

Vegetarian coffee shop

9 **Nether Edge Road**, Sheffield S7 1RU
Tel: 0114-258 1383
Open: Tue-Sun 10.30-18.30, Mon closed

A proper coffee shop where you can hang out, enjoy the papers or have a game of chess, backgammon, scrabble or go. They even photocopy the crossword so others can have a try. Many local actors and artists come here. They don't use eggs.

Cup of tea £1.20. Coffee, cappuccino, mocha etc £1.60-2.50. No soya milk. Bagels, beans on toast, toasted sandwiches all £2.95, made to order with brown bread. Cakes £1.50, probably not vegan.

Children welcome, kids' books. Outside seating, dogs welcome there. Bring your own alcohol evenings if they're open later.

Heeley City Farm Cafe

Vegetarian cafe

Richards Road, **Heeley**, Sheffield S2 3DT
Cafe: 0114-258 0244
Farm: 0114-258 0482
Cafe: every day 10.00-16.00
Farm: every day 9.30-17.00, 16.30 winter
www.heeleyfarm.org.uk

Amazing value, vegan-friendly cafe in a 2 hectare city farm and gardens, one mile from the city centre, with horses, cows, pigs, sheep. There are also an under 8's playground, peat-free garden centre, gift shop with local crafts and recycling centre. Wander around the aromatic herb gardens (mind the ducks!) humid polytunnels, demonstration gardens and vegetable plots. Renewable Energy Centre with information and demonstrations of wind and solar power.

Great breakfasts from 35p per slice for toast up to £1.80 for a cooked breakfast. Sausage sandwich £1.75.

Several salads and they can be unusual such as shredded cabbage with cranberries and caraway seeds; pasta with sweet chilli dressing; couscous with mint, roasted peppers and chickpeas. Mixed salad bowl £2.50 with bread. Soups are vegan £3. Toasties £3.95 on big granary bread with a plate of salad. Jacket potato with chilli or beans £1.75-£2.50, sometimes veggieburger £2.50 with bread and green salad. Specials most days £4 such as chilli, curry, bakes, can be with bread or couscous. Homemade cakes and flapjacks £1-£1.40, some vegan.

All tea and coffee is Fairtrade. Tea 90p, coffee £1.20. Soya milk available. Chocolate or banana soya milk, juice cartons 70p. Whole Earth organic cans £1.

Children's portions of anything from the main menu with juice £2-2.50, plus special kids' dishes or requests. High chair. Outside seating and playground, dogs welcome outside and they can provide water. Wheelchair friendly. Cash or cheque only.

If vegan readers are wondering, we were told that no animals are sent directly for slaughter, but some and "surplus" males are sold to individuals, who probably do not keep them as pets.

New Roots Wholefood

Vegetarian cafe & wholefood shop

86 Spital Hill, **Burngreave**, Sheffield S4 7LG
Tel: 0114-270 0972
Mon-Fri 11..00-17.00, Sat-Sun closed,
Open: Mon-Sat 11.30-15.30, Sun closed;
Sometimes open Fri evening
Can close a couple of weeks in August
www.newroots.org.uk

One of two New Roots vegetarian wholefood shops in Sheffield (the other is near the university, see below in Shops). This one is also a vegetarian cafe which massively expanded its range in 2010.

Soup £1.80 with homemade bread. Hot main £3.50 such as homity pie and salad with tea/coffee. Wide range of pasties 99p-£2.

Home-made puddings around £2 such as sticky pineapple upside down cake, rhubarb crumble. Cakes 80p, mostly vegan.

Vegan smoothies £1 using seasonal

fruit. Tea 75p, filter coffee 95p. Cake and coffee deal £1.60.

They are starting up Fri and Sat evening events from 8pm such as live music and story-telling, Sri Lankan curry night.

Cash only, cashpoint nearby. Dogs welcome. Children welcome, 2 high chairs, toys.

The **shop** carries the same range as their other shop near the university, see below, except that this one has no fruit & veg. Organic bread. Take-away salads 50p a portion, box of 4 portions £2, reusable tin £1.

Multi-faith chapel and library in the basement with seminars on various issues relating to different faiths.

World Peace Cafe, Sheffield

Vegetarian cafe

Gyaltsabje Buddhist Centre,
685-691 Ecclesall Road, **Hunters Bar**,
Sheffield S11 8TG
Tel: 0114 -266 1142
Open: Fri-Sun 11.00-16.00
www.meditateinsheffield.org.uk

Opposite beautiful Endcliffe Park, 20 minutes walk from the centre. Relaxing tranquil atmosphere. You can visit the meditation room. Meditation classes available. Gift shop with Buddhist books, statues, cards. The cafe vegetables come from local allotments.

Home-cooked soup £3.90 with homemade bread. Main meals £5.50 such as curries, chilli. Sandwiches £2.50 on their home-baked bread made on the premises.

Cakes £1.90-2.50, some vegan.

Pot of organic loose leaf tea £1.50, coffee £1.90, cappuccino £1.90, soya milk available. Juice £1.50.

Children very welcome, lots of space for them, high chairs, baby changing, toys, books, colouring stuff. Disabled access and toilet. Cash or cheque only.

Sheffield - omnivorous

The Bohemian Cafe

**90% vegetarian
cafe-bistro-restaurant**

53 Chesterfield Road, Sheffield S8 0RL
Tel: 0114-255 7797
Open: Tue-Sat 11.00-23.00, Sun 11-16.00, Mon closed
www.thebohemiancafe.co.uk

Opened 2006, a daytime cafe becomes a candlelit restaurant in the evening where you can save money by bringing your own alcohol. This is the closest Sheffield has to a vegetarian restaurant open late in the evening. Everything is veggie apart from 3 fish items and one meat dish, and it attracts 80% non-veggies looking for healthy food. Lots of vegan food, they make their own hummus and marinated olives.

Menu changes monthly. Sandwiches and wraps made to order £3.50-3.80 such as Cajun wrap with roasted carrot, aubergine, pepper, mushroom, courgette, onion. Light bites £3.00-3.25 such as soup with bread, Mediterranean veg tartlet, garlic mushrooms, falafel. Mains £7.25, vegan ones include moussaka, mixed bean burrito, chickpea goulash with rice, jambalay.

Half the cakes £3 are vegan such as chocolate or carrot cake, and they also have a gluten-free cake for example blueberry, lemon and coconut (also vegan). Sticky toffee pudding and apple crumble are also vegan and £3. They have soya cream.

Smoothies £2.80, fresh juices £2.30. Pot of tea (12 kinds) £1.40. Small coffee £1.50, large £1.80, cappuccino £1.90-2.10. Soya milk available. Small soya milkshake cartons £1.30. Whole Earth organic juice cans £1.20.

Children welcome if they don't run riot, 2 high chairs, facilities for baby changing upstairs if you have a mat, kids' menu meal and drink £2.50 . Cash or cheque only, cashpoint nearby. Outside catering, e.g. vegan weddings. Upstairs therapy rooms with massage etc.

Bilash Tandoori House
Omni Indian/ Bangladeshi take-away

347 **Sharrow Vale Road**, Sheffield S11 8ZG
Tel: 0114-266 1746
Open: Sun-Thu 17.30-24.00,
Fri-Sat 17.30-00.30

Take-away recommended by several readers for their separate veggie menu. Normal Indian starters around £1.30-2.20. Big range of different dishes around £4 such as Balti vegetables and ginger, veg katta masala, badami veg with mixed nuts and raisins, curries. Rice £1.70, lemon or coconut or onion rice £2.20, djipatti 70p, paratha £1.40. Desserts £1.20 include banana or pineapple fritter. Soft drinks 60p. Children welcome. MC, Visa.

East and West
Omnivorous South Indian & Sri Lankan restaurant

227 Abbeydale Road, Sheffield S7 1FJ (1.5 miles south of the centre)
Tel: 0114-258 8066
Open: Mon-Fri 12.00-14.30, 17.00-23.00,
Sat-Sun 12.00-23.00
www.eastnwest.net (menu)

Around half the menu is vegetarian, and most of that vegan. Usual Indian starters £1.95-4.25 plus cashewnut pakoda and gobi Manchurian. Main dishes £3.50-5.75 include dosas, uttappam, veg kotthu (chopped parota roti mixed with veg, tomato, onions and chilli), veg biryani. Curries £2.95-4.50. Rice, coconut, lemon or pilau £1.75-£2.75. Desserts include vegan gulab jamum £2.95. Juices £2.50, soft drinks £1, coffee £2. Bring your own alcohol, pay one or two pounds per table corkage. Children welcome. MC, Visa.

The Fat Cat
Omnivorous real ale pub

23 Alma Street, Sheffield S3 8SA (near Kelham Island Industrial Museum)
Tel: 0114-249 4801
Open: Mon-Sun 12.00-23.00, later weekends.
Food: Mon-Fri 12.00-15.00, 18.00-20.00;
Sat 12.00-20.00; Sun 12.00-15.00
www.thefatcat.co.uk

Friendly independent real ale pub with its own Kelham Island brewery attached, noted for cheap and healthy wholesome home cooking, with vegan and gluten-free dishes marked on the menu. Open fires, beer garden, family room, and conversation is encouraged by having no music and electronic machines. Winter lentil and veg soup £3. 3 vegetarian, of which two vegan, main dishes £4.50 such as leek & mustard pie with peas and gravy; vegetable burrito; parsnip & cashew roast; nutty parsnip pie; aubergine & mushroom casserole with herb dumplings; blackeye bean and pepper casserole. Sun lunch £5. Monday night quiz at 10pm, with 8-10pm veg curry, naan bread and onion bhajia £2.95, Kelham bitter £1.20 pint. You can have a birthday or other party here for 20+ with a buffet menu from 8pm: £5.50 for chilli, veg curry, potato wedges, Indian selection.

Ten draft ales from £1.95 pint. Prominence is given to small, independent brewers, also unusual bottled beers and traditional scrumpy. English country wines and some French wines around £2.75-2.85 glass. If you're lucky, the resident fat cat will come and sit on your lap!

Jhinook (Momtaz)

Omnivorous Indian/Bangladeshi restaurant and take-away

115-117 Chesterfield Road, **Heeley**, Sheffield S8 0RN (between Meersbrook Park Rd and Beeston Rd)
Tel: 0114-258 8822
Open: every day 18-24.00, -01.00 Fri-Sat

Previously called Momtaz until late 2010, now under new ownership but still aiming to cater for veggies and vegans. Recommended by local vegans for a big range of veggie food. Take-away prices in (brackets).

Starters include onion bhaji £2.50 (take-away £1.50), samosa 2.50 (£1.50) and they can make other dishes on request.

Lots of vegetarian main dishes £6-7 eat in, £1-1.50 cheaper as take-away, include Tandoori vegetable sizzler, medium bhuna, mild korma, hot Ceylon with coconut, hot samber, medium vindaloo, madras, sweet and sour dansak, medium dupiazza, bindi okra, hot sweet and sour pathia, veg balti jalfrazi, medium balti spi-cha with spinach and chickpeas, biryani.

Side dishes £3.50-4.50 (£2.30-3.50). Chips £2 (£1.10), 20 kinds of rice and breads £1.95-2.50 (£1.40-£1.90). Free delivery over £10 within 3 miles. Now has a vegan desserts, banana or pineapple fritters £2.50.

House wine from £9.95 bottle, £2.50 glass. Coffee £1.95. Children welcome, high chair. MC, Visa. Free car park opposite after 6.30pm.

UK Mama

Omnivorous African/Caribbean restaurant & take-away

257 Fulwood Road, **Broomhill**, Sheffield S10 3BD. Tel: 0114-268 7807
Hotline 07886 423785
Open: Every day lunch 11.00-15.00, evenings from 17.00 till late, last orders 23.00 (subject to revision)
advance booking highly recommended both lunch and evening;
www.ukmama.co.uk

Food from all over Africa, plus Caribbean dishes, with a separate vegetarian menu. Feel free to request a particular African dish not on the menu. These are take-away prices, add 25% for restaurant prices.

Start with unusual African soups or fried plantain £2. Main courses £4.40 such as couscous with veg sauce; Jallof rice with musrooms and mixed veg; fried or boiled rice with peanut casserole. Stewed mushrooms with yam, plantains and sweet potatoes £6.38; curried veg £2.80; Dodo fried ripe plantains £4.76 with beans with pepper sauce. Side veg 75p-£1.60 include yam, plantain, sweet potato, callaloo, okra, rice, couscous, blackeye or kidney beans. Early bird 5-7pm 2 courses £5.95. Budget menu 3 courses £8.95 includes glass of wine. Family African style 4-course mini buffet for 4 people £44.

Desserts £1.95-3.50, vegan ones include fresh mango papaw, banana split, fruit salad.

Teas and coffee 95p-£1.15, liqueur coffee £2.45. Wine £1.95-2.50 glass, £7.50-9.25 bottle.

Students can eat in for the take-away price, equivalent to 20% off. Children welcome. MC, Visa, cashpoints nearby. Outside catering for up to 3,000, with steel bands and drummers.

Wagamama, Sheffield

Omnivorous Japanese restaurant

2 Leopold Square, Sheffield S1 2JG
Tel: 0114-272 3615
Open: Sun–Wed 12.00–22.00,
Thu–Sat 12.00–23.00

The Oasis, Meadowhall Shopping Centre,
Sheffield S9 1EP
Tel: 0114-256 8033
Open: Mon–Sat 11.00–23.00,
Sun 11.00–23.00
www.wagamama.com

See Manchester for menu. Disabled access.

Sheffield shops
Beanies Wholefoods

Vegetarian wholefood shop

205-7 Crookes Valley Road, **Crookesmoor**, Sheffield S10 1BA (near Crookesmoor Road junction). Tel: 0114-268 1662
Open: Mon–Fri 9.00–20.00, Sat 9.00–18.00, Sun 10.00–16.00
www.beanieswholefoods.co.uk

Busy shop and an organic delivery service. Workers' co-op, since 1986. Soil Association Certified organic fruit & veg boxes for collection or delivery. Stacks of fruit and veg, both organic and non, dried and fresh herbs and spices, sprouts. They now have their own bakery and sell fresh bread in the shop Mon-Sat, all organic, pastries, cakes and biscuits, some organic, lots of them vegan-friendly. Lots of pasta including gluten-free. Chilled and frozen with extensive range of vegan cheeses and yoghurts, meat substitutes, pasties, burritos, wraps, Swedish Glace, Booja Booja, vegan cornettos.
Bodycare includes Tom's of Maine, Yaoh, Faith In Nature, Sheffield made Tanjero soaps containing essential oils, Natracare. Earth Friendly baby, Maltex nappies. Essential oils but not supplements. Cleaning products by Suma Ecoleaf, BioD.
Books on veggie and vegan nutrition and cookery including the Linda Majzlik *A Vegan Taste of* range. MC, Visa minimum £5.

Down to Earth

Wholefood shop

406 **Sharrow Vale Road**, Sheffield S11 8ZP
(near Bilash restaurant)
Tel: 0114-268 5220
Open: Mon–Sat 9.30–17.30, Mon 13.30–17.30, Sun closed

Big range of wholefoods. Fridge and freezer with pasties, vegan cheeses, meat substitutes, Swedish Glace ice-cream. Vegan chocolate. Shampoos and deodorants. Essential oils. Ecover cleaning products and refills. Cash or cheque only.

In a Nutshell

Wholefood shop

31 Chesterfield Rd, **Heeley**, Sheffield S10 0RL
Tel: 0114-250 8555
Open: Mon–Sat 9.00–17.00, Sun closed

A proper wholefood shop, with lots of take-away lunch possibilities too. Sandwiches made to order from £1.60. Fridge and freezer with wraps, sosrolls, vegan calzone, vegan homemade cakes, tofu, hummus, cheese and meat replacers, sausages, Redwood, Frys, Realeat, Swedish Glace. Local organic bread.
Vegan chocolate by Plamil, Organica and Booja Booja.
Some bodycare by Bioselect, Weleda, Natracare, some Weleda children's. A few supplements by Nature's Aid, Lanes, Biohealth. Essential oils. BioD, Ecover and refills. MC, Visa.

New Roots Wholefood

Vegetarian wholefood shop

347 Glossop Road, Sheffield S10 2HP (near the university). Tel: 0114-272 1971
Open: Mon-Fri 9.00-18.00,
Sat 12.00-17.00, Sun closed
Shop closed in August (student area)
www.newroots.org.uk

One of two volunteer-run, non-profit shops (the other in Burngreave is also a vegetarian cafe, listed earlier). Everything is vegetarian, half of it vegan and some organic. Fruit & veg, Organic bread. Fridge but not freezer with vegan yogurt, Redwood vegan cheeses, meat substitutes, cakes, lots of vegan pasties, drinks and snacks. Vegan chocolate. Cleaning products by BioD, Ecover and refills. Traidcraft and locally made cards and candles. This shop also sells plants. 10% discount for students, retirees and unwaged
Social justice displays in the window, petitions, magazines and campaign materials.
Downstairs is a "speakeasy" lounge area where you can have a warm pasty or a tea or coffee, though it's not an actual cafe.

Wicker Herbal Stores

Health food shop

117 Norfolk Street, Sheffield S1 2JE
Tel: 0114-272 1608
Open: Mon-Sat 08.50-17.15, Sun closed

Wholefoods but no fridge or freezer. Around 50 herbs and spices they pack themselves and 100 loose medicinal herbs. Bodycare include lots of Jason, Tints of Nature hair colours, Natracare. Supplements include Solgar, Quest, Lifeplan, Health Plan, Biona, Powerhealth, sports nutrition. Some homeopathy and remedies, essential oils. Ecover cleaning products. MC, Visa

Your Nuts, Broomhill

Health food shop

277 Fulwood Road, **Broomhill**, Sheffield
S10 3BD. Tel: 0114-266 5660
Open: Mon-Sat 9.00-17.00, Sun closed
www.yournuts.co.uk

Reopened under new management October 2009 and very open to customer suggestions. Fridge and freezer with vegan cheeses, hummus, meat substitutes, vegan ice-cream. Vegan chocolate by Plamil, Organica, Montezuma.
Bodycare by Dr Hauschka, Jason, Green People, Weleda, Faith In Nature, Natracare. Cleaning products by BioD, some Ecover and refills.
Supplements by Solgar, Terra Nova, Vogel, sports nutrition. Homeopathy, tinctures, Bach flower, essential oils. Consultation room added in 2010 with Reiki, reflexology, nutritionist, homeopathy, massage etc.
10% discount if you buy a full case of something such as 6 jars of tahini or 12 cartons of soya milk. MC, Visa. Two more branches in West Yorkshire.

Zed on the Edge

Wholefood shop

3A Nether Edge Rd, **Nether Edge**, Sheffield
S7 1RU (opposite Homemade Cafe)
Tel: 0114-255 2153
Open: Mon-Sat 9.00-19.00,
Sun 11.00-17.00

Cold pasties and wraps to take-away £1.10-2.39. Organic and non-organic fruit and veg. Organic veg box scheme. Local and organic bread. Fridge and freezer with Pulse burgers, (marinated) tofu, Redwood vegan cheeses and meat substitutes, Bute Island Sheese, Tofutti slices and cream cheese, sausages, burgers, Linda McCartney, Goodlife. Tofutti, Swedish Glace and Booja Booja ice- and rice-cream. Vegan chocolate by Plamil, Organica, Montezuma, Booja Booja and raw Ombar.

Some bodycare which includes Jason, Green People, Faith In Nature, Avalon, Natracare. A few supplements. Homeopathic creams, Bach Flower remedies, essential oils. BioD, Clearspring, Ecover and refills. MC, Visa.

Chain stores
Holland & Barrett

Health food shop

19 Cheapside, **Barnsley** S70 1RQ
Tel: 01226-770 069
Open: Mon-Sat 9.00-17.30, Sun 10-16.00

Unit 23 Frenchgate, **Doncaster** DN1 1ST
Tel: 01302-360 082
Open: Mon-Sat 9.00-17.30, Sun 10-16.00
The only health food shop in Doncaster

Unit 14 College Walk, **Rotherham** S60 1QB
Tel: 01709-828 114
Open: Mon-Sat 9.00-17.30, Sun closed

10 **Barkers Pool, Sheffield** S1 1HB
Tel: 0114-275 5438
Open: Mon-Sat 9.00-17.30, Sun 10-16.00

71 **The Moor, Sheffield** S1 4PF
Tel: 0114-276 2402
Open: Mon-Sat 9-17.30, Sun 10.30-16.30

21/22 **Hillsborough** Shopping Centre,
Sheffield S6 4HL
Tel: 0114 -234 4462

Unit 178, 87 High Street, **Meadowhall Centre**
Sheffield S9 1EN. Tel: 0114-256 8752
Open: Mon-Fri 10.00-21.00, Sat 9.00-19.00, Sun 11.00-17.00

47 Crystal Peaks, **Mossborough**, Sheffield
S19 6PQ. Tel: 0114-251 0369.
Open: Mon-Sat 9.00-17.30 Thu-Fri 20.00,
Sun 10.00-16.00

Local Groups
Sheffield Animal Friends

Animal rights group

www.myspace.com/sheffieldaf
www.yorkshireveggievegan.veginfo.org.uk

Weekly demos to make Sheffield foie gras free, stalls and demonstrations against fur, vivisection and meat industries. Join the mailout list by emailing sheffieldanimalfriends@gmail.com

Sheffield Vegetarian Soc

John Nicholson, Tel: 0114 230 4267 (no media calls please)
www.vegsoc.org/network/yorkshire.html
Email: sheffveg@daize.plus.com

Coffee mornings last Saturday of the month 10.45 at Blue Moon Café. Walks, trips and meals.

West Yorkshire Introduction	**187**
Hebden Bridge veggie hotspot	**188**
Accommodation	**·194**
Boston Spa	**194**
BRADFORD	**194**
Brighouse	**197**
Cleckheaton	**198**
Denby Dale	**198**
Dewsbury	**198**
Halifax	**199**
Haworth	**200**
Holmfirth	**201**
HUDDERSFIELD	**201**
Ilkley	**203**
Keighley	**204**
LEEDS	**204**
Otley	**210**
Shipley	**213**
Slaithwaite	**212**
Sowerby Bridge	**213**
Wakefield	**213**
Wetherby	**214**
Chain stores	**216**
Local groups	**216**

West Yorkshire

West Yorkshire

West Yorkshire has so many attractions, including some of the country's best gourmet vegetarian restaurants, and at 25 pages this county now boasts a hugely increased range of country and city vegetarian delights. Top of the must-visits has to be **Hebden Bridge**, where you can enjoy the breath-taking scenery of the Pennines. Stay in **Myrtle Grove** if you have time to spare and explore the town which offers live music, theatrical performances, heaps of cafes and an Alternative Energy Centre. If you plan a June/July visit, don't miss the Arts Festival. **Greens** is a great new cafe (replaces Relish) and there are lots more places to eat and shop, see our 6-page Hebden Bridge hotspot starting on the next page.

Nearby is **Bronte country**, centered on the village of **Haworth**. Lush green hills spill over into the magnificent valleys and villages of **the Dales**. The Dales are a wonderful place to spend the night and **Archway Cottage** in Ilkley does it in style. This early Victorian home in Ilkley offers B&B from just £25 per person and you can dine at the wonderful restaurant **The Veggie**. Two other outstanding restaurants are **Cheerful Chilli** in Otley and **Dandelion & Burdock** in Sowerby Bridge.

If you love Indian food, be sure to try **Hansa's** in Leeds, **Prashad** and **Tulsi** in Bradford and **Mango** in Wetherby.

The industrial cities of Bradford and Leeds were major centres of the late-medieval wool trade and the 19th-century Industrial Revolution, and have evolved into two separate worlds.

Bradford has the world renowned National Museum of Film & Television, the most visited museum outside London. Or make the short trip to nearby Saltaire to soak up the fascinating history of the industrial revolution, or visit the David Hockney exhibition at the 1853 gallery. There are only three completely vegetarian places to eat: **South Square** vegetarian cafe is good for daily lunch specials, **Treehouse** at the university is great for vegan cakes and now has a wholefood store downstairs, and **Prashad** Indian vegetarian restaurant starred in channel 4's *Ramsay's Best Restaurant* at the end of 2010. In the centre a good bet is **Tulsi**, a formerly vegetarian Indian restaurant now under new ownership which has an all-vegetarian all-day buffet every day.

Leeds has evolved into one of the trendiest, hippest cities in England, where **Hansa's** is famous for its traditional Gujarati vegetarian cuisine; while **Roots and Fruits** offers veggie breakfasts and lunches.

www.city-of-bradford.com
www.bronte-country.com
www.bronte.org.uk
www.haworth-village.org.uk
www.visitbradford.com
www.visitleeds.co.uk
www.nationalmediamuseum.org.uk
www.hebdenbridge.co.uk
www.visitilkley.com
www.ilkley-online.co.uk

Hebden Bridge veggie hotspot

Hebden Bridge, on the west side of Halifax, is at the heart of the Pennines and could be called the Brighton of the north, a counter-culture paradise and "Sapphic capital of Britain" according to the Guardian. It is surrounded by beautiful walking country and cycle routes, including the Pennine Way and the Calderdale Way. The Bronte sisters' home village of Haworth is a few minutes' drive away.

In the town are art galleries, independent shops, real ale pubs and wine bars. Eating out is excellent. There are two superb veggie places to feast and drink: **Greens Vegetarian Cafe**, run by the founder of Ilkley's The Veggie, opened in October 2010 in the premises previously occupied by Relish vegetarian restaurant, while **Nelson's** vegetarian wine bar is open late and has mainly Mediterranean food. **Mooch** cafe-bar is open daytimes till 8pm and does vegetarian tapas. Other restaurants have ample veggie options, for example the average looking curry house **Eastern Spice** is truly fantastic in terms of the food, and there is even a chip shop with vegan options. (Owners of our last edition be aware that Laughing Gravy has closed and Organic House has gone over to the dark side.)

For self-catering, picnics and guest house midnight feasts, around the high street are a Co-op, two wholefood stores (one with a deli), and the **Saker** organic vegetarian bakery sells pasties, pies and vegan cakes and desserts.

100% vegetarian accommodation is offered at **Myrtle Grove** (which has added a self-catering cottage) and, for women only, **Thorncliffe**, but almost every B&B in Hebden Bridge will do some sort of vegetarian breakfast. There are other self-catering apartments and cottages, though the ones we investigated had leather sofas.

Hebden Bridge station is on the Caldervale Line from York and Leeds towards Manchester Victoria and Blackpool North. It is 8.5 miles (14 km) west of Halifax and 26 miles (42 km) west of Leeds.

Tourist info, self-catering, walking info and what's on:
www.hebdenbridge.co.uk
www.hebdenbridge.co.uk/festival
(in 2011 25th June-10th July)
www.hbwalkersaction.org.uk
www.hebdenbridgelist.com
www.visitcalderdale.com
www.calderdale.gov.uk/leisure

Myrtle Grove

Veggie B&B set in the busy thriving town of Hebden Bridge. There is one spacious double ensuite room with views over the garden, the town and across the valley to Heptonstall. Price depends on season and length of stay, £25-£35 per person per night as a double, single occupancy £35-50 Sun-Thu, £50-55 Fri-Sat, £50-60 bank holidays. Up to two children can be accommodated at an extra charge.

Begin your day with home grown organic fruit with soya yoghurt and cereal followed by a full cooked breakfast. Soya milk, vegan margarine and vegan muesli are available. The veggie proprietor uses organic produce where possible, bakes her own bread and makes preserves.

Walk from the B&B down to the canal and town centre to do some shopping, or eat dinner at one of the many restaurants providing veggie food. The town of Hebden Bridge promotes the arts and has theatrical performances, poetry readings, story telling and live music. There is an arts festival every June/July. There are alternative therapy and healing clinics as well as an Alternative Energy Centre, canal boats, a marina and a cinema providing a varied selection of films.

For walkers, Hardcastle Crags are nearby and there are footpaths beginning at the house. You could take easy and relaxing strolls along the canal or more challenging walks into the hills and onto the moors.

Also **Lumb Cottage**, a grade 2 listed 18th century cottage in a quiet rural location one mile from the centre of Hebden Bridge, with oak beams and an open stone fireplace with a wood/coal stove. It sleep 4 or 5 in two bedrooms. Two bathrooms, fully equipped kitchen, dining/study/third bedroom, lounge. Central heating, washing machine, TV, CD/tape player, garden. £250-460 per week. Weekend or part week may be possible. Linen hire by agreement.

Hebden Bridge

Vegetarian B&B and self-catering cottage

Old Lees Road
Hebden Bridge
West Yorkshire HX7 8HL
England

Tel: 01422 846 078
Mobile 07905 174902

www.myrtlegrove.btinternet.co.uk

Email: myrtlegrove@btinternet.com

Train Station: Hebden Bridge, 1km, then bus or taxi or collection is possible.

Open: all year

Directions:
At Hebden Bridge (A646) take A6033 to Haworth after the first set of traffic lights. Myrtle Grove is 200 metres on the right. (A B&B sign hangs from the railings.)

Parking: available on the street

Dogs welcome by arrangement

No smoking throughout

Special dietary requirements catered for with notice

The room has tea and coffee making facilities, television and radio

For places to eat out see the rest of this section

Hebden Bridge Accommodation

Thorncliffe Bed & Breakfast for Women

Vegetarian B&B for women

Alexandra Road, Birchcliffe Road
Hebden Bridge HX7 8DB
Tel: 01422-842163
Mobile: 07949729433
Open: all year
www.thorncliffe.uk.net
carmelandjo@btopenworld.com
See website for detailed directions

Spacious Victorian house in the Birchcliffe area, a few minutes from the centre, with views over Hebden Bridge. Exclusive use of attic floor with double bedroom with king sized bed and own bathroom. £30 per person, or £40 as single, reduced rates for 3 or more nights midweek. Fridge, toaster, tea/coffee making, TV, hairdryer, wifi. Another double (not ensuite) sometimes available. No smoking. Continental breakfast in room, vegan and special requirements no problem.

Kersal House B&B

Omnivorous bed & breakfast

Hangingroyd Lane, Hebden Bridge HX7 7DD
Tel: 01422-842664, Mobile: 07871 938766
www.kersalhouse.co.uk
roma11 4@hotmail.com

In the centre of Hebden Bridge. Vegetarians and vegan breakfasts. One twin with balcony, one double with extra single bed, both en suite. Sun-Thu £30 per person, £38 single; Fri-Sat and public holidays £32.50 each, single £45. Children welcome, £10 per night for under 16's sharing. Rooms have tv/dvd, tea/coffee maker, hairdryer, wifi. Secure cycle storage. Drying facilities. Maps and guidebooks to browse.

Prospect End B&B

Omnivorous bed & breakfast

8 Prospect Terrace, Savile Road, Hebden Bridge HX7 6NA (3/4 mile west of town centre). Tel: 01422-843586
www.prospectend.co.uk

Victorian house 3/4 mile west of the town centre. Twin/double ensuite from £27.50 per person, £35 single. Tv/radio, alarm clock, hairdryer. Vegetarian and vegan full cooked breakfast available, any diet catered with advance notice. No smoking. Very private with own entrance.

Almost every B&B in Hebden Bridge will do some sort of vegetarian breakfast. There are also self-catering apartments and cottages, though the ones we investigated had leather sofas.

Hebden Bridge vegetarian

Greens Vegetarian Cafe

Vegetarian cafe

Old Oxford House, Albert Street, Hebden Bridge HX7 8AH. Tel: 01422-843 587
Open: Thu-Sat 10.30-15.00, Fri-Sat also 18.30-late (last orders around 20.30), Sun 12.00-16.00, Mon-Wed closed
www.greensvegetariancafe.co.uk

Opened October 2010, in the premises formerly occupied by Relish vegetarian restaurant, by the founder of the fabulous Ilkley cafe The Veggie, with a similar menu in this bigger space. Daytime cafe Thu-Sat, cosy bistro candlelit dining Fri-Sat evening, with a menu that changes regularly. They use local, Fairtrade and organic produce where possible. Gluten, dairy-free and vegan options always available. All food prepared from scratch on the premises.

Breakfast till 12.00 includes wholemeal toast £2.50, organic beans on toast £3.50, sausage sandwich £3.75.

Lunch includes a hot dish of the day, soup with bread £4.25. Sandwiches with side salad £4.95, such as falafel with hummus and sweet chilli sauce; grilled marinated tofu; veggie sausage; hummus and avocado. Main course salads £7.95 such as hummus, olives, two salads or dip of the day with warm pitta and green salad; quinoa and grilled tofu with beans, toasted pumpkin seeds and green salad. Home-made raw nut and seed pate with crudites £4.95.

Cakes and desserts from £2.95 such as scones, vegan cakes such as chocolate, coffee and walnut; carrot, walnut and coconut; flapjacks.

Juices and smoothies made to order £3.25-3.50. Coffee, cappuccino, latte, hot choc etc £1.45-2.25. Pot of tea £1.75-1.95. Green tea and fresh ginger £2.25. Bottled fruit juices and sodas.

Greens inside and out

Evening starters £4.50 such as fennel, cardamon and coconut soup with home-made soda bread; carro tpancakes with hummus and sprouted salad. Mains £8.95 such as thali; penne with fennel and green peppers.

Desserts £4.50 such as apple and blackberry crumble.

Evenings bring your own alcohol, no corkage, off-licence nearby. Children welcome, high chairs. Well-behaved dogs welcome. Booking advisable. MC, Visa.

Nelson's Wine Bar

Vegetarian wine bar

Crown Street, Hebden Bridge HX7 8EH
(off St George's Square, under an off-licence)
Tel: 01422-844782
Open: Tue-Thu 17.00-23.00, Fri-Sat till 01.00, Sun 17.00-23.00, Mon closed

---

Fantastic, this basement wine bar in the centre has a completely vegetarian menu with mainly Mediterranean food. Wooden floors and furniture. Art exhibition on the walls changes monthly, and it's for sale. DJ's and sometimes acoustic live music.

Tapas dishes £2-3 such as olives, hummus, stuffed vine leaves, tapenade, baba ghanoush. Leek and potato soup £3 with bread. Wraps £4.50 such as hummus and red pepper.

Mains around £7 such as Greek platter, Mexican pancakes with veggie chilli in tortilla, bake, falafel salad, couscous, Thai red curry. A few desserts, occasionally vegan, £3.

Wine from £2 glass, £4 large glass, £10 bottle. Bottled beers from around the world £2.60-£4. Organic beer and wine.

Hebden Bridge omnivorous
Eastern Spice

Omnivorous Kashmiri restaurant

19 Market Street , Hebden Bridge HX7 6EU
Tel: 01422-844319
Open: Mon-Sun 17.30-24.00, Fri-Sat 01.00

This average looking curry house offers truly fantastic value with freshly prepared chunky vegetables and fresh coriander. Most dishes come in a vegetable or mushroom version, and you can ask for anything you like such as chickpea rogan josh. Most dishes are dairy-free apart from those that world normally contain it such as a creamy korma. Two people can eat well for under £15. Starters £1.70-1.80. Main courses £4.50-5.60 includes rice or chapatis. All desserts contain dairy.

No alcohol, bring your own, no corkage. Soft drinks 60p, coffee 70p. Children welcome, high chairs. Cash or cheque only.

Mooch Cafe

Omnivorous cafe-bar

24 Market Street, Hebden Bridge HX7 6AA
Tel: 01422-846 954
Open: Mon, Wed-Sat 9.00-20.00;
Sun 10.00-19.00; Tue closed
Last food orders 1 hour before closing
www.moochcafe.co.uk

Good music and great atmosphere. European menu. Full veggie or vegan breakfast £7 till 12.00. Lunch ciabatta with salad £4.95 cold, £5.35 hot, falafel with tabouleh £6.95, soup £4. The house dish is tapas platters £7 served with salad, tortilla and warm pitta, choose hummus, olives, stuffed vine leaves, artichoke hearts, tabouleh, piquant peppers, sundried tomatoes etc. Hummus with pitta or tortilla chips £3.50. Bowl of olives £2.95. Cakes £1.80-2.50 not vegan.

Tea, chai, coffee £1.80-2.75, soya milk available. Wines from £11.50 bottle, £2.40 small glass, £3.90 large, other wines by the bottle up to £15. German beer on tap from £1.70 half, bottled beers £2.70-3.00.

Children welcome, high chairs. Some outside seating in garden, dogs welcome there. MC, Visa £5 minimum.

Also recommended by local veggies:

Paradise Indian at 18 New Road HX7 8AD. Tel: 01422-845823.

Rim Nam Thai by the canal at Butlers Wharf, New Road HX7 8AF, Tel: 01422-846 888.

JK's Chinese take-away opposite Mooch has some veggie dishes.

AJ's chip shop and restaurant at 1 Bridge Gate HX7 8EX on Market Street, does deep fried tempura, vegan sausages and burgers, with a separate fryer for chips and veggie stuff. Tel: 01422-846755. Every day 11.30-19.30, Sun 12.30-19.00, take-away till half an hour later.

Hebden Bridge shops
Pennine Provisions

Omnivorous delicatessen, take-away and wholefood shop

21 Crown Street, Hebden Bridge HX7 8EH
Tel: 01422-844 945
Open: Mon-Sat 9.00-17.00, Sun 11-17.00

Not just a deli but a full scale wholefood store too with lots of Suma groceries. In 2010 they added more local products such as jams, and Saker vegan pies, pasties and cakes.

Deli has lots of Mediterranean ingredients for picnics, salad boxes £3 or sandwiches £2.30–2.50, such as hummus and salad, sundried tomatoes, olives, smoked and braised tofu, vegan cheeses, Redwood celebration roast, Cheatin' ham and bacon, vegetarian haggis (all year), vegan sausages, pasties, burgers, nut roast and sausage mixes. Full Provamel range. Suma tinned soups. Vegan flapjacks and cakes. Fresh bread, some organic. Fairtrade organic coffee and tea. Booja Booja truffles, full Montezuma range, Swedish Glace vegan ice-cream. Baby foods. Supplements all vegetarian, mostly by Nature's Aid. Bodycare by Weleda, Tom's, Sarakan, Natracare. Full Ecover range, Suma Ecoleaf.

Saker Organic Bread Shop

Vegetarian bakery

30 Market Street, Hebden Bridge HX7 6AA
Tel: 01706-818189 Todmorden H.Q.
Open: Tue–Sat approx 9.30 –16.30,
Sun–Mon 11.00–16.30, though bread may sell out earlier

The legendary Saker vegetarian bakery in Todmorden, 5 miles away in Lancashire, supplies many places listed in this book and now has its own retail outlet in Hebden Bridge. It sells organic vegan bread, vegan and vegetarian savouries such as pasties, pies and flans, with pasties baked on the premises in the morning if you fancy a warm one for lunch. All the sweets are vegan such as whole cakes and slices, flapjacks, fruit crumbles and fruit scones. Their specialities include blueberry and caramel crumble, and black cherry and chocolate crumble.

Valley Organics

Omnivorous organic wholefood shop

31 Market St, Hebden Bridge HX7 6EU
Tel: 0778 817 0456
Open: Mon–Tue 13.00–18.00, Wed–Fri 9.30–18.00, Sat 9.30–17.30, Sun 11.30–16.30
www.valleyorganics.co.uk

Since Organic House vegetarian cafe and wholefood store became an omnivorous American cafe, this has become the best place for organic wholefoods and fresh fruit and veg. Lots of vegan, gluten-free, special diets.
Fridge and freezer with vegan cheeses, tofu, hummus, meat substitutes, Taifun, Clearspot, Cauldron, Booja Booja and Swedish Glace ice-cream. Vegan chocolate by Booja Booja and Montezuma. All organic fruit and veg, with a box scheme delivered throughout Calderdale and some surrounding areas. Paul's organic bread.
Bodycare by Faith In Nature, Tom's, Natracare. Cleaning by BioD, Clearspring, Ecover and Suma Ecoleaf, with refills for the last two. No supplements. MC, Visa.

The Book Case

Independent book shop

29 Market Street, Hebden Bridge HX7 6AA
(next door to Valley Organics)
Tel: 01422-845 353
Open: Mon, Wed–Fri 9.30–17.30;
Sat 10.00–17.00; Sun, Tue normally closed, but in summer and towards Christmas also open Sun 14.00–16.30, Tue 14.00–17.30
www.bookcase.co.uk

Wide selection of new fiction and non-fiction for all ages. They stock all current local history titles, and local guide books if you are using Hebden Bridge as a base for walking in the Pennines.

Yorkshire Dales Accommodation
Archway Cottage
Omnivorous bed & breakfast

24 Skipton Road, **Ilkley**, West Yorkshire
LS29 9EP. (on A65, 2 mins from Ilkley
town centre) Tel: 01943-603 399
Mobile: 07960 452643
Train: Ilkley, 1/4 mile
Open: all year, except Christmas
www.archwaycottageilkley.co.uk
archway@ilkley1.wanadoo.co.uk

Two early Victorian cottages linked together make this large family home and B&B in the heart of Ilkley.
1 twin, 1 family with double and single (these two rooms share a bathroom), 1 ensuite double, 1 family suite with a bathroom and a double and a single bedroom. Around £25 per person.
Vegan breakfast with prior notice. Packed lunches available. Tea and coffee making facilities, washbasins, TV and dvd player in rooms. Children welcome, high chair. No smoking throughout. Cash and cheque only.

Bradford Accommodation
Ivy Guesthouse
Omnivorous bed & breakfast

3 Melbourne Place, **Bradford** BD5 0HZ
Tel: 01274-727060
Open: **all year**
Train & bus: Bradford Interchange 10 mins walk
www.ivyguesthousebradford.com

Grade II listed building near the city centre, handy for the Bradford Interchange bus and rail station, film museum and Alhambra theatre. Single £25, twin and double £19 per person. Vegetarian or vegan full English breakfast. MC, Visa.

Haworth Accommodation
The Kings Arms
See page 200.

Boston Spa (Wetherby)
Thai Jantra
Omnivorous Thai restaurant

202 High St, Boston Spa, near Wetherby,
LS23 6BT (near Stables Lane)
Tel: 01937-845 827
Dinner: Fri-Sat 18.00-22.00 (last orders),
Sun-Thu 18.00-21.30 (last orders);
Lunch: Wed-Sat 12.00-14.00,
closed Sun-Tue lunchtime
www.thai-jantra.co.uk

Recommended by Mungo Deli in North Yorkshire since they get organic veg from the same supplier and have a mostly organic wine list. Vegan dishes £5.50-6.50 include stir-fry veg; mushrooms with glass noodle salad; aubergine, potato and peanut coconut curry; fried tofu with red curry; spicy yard long beans, mushroom and peppers. Rice £2-2.50. Desserts £3.50-4.50 include for vegans bananas in coconut milk with toasted sesame seeds £3.50, sticky coconut rice with mango £4.50.

"Early bird" (actually all night) midweek menu changes every 2 weeks, £16 for 3 courses including a glass of house wine, Sun-Thu.
Organic wine from £12 bottle, £3.75 small glass (175ml), £4.50 large glass (250ml). Beer £2.75. Spirits from £2.50. Soft drinks £1.50-2.00. Tea £1.20, coffee £1.50, liqueur coffee £4. No soya milk.

Service not included. The takeaway has additional dishes such as green curry with tofu, massamam curry, sweet and sour veg all £5.50, which you can also ask for in the restaurant. rice £1.75-2.25. Children welcome, high chairs. MC, Visa.

Bradford - vegetarian
Prashad
Vegetarian Indian restaurant

86 Horton Grange Road, Bradford BD7 2DW
Tel: 01274-575 893
Open: Tue-Fri 11.00-15.00, 18.00-22.30;
Sat-Sun 11.00-22.30, Mon closed
www.prashad.co.uk (menu & video recipes)

Award-winning Gujurati vegetarian restaurant, with dishes from north and south India and the Punjab. Vegan, wheat or onion/garlic free marked on menu. After coming a very close second in Channel 4's Ramsay's Best Resaurant in 2010 (which you can watch on their website), they have closed their deli and added a second restaurant seating area. A dozen kinds of starters £4.75 include unusual ones such as dhokra, pea and garlic kachori, courgette bhajia, dhal kachori, corn roll, stuffed chilli, aubergine bhajia, or share a mixed platter for £8.95.

Gujarati and Punjabi curries £7.95-8.95 include black eyed bean; aubergine and pea; courgette and lentil; okra; chickpea. Other mains £7.95 include dosa with lentil soup, veg curry, uttapam, spicy pea and cauliflower burger with spciy massala chips, idli sambar. Monster dosa for two £9.50, extra fillings 60p. Special thali £13.50 with starter, two curries, 3 rotis, rice, dhal or khadi, papodom and dessert.

Rotis and breads 80p-£1.95. Basmati rice £2, pilau £2.50, kichdi rice with lentil dhal £2.50.

Desserts £4.95, gajar halva hot carrot cake is vegan. Soft drinks and orange juice £1.75. Tea, coffee £1.75. No alcohol.

Children welcome, high chair. Take-away prices are cheaper, free delivery within 3 miles, minimum order £10.50. Gift vouchers. Corporate catering up to 1,000. MC, Visa.

South Square Vegetarian Cafe
Vegetarian cafe

South Square, Thornton Road, **Thornton**, Bradford BD13 3LD (west side of Bradford)
Tel: 01274-834 928
Open: Tue-Sat 11.30-15.00, Sun 12-15.00, Mon closed; also open 1st and 2nd Friday nights each month 18.00-20.00.
Last orders 30 mins. before closing.
www.southsquarecentre.co.uk

Vegetarian cafe in the same building as art galleries and craft shop. Mix of British, Italian, Indian, Mediterranean and Mexican dishes, with a wholefood approach. Fixed menu and daily specials, All food cooked on premises. Always have vegan options.

All soups vegan and gluten-free £3.05 include: lentil & tomato soup, carrot and coriander, green pea and more.

Bowl of mixed salads of the day £2.50 small, £5 very big, such as celeriac, beetroot and red onion; mung bean and coriander; couscous.

Main courses £6.50 include potato, pea, spinach and chickpea vegan curry; butternut squash, aubergine and mushroom crumble; spicy bean enchilada. Panini £3.95, toasties £3.75. Filled baked potato £5.95 with full salad.

Homemade cakes £2.75 include two vegan ones such as oat and orange, or date and apple crumble slice, vegan crumble £2.20, all come with (soya) cream or ice-cream.

Usually on the first and third Friday of the month they are open from 6pm for art exhibitions which change on the first Friday. There are four galleries here with free entry, see website for details.

Bring your own booze with free corkage. Fairtrade organic tea £1.10, coffee £1.20 with free refill. Soya milk available. Lots of cold drinks such as

NORTH West Yorkshire

James White organic fruit juices £1.60, other juices £1.20, shakes £1.50.
Wheelchair access. Children welcome, high chair, little table with children's and recipe books and dominoes. 10% discount for Vegetarian Society and Viva! members.

Treehouse
Vegetarian organic Fairtrade cafe

In Desmond Tutu House, 2 Ashgrove, Bradford BD7 1BN (opposite University of Bradford. Use entrance on Great Horton Road, opposite Chesham Building.
Tel: 01274-732354
Open: Mon-Fri 10.30-15.00 during term;, also Thu evenings and events, see website; Sat-Sun usually closed
www.treehousecafe.org
also on Facebook

It doesn't get much better than this, a small, friendly organic and Fairtrade vegetarian cafe opposite the university campus but open to everyone, run mainly with the help of volunteers. Lots of vegan options. Great food on a shoestring. From autumn 2010 there is a greater emphasis on sandwiches, soups, cakes and drinks rather than hot meals.

Soup with bread £1.90. 3 platters such as falafel, hummus, salad and bread. Sandwiches made to order, 1 filling £2, 2 for £2.40, 3 for £2.70, 4 for £3.

The cakes £1.70 and flapjacks £1.10 change regularly and are all vegan, such as chocolate cake, cheesecake, carrot cake.

Tea 90p, coffee £1.10, cappuccino or latte £1.40, Treehouse latte with vanilla syrup £1.55. Whole Earth cans £1, organic cordial 50p.

Regular themed daytime and evening events - see website, you can bring your own alcohol.

No credit cards. Children welcome, high chair. If you volunteer for 3 hours you get a free meal. Outside catering.

This is also the Bradford Centre for Non-Violence which includes a Children's Peace Library and resources for non-violence. It's a non-profit community interest company. It is a welcoming and attractive space, eco-refurbished, with organic paint and wood recycled from schools, old houses and even an army barracks.

From autumn 2010 there is **The Olive Branch** wholefood store in the basement, see below.

Bradford - omnivorous
Tulsi
Omnivorous Indian restaurant

9 Aldermanbury, Centenary Square (opposite the Town Hall), Bradford BD1 1SD
Tel: 01274-727247
Open: Mon-Sun 12.00-23.00
www.tulsirestaurantandbar.co.uk

Bradford city centre, the curry capital of Yorkshire, finally had an Indian vegetarian restaurant, opened in late 2008, which in June 2010 went under new management who have expanded the vegetarian menu while reducing the price of the buffet, increased the opening times, but also have added some non-veg dishes to the a la carte menu which they say are cooked separately. It's near the Alhambra, St Georges Hall and the National Media Museum with its IMAX cinema.

Best value is the eat as much as you like all-day all-vegetarian buffet with Gujarati, Punjabi, South Indian and Indian-Chinese starters, mains and desserts including dosas, uttapam, idli, curries. £5.70 until 6pm, then £9.30 after 6pm. Children 5-14 £3.95 then £5.95.

None of the desserts are vegan, but they are looking into fixing that.

Draft cobra beer £2.70 pint. House wine

£3.50 glass, from £5.75 bottle, premium wines from £13. Coffee and tea £2.20.
Children welcome, high chairs. MC, Visa.

Rawal Restaurant
Omnivorous Balti restaurant

3 Wilton Street, Bradford BD5 0AX
Tel: 01274-720 030
Open: Sun–Wed 17.00–01.00, Thu–Sat 17.00–02.00 or later
Menu at www.just-eat.co.uk, search on BD6

Locals love that they have 40 vegetarian and vegan dishes here, all £5.00-6.50 (towards the end of the online menu). Veg or mushroom masala, bhuna, dupiaza, dansak, rogan josh or vindaloo all £5 and come with rice or 2 roti or 3 chappatis or naan. Also take-away and delivery. Bring your own alcohol, no corkage. MC, Visa.

Bradford shops
The Olive Branch
Vegetarian wholefood shop

in basement of Treehouse vegetarian cafe, Desmond Tutu House, 2 Ashgrove (coner of Great Horton Road, entrance on this road), Bradford BD7 1BN
Tel: 01274-732354
Open: Mon-Fri 10.00-16.00, Thu also 19.00-21.00, Sat-Sun closed. Sometimes open evening or weekend for events.
www.obranch.co.uk coming soon

Vegan owned wholefood shop (moved 2010 from Shipley) in the basement of Treehouse vegetarian cafe, with Fairtrade and organic food and drink, and also a wide range of Fairtrade gifts, stationery, Traidcraft clothes, vegetarian shoes, jewellery, gifts, sports balls, books and CDs.
Almost everything is vegan, with lots of wheat/gluten-free. Fridge with vegan cheeses, meat substitutes. No freezer. Vegan chocolate by Plamil, Divine, Organica.
Organic and Fairtrade bodycare, Faith In Nature, some Natracare. Cleaning by BioD, Ecover, Suma Ecoleaf. Traidcraft tissues and kitchen paper. Cash or cheque only.

The Olive Branch and Holland & Barrett (see end of chapter) are the only wholefood shops we know of in Bradford. But if you are not near the university, there are lots of Asian and other international shops and supermarkets.

Brighouse
Ryecorn Wholefoods
Wholefood shop & herbalist

112 Commercial Street, Brighouse, Calderdale, HD6 1AQ (between Huddersfield and Bradford)
01484-711 835
Open: Mon-Sat 9.00-17.30, Sun closed

Organic and non-organic wholefoods. Organic fruit and veg boxes to West and South Yorkshire. Local organic bread. Fridge with vegan cheese and meat substitutes. No freezer. Vegan chocolate by Plamil, sometimes Booja Booja. Over 200 different herbs.
They make their own shampoos, creams and body washes using coconut and essential oils. Local soaps. Natracare.
Supplements by local firm Gemini Health Care, Quest, FSC, Bioforce, Nature's Aid. Weleda and their own tinctures and homeopathy, Bach flower remedies. Their own essential oils. There is a room for reflexology, Reiki, aromatherapy, homeopathy, allergy testing.
Cleaning products by BioD and Ecover and refills. MC, Visa.

Cleckheaton
The Green Health Shop
Health food shop

27 Northgate, Cleckheaton BD19 3HH
(between Dewsbury and Bradford)
Tel: 01274-871 488
Open: Mon–Fri 9.00–17.00, Sat 9.00–16.30,
Sun closed
www.greenhealthshop.co.uk
www.healthfoodonline.co.uk

Fridge and freezer with vegan cheeses, meat substitutes, Swedish Glace. Wheat, gluten and dairy-free products. Plamil and Booja Booja vegan chocolate.
Bodycare includes Jason, Weleda, Giovanni, Natracare. Supplements by Solgar, A.Vogel, Natures Plus, Udo's, Kordels. Complementary medicines and therapies. Essential oils. Ecover and refills. Therapy room. MC, Visa.

Denby Dale
Your Nuts, Denby Dale
Health food store

Springfield Mill, Norman Road, Denby Dale,
Huddersfield HD8 8TH
Tel: 01484-864 902
Open: Mon–Sat 9.00–17.00, Sun 11–16.00
www.yournuts.co.uk

Fridge and freezer with vegan cheeses, meat substitutes, vegan ice-cream. Wheat, gluten and sugar-free foods. Vegan chocolate by Plamil, Organica. Baby foods. Bread from the Village Bakery.
Bodycare by Green People (including makeup), Nelson's Pure and Clear, Optima, Weleda, Faith In Nature, Natracare. Cleaning products by BloD, Ecover and some refills.
Supplements by Nature's Aid, Solgar, Vogel (Bioforce). Small homeopathy section, remedies, essential oils. Allergy testing once a month. Some books and meditation/relaxation CD's.
10% discount over £5 for Vegetarian or Vegan Society members, and on Friday for senior citizens. 10% discount if you buy a full case of something such as 6 jars of tahini or 12 cartons of soya milk.
MC, Visa over £5. Two more branches in in Sheffield (South Yorkshire) and Holmfirth.

Dewsbury
C L Brimelow & Sons Ltd
Herbalist

1 Crackenedge Lane, Dewsbury WF13 1QD
Tel: 01924-463612
Open: Mon 9.30–15.30, Tue usually closed,
Wed 9.00–16.00, Thu 9.30–15.00, Fri–Sat
9.00–16.00, Sun closed

Lots of medicinal herbs, own brand tinctures and advice. Supplements include thier own brand, Quest, FSC, Lifeplan, Nature's Aid. They don't sell wholefoods apart from dried fruit and nuts. MC, Visa.

Dewsbury is famous for its huge **market**, they even get coach parties, Wed and Sat 9.00–16.00 with fruit and veg, bakers with nice Italian breads, clothing, homewares, all sorts. Friday is the secondhand market which is half the size.

Halifax – eating out
Ginger Vegetarian Cafe
Vegetarian cafe

Above Food Therapy health food shop,
11 Northgate, Halifax HX1 1UR
Tel: 07775 570 923
Open: Tue-Fri 9.30 till 16.00,
Sat 9.30-15.30, Sun-Mon closed
On Facebook and Myspace

This new vegetarian cafe fills the gap left by the closure of Laughing Gravy and Okra House, and was a finalist in the Vegetarian Society 2009 and 2010 awards for best catering. They are big on local, seasonal and Fairtrade ingredients, including from a nearby organic farm. Mainly table service.

Full cooked breakfast £5 includes sausages, mushrooms, tomato, beans, toast. Beans on toast £2.20.

Light lunch starts around £3.50 for sandwiches, jacket potatoes, filled pitta. 2 or 3 specials daily £5.50 such as smoked tofu and mushroom pie with roast potatoes and seasonal local veg; beetroot and roast potato salad on local leaves with red onion and pepper; cauliflower and coconut curry.

Lots of cakes, all vegan, £1.50, such as fridge cake, chocolate orange torte, orange sponge, plum and almond upside down cake. Crumble made with local apples £3, summer soft fruit crumble £2.50, both with vegan ice-cream. Gluten-free vegan cookies £1.50.

Fairtrade tea £1.10, coffee £1.30, cappuccino £1.50, latte £1.60, they have soya milk. Whole Earth cans, English apple juice and Fairtrade orange £1.

Children welcome, high chairs. Disabled note it's first floor, no lift. Cash only, cashpoint nearby, or pay downstairs with credit cards.

World Peace Cafe & Meditation Centre
Vegetarian cafe in Buddhist meditation centre

in Ganden Buddhist Centre, 5 North Bridge,
Halifax HX1 1XH
Tel: 01422-353 311
Open: Wed & Fri 9.30-15.30,
Sat 9.30-16.30;
also once a month Fri evening;
closed Sun-Tue, Thu;
www.worldpeacecafehalifax.com
/PeaceCafe.htm

Many vegan options, organic and local where possible, including falafels £4.50. 3 specials daytime £5 such as pie, Thai or Indian curry, all served with 3 salads. Most salads are vegan. Veggieburger £3.20 and hot dog £3. Sandwiches £3 made to order. Soups are almost all vegan £3, and salads mostly vegan £4. Mostly Fairtrade tea £1.20, coffee £1.30, cappuccino and latte £1.50, they have soya milk. Sparkling elderflower, cranberry, cola, lemonade, organic juices all £1, bottled smoothies £1.80.

Once a month on a Friday evening at 19.30, **Stop the Week**, a 3 course meal with coffee and meditation costs £15.

Children welcome, high chairs, a few toys. Sofas and comfy chairs. Staffed by volunteers Take-away available. Cash only.

The centre sells Buddhist and meditation books and CDs, Fairtrade crafts. Meditation classes, retreats. Meditation room. Wed and Fri lunchtime meditation 12.30, 45 minutes, £2.

Halifax isn't great for evening eating out but you could try **East View** in Halifax's "Little India" at 12a Bull Close Lane, HX1 2EF. Tel: 01422-368800. Lots of veggie and some vegan food. Also **Cactus Joe's** Mexican at 5 Central Street HX1 1HU, Tel: 01422-300030, open every day 11.30-23.30. www.cactusjoes.co.uk

Halifax - shops

Modern Herbals

Health food shop

20-22 Market Arcade, Halifax HX1 1TJ
Tel: 01422-353 991
Open: Mon-Sat 9.00-17.00, Sun closed
www.modernherbals.com

Fridge (but not freezer) with soya yogurt, but no vegan cheeses or meat substitutes which you can get at Food Therapy. Vegan chocolate by Plamil, Montezuma and Blakes. Bodycare including Lavera, Jason, some Natracare, Bush Baby. Supplements by Solgar, Lifeplan, their own brand, Nature's Aid, A.Vogel. Weleda homeopathy. Essential oils. Top nutritionist Gareth Zeal is here once a month for consultations. Cleaning by Ecover. MC, Visa.

Food Therapy

Wholefood/health food shop, vegetarian take-away & organic baker

11 Northgate, Halifax HX1 1UR
(downstairs from Ginger vegetarian cafe)
Tel: 01422-350 826
Open: Mon-Sat 9.00-17.30, Sun closed
www.foodtherapyhalifax.co.uk

Downstairs from Ginger vegetarian cafe, but the food here is quite separate with on-site overnight baking. Take-away savouries include pies, pasties, bhajias and samosas, from £1 to £2.85 for a sandwich such as veggie BLT in a huge teacake roll. Soup £1.10 small, £1.30 large. Vegan desserts include fruitcake £1.05, all flapjacks 70p, scones 60p. Organic bread made on the premises. They can make virtually anything to order, including gluten-free.
Fridge and freezer with vegan cheeses, meat substitutes, soya yogurt, tofu, hummus, pates, Linda McCartney, Frys, Swedish Glace.

Vegan chocolate by Plamil, Organica, Divine, Montezuma, and towards Christmas also Booja Booja.
Lots of bodycare by Faith In Nature, Akin, Weleda, Jason, Green People, Tom's, Urtekram, Natracare, and they can order in anything you want. Children and babies bodycare section with Weleda and Green People, but not foods or nappies.
Lots of supplements by Solgar, Viridian, Biocare, Lamberts, Vogel, own label. Some Weleda and New Era homeopathy, remedies, tissue salts, essential oils. Treatment room with practitioners including ozone therapy, Alexander technique, Bowen, massage.
Cleaning products by Attitude, Ecoleaf and refills, Ecover and refills.
MC, Visa over £3.

Haworth - Bronte country

The Kings Arms

Omnivorous pub & accommodation

2 Church Street, Haworth. BD22 8DR (corner of Main Street, opposite tourist info centre)
Tel: 01535-647302
Restaurant open: Mon-Sat 12.00-20.00, Sun 12.00-17.00 (last order 15 mins before)
www.thekingsarmshaworth.com (menu)
www.oldsunhaworth.com

Olde Worlde inn in a 17th century building. 1 double ensuite £65, £45 as a single. Vegetarian breakfast, vegan with notice.
The pub menu has five vegetarian main courses £6.50-8.25 including balti veg curry with naan and chips or rice. House wine £10.95 bottle, £3.70 glass.
Free wifi. Children welcome, 2 high chairs. Dogs welcome. MC, Visa over £10, cash machine.
They own another pub nearby called **The Old Sun Hotel** which has 5 more rooms and a car park with CCTV, where you can leave your car if staying at the Kings Arms.

Holmfirth
Your Nuts, Holmfirth
Health food store

11 Victoria Square, Holmfirth HD9 2DN
Tel: 01484-680 126
Open: Mon-Sat 9.00-17.30, Sun 10.00-16.00
www.yournuts.co.uk

Reopened under new management October 2009 and very open to customer suggestions. Fridge and freezer with vegan cheeses, meat substitutes, vegan ice-cream. Vegan chocolate by Plamil, Organica. Baby foods. Fresh bread by Village Bakery on Thursdays.
Bodycare by Dr Hauschka, Jason, Green People, Weleda, Faith In Nature, Natracare. Cleaning products by Ecover and refills.
Supplements by Solgar, Nature's Aid, Vogel. Homeopathy, tinctures, Bach flower, essential oils. Occasionally practitioners in the shop such as medical herbalist, homeopath, reflexologist, food sensitivity testing.
10% discount if you buy a full case of something such as 6 jars of tahini or 12 cartons of soya milk. 10% discount for senior citizens Thursday. MC, Visa over £5. Two more branches in Sheffield and Denby Dale.

Rotcher Coffee Bar
Omnivorous cafe-bar

Rotcher, Holmfirth, HD9 2DL
Tel: 01484-685 512
Open: Mon-Sat 08.00-18.00,
Sun 9.00-17.00

Since Wow vegetarian cafe closed, this is your best bet with a modern, contemporary feel compared to the other local cafes. Nice view of the town from the window. Vegetarian but not vegan sandwiches on the menu, however they do a roast veg panini for a local vegan or can make something special for you. Lots of cakes, gluten-free available but nothing vegan.
Fruit smoothie £2.60. Pot of tea £1.40-1.60, coffee £1.90-2.20, soya milk available at no extra charge. Bottled beer £2.80. Wine £3.80 for a small bottle.
Children welcome, high chairs. MC, Visa.

Huddersfield
World Peace Cafe
Vegetarian cafe

in Vajrapani Kadampa Buddhist Centre, Wheathouse Terrace, Birkby, Huddersfield HD2 2UY
Tel: 01484-469 652
Cafe: Fri-Sun 10.00-17.00, Mon-Thu closed
www.vajrapanicentre.org/world-peace-cafe.html

A peaceful oasis where you can relax and unwind in the comfortable surroundings of their recently converted church, now a residential Buddhist centre, which was built in the William Morris "Arts & Crafts" style in 1910. In winter the cafe has a wood burning fire, and in summer you can picnic in the gardens. All food is home cooked.
Most savoury food is around £3.50 such as soup with bread, bakes, bean and veg pie with salad, salads. Filled pitta or toasted bagel with salad and homemade hummus £2, or £2.50 with roasted veg. Homemade cakes £2.50.
Fairtrade organic Rainforest Alliance coffee, tea and herbal teas £1.50. Fruit juices £1.35.
Children welcome, especially Friday morning. Dogs welcome outside. Good for cyclists. No alcohol. Free wifi.
Classes, events and day courses at the centre and in Marsden, Wakefield and Holmfirth. They sell Buddhist meditation books.

The Kwerki Cafe & Deli

Omnivorous cafe and deli

9-10 Byram Arcade, Huddersfield HD1 1ND (ground floor). Tel: 01484-537699
Open: Mon-Thu 10.00-16.00,
Fri-Sat 9.00-17.00, Sun closed
www.thekwerkicafe.co.uk

In an old Victorian Arcade with plenty of seats inside and out, ideal if you have a dog with you. Previously the Blue Rooms vegetarian cafe, then The Oak Rooms and Number 10 Deli, in 2010 under new ownership and with some of the old recipes plus new ones. They make everything from scratch, no processed food, and there's a veggie version of almost every dish and they will make dishes not on the menu to order.

Cooked veggie delight **breakfast** 7.30-11.30a.m. £5.50 includes lentil cakes, beans, tomato, mushrooms, toast, fruit juice and tea or coffee. Double portions £8.95. Or treat yourself to a leisurely, romantic **6-course champagne breakfast** £49.95 for two with half-bottle of champagne, half toasted grapefruit, juice, cereal or porridge, croissants, cakes, unlimited tea and coffee. Allow 2 hours.

Starters £3.95, two for £5.95, include Italian bread with olives or tapenade and oil dip, bruschetta, hummus with toasted pitta fingers. Soups with bread £3.75. Chilladas lentil rissoles with tomato and chilli sauce, salad and warmed pitta £6.25. Deli salad, your choice of four items £7.50. Real chips £2. Daily veggie special £7.50-8.50, 2-course set menu £9.95 (main plus starter or dessert).

Sandwiches on bread of your choice such as hummus £4, or hummus, roasted veg and capers £5.50, all served with salad and dressing. Add £2 for soup with your sandwich.

Daily hot pudding £2.95-3.95 but not vegan, though they are looking into making vegan cake.

Pot of tea for one £2. Coffee £2. Cappuccino/latte £2.25 12oz, £2.75 16oz. 3 kinds of hot chocolate. They have soya milk, fruit and decaf teas and coffee. Hot spiced apple with cinnamon and clove £2. Fruit smoothies £3.25. Wine from £2.45 glass, £8.95 bottle.

Children welcome, 2 high chairs, smaller portions from adult menu, baby changing. Dogs welcome outside. Outside catering, or hire the cafe for your reception or meeting with your own menu. MC, Visa.

Deli: Soup from £1.75. Hot, deli and breakfast sandwiches from £2.55. The deli sells hummus, olives, make their own pickles, jams and chutneys, cakes including gluten-free to order but not vegan (as yet), local bread. Build your own hampers, especially at Christmas, with your choice from their list of possibilities including chutneys, nut roast, cakes.

Half Moon Healthfoods

Organic health food store

6 Half Moon Street, Huddersfield HD1 2JJ
Tel: 01484-456 392
Open: Mon-Sat 9.00-17.30, Sun closed
www.halfmoonhealthfoods.co.uk

Fresh organic fruit & veg and box scheme. Big range of wholefoods. Organic vegan pasties from Saker bakery in Todmorden. Fridge and freezer with vegan cheeses, meat substitutes, Swedish Glace and Booja Booja ice-cream. Vegan chocolate by Plamil.

Bodycare by Faith In Nature, Jason, Weleda, Simply Gentle, Natracare. Supplements by Solgar, Viridian, A.Vogel, Nature's Aid, FSC, Nature's Plus, Kordels. Some Weleda homeopathy, Bach flower, Aqua Oleum essential oils. Nutritionists Gareth Zeal and others are in the shop once a month, and staff are very knowledgeable about products. Organic wines and cider.

Ecover and refills, BIoD and washing up refills, Faith In Nature cleaning. Some books. MC, Visa.

Ilkley
The Veggie
Organic vegetarian cafe

32 Leeds Road, Ilkley LS29 8DS
Tel: 01943-600 245
Open: Mon-Thu 10.00-17.00, Fri-Sat 10.00-20.00 (last orders), Sun closed
Directions: heading west on the A65 Leeds Road towards Ilkley, pass Booths Supermarket and The Veggie is 2 mins further up the road, on the left hand side.
www.theveggiecafe.co.uk

Daytime cafe, plus cosy candlelit evening restaurant on Fri-Sats. All food made on the premises, always vegan options. Local and Fairtrade where possible. Under new management from October 2010 with longer opening hours but still the same great veggie food. (The previous owner has just taken over Relish in Hebden Bridge.)

Breakfast: the massive English cooked £6.95 is now available all day every day, includes tea or coffee. Lighter breakfast such as toast with spread £2.50.

Lunches: Soup of the day with homemade wholemeal bread £4.25. Falafel with hummus £4.95. Avocado and olive salad with sprouts £6.95. Organic 3-bean burger £5.95 with salsa, mixed leaves & potato wedges. Daily specials £4.25-5.95, call for what is on the black board today. Sandwiches with side salad £4.50 made with wholemeal bread by the award winning Bondgate Bakery of Otley, gluten-free on request.

Cakes and desserts £1.80-3.95 include scones and vegan cakes.

Soft drinks £1.60-1.85 include Whole Earth cans, James White organic fruit juices, Belvoir presse such as elderflower or orange and jasmine. Filter coffee, cappuccino, latte, mocha, macchiato, hot chocolate £1.95-2.30. Pot of tea and herbal teas per person £1.75. Soya milk available.

Fri-Sat night has a different menu every week, starters £3.50, mains from £7.95. Bring your own booze and pay corkage. Children welcome, high chair. Outside seating in summer. Take-away prices are cheaper. They also sell coffee, tea, cordials, jam. Cakes to order, outside catering, private hire. MC, Visa.

The Green Health Shop
Health food shop

Unit 9, The Moors Centre, Ilkley LS29 9LB
Tel: 01943-816435
Open: Mon-Sat 9.30-17.00, Sun closed
www.healthifoods.com

Large health food shop with mainly dry foods. Products for diabetics and food intolerance sufferers. Plamil vegan chocolate.
Bodycare includes Jason, Weleda, Giovanni, Natracare. Supplements by Bioforce, Solgar, Terra Nova, Nature's Plus, Kordel's. Complementary medicines and therapies. Essential oils. Ecover.
Mail order from the website. MC, Visa.

Keighley
Offshoot Wholefoods
Wholefood and health food shop

18-20 Cavendish Street, Keighley BD21 3RG (near Sainsbury's)
Tel: 01535-606 589
(on A629 Halifax to Skipton and the Dales)
Open: Mon-Sat 9.00-17.00, Thu till 18.00, Sun closed
www.offshootonline.co.uk

Fridge and freezer with vegan cheeses and meat substitutes, pasties, sprouts, tofu, Swedish Glace, sometimes Booja Booja. Lots of vegan chocolate including Plamil, Montezuma, Organica, Divine, Booja Booja.
Bodycare by Faith In Nature, Jason, Weleda and they can order others, Natracare, some Weleda baby.
Supplements include Solgar, Nature's Aid, Bioforce, Nature's Answer. Weleda homeopathy, Bach flower remedies. Hermitage essential oils and some Aqua Oleum. Food sensitivity testing and acupuncture, sometimes other practitioners. Ecover and refills, Clearspring cleaning products. Books and magazines. MC, Visa.

Leeds - vegetarian
Hansa's
Gujarati vegetarian restaurant

72-74 North Street, Leeds LS2 7PN
Tel: 0113-2444 408
Open: Mon-Fri 17.00-23.00, Sat 18.00-23.00 (last orders Mon-Thu 22.00, Fri-Sat 22.45,); Sun 12.00-14.00 buffet
www.hansasrestaurant.com (menu)

Since 1986. All dishes made to order.
Starters £3.75-4.50 include samosas; makai-no-chevdo sweetcorn; patra tropical colocasia leaves with curied batter rolleed, steamed and stir-fried with mustard and sesame seeds; fafda ghathiya gram flour wafers with fried chillies, chutneys and sambar; pau bhaji spicy mixed veg on toasted mini baps. Platter of starters for two £7.95.
Specialities (larger starters) £4.50-5.95 include ragda petis mashed potato cake with pea and tamarind sauces; masala dhosa; Maharastran sabudana khichadi potatoes with sago and ground peanuts.
Mains from £5.75-7.50 such as Paletta aubergine and potato dry curry masala; Bateta-nu-Shak potato with sweet corn and crushed peanuts; Tuwer beans with aubergine; daals and pulses.
Desserts £3.75-5.25 and uniquely for Indian restaurants, a separate **hot vegan dessert** menu with sweet vermicelli or semolina cooked in vegetable ghee with sultanas, almonds and cardamon; bulgar with cinnamon, fennel, sultanas and cardamon.
Special thali with 2 curries, rotli or puri, rice, daal or kadhi, farsan, shrikhand or mango pulp, papad and drink £10.95. Banquet for six £12.95 served in large portions to share with any 2 starters, 2 specialities, 2 curries, rotli, puris and pilau rice. Surprise meal £64.95 for 4 persons with starters, mains and desserts.
All you can eat Sunday buffet £8.75, children 6-12 £4.50.

Organic, vegetarian and vegan wine from £2.95 glass, £13.95 bottle. Beer £2.95 bottle. Juices and soft drinks £1.95. Tea or coffee £1.75, liqueur coffee £3.95. No soya milk available.

High chairs for children. 10% service charge. 10% discount for members of Animal Aid, PETA, Vegetarian or Vegan Society, Viva! Gift vouchers available. Cookery demos. Outside catering. MC, Visa.

Roots and Fruits

Vegetarian cafe

10-11 Grand Arcade, Leeds LS1 6PG
Tel: 0113-242 8313
Open: Mon-Fri 11.00-19.00,
Sat 10.00-19.00, Sun closed
www.rootsandfruits.net

Since 1989 in one of Leeds' covered arcades near the Grand Theatre. GM-free. Snacks, sandwiches and hot dishes, with the many vegan options marked on the menu.

All day full English cooked breakfast £5.95 includes tea or filter coffee.

Baguette and focaccia sandwiches £4.95 include wild mushroom pate with lettuce and red onion; hummus with roast peppers and olives.

Snacks and starters from £3.75 include soup of the day with bread, Mexican bean and tomato soup with tortilla chips, samosas, spring rolls, pate with toast and leaf garnish, New York wedges.

Mains served with salad £4.95-£6.95 such as falafel, pasta with roast peppers, burger, jacket potato with two fillings. Main course salads £4.60-5.95, side £1.95.

Desserts £3.95 such as vegan crumble with custard.

Juices £1.60, Fentiman's lemonade and ginger beer £1.95. Filter coffee £1.80, cappuccino/latte £2.30, hot chocolate or mocha (cappuccino with hot choc) £2.60. Teas £1.30. Soya milk available. Bring your own wine, £3 de-corking charge per bottle. Children welcome, high chair. Two outside tables but no smoking as in covered arcade, dogs welcome. Wheelchair access. 10% discount (food only) to Vegetarian Society members and students. Private parties for up to 30 people. Visa, MC, debit cards £10 minimum.

The Common Place

Vegan co-operative cafe

23 Wharf Street, Leeds LS2 7EQ
Tel: 0845-345 7334
Open most evenings for events such as films and bike repair workshops. Vegan food sometimes served at these events.
www.thecommonplace.org.uk

Leeds' autonomous, collectively run, radical social centre in an old textile mill sometimes has a vegan cafe run by volunteers, such as when they have their fortnightly Cafe Politique discussion and at other events, with the intention to be open more often. Around £1.50-2.50 for a meal such as curry with rice and salad. Really tasty cakes 50p-£1. Sometimes Sunday brunch. Cinema, bookshop, internet, meeting rooms, art space and a music venue.

Anand Sweets

Vegetarian Indian take-away in shop

109 Harehills Road, Leeds LS8 5HS
Tel: 0113-248 1234
Open: Tue-Sun 10.00-20.00, Sun till 19.00, closed Mon

Mainly sweets including vegan ladhu. Samosas, pakoras, allu tikki. Cold curry and rice £2.80-3.50. Take-away only. Cash only.

That Old Chestnut
Vegan market stall

Leeds Farmers Market, Kirkgate, Leeds
First Sunday of the month 9.00-14.00
www.thatoldchestnutishere.com

Monthly vegan market stall with a big spread of take-away food. Seasonal hot soups £1.50, with bread £2. Slice of cake such as coffee and walnut £1. Box of 4 muffins £1.50. Also flapjacks and more tasty treats. See website for next event and email them if you'd like to order and collect any of their cakes. Their cakes are also available in shops including (see below) Love Organic, Pomegranate Organics, Natural Food Store and Green Action Co-op

Leeds - omnivorous
The Corner Cafe
Omnivorous Indian cafe

104 Burley Road, Leeds LS3 1JP
Tel: 0113-234 6677 Open: Tue-Sat 18.00-22.30 (last orders 22.15), Sun-Mon closed
www.cornercafeleeds.co.uk

Since 1985, restaurant food in a relaxed atmosphere with grandmother's recipes from Delhi. They sell out every night and cook fresh every morning. They use different batters for the different vegetabale bhajia starters, for example the popular mixed bhajia uses three different batters, with everything made fresh to order and not at all oily. Lots of gluten-free options.

60 items on the separate vegetarian menu, of which most are vegan (apart from korma dishes), such as shimlas (red, yellow and orange peppers with baby aubergines), dal made with 7 or 8 kinds of lentils, or spicier dal haleem with ground cloves and cumin. Starters £2.60-4.50, average main dish £7. Starter and main with rice and popadoms around £12. Instead of one main you could have a starter and two half portions, which is good for couples who don't want a belt-buster. Desserts £1.95-3.50 include for vegans mango and passion fruit sorbet, Swedish Glace raspberry ice-cream or Neapolitan (gluten-free, dairy-free).

Now licensed. Wine from £2.95 glass, £9.45 bottle. Bottle of local Saltaire beer from £2.95. Soft drinks £1.20-1.75 for Australian ginger beer or J20. Coffee or fresh mint tea £1.50. No soya milk.

Children welcome, 3 high chairs, you can see 3 or even 4 generations of the same family eating together here. MC, Visa.

Little Tokyo
Omnivorous Japanese restaurant and take-away

24 Central Road, Leeds LS1 6DE
Tel: 0113-243 9090
Open: Sun-Thu 11.00-22.00, Fri-Sat 11.00-23.00 (last orders)
Menu online at http://eatitnow.co.uk

Popular with local vegans. Starters and snacks £3.65-4.99 such as edamame green soya beans, dumplings with glass noodles. spring rolls, deep fried sushi, soya chicken legs, avocado tempura. Ramen soup-noodles with Japanese veg £7.55. Vegan's Paradise tofu and veg £8.55. Shallow-fried yaki soba buckwheat noodles and veg £8.85. Japanese curry £8.55. Sushi set £8.35. 4-course bento box set with tofu steak £12.85, with vegan roast duck with mango £15.95.

Desserts £3.95 but not vegan.

House wine £2.85 (125ml), £3.55 (175ml), £4.55 (250ml), £13.95 bottle. Kirin beer £3.20, pint Asahi £3.75. Japanese green tea is free. Coffee £1.75. Children welcome, high chairs. Take-away discount Mon-Wed 15%, Thu-Sun 10%.. MC, Visa.

The Grove Cafe

Omnivorous cafe & take-away

133-135 Cardigan Road, **Headingley**, Leeds
LS6 1LJ. Tel: 0113-230 2727
Open: Mon-Sun 17.00-24.00
www.hungryhouse.co.uk/grove-cafe/menu

All kinds of food including curries with vegetarian and lots of vegan dishes marked on the menu. Samosas and bhajias £1.90, platter £3.50. Curries £4.50-5.50 include veg bhuna, madras, vindaloo, dopiaza, masala, rogan josh, jalfrezi, dhansak, palak; roasted soya and veg. Roasted tofu, mushroom and pepper biryani with basmati rice and curry sauce £5. Rice £1.50-2.50. Chips £1.20.

Vegan, yes vegan, we kid you not, VEGAN soya delight pizza is on the main menu, £5 9", £6 12", such as vegan cheese with roasted tofu, mushrooms, peppers; or vegan cheese with courgettes, onions, olives, tomatoes and herbs. Vegan chapati 50p, tandoori roti 70p. Cans 80p, litre carton juice £2.

Hawkers Green

Omnivorous cafe & take-away

Headingley Enterprise and Arts Centre (HEART) Building, Bennett Road, **Headingley**, Leeds LS6 3HN
Open: Mon-Tue 9.30-18.00, Wed-Sat 9.30-21.00, Sun closed.
Tel: 0113 275 10 80
www.heartcentre.org.uk (centre)

New cafe opened February 2011 just inside the new Headingley Enterprise and Arts Centre. They do veggie and vegan food from around the world, using local produce, cakes and teas, and are already attracting lots of Leeds vegetarians and vegans.

Full vegan cooked breakfast £4.50 with sausages, fried potatoes, tomatoes, mushrooms, guacamole and sweet chili sauce with toast and dairy-free spread. Examples of main meals are gobi cauliflower and sweet potato coconut curry, stuffed butternut squash with rice and veg, £4.50 lunchtime bowl or £6.80 for a large plate lunch/eve. Sandwiches from £3.20, sweet potato falafel wrap £3.60, pastries and pies from £3 such as beetroot, spinach and squash.

Lots of cakes £1.20-2.60, some unusual ones, some vegan or gluten-free, such as banana loaf, fruit loaf, vegan gluten-free raspberry and syrup slice with coconut milk custard.

Lots of leaf teas, Chinese, Japanese and English staples, from £1.60. Coffees £2 including (soya) cappuccino. Bottled ales and vegan wines, some organic. Glass of wine £3.20, bottle from £13.50 Secluded outdoor seating area. Al fresco off street area where children can play outside. Children's corner, high chairs.

Love Organic

Omnivorous wholefoods and health foods plus delicatessen/cafe

4 Regent Street, **Chapel Allerton**, Leeds LS7 4PE. Tel: 0113-266 3030
Open: Mon-Fri 9.30-17.30, Sat 10.00-17.00, Sun 10.00-16.00

Deli with one table and 6 chairs outside, adding a breakfast bar at the end of 2010. See below under shops.

Pomegranate Organics Etc

Omnivorous organic food shop, deli/cafe, juice bar & holistic treatment centre

79 Great George Street, Leeds LS1 3BR (opposite LGI Hospital near Millenium Sq)
Shop, deli/cafe, treatments: 0113-234 7000
Shop: Mon-Fri 9.00-18.30,
Sat 11.00-17.30; Sun closed
Deli:/cafe Mon-Fri 9.30-17.30,
Sat 10.00-16.00, Sun closed
www.org-organics.org.uk

Previously called Org Organics, now

NORTH West Yorkshire

under new ownership but still two-thirds the same items with lots for veggies and vegans.

Deli/cafe has seating for 8 people. Take-away and eat-in veggie and vegan sandwiches. Vegan-friendly salad bar offering a wide range of salads, some also wheat/gluten free. Hot food typically includes vegiburger, soup, bean flans.

Sweet stuff includes flapjacks and selection of cakes (vegan included).

Fresh juices, smoothies, tea, infusions, coffee, coffee alternatives. Soya milk available.

Shop sells eco, ethical and organic products (including household, personal care and vitamins/supplements). Refills for Ecover laundry liquid and washing up liquid.

Chilled products include veggie burgers, tofu, falafel, soya yoghurt. Montezuma and Booja Booja chocolates.

Bodycare by Dr Hauschka, Lavera, Natracare, with some Jason, Weleda, Green People, Faith In Nature etc. Supplements by Bioforce/Vogel, Viridian.

Treatment rooms downstairs with massage, reflexology, acupuncture, reiki, kinesiology, hypnotherapy, aromatherapy, call for appointment. Visa, MC.

Stop press: **Primo's Gourmet Hot Dogs** in the Corn Exchange, Leeds LS1 7DA has just added an organic vegan tofu dog. Tel: 0113-345 8901.
Open Mon-Wed 9.00-17.30, Thu-Sat 9.00-22.30, Sun 10.00-16.30. And you can do your food shopping at Out of This World nearby (see below).

Leeds shops

The Third Estate
Ethical fashion shop

102 Merrion Centre (at the back), Leeds LS2 8NG. Tel: 0113-244 8896
Open: Tue-Sat 10.00-17.30, Sun-Mon closed. www.vegetarian-shoes.co.uk

All the shoes here are vegan, with a selection from the *Vegetarian Shoes* brand (which has a shop in Brighton) and they can order in the whole range. Also other ethical and Fairtrade clothing.

The Beehive
Fairtrade shop

67 Potternewton Lane, **Chapel Allerton**
Leeds LS7 3LW
Tel: 0113-262 2975, call first to check
Open: Wed 10.00-16.00, Thu-Sat 10.00-13.00, may change, call to check

Small Fairtrade shop run by volunteers with Traidcraft crafts, gifts, jewellery, handmade cards from developing countries, some organic and wholefoods, tea, coffee, chocolate by Divine. Food is clearly labelled if dairy-free, gluten-free and nut-free. Chilled drinks.

Green Action Food Co-op
Vegetarian wholefood shop

based in Leeds **University Union**, under the stairs, opposite the Old Bar (plenty of maps around campus, then ask at reception)
Open: Mon-Fri 10.00-18.00 term-time, sometimes 17.00 depending on volunteers; Sat-Sun closed
www.greenactionleeds.org.uk
www.luuonline.com

You don't have to be a student to shop here. The Green Action Food Co-op is run solely by volunteers and sells cost-price food that's vegan and organic or Fairtrade wherever possible. It costs £1 to join for a year. No GM.

Wholefoods include loose grains, dried beans, dried fruit, nuts, muesli and flours by weight. Fridge with tofu, soya yogurt, hemp oil, pasties, sos rolls, cakes. Chocolate by Plamil and Divine. Herbs. Fruit & veg boxes by Goosemoor smallholding in Wetherby: www.goosemoor.co.uk
Non-food items include toilet roll, Mooncups, Natracare, Condomi, recycled paper, bio-degradable bin liners and cleaning products in bulk for you to fill your own container. BioD. Essential oils. High capacity rechargeable batteries. See website for stock list. Cash only.

The Healthfood Co
Wholefoods & health food shop

16 Ludgate Hill, Leeds LS2 7HZ (near Millies)
Tel: 0113-245 3145
Open: Mon-Sat 9.00-17.30, Sun closed

Owned by the same people as Millies, this had previously been a herbal shop since 1857 and still stocks 150 herbs, medical herbs and spices. Massive range of nuts and fruit. Fridge with drinks. Vegan chocolate.
One of the best places in the country for vitamins with nearly every make including Higher Nature, Lifeplan, Vogel, own brand, Solgar. Nelsons and Weleda homeopathy. Lots of essential oils.
Bodycare by Giovanni, full Jason range and others, Natracare, some baby. Ecover cleaning. MC, Visa.

Love Organic
Omnivorous wholefoods and health foods plus delicatessen/cafe

4 Regent Street, **Chapel Allerton**, Leeds LS7 4PE. Tel: 0113-266 3030
Open: Mon-Fri 9.30-17.30, Sat 10.00-17.00, Sun 10.00-16.00

Deli with bhajias, samosas, sos rolls, winter soups, summer salads, hummus, pates, olives, artichokes, sundried tomatoes. One table and 6 chairs outside, adding a breakfast bar at the end of 2010.
Full range of wholefoods with lots of organic and Fairtrade. Organic fruit and veg. Bread. Fridge and freezer with vegan cheeses, meat substitutes, Swedish Glace and Booja Booja vegan ice-cream. Organic olive oil and refills. Vegan chocolate by Montezuma, Booja Booja. Organic wine and ales on the way.
Bodycare by Faith In Nature, Lavera, Suma, Natracare, some baby products. Supplements by Viridian and Nature's Aid. Essential oils.
Cleaning by Ecover and refills, BioD. MC, Visa.

Millies
Omnivorous organic food store

109 Vicar Lane, Leeds LS1 6PJ (city centre)
Tel: 0113-2429 217
Open: Mon-Fri 08.00-19.00,
Sat 09.00-18.00, Sun 11.00-16.30
www.milliesfreshandorganic.co.uk

Seasonal organic veg from the Organic Pantry in Tadcaster and also local non-organic veg from Whiteleys at Pudsey.
Deli counter is not vegetarian but does have pies, pasta, tapas, salad bars. Sandwiches from £2.20 such as vegan spreads, roasted organic vegetables. Also healthy oils, sauces, soups, curry sauces. Gillian McKeith range. Local bread. Big new chocolate section includes for vegans the full range of Plamil, lots of Booja Booja and Divine.
Organic cosmetics by Dr Hauschka, Barefoot Botanicals, Jason, Giovanni, Elysambre. Consultants and makeup artists sometimes available.
Ecover cleaning products and refills.
Supplements include Viridian, Health Aid, Natures Aid, Solgar, Bioforce and own label. Sports nutrition. Essential oils

and emergency essences. Help for snorers and smokers, gentle remedies for children. Lifestyle and healthy eating books. Therapy and beauty rooms with full time beauty technician using organic products. MC, Visa.

The Natural Food Store

Cooperative wholefood store

23 North Lane, **Headingley**, Leeds LS6 3HW (at Rose Garden, corner of Ash Road, north of the university near Headingley cricket ground)
Tel: 0113-278 4944
Open: Mon–Fri 9.00-17.30, Sat 9.00-17.00, Sun closed
www.naturalfoodstore.coop

Almost vegetarian store with lots for vegans and gluten-free. Groceries, wholefoods and food for special diets, as well as Fairtrade and ethical goods. They bag their own wholefoods. Over 100 herbs and spices.
Fridge and freezer have frozen pies, pasties, sos rolls, Redwood cheese and meat substitutes, Beanies, full range of Swedish Glace and Booja Booja vegan ice-creams. Bread from three local bakeries. Montezuma, Divine, Organica and Booja Booja chocolate.
Bodycare by Faith In Nature, Green People, Weleda, full Natracare range, Green People baby.
Supplements include Quest, Nature's Aid, Solgar, sports nutrition. Bioforce/Vogel remedies, Weleda homeopathy, essential oils. They sell their own vegetarian recipe book.
Full Ecover, BioD and Clearspring cleaning products. MC, Visa.
Monthly **farmers' market** outside on the Rose Garden every second Saturday 8.30-12.30.

Oakwood Health Foods

Wholefood and health food shop

458 Roundhay Rd, **Oakwood**, Leeds LS8 2HU
Tel::0113-217 9977
Open: Mon-Sat 9.00-18.00, Sun closed

Organic fruit and veg. Organic bread, gluten and wheat-free, fresh daily. Fridges and freezers with sandwiches, lots of vegan foods such as cakes, buns, burgers, cheeses, yogurts, Swedish Glace, Tofutti, Booja Booja. Vegan chocolate by Plamil, Divine. Organic vegetarian and vegan wine, beer, cider, spirits.
Bodycare and makeup by Weleda, Jason, Toms, Saaf, Faith In Nature, Suma, Natracare, baby things. Natural hair dyes for men and women.
Supplements, especially by Lamberts, Solgar, Biocare. Sports nutrition. Homeopathy. Lots of essential oils.
Upstairs therapy rooms with acupuncture, counselling, beautician, Reiki, massage
Ecover and all the refills, BioD. Books and CD's. Deliveries. MC, Visa, Amex.

Out of This World

Vegetarian organic supermarket, deli and take-away

20 New Market St, Leeds LS1 6DG (opposite the Corn Exchange, next to the market)
Tel: 0113-244 1881
Open: Mon-Sat 9.00-18.00, Sun 11-16.00

Now completely vegetarian and heaven for vegans and people with intolerances. Full range of wholefoods. Lots of Fairtrade and local. Deli section with different coloured labels for vegan or gluten-free, such as vegan gluten-free chocolate cake £2.29, sandwiches such as BLT or sausage and falafel £2.85, pasties such as chickpea or aduki bean, bhajias, samosas, 3 kinds of vegan pizza, olives, hummus, salads, vegan crumbles, vegan fudge.

All organic fruit and veg. Local bread every day including gluten-free. All the Clearspring Japanese foods. Suma branded products. Orgran free-from foods. Fridges and freezer with vegan cheeses, yogurts, meat substitutes, lots of tofu, burgers, veggie bacon, pate, Swedish Glace, Booja Booja. Wide range of vegan chocolate by Organica, Plamil, Montezuma, Divine, Booja Booja.

Organic Fairtrade wine, Sam Smith's cider and beers, rum, vodka, whisky, all are vegetarian and labelled if vegan.

Bodycare by local Bentley Organics, Organic Blue, Urtekram, Faith in Nature, Lavera, Australian Organics, Beauty Without Cruelty, Weleda, Yaoh, Natracare, Weleda baby.

Supplements by Nature's Aid, Kordels, Viridian.

Household and baking stuff. Ecover and refills, BioD, Simply Active cleaning.

Books. Permaculture, Green Parent, The Vegan and Ethical Consumer magazine. They can order in anything else you need. MC, Visa over £5.

Purely Natural

Health food shop

98 Town Street, **Horsforth**, Leeds, LS18 4AP
(6 miles north-west of the centre towards Otley and Ilkley or Harrogate)
Tel: 0113-258 0283
Open: Mon-Tue, Thu-Fri 9.00-17.00;
Wed, Sat 9.00-16.00; Sun closed
www.purelynaturalonline.co.uk (online shop)

Small chiller with vegan cheese, meat substitutes, tofu, dairy-free yogurts. Plamil vegan chocolate.

Bodycare includes Faith In Nature, Weleda and Green People and their baby things. BioD and Ecover cleaning products.

Supplements by Lifeplan, Nature's Own, Nature's Aid, Kordel, Quest, Vogel/Bioforce, Floradix. Weleda homeopathy, Ainsworth Bach flower remedies. Aqua Oleum essential oils. MC, Visa.

For the latest on Leeds check out:
www.leedsveg.co.uk/eatingout.htm

Otley
The Cheerful Chilli

Vegetarian restaurant & tea rooms

Yorkgate Farm, East Chevin Road, Otley
LS21 3DD. Tel: 01943-466 567
Tea rooms: Sat 11.00-16.00, Sun 11-17.00.
Restaurant: Tue-Sat 18.30-late,
last orders 21.30.
Mon closed
Location: on the right-hand side of East Chevin Road, which comes south out of Otley and eventually, after changing its name to Otley Old Road, joins the A658 airport road a mile or so N.E. of the airport.
www.thecheerfulchilli.co.uk (menus)
and on Facebook

Weekend daytime tearooms, plus evening vegetarian restaurant, in a converted farmhouse with a courtyard for outdoor dining. Plenty for vegans or allergies.

The **tea rooms** offer light lunches, puddings and cakes. The menu changes weekly and favourites around £5.50 include for example red Thai curry, or Moroccan baked veg with tomato sauce and breadcrumb topping. Scones (not vegan) and toasted teacakes (vegan) £1.60-1.90. Desserts £2-3 include vegan fruit crumble or chocolate cake.

Pot of tea £1.20, large to share £2. Coffee, latte, cappuccino £1.20-1.75, they have soya milk. Fruit juices and soft drinks £1-£1.20.

In the evening **restaurant** starters £5-5.50 include parsnip and sweet potato crips with hummus or pesto; seasonal soup; falafels with couscous, hummus, salad and chilli peanut dip; hot char-griddled Mediterranean vegetable salad. Main courses £8.50-8.75, if not already vegan, can be made so with vegan sour cream or cheese, such as pizza, tacos, chimichanga, enchilada, fajitas, chilli, Kerala curry, or aubergine involtini.

Several proper puddings £4.75 include a vegan crumble and they always have vegan ice-cream.

Bring your own alcohol, 50p corkage per person. Banquet menu £16.50 each for 4+ people, the more of you there are the more dishes. The restaurant gets heavily booked so call to reserve and they'll call you back. Two private dining rooms for 20 or 25 people or book the whole restaurant for up to 70.

Children welcome, high chairs, low table for drawing. Dogs welcome outside. Free car park. MC, Visa.

Also summer picnic boxes made to order with savoury tarts, couscous salad, chutneys, fresh bread, cake and homemade lemonade. Take-home Christmas puddings, nut roasts and cakes, and the rest of the menu throughout the year. Outside catering.

Chevin Health Store

Health food shop

44 Boroughgate, Otley LS21 1AE
Tel: 01943-850 323
Open: Tue, Thu, Fri 10.00-16.30
Wed 10.00-12.30, Sat 10.00-16.00, closed Sun and Mon

Full range of wholefoods. No fridge of freezer. Vegan chocolate by Plamil, Siesta. Bodycare by Faith In Nature, Weleda, Bentley including baby stuff.

Supplements include their own brand, Lifplan, Solgar, Kordel, Weleda, Nature's Aid, Vogel, Lanes. Weleda homeopathy. Country Harvest essential oils. Cleaning by Ecover. MC , Visa.

Otley Apothecary

Natural health store & treatment centre

16 Bondgate, Otley, LS21 3AB (near Harrogate and Ilkley)
Tel: 01943-465544
Open: Mon-Sat 9.30-17.30, treatments till 21.00. Also open last Sun of the month for farmers' market 12.00-16.00.
www.otleyapothecary.co.uk

Wholefoods, organic, Fairtrade, gluten-free and dairy-free products, lots vegan. No fridge or freezer, but if you need a snack they have grain bars and Montezuma chocolate. They can order in anything else you need.

Bodycare and make-up by Dr Hauschka, Jane Iredale, Lavera, Green People, Faith In Nature, Avalon Organics, Weleda, Natracare. Comprehensive range of baby products.

Ecover and some refills, BioD and washing up refills. Health, healing, herbal medicine and alternative diet books.

Big range of supplements by Lamberts, Viridian, Solgar, Nature's Aid, Biohealth, Bioforce, Nature's Plus including children's.

Weleda homeopathy. Jan de Vries flower essences. Essential oils. Herbal pharmacy, dried herbs, teas, creams, oils & tinctures with professional advice from the owner who is a qualified medical herbalist and nutritionist.

Treatment centre with aromatherapy, chiropractic, clinical hypnotherapy, counselling, herbal medicine, life coaching, NLP, massage, Indian head massage, mediation (that's mediation not meditation), shamanic energy healing, spiritual healing, Reiki. Events and courses, see website. Online shop. MC, Visa.

Local walks: www.waw-otley.org.uk

Shipley
The Health Shop
Health food shop

40 Westgate, Shipley BD18 3QX
Tel: 01274-582 635
Open: Mon-Fri 9.00-17.00, Wed 9.00-13.00,
Sat 9.00-16.00, Sun closed
www.vitaminsforall.co.uk

All the usual wholefoods. Fridge with Bute Island Sheese, tofu. Vegan chocolate by Plamil. Lots of specialist teas. Fairtrade teas and biscuits and may increase the range now that the other wholefood store Olive Branch has moved to Bradford. Gluten-free baking flours.
Bodycare by Skin Blossom, Faith In Nature, full range of Natracare.
Supplements by Nature's Aid, Solgar, full range of Vogel, Potters. Nelsons and Weleda homeopathy, Pharmanord, essential oils.
Specialist orders always welcome. MC, Visa.

Shipley has lots of cafes and restaurants including Indian. The Olive Branch wholefood shop in Westgate moved in 2010 to Treehouse Cafe in the university, see Bradford shops.

Slaithwaite
Green Valley Grocer
Cooperative grocer & greengrocer

14 Carr Lane, Slaithwaite HD7 5AN
(on the A62 Huddersfield Oldham Road)
Tel: 01484-844 417
Open: Mon-Sat 08.30
Mon-Wed, Fri 08.30-17.30;
Thu 08.30-19.00;
Sat 08.30-15.30; Sun closed
www.slaithwaite.coop
www.thehandmadebakery.coop

Mainly fruit and veg, much of it organic or local, including allotment and garden surplus. Suma wholefoods. Lots of bread from The Handmade Bakery at the back. Jams and chutneys. Hummus. Bodycare by Faith In Nature, Suma, Natracare. Ecover and Ecoleaf cleaning products. In 2010 they started to also sell fish. MC, Visa.

Sowerby Bridge
Dandelion and Burdock
Vegan wholefood organic restaurant

16 Town Hall Street, Sowerby Bridge
HX6 2EA (near Halifax, half way between Leeds and Manchester, 45 mins)
Tel: 01422-316000
Train: Sowerby (Manchester-Leeds line)
Open: lunch Sat-Sun 11-15.00; dinner Wed-Sat 18.00-close (licensed till midnight, food served till 9 Wed-Thur, till 10 Fri-Sat);
Mon-Tue closed
Sign up to receive monthly menus:
dandelion.burdock@yahoo.co.uk

Fully licensed new all-vegan restaurant with a lovely view of the rivers Ryburn & Calder. The mostly organic, international gourmet menu changes daily, phone for details. Some examples follow.
Small plates £4.50 such as beetroot cakes with sour cream, mixed baby leaf and rhubard dressing; red onion soup with bean roast garlic spread rosemary bread; Cuban potato salad with avocado, pecans, lemon and lime

Dandelion and Burdock

dressing; sauteed curly kale and celeriac root with sesame oil, ginger, tamari.

Large plates £8.50 such as purple potato hash with collard greens, fried tofu and cream tarragon sauce; Mandarin stir-fry with soya chicken; dal, sweet potato bhajia and basmati rice; Tuscan tart with roast garlic mash and spinach sauce; linguini bolognese with soya mince.

Desserts £4 such as lemon puding with vanilla custard; almond and cranberry tart with ice-cream; orange and pomegranate chocolate cake with ice-cream and chocolate sauce.

Organic vegan house wine glass £4.50, bottle £12.80. Beer £2.30. Coffee £1.80.

They make their own bread. A bench for drinks on balcony. High chairs. Vegetarian Society 2008 Vegetarian Independent Restaurant of the Year. No credit cards.

Wakefield

Healthy Option

Mobile catering trailer in market

in Wakefield Market, Union Street
Open: Mon-Tue, Thu-Sat 9.00-16.00
not Wed, Sun
Debra Lowe Tel: 01924-783993

Look for the green chickpea on the trailer, an oasis in the midst of not much for veggies. Debra has done catering for years abroad including many years working in a kosher vegetarian restaurant. Most of the food is vegetarian and some of the veg are from the family allotment. Vegan soup £1. Home-made falafel with hummus, salad, sauerkraut, chopped onions and choice of home-made chilli sauces £2. Traditional hotbreads £2.30. Cake (not vegan) £1. Freshly made orange or carrot juice £1.50, Fairtrade tea and coffee 60p. No soya milk. 100% biodegradable packaging.

Also available for catering within a 10 mile radius with an exclusively vegetarian second trailer and menu.

Wetherby

Mango Vegetarian Restaurant and Cafe

Vegetarian Indian restaurant & deli

12 Bank Street, Wetherby LS22 6NQ
Tel: 01937-585 755
Cafe and deli open: Mon-Sat 9.30-16.00, closed Sun;
Restaurant: Tue-Sat 18.00-23.00 (21.30 last orders), closed Sun-Mon.
Buses from Leeds, Harrogate, York, Otley, Wakefield
www.mangovegetarianlimited.co.uk
Email: info@mangovegetarian.co.uk

New family-run licensed vegetarian restaurant opened 2008, on two floors, near the market place. Daytime it is a cafe with Indian food. In the evening it turns into a restaurant with food from all over India. They specialise in gluten-free and vegan, which are marked on the menu.

Cafe: Have an Indian style breakfast at any time of day such as uthapam, aloo paratha, mushrooms on toast, idli sambhar.

Lunch buffet 12.00-15.00, £7.99 for 3-courses eat as much as you like, you can come back for more.

Mango

Vegan soups £3.50-4.50 with bread. Bombay sandwich £5.50. Falafel wrap with hummus and fenugreek leaves £4.50. Indian vegatable wraps £6.50 in gram flour fenugreek pancake, served with salad. Salads £3.50-4.95.

Chaats (Indian street food) £4.95-5.50 include pani puri pastries with brown chickpeas, spiced potatoes, sweet and sour tamarind sauce and dressing; ragda pettis potato rounds and white peas with tomato curry sauce, tamarind chutney and crunchy gram vermicelli; Mumbai chaat with peanuts. Snacks £1.55-1.75 such as samosa, spicy rolls, onion bhajia, kachori, dhokra.

South Indian specialities include idli savoury steamed rice and lentil flour cakes £6.50, sada dosa £6.50, masala dosa £8.50, mysore masala dosa £9.50, uthapam rice and lentil vegetable pancake £8.50.

Vegan and gluten-free cakes from £2.45, cupcakes from £1.75.

Restaurant: 11 starters, most £3.50-3.99, include samosas, yellow moong daal kachori, onion bhajia, spicy vegetable rolls, maroo potato bhajia in gram flour batter with ginger, coriander and garlic , or a mixed platter for two £8.50, for three £12.50. 6 kinds of chaats £5.50-6.75 such as pani puri with sweet and sour tamarind sauce; or a platter for 2 or 3 people for £12.50 or £15.50.

Gujarati and Mango's main course specialities £6.50-7.50 include daals, baby aubergines stuffed with Mango's masala, white chickpea curry, smoked aubergine Aurro. Lots of dosas £6.99-12.95 made from rice and lentil flour filled with spicy vegetables. Uthapam £10.95 Idli sambhar £6.50.

Main course thalis £13.50, £18.99, including dessert.

Rice £2.99, spicy rice £3.50, pilau rice with peas £3.75, mushroom rice £3.99, vegetable biryani £5.95. Indian breads £1.50-4.50 include rotis, puris, parathas and stuffed parathas, naan, bhatura.

Desserts £3.25-4.25 include for vegans Indian halva carrot cake with flaked pistachios and almonds; shiro semolina with saffron and cardamon; home-made cakes; and Swedish Glace ice-cream.

Vegetarian, vegan and organic wines. House wine from £3.25 glass, £13.50 bottle. Beer £2.85. Soft drinks £2.25. Tea £1.95. Coffee £2.45. They have soya milk.

Children welcome, high chairs. Optional service charge 10%.. MC, Visa, Amex.

The Good Life

Health food shop

32 Market Place, Wetherby LS22 6NE
Tel: 01937-587564
Open: Mon-Sat 9.00-17.00, Tue from 9.30, Sat 9.00-16.00, Sun closed

---

Wholefoods, flapjacks, protein and energy bars, Bounce energy balls, Clif bars. Small fridge with dairy-free cheeses, tofu. No freezer. Bodycare by Faith In Nature, Avalon, Dead Sea Magik. Supplements by Nature's Aid, FSC, Solgar. Homeopathy. Essential oils. They can order in anything you need. MC, Visa.

Mango

Local groups
Leeds Vegetarian & Vegan Society
Sophie Krank 07513 592188
sophie.krank@hotmail.co.uk
www.leedsveg.co.uk
Facebook: Leeds Vegans and Veggies

Social events, themed potluck meals, visits to veggie friendly events and restaurants. Website has lots of places to get organic fruit & veg. Affiliated to the Vegetarian Society.
They produce a 60 page recipe booklet called *A Taste Of Leeds*, containing 90 vegan recipes from their get togethers, available for £3 from
www.vegetarianguides.co.uk

Leeds Animal Protection
www.leedsanimalprotection.org.uk

Against all animal abuse such as labs, food or entertainment. Open meetings 4th Wednesday of the month (3rd Wed in Dec), from 7pm in the Civic Hall, Leeds. Regular stalls in and around Leeds. They also attend events in other parts of the country. Register to receive notice of forthcoming events.

Bradford Animal Rights
Meets at 7.30pm on the fourth Thursdsay of the month at CVS, 19-25 Sunbridge Rd, Bradford City Centre (not Dec)
email: sm014j6481@blueyonder.co.uk

Well established group that has been campaigning for over 20 years. Bradford is on the up veggie-wise and is full of vegans attracted by cheap rents, a vegan housing co-op and social centre, and this thriving AR group.

West Yorks AR Group
westyorkshireanimalrights.wordpress.com

Regular Saturday stalls in Leeds city centre, demos, leafletting, films.

West Yorks Hunt Sabs
westyorkshirehuntsabs.wordpress.com
westyorkshuntsabs@yahoo.co.uk.

Non-violent direct action to stop illegal blood sports.

Chain stores West Yorkshire
Holland & Barrett
Health food shop

Unit 1, 58 Kirkgate, **Bradford** BD1 1QT
Tel: 01274-723 289
Open: Mon-Sat 9-17.30 Sun 10.30-16.30

Unit 14 Carlton Lanes Shopping Centre
Carlton Street, **Castleford** WF10 1AD
Tel: 01977-603 858
Open: Mon-Sat 9.00-17.30, Sun closed

1 Princess of Wales Precinct, **Dewsbury** WF13 1NH. Tel: 01924-462 625
Open: Mon-Sat 9.00-17.30, Sun closed

4 Crown Street, **Halifax** HX1 1TT
Tel: 01422-365 794
Open: Mon-Sat 9.00-17.30, Sun closed

95 New Street, **Huddersfield** HD1 2TW
Tel: 01484-548 963
Open: Mon-Sat 9-17.30 Sun 10.30-16.30

19 Brooke Street, **Ilkley** LS29 8AA
Tel: 01943-817 162
Open: Mon-Sat 9-17.30, Sun 10.30-16.30

64 Towngate, **Keighley** BD21 3QE.
Tel: 01535-663 338
Open: Mon-Sat 9-17.30, Sun closed

11 **Crossgates Shopping Centre, Leeds** LS15
Tel: 0113-264 8326 (no fridge/freezer)
Open: Mon-Sat 9-17.30, Sun 10.00-16.00

Unit 22, **Bond Street Mall, Leeds** LS1 5ER
Tel: 0113-246 1856
Open: Mon-Sat 9.00-17.30, Sun 11-17.00

37 **The Merrion Centre, Leeds** LS2 8NG
Tel: 0113-234 2828
Open: Mon-Sat 9.00-17.30, Sun 11-17.00

11 All Saints Walk, The Riding Centre,
Wakefield WF1 1US. Tel: 01924-367 195
Open: Mon-Sat 9-17.30, Sun 10.30-16.30

The Isle of Man is so different, with a history that stretches right back to the Vikings. The island is also very scenic, with beautiful coastal walks. Being in the Gulf Stream the weather is mild. There is lots of sea wildlife such as seals and basking sharks.

Fly there from Manchester, Birmingham, Liverpool or London, or get the ferry or Seacat from Liverpool, Heysham (Lancashire), Belfast or Dublin.

Green's was the only vegetarian restaurant on the island but the local council refused to renew their lease after 21 years at the end of 2010. However the owner has opened a new place **Tynwald Hill Tea Rooms** in St Johns on the west side of the island. In the evenings and on Sundays in Douglas you'll find plenty of pizza places, Italian and Indian restaurants.

www.gov.im/tourism
www.isleofman.com
www.touristnetuk.com/NW/isleofman
www.cottageguide.co.uk

Accommodation	**218**
Castletown	**218**
Douglas	**218**
Port Erin	**219**
Ramsey	**219**
St Johns	**220**

Isle of Man

Peel – accommodation
Fernleigh Hotel
Omnivorous hotel

Marine Parade, Peel, Isle of Man IM5 1PB
Tel/fax: 01624-842 435.
Open: all year except around Christmas
fernleigh@manx.net
www.isleofman.com then search "Fernleigh"

On the sunny West side of the island with a panoramic view of the bay, 12 miles from both the Douglas sea terminal and Ronaldsway airport in Castletown. Happy to do vegetarian or vegan breakfast if you let them know in advance. 4 en suite rooms £33 per person. 8 standard rooms £27. No supplement for single occupancy. Children welcome. Extra bed available. They make their own Glamorgan and chickpea vegetarian sausages, vegan lentil and carrotburgers, oat cakes, a different breakfast every day. Soya milk and soya cream available and they will get soya margarine if you ask beforehand. Central heating. Hairdryers. Drying and ironing facilities. No smoking. Cash or cheque only.

Castletown
Castletown Health Store
Health food shop

8 Malew Street, Castletown IM9 1AB (near the airport)
Tel: 01624-825 812
Open: Mon-Sat 9.00-17.00, usually closed Sun
www.health-store.co.uk

The biggest independent health store on the island. All kinds of wholefoods apart from fruit and veg, bread and chilled/frozen (get these at Good Health in Port Erin). Vegan chocolate by Plamil, Montezuma, full range of Divine. Ella's Kitchen and Plum baby foods. Bodycare by Barefoot Botanicals, Jason, Tom's, Dead Sea Magik, Faith In Nature, Green People, Weleda, extensive range of Natracare, Mooncup. Green People, Weleda and Avalon baby. Optima tea tree oil, shampoos, creams, soaps.
Supplements by Solgar, Vogel, Pharma Nord, Quest, Viridian, Lifeplan, nature's Aid, Lifestream. Ainsworths and Nelson homeopathy, Bach and Ainsworth flower remedies.
They can order in for you with weekly deliveries of food and daily of supplements. 10% discount over-60's on Thursday. Loyalty card. MC, Visa, Amex.

Douglas
Millennium Saagar
Omnivorous Indian restaurant

1 Sherwood Terrace, Broadway, Douglas, Isle of Man IM2 4EN (other side of Villa Marina)
Tel: 01624-679 871
Open: Mon-Sun 12.00-14.00,
18-23.00 (Fri-Sat till 24.00)
www.millenniumsaagar.co.uk

Ground floor lounge-bar and upstairs dining room. Starters £3.95-5.75 include samosa, pakora, onion bhajia, garlic mushrooms with red wine, spiced aubergine with deep-fried puri bread, vegetable stuffed pepper. Vegetable balti, biryani, karahi, jalfrazi, masala, pasanda £8.75; bhuna, dansak, dupiaza, korma, pathia, sagwala, zaal (Madras or vindaloo) £7.50. Thali £11.50. 12 veg side dishes £4.50-5.25. Rice and pilau rice £2.50-3.95, Indian breads £2.50-2.95.
All desserts contain dairy products.
House wine from £2.95 125ml glass, £11.95 bottle.
Children welcome, half portions, no high chair. Take-away cheaper. Vegans should ask for no butter ghee before ordering. MC, Visa.

Isle of Man Health Food Centre

Health food shop

90 Bucks Road, Douglas, Isle of Man IM1 3AG
Tel: 01624-675 647
Open: Thu 10.30-13.00, Mon-Sat 10.30-17.30, Sun closed

No fridge or freezer. Multi-vitamins, health food supplies. Good for veggies. Bodycare mainly by Green People, including children's range. Supplements by Lamberts, Biocare. Weleda homeopathy, Bach flower, essential oils. Kindred Spirit magazine. They can refer you to a local naturopath and have cards for other local practitioners. Home brew beer and wine-making kits. Ecover and washing-up refillls. MC, Visa 50p under £5.

Holland & Barrett

Health food shop

Unit 2, 26-30 Strand St, Douglas IM1 2EG
Tel: 01624-676 527
Open: Mon-Sat 9.00-17.30.
Sun11.30-16.30

Julian Graves Health Store

Health food shop

62 Duke Street, Douglas, Isle of Man
Tel: 01624-616 933
Open: Mon-Sat 9.00-17.30, closed Sun

Savoury pre-packed foods, dried fruits and nuts, snacks, flapjacks.

Port Erin

Good Health

Health food shop

Shop F, Museum Buildings, Church Rd, Port Erin IM9 6AH
Tel: 01624-832 865
Open: Mon-Sat 9.30-17.00, Sun closed
www.shopiom.com
www.thegoodhealthstore.co.uk

Fridge and freezer with Redwood with vegan cheese and meat replacers. Veg from a local farm. Frozen Country Choice stoneground organic bread. Plamil vegan chocolate. Flapjacks, organic drinks.
They do not sell bodycare but do have some Natracare women's products. Nappies. Supplements by Health Aid, Healthwise, Power, Good Health, Lifeplan, Weleda homeopathy. Ecover and Method cleaning products. MC, Visa, Amex.

Ramsey

Mother Nature

Health food shop

1 Victoria Buildings, Parliament Street, Ramsey IM8 1AX
Tel: 01624-815 118
Open: Mon-Sat 9.00-17.00, Sun closed

Small shop with big range of foods and drink. No fridge or freezer.
Bodycare by Jason, Dr Hauschka, Giovanni, Avalon, Elsambre, Natracare, baby things. Supplements by Nature's Aid, Viridian, Quest, Nature's Answer, Pharmanord.
Homeopathy and remedies by Weleda, New Era, Vogel Jan de Vries and Nelsons.
Cleaning by Method, BioD and Ecover. Some health books. MC, Visa.

St Johns
Tynwald Hill Tea Rooms
Omnivorous cafe

Main Road, St Johns, Isle of Man IM4 3NA
Tel: 01624-800 129
Mon-Sun 9.00-17.00, maybe Fri-Sat evenings in future
www.greensiom.com

New 50% vegetarian cafe opened May 2010 on the west side of the island with the same owner as Greens, which was the vegetarian cafe in Douglas (until the Council did not renew their lease at the end of 2010), with similar food and prices. It's quite big with a large conservatory and seats about 100.

Main courses £6.95-7.95 such as Homity pie, Red Dragon pies. Usually they have a vegan dish. Soups £3.95 with bread, baked potatoes, 6 salads. Cakes £1.90.

Soya milk available. £1.10 cup of tea, £1.50 pot £1.80 cappuccino or latte. Soft drinks £1-2.

The cafe has a pub licence, wine £3 glass, beer £2.80 pint.

Children's area, high chairs, babies welcome. Garden with outside seating, dogs welcome. Take-away. MC, Visa.

CATERERS INDEX

Cheshire	
The Greenhouse	5
Lucy's Grocer	35
Waterside Wholefood	41
Lakeland Pedlar	42
Derbyshire	
The Buxton Tram	61
Co Durham & Cleveland	
The Waiting Room	66
Lancashire	
Surya	73
RK Sweet	77
Bear Café-Bar	79
Manchester	
Eighth Day	92
Greens	93
The Thirsty Scholar	95
Sweet Tooth Cupcakery	98
Something Fishy	102
Merseyside	
Cooks Catering	106
Maharajah Restaurant	109
Nottingham	
Crocus Café	126
Alley Café	127
Veggies, Sumac Centre	134
Tyne & Wear	
Jack Sprats	137
Khan's Restaurant	138
The Sky Apple	139
The All Good Catering Co	145
North Yorkshire	
El Piano, York	161
East Yorkshire	
Seasalt & Passion, Bridlington	169
Hitchcocks, Hull	171
South Yorkshire	
Blue Moon Café, Sheffield	177
Homemade Café, Sheffield	177
The Bohemian Café, Sheffield	180
UK Mama, Sheffield	183
West Yorkshire	
Prashad, Bradford	195
Treehouse, Bradford	196
Kwerki Café, Huddersfield	202
The Veggie, Ilkley	203
Hansa's, Leeds	205
The Cheerful Chilli, Otley	211
Healthy Option, Wakefield	214

www.vegetarianguides.co.uk/updates for new places

A-Z INDEX

33 Newgate B&B, Barnard Castle	63
9 Green Lane, Buxton	52

ABC of Health, Harrogate 151
Acorn Guest House, Hull 168
Advanced Nutrition, Morpeth 123
Airedale Guest House, Scarborough 148
Airy Fairy, Sheffield 176
Aisseford Tea Rooms, Ashford 53
AJ's chip shop, Hebden Bridge 192
Alhana Falafel, Durham 64
All Good Catering Co., Newcastle 145
Alley Café, Nottingham 127
Alligator Wholefoods, York 165
Almonds & Raisins, Newcastle 142
Alms Houses, Durham 64
Alternative Stores, Newcastle 143
Anand Sweets, Leeds 205
Aphrodite HF, Penwortham 78
Appleseeds, Ulverston 46
Archway Cottage, Ikliey 192
Ardrig Vegetarian B&B 32
Arthur Street Trading, Hull 173
Ask, Hull 172
ASM, Ashton-uner-Lyne 70

Bailgate Health Store, Lincoln 86
Balti House, Nottingham 130
The Bar (Marble Brewery), Manchester 96
Barburrito, Manchester
  Deansgate 97
  Piccadilly 97
  Trafford Centre 97
The Barn at Ashe Hall, Etwall 51
The Barnacle, Whitley Bay 144
Bawtry Deli & Cafe 175
Bawtry Natural Health 175
Bay Horse Inn, West Woodburn 118,123
Bean There, Bridlington 168
Beanies Wholefoods, Sheffield 183
Bear Cafe-Bar, Todmorden 79
Bear Healthfoods, Todmorden 80
Beech Tree Guest House, Coniston 22
The Beehive, Leeds 208
Bella Italia
  Blackpool 72
  Lancaster 76
Bempton Cafe, East Yorks 169
Bilash, Sheffield 181
Birds Nest Cottage, Glossop 51
Bistro 1847, Manchester 95
Blackpool Nutrition Ctr, Blackpool 72
Blake Head, York 158
Blue Moon Café, Sheffield 177
Bob Trollop's Pub, Newcastle 141
Bohemian Cafe, Sheffield 180
The Book Case, Hebden Bridge 193
Briar Lea Guest House, York 160
Brimelow C L, Dewsbury 198
Broadway Media Ctr, Nottingham 130
Buddhist Centre Café, Buxton 53
Burnley House, Hutton-le-Hole 149
Bury Natural Health Store, Bury 74
Butterfly Cabinet, Newcastle 138
Buxton Tram, Derbys 61

Cafe @ Green Pavilion,Buxton 53
Cafe Curio, Berwick 120
Cameo Hotel, Blackpool 72
Carriages, Knaresborough 153
Castletown Health Store 218
Caudwell's, Rowsley 52
Chantry Tea Room, Morpeth 123
Cheerful Chilli, Otley 211
Chevin Health Store, Otley 212
Chorley Health Foods, Chorley 74
Chrysalis Wholefoods, Wigton 47
Coach House, Cornhill-on-Tweed 118
The Common Place, Leeds 205
Conishead Priory, Ulverston 45-6
Conservatory Cafe, Ulverston 45
Corner Cafe, Leeds 206
Coven Delicatessen, Wigan 80
Crazi Carrots, Bolton 69
Crewe Hall, Crewe 7
Crocus Café, Nottingham 126
Croft Gueste House, Cockermouth 18
Curio Cafe, Berwick 120

Dairy Guest House, York 160
Dandelion & Burdock, Sowerby Br 213
Derby Animal Rights 61
Derbyshire Vegetarians 61
detoxretox, Manchester 95
Dhesi Sweet Centre, Derby 57
Dilli, Altrincham 5
Dog & Partridge, Ashbourne 52
Doi Intanon, Ambleside 34
Dosa House, Middlesbrough 65
Dough, Manchester 97
Down to Earth, Sheffield 183
Dragon Indulgence, Liverpool 111

Earth Café, Manchester 91
Earth Mother, Bury 74
East and West, Sheffield 181
East Midlands Vegan Festival 135
East Riding Vegans 173
Eastern Spice, Hebden Bridge 192
Eat Me, Scarborough 155
Eating Whole, Doncaster 176
Edendale House, Southport 106
Edwardene Hotel, Keswick 28
Egg Café, Liverpool 106
Ego
  Bramhall 5
  Heswall 113
  Liverpool 108
Ego, Warrington 9
Eighth Day café, Manchester 92
Eighth Day shop, Manchester 100
El Piano, York 161
Elliotts's, Chesterfield 54
Encounters, Nottingham 130

Fairchild's, Scarborough	154
Falcon Guest House, Whitby	148
Falstone Tearoom, Falston	121
Farmer's Arms, Bispham Green	71
Fat Cat, Sheffield	181
Feathers Inn, Hedley on the Hill	122
Feel Good Factory, Appleby-in-Westmoreland	36
Fellinis	33
Fenwicks Food Hall, Newcastle	144
Fernleigh Hotel, Peel, Isle of Man	218
Fiesta Mehicana, York	164
Firenze, Buxton	54
First Season, Whitby	156
Flamenco, Buxton	54
Flying Goose	126
Food From Nowhere, Liverpool	107
Food Therapy, Halifax	200

For Goodness Sake
Coulby Newham 65
Guisborough 65
Middlesbrough 65

Forum, Lincoln	86
Fountains Court, Scarborough	149
Fountains, Ripon	154
Fox Hall Vegan B&B, Kendal	24
Fuel, Manchester	94
Gaia Wholefoods, Lincoln	87
Garden Station, Hexham	122
Garstang Nat Health, nr Preston	78
Gekko, Newcastle	140
Gianni's, Whitby	150
Gillam's Tearoom, Ulverston	44
Ginger Vegetarian Café, Halifax	199
The Globe pub, Glossop	58
Goji, York	163
Golden Harvest, Workington	47
Good Health, Port Erin	219
Good Life, Wetherby	215
Goodbody's Café, Middlesbrough	65
Grain Wholefoods, Hull	173
The Granary, Chester	6
The Granary, Cockermouth	37
Granny Smiths, Ambleside	36
Great Panda, Buxton	54
Green Action Food Co-op, Leeds	208
Green Days, Aigburth	108
Green Fish Café, Liverpool	107
Green Ginger, Hull	172
Green Health Shop, Cleckheaton	198
Green Health Shop, Iklley	204
Green Pavilion Cafe, Buxton	53
Green Shop, Berwick	121
Green Valey Restaurant, Grasmere	39
Green Valley Grocer, Slaithwaite	213
Green Way Café, Matlock	59
The Greenhouse vegetarian restaurant, Altrincham	5
Greenhouse Natural Healthstore, Longridge	78
Greenhouse Restaurant, Manchester	93
Greens Cafe, Hebden Bridge	190
Greens, Lincoln	86
Greens Restaurant, Manchester	93
Gregson Centre, Lancaster	76
Grimsby Vegetarians	88
Grove Cafe, Leeds	207

Gusto
Alderley Edge 5
Heswall 113
Knutsford 7
Liverpool 108

Half Moon Wholefoods, Brampton	37
Half Moon, Huddersfield	202
Hall Croft, Appleby-in-Westmoreland	17
Hanni's, Sale	8
Hansa's, Leeds	204
Hanuman Thai, Todmorden	80
Hawkers Green, Leeds	207
Hazelmere, Keswick	32
The Headless Woman, Tarporley	9
Health & Vegetarian Store, Manc	100
The Health Shop, Shipley	213
The Health Store, Nottingham	133
Health Warehouse, Darlington	64
Healthfood Co, Leeds	209
Healthy Life, Skipton	156
Healthy Option, Wakefield	214
Heeley City Farm Cafe, Sheffield	179
The Heights Hotel, Keswick	26
Hellon's Health, Blackpool	72
Heswall Health	115
Hexham Tans, Hexham	122
Hitchcock's, Hull	171
Holbeach Wholefoods, Holbeach	85

Holland & Barrett
Cheshire 9
Cumbria 47
Derbys 61
Co. Durham 67
Isle of Man 219
Lancs 82
Lincs 88
Liverpool 110
Manchester 102
Northumberland 124
Notts 134
Southport 112
Tyne & Wear 145
Wirral 116
East Yorks 173
North Yorks 157
South Yorks 185
West Yorks 216
York 165

Homemade Café, Sheffield	177-8
Honest to Goodness, Hoylake	115
Honey Tree, Newcastle	140
Honister House, Keswick	28

Host, Liverpool	108
Hotel Roma, Chester	6
In a Nutshell, Sheffield	183
In the Peak of Health, Glossop	59
Isle of Man Health Food Centre	219
Ivy Guesthouse, Bradford	192
Jack Sprats, Newcastle	137
Jhinook, Sheffield	182
Jim Skaffy, Colne	74
JK's Chinese, Hebden Bridge	192
Julian Graves	
East Yorkshire 173	
Douglas, Isle of Man 219	
Morpeth, Northumberland 124	
Scarborough, N Yorkshire 157	
Wigan, Lancas 81	
Jumbo Buffet, York	164
KAN Health Foods, Kendal	41
Kayal, Nottingham	130
Kerala Kitchen, Prenton	113
Kersal House B&B, Hebden Bridge	190
Kershaw's, Whitehaven	46
Khan's, Newcastle	138
Kielder Youth Hostel, Kielder	119
Kings Arms, Halifax	200
Kings Head, Tealby	88
Kirkwood Guest House, Windermere	32
Kitchen on Great Moor St, Bolton	72
Kro, Manchester	
Kro Bar 96	
Old Abby Inn 96	
Piccadilly 96	
Trafford Centre 96	
Kro2 96	
Kwerki Café & Deli, Huddersfield	202
Lakeland Living, Cockermouth	19
Lakeland Pedlar, Keswick	41
Lam's, Crewe	7
Lancrigg	20
Langtong Thai, Nottingham	131
Laughing Lentil, Salford	101
Leeds Farmers Market	206
Leeds Veg & Vegan Society	216
Libra, Tarleton	79
Lidmoor Farm, Bransdale	147
Lily's, Ashton-uner-Lyne	70
Little China, Grimsby	85
Little Tokyo, Leeds	206
Living Well, Milnthorpe	41
The Long View, nr Berwick	118
Louth Vegetarian Group	88
Louth Wholefood Co-op	87
Love Organic, Leeds	207,209
Lucy's, Ambleside	
Lucy's on a Plate 34	
Lucy4 Wine Bar & Bistro 36	
Lumb Cottage, Hebden Bridge	189

Lush	
Arndale, Manchester 101	
Royal Exchange, Manchester 101	
Trafford Centre, Manchester 101	
York 165	
Maharajah, Liverpool	109
Man Zen, Hale	7
Man Zen, Knutsford	7
Manchester Veg & Vegan Group	102
Manchester Vegan Society	102
Mango cafe, Wetherby	214
Mango restaurant, Wetherby	215
Manuka Health Store, Windermere	47
Manzil Tandoori, Morpeth	123
Marina Arms, Amble	120
Market Shop, Berwick	121
Mattas, Liverpool	111
Maud's Tearoom, Boston	84
Mayson's Restaurant, Kendal	41
McQueens, Knaresborough	153
Meeting House Cafe, Kendal	41
Meltons Too, York	164
Mezze, Wallasey	113
Michelango, Buxton	54
Millennium Saagar, Douglas	218
Millies, Leeds	209
Mimosa, Hull	172
Ming Vase, Birkenhead	113
Mm... Deli, Nottingham	128
Modern Herbals, Halifax	200
Moguls, Lancaster	76
Mojo's Music Café, Scarborough	154
Momtaz, Sheffield	182
Monk Bar Chocolatiers, York	
Goodramgate 165	
Shambles 165	
Monsell, Skegness	84
Mooch Cafe, Hebden Bridge	192
Mooreys Health Stores, Preston	78
Mooreys, Blackburn	72
Mooreys, Rossendale	79
Morrisons Café	7
Mother Nature, Ramsey	219
Mungo Deli, Knaresborough	152
Myrtle Grove, Hebden Bridge	189
Nab Cottage, Ambleside	32
Nag's Head, Edale	58
Natural Choice, Knaresborough	152
Natural Food Co, Nottingham	133
Natural Food Store, Leeds	210
Nature's Best, Wigan	81
Nature's Boutique	116
Nature's Health Store, Penrith	44
Nelson's, Hebden Bridge	191
New Roots cafe, Sheffield	179
New Roots shop, Sheffield	184
New Water Margin, Derby	56
Newgate Market, York	166
News From Nowhere, Liverpool	111

www.vegetarianguides.co.uk/updates for new places

Ning, Manchester	98	Prima, Ripon	153
Noah's Place, Berwick	119	Prospect End B&B, Hebden Bridge	190
Nomad, Nottingham	128	Purely Natural, Leeds	211
North Cliff, Robin Hood's Bay	149	Pyewipe Inn, Lincoln	84
Northumbria Veg*ns	124, 145		
Nottingham Animal Rights	135	**Q**uality Health Foods, Harrogate	151
Number 9, Sheffield	178	The Quarter, Liverpool	109
Number 37 B&B, Wirksworth	52	Quince and Medlar, Cockermouth	38
Nutmeg Café, Scarborough	154		
		Rattle Gill Café, Ambleside	34
Oakwood Health Foods, Leeds	210	Ravensdowne GH	119
Oast Guest House, Settle	150	Rawal Restaurant, Bradford	197
Odd, Manchester	96	The Red Cow, Nantwich	8
Odder, Manchester	96	Red Hot World, Nottingham	131
Oddest, Manchester	97	Red Triangle, Burnley	73
Offshoot Wholefoods, Keighley	204	Relish (now Greens), Hebden Br	190
Oklahoma, Manchester	94	Retreat Cafe, Grassington	150
Old Sun Hotel, Halifax	200	Review Coffee Bar,	
Old Water View, Patterdale	23	Barrow-in-Furness	36
Olde Barn, Tealby	87	Rim Nam Thai, Hebden Bridge	192
Olive Branch, Bradford	197	Ritz, Lincoln	86
Olive Deli, Manchester	101	RK Sweets, Preston	77
Only Natural, Wigan	81	Hotel Roma, Chester	6
The Orange Peel, Derby	56	Roots and Fruits, Leeds	205
The Orange Tree, Rosedale	148	Roots Natural Foods, Nottingham	133
Organic Direct, Liverpool	116	Rosemary's, Nottingham	133
Organic Kitchen, Chesterfield	55	Rotcher Coffee Bar, Holmfirth	201
Otley Apothecary, Otley	212	Rowan Tree, Grasmere	39
Out of This World, Leeds	210	Roya's at The Flying Goose,	
Outside Shop Café, Hathersage	59	Nottingham	126
		Royal Thai, Nottingham	131
Palm Tree, Nottingham	131	Ruffi, Buxton	54
Paprika, Bury	73	Ryecorn Wholefoods, Brighouse	197
Paradise Indian, Hebden Bridge	192		
Pastures New,		**S**abai, Liverpool	109
Appleby-in-Westmoreland	36	Saker, Hebden Bridge	193
Pennine Provisions, Hebden Br	192	Saltburn Health Foods	153
Peppercorn, Goole	170	Sanders Yard GH, Whitby	150
Peppermill, Northallerton	152	Sanders Yard restaurant, Whitby	156
Perkins' Pantry, Louth	87	Scarthin Books, Scarthin	60
Phoenix Court, Scarborough	149	Scouseveg	116
Pimento Tearooms, Lincoln	85	Screaming Carrot, Nottingham	134
Pizza Express		Scrumpy Willow & Singing Kettle,	
Menu 6		Newcastle-upon-Tyne	142
Cheadle, Cheshire 6		Seasalt & Passion, Bridlington	169
Manchester (8 branches) 98		Seasons, Chester-le-Street	63
Darlington 63		Sefton House, Ulverston	32
Derby Irongate 56		Shahensha, Derby	56
Derby Westfield 56		Shalimar, Derby	56
Durham 64		Sheffield Animal Friends	185
Gosforth 137		Sheffield Vegetarian Soc	185
Hale, Cheshire 7		Sheldon's Luxury Retreat, Sheldon	51
Knutsford, Cheshire 8		Shepherd's Purse B&no-B, Whitby	148
Macclesfield, Cheshire 8		Shepherd's Purse shop, Whitby	157
Newcastle-upon-Tyne 140		Sheriff Lodge, Matlock	51
Wilmslow, Cheshire 9		Simply Natural, Kirkham	79
Pizza Margherita, Lancaster	76	Simply Thai, Buxton	54
Plough Inn, Euxton, Lancs	75	Single Step, Lancaster	77
Pomegranate Organics Etc, Leeds	207	Sinners Café, Berwick	120
Prashad, Bradford	193	Sky Apple, Newcastle	139
Preston Health Food Store	77	Sokrates, Bolton	73

www.vegetarianguides.co.uk/updates for new places

Sokrates, Sale	8
Something Fishy, Manchester	102
Sonargaon, Cleethorpes	85
Sound Bites, Derby	57
South Square Café, Bradford	193
Southwell's, Bispham Green	71
Spice of Life, Bourne	84
Spurriergate Centre, York	165
Square Sail, Lincoln	86
Squeek, Nottingham	128
St John Street Gallery, Ashbourne	52
St John's Lodge, Windermere	30
Stonecrofhe, Edale	50
Studio2@Parr Steet, Liverpool	106
Sultan Food Court, Lancaster	76
Sultan of Lancaster	76
Sultan's Palace, Liverpool	110
Sumac Centre, Nottingham	129
Surya Snack Bar, Bolton	73
Sweet Tooth Cupcakery, Chorlton	98
Sweet Tooth Cupcakery, N Qtr	98
Swinton Health Foods, Swinton	101
Tamatanga, Nottingham	132

Tampopo, Manchester
City Centre 99
Trafford 99
Triangle 99

Tapestry Tearooms, Kendal	41
Tees Veg	65
Thai Boran, Derby	57
Thai House Restaurant, Hull	172
Thai Jantra, Boston Spa	192
Thailand No.1, Nottingham	132
Thailand Number One, Lincoln	85
That Old Chestnut, Leeds	206
The Third Estate, Leeds	208
Thirsty Scholar, Manchester	95
Thorncliffe B&B, Hebden Bridge	190
Three Wheat Heads, Thropton	123
Tikka Tikka, Whitby	150
Topaz Café, Ashton-uner-Lyne	70
Treehouse, Bradford	196
Tullivers, York	166
Tulsi, Bradford	196
Tynwald Hill Tea Rooms, St Johns	220
UK Mama, Sheffield	182
Unicorn Grocery, Manchester	102
Upfront Gallery, Unthank, Penrith	41
Va Bene, Glossop	59
Valley Organics, Hebden Bridge	193
Valparaiso, Liverpool	110
Veg NE	67,124,145
Vegan Cake Direct, Matlock, Derbys	61
Vegan Hot Dog Stall, Manchester	95
Vegan Lincs	88
Vegan Nottingham Guide	135

Vegge B&B, Durham	63
Veggie, The, Ikley	203
Veggies, Nottingham	134-5
Vegonia Wholoefoods, Nantwich	8
Venus Cafe, Scarborough	154
V-Fresh, Blackburn	71
Victoria Hotel, Nottingham	132
Vinehouse Café, Helmsley	151

Wagamama
Menu 99
Corporation St, Manchester 99
Spinningfields, Manchester 99
Meadowhall, Sheffield 183
Newcastle-upon-Tyne 142
Nottingham 132
Sheffield centre 183

The Waiting Room, Stockton on Tees	65
The Watermill Café, Caldbeck	37
The Watermill, Little Salkeld	44
Waterside Wholefood, Kendal	40
Well Bean, Scarborough	154
The Whale Tail, Lancaster	75
White Rabbit Chocolate, Beverley	168
Wicker Herbal Stores, Sheffield	184
Wild Carrot, Buxton	54
Wild Oats, Skipton	156
Windmill Wholefoods, Wavertree	112
Wirral Veggies	116
Wok 1, Derby	57
Wolds Retreat, Pocklington	147
Women's Holiday Centre, Horton-in-Ribblesdale	147

World Peace Café
Etwall, Derbys	51
Halifax, W Yorks	199
Huddersfield, W Yorks	201
Nottingham	129
Pocklington, N Yorks	153
Sheffield, S Yorks	180
Ulverston, Cumbria	45
World Peace Shop, Gosforth	137

Yaffle, Derby	55
Yewfield Vegetarian B&B, Ambleside	14
York Alternative B&B, York	160
The York Nut Centre	166

Your Nuts
Broomhill, Sheffield 184
Denby Dale 198
Holmfirth 201
Yuet Ben, Liverpool	110
Zed on the Edge, Sheffield	184
Zeffirelli's	33
Zoo Café, Hull	170

www.vegetarianguides.co.uk/updates for new places

LOCATIONS INDEX

Accrington	82
Aigburth	108
Alderley Edge	5
Altrincham	5,9
Amble	120
Ambleside	14,32-5,47
Appleby-in-Westmoreland	17,36
Ashbourne	52
Ashford-in-the-Water	53
Ashington	124
Ashton-under-Lyne	70-1,82
Bakewell area	51-53,61
Barborough	61
Barnard Castle	63,67
Barnsley	185
Barrow-in-Furness	36,47
Bawtrey	175
Beeston	126,132,134
Belper	61
Bempton	169
Berwick upon Tweed	118-121,124
Berwickshire	118
Beverley	168,173
Birkenhead	113,116
Bispham Green	71
Blackburn	71-2,82
Blackpool	70,72,82
Blyth	124
Bolton, Lancs	69,72-3,82
Bootle	116
Boston Spa	194
Boston, Lincs	84,88
Bourne	84
Bradford	193-7,216
Bramhall	5
Brampton	37
Bransdale	147
Bridlington	168-9,173
Brighouse	197
Broomhill, Sheffield	182,184
Burngreave, Sheffield	179
Burnley	73,82
Bury, Lancs	73-4,82
Buxton	52-4,61
Caldbeck	37
Carlisle	47
Carrington	128
Castleford, W Yorks	216
Castlerigg	26
Castletown, Isle of Man	218
Chain stores	9
Chapel Allerton	207-9
Cheadle	6
CHESHIRE county	4-9
Chester	6,9
Chesterfield	54-5,61
Chester-le-Street	63
Chirnside	118
Chorley	74,82
Chorlton on Medlock	96
Chorton-cum-Hardy	95-8,102
Cleckheaton	198
Cleethorpes	85
Cleveland	62-7
Cleveleys	82
Cockermouth	18-19, 37-9
Colne	74
Coniston	22
Cornhill-on-Tweed	118
Cottingham	173
Coulby Newham	66
Crewe	7,9
Crookesmoor	183
Crookham	118
CUMBRIA county	10-47
Darlington	63-4.67
Denby Dale	198
Derby	55-7,61
DERBYSHIRE county	49-61
Dewsbury	198,216
Doncaster	176,185
Douglas, Isle of Man	218-9
Durham city	63-4,67
DURHAM county	62-7
Easedale, Grasmere	20,39
East Retford	134
EAST YORKSHIRE	167-173
Edale	50,58
Ellesmere Port	116
Etwall	51
Euxton	75
Falstone	121
Forest Fields	134
Forest Fields, Notts	129,134
Formby	116
Gainsborough	88
Garstang	78
Gateshead	145
Glossop	51,58-59
Goole	170
Gosforth	137
Grasmere	20,39
Grassington	150
Grimsby	85,88
Guisborough	65,67
Hale	7
Halifax	199-200,216
Harrogate	151,157
Hartlepool	67
Hathersage	59
Haworth	200
Headingley, Leeds	207,210
Headley on the Hill	122
Heaton	137-140
Hebden Bridge	188-193
Heeley, Sheffield	179,182-3
Helmsley	151
Helsington	24
Heswall	113,115
Hexham	122.124
Hockley	127-8,130-4
Holbeach	85
Holmfirth	201
Hope Valley	50
Hornsea	173
Horsforth, Leeds	211
Horton-in-Ribblesdale	147
Hoylake	115
Hucknall	134
Huddersfield	201-3,216
Hull	168,170-3
Hunters Bar, Sheffield	180
Hutton-in-the-Forest	43
Hutton-le-Hole	149
Ilkeston	61
Ilkley	192,203-4
ISLE OF MAN	217-220
Keighley	204,216
Kendal	24,32,40-41,47
Keswick	26-9,32,41-2,47
Kielder	119
Kingston upon Hull	168,170-3
Kirkham	78
Knaresborough	152
Knutsford	7-8
Lake District	10-47
LANCASHIRE county	68-82
Lancaster	75-77,82
Langley on Tyne	122
Leeds	204-211,216
Leigh, Lancs	82
Lenton	126
Lincoln	84,85-88
LINCOLNSHIRE county	83-8
Little Salkeld	44
Liverpool	104
Long Eaton	134
Longridge	78
Louth	87-9
Macclesfield	8,9
MANCHESTER	89-102
Mansfield	134
Matlock	51,59,61
MERSEYSIDE county	103-116
Middlesbrough	65-7
Middleton, Lancs	82
Milnthorpe	43
Morecambe	82

www.vegetarianguides.co.uk/updates for new places

INDEX LOCATIONS

Morpeth	120,123	Rossendale	79	Tarleton	79
Mossborough	185	Rothbury	123	Tarporley	9
Nantwich	8,9	Rotherham	185	Tealby	87-88
Nether Edge	177-8,184	Rowsley, nr Bakewell	52	Teesside	67
Newark	134	Runcorn	9	Thirsk	157
Newcastle-upon-Tyne	140-145	Rusholme	93	Thornton, Bradford	195
Newton Heath	100	Sale	8,9	Thropton	123
North Shields	145	Salford	82,98,101	Todmorden	79-80
NORTH YORKSHIRE	146-166	Saltburn by the Sea	153	**TYNE & WEAR**	136-145
Northallerton	152,157	**Scarborough**	148-9,154-5/7		
NORTHUMBERLAND	117-124	Scarthin	60	**Ulverston**	32,44-6
Northwich	9	Scunthorpe	88	Unthank, Penrith	43
Nottingham	125-135	Selby	157		
NOTTINGHAMSHIRE	125-135	Settle	147,150	Wakefield	214,216
		Sharrow Vale	181,183	Wallasey	113,116
Oakwood, Leeds	210	**Sheffield**	176-185	Warrington	9
Oldham	82	Sheldon, near Bakewell	51	Washington	145
Ormskirk	82	Sherwood	128-130,133-4	Wavertree, Liverpool	112
Otley	211-212	Shipley	213	West Bridgford	133
		Skegness	84,88	West Didsbury	93,98
Parbold	71	Skipton	156-7	West Woodburn	118,123
Parbold, Lancs	71	Slaithwaite	213	**WEST YORKSHIRE**	186-216
Patterdale	23	South Shields	145	Wetherby	194,214-5
Peak District	49	**SOUTH YORKSHIRE**	174-185	**Whitby**	148,150,156-7
Peel, Isle of Man	218	Southport	106,112	Whitehaven	46
Penrith area	43-4,47	Sowerby Bridge	213	Whitley Bay	144-5
Penwortham	78	Spalding	88	Wideopen, Newcastle	143
Pocklington	147,153	St Annes	82	Wigan	80-82
Port Erin, Isle of Man	219	St Helens	82	Wigton	47
Prenton	113	St Johns, Isle of Man	220	Wilmslow	9
Preston area	77-78,82	Stamford, Lincs	88	Windermere	30,32,47
Prestwich	98	Stockport	9	Wirksworth	52
Ramsey, Isle of Man	219	Stocksfield	122	**Wirral**	113-116
Redcar	67	Stockton-on-Tees	66-7	Withington	94
Ripon	153	Stretford	82	Workington	47
Robin Hood's Bay	149	Sunderland	145	Worksop	134
Rochdale	82	Sutton in Ashfield	134	**YORK**	158-166
Rosedale	148	Swinton	101	**YORKSHIRE**	146-216

HELP MAKE THE NEXT EDITION EVEN BETTER

Please send corrections and new entries to
updates@vegetarianguides.co.uk

and we will post them up at
www.vegetarianguides.co.uk/updates

227

All you need on the road

160 vegetarian restaurants, cafes and take-aways, 25 of them vegan.
200 more with huge veggie menus.
300 shops.
Accommodation.
15 local maps.

"More important than the A-Z."
The Vegetarian Society

300 entries.
48 tourist destinations.
23 countries.
Includes giant Paris section.

"An ideal springboard for that European holiday you always wanted to take, but were unsure about the food."
The Vegetarian Society

44 vegetarian restaurants & cafes.
90 more with big veggie menus.
12 city and country pubs.
Vegetarian city and country B&Bs.
160 shops and delis.

Coming soon: Scotland, Wales, South and Vegetarian Britain 4

We also sell vegetarian guides to Spain, Brighton, Bristol & Bath, Lake District, New York, USA/Canada, the Vegan Passport and the Scoffer vegan cookbooks.
Read our monthly restaurants page in *Vegetarian Living* magazine.
Visit our /links page for websites covering the whole world.

**See the latest guides and print off updates at
www.vegetarianguides.co.uk**